Exodus and Its Aftermath

Exodus and Its Aftermath

Jewish Refugees in the Wartime Soviet Interior

Albert Kaganovitch

THE UNIVERSITY OF WISCONSIN PRESS

publication supported by
Figure Foundation

The University of Wisconsin Press
728 State Street, Suite 443
Madison, Wisconsin 53706
uwpress.wisc.edu

Gray's Inn House, 127 Clerkenwell Road
London EC1R 5DB, United Kingdom
eurospanbookstore.com

Copyright © 2022 by Albert Kaganovitch
All rights reserved. Except in the case of brief quotations embedded in critical articles and reviews, no part of this publication may be reproduced, stored in a retrieval system, transmitted in any format or by any means—digital, electronic, mechanical, photocopying, recording, or otherwise—or conveyed via the Internet or a website without written permission of the University of Wisconsin Press. Rights inquiries should be directed to rights@uwpress.wisc.edu.

Printed in the United States of America
This book may be available in a digital edition.

Library of Congress Cataloging-in-Publication Data
Names: Kaganovich, Albert, author.
Title: Exodus and its aftermath : Jewish refugees in the wartime Soviet interior / Albert Kaganovitch.
Description: Madison, Wisconsin : The University of Wisconsin Press, [2022] | Includes bibliographical references and index.
Identifiers: LCCN 2021009803 | ISBN 9780299334505 (hardcover)
Subjects: LCSH: Jewish refugees—Soviet Union—History. | Jews—Soviet Union—History. | World War, 1939–1945—Jews--Soviet Union.
Classification: LCC DS134.85 .K34 2022 | DDC 940.53/145089924047—dc23
LC record available at https://lccn.loc.gov/2021009803

ISBN 9780299334543 (paperback)

To the memory of my grandmothers

Contents

List of Illustrations and Tables	ix
Acknowledgments	xi
Transliteration Notes, Names, and Places	xiii
Introduction	3
1 Wartime Migration to the Eastern Regions of the USSR	14
2 The Local Authorities Facing Refugees	47
3 "He who does not work, does not eat"	77
4 Famine, Mortality, and Some Help	104
5 Orphanages, Adoption, and Jewish Children	123
6 Culture Clashes	143
7 Statistics on Refugees and Their Migration	188
8 The Difficult Road Back	210
Conclusion	235
Notes	239
Selected Bibliography	297
Index	309

Illustrations and Tables

Jewish refugees, Irkutsk	89
Polish Jewish refugees bake matzah for the Passover holiday, Samarkand	178
Jewish refugees celebrate a wedding, Bukhara	183
Map of German invasion of the Soviet Union, 1941 and 1942	204
Table 1. The share of Jews among refugee doctors in several areas of Kazakhstan in January 1943	85
Table 2. Mortality and its most common causes in unoccupied urban settlements of the USSR in 1941–1945	115
Table 3. Orphanages in the Chuvash ASSR with a large proportion of Jews, September 19, 1941	140
Table 4. Changes in the number of Jews among refugees in the Shemursha district of the Chuvash ASSR, 1941–1943	195
Table 5. Changes in the number of Jews among refugees in Cheboksary, Chuvash ASSR, 1941–1942	196
Table 6. Distribution of refugees arriving in Kzyl-Orda in September 1941, according to their place of origin	197
Table 7. Distribution of Jewish refugees in several places in Turkmenistan and Kazakhstan according to a place of departure by summer 1942	198

Table 8. Distribution of registered refugees in the Central Asian republics as of January 20, 1942, according to official data — 200

Table 9. The total number of all evacuees who had been and were in the status of evacuees, among them Jews and their percentage — 207

Table 10. Distribution of Jews evacuated as of January 1, 1943, according to their place of residence in the summer of 1939 — 208

Table 11. The number of Jewish refugees in Central Asia and their percentage of all Jewish refugees in the USSR — 209

Table 12. Changes in the number of refugees and Jews among them in the Kuvakino district of the Chuvash ASSR, 1941–1944 — 211

Table 13. Changes in the number of refugees and Jews among them in the Tsivil'sk district of the Chuvash ASSR, 1941–1945 — 212

Table 14. Changes in the number of refugees and Jews among them in the Chuvash ASSR, 1941–1946 — 213

Acknowledgments

This study is the result of my many years, including research at the Center for Advanced Holocaust Studies of the United States Holocaust Memorial Museum, the International Institute for Holocaust Research of Yad Vashem, and the Institute for the Humanities of the University of Manitoba. I am very grateful to the sponsors for fellowships and to the staff of these institutions and centers for their attentiveness and professionalism. This book was made possible by funds granted to the author through a Matthew Family Fellowship at the Center for Advanced Holocaust Studies of the United States Holocaust Memorial Museum, and the Memorial Foundation for Jewish Culture.

I am deeply grateful to Dan Michman, Antony Polonsky, Lionel Steiman, Shaul Stampfer, and Martin Dean for their advice and recommendations, and I'd like to thank Michael Gelb, Benton Arnovitz, Benjamin Baader, Myroslav Shkandrij, Daniel Stone, Mordechai Altshuler, Natalie Johnson, Suzanne Brown-Fleming, Vadim Altskan, and Mary Ginzburg for their moral support and help with materials. Some highlights of this study appeared in *Yad Vashem Studies* 38, no. 2 (2010), and I publish them here in the expanded version.

My thanks go to two anonymous reviewers, whose recommendations I found to be both relevant and very useful. I am very appreciative of the editorial staff at the University of Wisconsin Press and particularly copyeditor Anna Paretskaya for her careful and caring reading of the manuscript.

It is a particular pleasure to acknowledge my debt to my daughter Ayala for her preliminary editing of the text, creating the map illustration, and translating the poems. I am indebted to her and my son Benjamin for the many evenings I spent away from them working alone at my desk. I am endlessly grateful to my wife Svetlana for her patience with this study and for the many valuable suggestions she made as she kindly read the manuscript multiple times.

Transliteration Notes, Names, and Places

To make it easier for the reader, I have used familiar Anglicizations of the names of well-known figures like Ilya Ehrenburg, Lavrenty Beria, Menachem Begin, and Yosef Yitzchak Schneersohn. Given names like Maria and Iulia are rendered without the extra "i" that a strict transliteration requires. For other proper names, as well as for place names, except for those already in common use in the West, I have followed the standard transliteration model set by the Library of Congress, including the letter "ё" but excluding diacritical mark for the "й" (using "i"). Hebrew transliteration follows the standards of the Library of Congress too (for details see Paul Maher, *Hebraica Cataloging: A Guide to ALA/LC Romanization and Descriptive Cataloging* [Washington, DC: Library of Congress, 1987]).

Following convention, I have used the geographical names that were current in the USSR in the period discussed in this book, like Leningrad, Kiev, Odessa, Molotov, Alma-Ata, and Belorussian SSR (BSSR).

Exodus and Its Aftermath

Introduction

"We are ready to take in the homeless
There will be a home for the orphans!"—
Receiving the bereaved,
Answering to Kazakhstan,
Swore an oath Uzbekistan.

—SERGEI MIKHALKOV, from the poem "A True Story for Children," 1944

IN THE YEARS 1941 AND 1942, more than two million Jewish refugees moved from the western regions of the USSR to its inner territories in the largest and most intensive Jewish migration in history. Such a massive migration was made possible by the territorial expanse of the USSR, its military might, production resources, and harsh winters that hindered the swift German offensive. Among the migrants were those from regions not yet captured by the Wehrmacht but under the threat of occupation. Jews fled from dangerous areas on their own, or they were taken out in an organized manner together with others. In organizing the evacuation, the central Soviet authorities did not prioritize Jews.[1]

All the Jews who ended up in the eastern regions during the war can be divided into three categories: (1) those who were Soviet citizens before 1939; (2) new Soviet citizens from the territories annexed by the Soviet Union in 1939–1940: Latvia, Lithuania, Estonia, the eastern parts of Poland and Romania; (3) foreigners who escaped to Soviet territory between September 1939 and the summer of 1940, mostly from German-occupied regions of Poland. The second and (generally) third categories also included the survivors from among the 100,000 Polish Jews who were deported to the east—to labor camps, special labor settlements, and places of exile—between the autumn of 1939 and the summer of 1941.[2]

Jews, Ukrainians, and Belorussians who resided in eastern Poland before November 2, 1939, were recognized as Soviet citizens under the decree of the Supreme Soviet of the USSR, which went into effect on November 29, 1939. In contrast, ethnic Poles who resided in the same territory from August 1941 through January 1943 enjoyed certain rights granted to Polish citizens, the most important being an exemption from conscription into the Red Army. For almost the entire duration of the war with Germany, these same rights were also enjoyed by Poles and Polish Jews who arrived in the territory of the USSR after November 2, 1939.³ However, these rights did not grant full-fledged diplomatic protection, although these refugees received many of the rights of Soviet citizens: work permits, provision of food rations, free medical care, and education. In order to combine different categories of those from prewar Poland, we shall conditionally call all the natives of Poland "former Polish citizens."

In the official Soviet lexicon, flight and the organized removal of the population were deemed "evacuation," which was an alternative to the negatively tinged "flight," which implied the authorities' miscalculations. Along with those who voluntarily arrived in the east, those who were deported from the western regions of the USSR were also sometimes officially referred to as evacuees (*evakuirovannye*). The local residents of the eastern regions often confused this word with "picked out" (*vykovyrovannye*) or "out-picked" (*vykovorennye*) and often replaced "evacuees" with a more appropriate one—"refugees." Major of Communications Vasilii Agafonov, who fought in 1941 in Lithuania, commented in his memoirs: "Women, children, and the elderly wandered along the roads . . . the word 'evacuees' was often used in the early days of the war. The common people used a simpler word—'refugees'—and this simple word described what was happening more accurately. We saw *refugees* of the war on the roads. Oh, if only it were possible to evacuate these people!"⁴ Therefore in this study, refugees, evacuees, Romanian and Polish citizens deported from the USSR's western regions before the war or liberated in the course of the war united under the name "refugees." Referring to all these people by a common name is fairer, as, furthermore, evacuees received minimal assistance in transit and very poor government care upon arrival. If necessary, I shall also use the term "evacuees," referring to the same population.

Many of the authorities' actions regarding evacuation and placement of refugees were poorly thought out and coordinated. Often, due to lack of awareness, refugees were sent to places where many other refugees already resided, resulting in difficulty finding housing and work. Besides the usual carelessness, this type of situation also facilitated the deliberate distortion of some administrators' reports on the resources available to accommodate refugees. Regarding those refugees who had already arrived, local authorities often employed poor migration tactics. For example, in Uzbekistan, refugees were deported from cities to kolkhozes (collective farms), and kolkhozniks (farmers) were sent to the cities to work in factories.

Regardless of the hunger and disease that led to an enormous number of refugee deaths—a staggering figure even compared to the high mortality in the prewar years—the Soviet authorities in the war years, and especially in the postwar years, managed by means of information manipulation to introduce into the mass consciousness the myth of the successful accommodation of over ten million evacuees. This mechanism of the formation of controlled memory by a totalitarian society was evinced in George Orwell's novel *1984*. Therefore, to paraphrase the title of Terry Martin's well-known book *The Affirmative Action Empire*, the Soviet Union can be called *The Fictional Action Empire*. Examples of this shall be discussed in this book.

Although the conditions of accommodation in different eastern regions had little variation, the discourse about the selfless assistance to refugees offered by the entire Republic of Uzbekistan has become one of the important components of this myth. It was highly regarded even by Stalin's successors insofar as it perfectly served the official ideal of the "friendship of the peoples" and mutual assistance. Having been planted successfully in the mass consciousness, this discourse is widespread even today among former Soviet citizens: Russians, Uzbeks, Jews, and others. Its foundations were laid in 1943 when the official poet Sergei Mikhalkov wrote "A True Story for Children," a stanza from which serves as the epigraph for this introduction. It is symptomatic that in the author's roll call of regions and republics, only Uzbekistan offered help to evacuees, while other regions and republics dedicated their material resources to the cause of victory.

The same year, little-known writer and journalist Nikolai Strakovskii, having been evacuated to Tashkent, correctly understood the discourse and seized on the story of a childless Uzbek couple—Sha'khmed and Bakhri Shamakhmudovs—who raised foreign children. His story "A Big Family" was published by *Izvestiia* in May 1943.[5] By that time, the family had adopted eight children of various nationalities. However, this story remained ignored by the Agitprop (Department of Agitation and Propaganda), possibly because of the growing role of the Russians, which was a new trend. This trend of Russian national chauvinism had already manifested in that same newspaper issue, which published an article by the writer Arkadii Perventsev with a headline that would have been unthinkable before that time: "We Are Russians." In it, after a reminder of the difficult struggle against the Golden Horde, the author called upon the Russian population to protect not the Soviet but the *Russian* land.[6] Unsurprisingly, Perventsev was later involved in the "anti-cosmopolitan" campaign of the late 1940s and early 1950s.

It was a decade after the war when the central authorities turned their attention to the story of the Shamakhmudovs, as the height of the Cold War deemed it necessary to reinforce the solidarity of Soviet republics in the population's consciousness. In 1955 the Telegraph News Agency of the Soviet Union (TASS) published a feature essay on the Shamakhmudovs' adoption of eleven children during the war and three more after the war.[7] The couple became the prototypes of the main characters of Rakhmat Faizi's novel *His Majesty the Man* and the 1962 feature film *You Are Not an Orphan*, directed by Shukhrat Abbasov. In the film the couple adopt fifteen children, and in the book they are also given a child of their own, who returns from the front in the final scene bringing another orphan with him—a rescued German boy. The arrival of the latter causes a conflict between the adults and the other children—especially with the Jewish boy Abram (who is not mentioned in the 1955 TASS essay), whose parents were killed in the occupied territory and who, in an inexplicable way in the film, turned up in Tashkent before the end of the war.[8] In 1964, at the Film Festival in Leningrad, the film won the award for best screenplay, in 1972 it was awarded the Uzbek SSR's Lenin Komsomol Prize, and two years later it was the winner of the State Hamza Prize of the Uzbek SSR. The pinnacle of this discourse was the placement of a monument to the Shamakhmudovs on Tashkent's Friendship of the Peoples Square in 1982.

While the Soviet mass media was portraying the evacuation and movement of Jews to the home front as a happy and peaceful process, Soviet historiography erected a pseudoscientific shield over this myth. At that time in the USSR, and later in Russia, more than a thousand books were published about the selfless help offered to evacuees. Almost all this research is based on official administrative orders that likely were never carried out and on falsified and exaggerated reports. It is characteristic that under the term "evacuation," many Soviet authors first and foremost had in mind the removal of factory equipment, and not the evacuation of the population, reflecting priorities of those who developed the evacuation plans. Incidentally, the organization responsible for the people's evacuation from dangerous territories was exempt from criticism in the USSR, both during and after the war. Perhaps the only Soviet author who went beyond the common framework of criticizing objective difficulties with train cars, locomotives, fuel, and human resources was I. I. Belonosov. In *The Period of Stagnation*, he was cautiously able to recognize the poor performance of evacuation centers in terms of securing food, medicine, and hot water for the refugees.[9]

Georgii Kumanëv, Mikhail Likhomanov, Marina Potëmkina, and Elena Krasnozhënova became contemporary apologists for the notion of the successful accommodation of the evacuated population.[10] In general, they consistently adhered to the patriotic principle of "not airing dirty laundry in public," though they allowed the use of certain materials on the costs and mistakes of the evacuation effort. Although in the post-Soviet years more critical studies appeared, they also sometimes followed the same ideological construct.[11] Research on this topic carried out in Russia today suffers from even greater local patriotism. In this, it resembles the studies of the wartime home front that are conducted today in those few former Soviet republics where the subject receives attention.[12]

Modern Russian historiography also inherited the false optimism of Soviet historiography in the description of the economic achievements of the agricultural and industrial enterprises at the home front. Many Soviet and Russian authors have reported about the kolkhozes' and factories' fulfillment and surpassing of plans uncritically using reports of the time. Against this background of rosy-colored works, there are several sober monographs on the home front industry. They show that a large proportion of production was defective, that a shop exploded from neglect of safety precautions, and that plans were often not fulfilled. Inspections have revealed numerous violations of the technological processes, deception by factories' directors of their superiors, additions and gross distortions in reporting, as well as mismanagement and negligence on the part of the officials responsible for the implementation of defense tasks.[13]

Polish scholars have also explored the topic of the Soviet rear. The study by Grzegorz Hryciuk and Stanisław Ciesielski stands out for its thorough investigation of the economic assistance to the former Polish refugees and their living conditions during the war.[14] Ciesielski also examined the relations of the local populations and authorities' attitudes toward the Polish refugees.[15] Another Polish researcher, Alexander Srebrakowski, concluded that, based on the data, disease and mortality were very prevalent among Polish refugees.[16] However, he missed the opportunity to compare their situation with other ethnic groups among the refugees, which makes his description of the xenophobia and the Soviet anti-Polish propaganda as an explanation for it somewhat lopsided.

The attempts of Israeli researchers to depict the history of Jewish refugees are marked by the same limited approach, even when they focus on specific groups of refugees and not the entire refugee population. Yosef Litvak dedicates his work to Polish Jews, focusing mainly on their statistics, public organizations, and relations with the Polish authorities.[17] Dov Levin conducted a similar study of the Jews from the Baltic republics and Bessarabia.[18] Shlomo Kless, in his doctoral dissertation, focuses on the Zionist activities of Jewish refugees from the western republics of the USSR.[19] Semën Shveibish considers the state's approach to the evacuation, but only of Jews alone.[20]

Kiril Feferman touches on the Kremlin's general evacuation policy, considering the issue of refugees in the North Caucasus. Reflecting on the benefits of a total evacuation as a means to fully preserve the USSR's human resources and deprive the German side of being able to use them in the occupied lands, he also notes the benefit of leaving the Soviet population under occupation as saboteurs in the struggle against Germany.[21] Although he recognizes the logistical difficulty of a total evacuation (calling it the policy of scorched earth), he does not take into account that, on the one hand, the majority of the population did not want to leave, and, on the other, the administrations and populations of the eastern regions would have been unable to accommodate over a hundred million people. As we shall see, the majority of the locals of those eastern provinces responded negatively to even a tenth of that number of refugees. In addition, such enormous resettlement would have caused panic in the country, where a well-known prewar strategy was to "drive the enemy back to fight on their own territory." I note in passing that this initial strategy led to flight "without luggage." Many refugees assumed that the war would be over quickly, taking with them only summer clothes and footwear. Because of this misconception, up until August 1941, Soviet authorities in Belorussia and Ukraine, which had not yet been fully subdued by the Wehrmacht, failed to prepare organized resistance groups for the approaching German occupation.

Feferman also believes that the evacuation of the population from the North Caucasus was a purely humanitarian action because the population there consisted mainly of women, children, and the elderly.[22] In fact, given the difficulties the USSR had with the supply of labor, the authorities were happy to put to work whatever refugees there were. Of course, the authorities somewhat overestimated the labor potential of the refugees, believing that they would work "wherever the party sent them." In this regard, it is worth noting another aspect that has not yet been discussed by historians. The authorities must have expected that soldiers would be able to fight better knowing that their families were living in unoccupied territory. Officers in particular sought the evacuation of their families, as it was well known how the Germans would deal with them.[23] The converse also supported such reasoning: the refusal of a family to evacuate often led to its sons being drafted in the Red Army to evade mobilization.

In spite of the unprecedented scale of this migration, only a few attempts have been made in the West to reveal certain aspects of this history. Shimon Redlich, in his 1968 doctoral dissertation, examined the attitudes of the Soviet authorities toward the Jewish refugees, mainly those from Poland.[24] Although many aspects were touched upon only superficially in his work and the author had few sources, for the next four decades his dissertation became the starting point for all researchers interested in the topic. Rebecca Manley was the first to impartially and comprehensively review the policy of the Soviet authorities regarding all refugees,[25] although her study did not cover all the nuances of this policy, in particular, the situation in provincial parts of the Soviet Union. Manley makes no distinction between the central and local authorities' positions on refugees. Although she discusses the specific situation of Jewish refugees, this topic remains secondary. Paul Stronski considers the situation of refugees in Tashkent and the surrounding area in several chapters of his book. He concludes that in general Central Asians did not care about refugees and that the Uzbeks greatly disliked them,[26] which, while being the polar opposite of the Soviet mythology on the subject, is far too oversimplified of a conclusion.

The studies dedicated to Soviet wartime economics published in the West tend to trust Soviet sources and propagandistic publications without a shadow of a doubt, despite all their critical approaches.[27] Meanwhile, public statistics in the USSR (including economic statistics) over the years were an important means of propaganda and therefore widely used for manipulation of public opinion. That said, this study doesn't set itself the task of checking all the relevant statistics, but only the data that can be verified by other sources, confirming that manipulations have occurred and providing a basis to at least question all the official statistics.

A separate—and difficult—matter is the data on the evacuees, and even more so the proportion of Jews among them and their mortality. These statistics are very important for calculating the loss of life during the war. Israeli researcher Vadim Dubson has recently proposed a method of counting refugees, but he failed to take some very important points into account, one of which being the Soviet authorities' underestimation of the evacuated population, which we shall consider in detail. Neither Dubson nor the demographers who studied the eastern regions of the USSR during the war paid attention to the overall mortality statistics among the refugees.[28] This is rarely considered to be a separate issue by Russian researchers engaged in estimating deaths in the rear areas during the war.[29] Although their assertions about high mortality among kolkhozniks and townspeople are valid, the living conditions of refugees were much worse.

Because of the peculiarities of Soviet propaganda, the population, now liberated from the German occupation, knew almost nothing about these deprivations and didn't want to. When after the liberation of the USSR's western regions refugees began to return and reclaim their property, it was precisely this liberated population that was among the first to catch on to the myth of good life in evacuation—"the Jews fought in Tashkent." I did not set out to expose the part of the myth whose aim was to diminish the degree of Jewish resistance against the Nazis. Much has already been written about this, and, moreover, the currently available statistics speak for themselves.[30] One of the goals of this work is to show the struggle for survival of refugees (among them Jews) in

Tashkent and Central Asia as a whole, as well as in the eastern regions of the USSR more generally. Many of them suffered every day for four long years, and some were only able to return after six years. It was a real front, with victories and victims. No less than 15–20 percent of the refugee population died of hunger and disease. Of course, the difficult situation in which Jewish refugees found themselves in the rear was preferable to what befell the Jews who remained under occupation, who almost completely perished by starvation and torture in concentration camps and ghettos, in the gas "showers," or by bullets from German machine guns.

The Soviet central authorities did attempt to help the "evacuated population," but they did so not out of a sense of compassion but rather by looking out for the military industry and agriculture of the areas of the rear. These attempts were not very effective since they were often not supported by local administrators, some of whom did not hide their hostility to refugees. They were hardly better perceived by the local populations, who saw them as essentially others. Although this was a very common attitude, the hostility specifically toward the Jews was often aggravated by antisemitism. Despite the failure of the Soviet state to care for the refugees, the main and the greatest responsibility for the death and suffering of some among them lies with Germany. The refugees who perished in the rear were indirect victims of the Second World War.

A comprehensive study of the migration of Jewish refugees to the eastern regions of the USSR and the conditions of their life during the war still has not been done, largely due to the full or partial unavailability of archival sources. Actively engaged in the project of constructing collective memory, the Russian governmental and archival authorities practice selective screening of documents for research access. Prior to the 2010s, this topic had been so poorly studied that publications based on archival sources that shed even the slightest light on the issue were welcomed.[31] The absence of a sufficient number of sources precluded large general studies of the issue and analysis of the overall situation. A lack of available official sources and methodological difficulties have prompted researchers to study refugees' family histories. Some substantial works have appeared only in recent years analyzing the personal experiences of Jewish refugees in the Soviet rear.[32]

Based on multiple sources, this book examines the impact of the war on Jewish refugees. Its purpose is to provide the reader with a complete picture of the history of Jewish refugees along with its many nuances. The research destroys the myth about the unity of the population and authorities during the war, which was built in the USSR for many decades. It shows the crisis of the administrative apparatus and reveals acute contradictions in Soviet society.

This book contains eight chapters. In chapter 1, I discuss five main questions: How did the authorities deal with the issue of civilian evacuation, Jews in particular? How did different groups of the Jewish population decide to flee or stay? What was their motivation? What difficulties did refugees face? How many refugees hailed from Ukraine and Belarus, and how many among them were Jews? This chapter also covers another unexplored topic—the high mortality rate of refugees on the road, first from targeted Wehrmacht aerial bombardments and then from starvation. Chapter 2 shows what needs and struggles refugees faced in their new places of residence, how local administrations helped to resolve them, and how they treated the refugees.

Chapter 3 compares attitudes toward refugees at different levels of government and explains the different approaches. Special attention is paid to refugees' responses to the poor attitudes of local authorities. Chapter 4 argues that a well-chosen profession or enterprise helped refugees settle. It discusses the attitudes of the authorities toward refugees' aspirations for a better place to live and thus a boost in their chances of survival. In turn, many administrators themselves did not miss out on the opportunity to steal food and goods. The central authorities were aware of this problem, and the attitude toward it is also a subject of study in this chapter. Chapter 5 shows that children from the western regions' orphanages, where theft flourished at various levels, were in an even worse situation. Because of antisemitism, it was particularly difficult for Jewish orphans. Was this a unique situation? This question is answered in chapter 6. Here I discuss the attitudes of the local population toward all refugees and whether attitudes toward Jews were different. This chapter also analyzes how the attitude toward Jewish refugees ranged among officials at different levels. The chapter discusses the growth of Jewish identity and mutual assistance during the war.

In the seventh chapter, I address other critical issues. What difficulties did relatives of Jewish refugees have to go through to move in and fight for survival together? How did the communication between people develop during these years of permanent population movement? How many people were evacuated during the war? How many of them were Jews? Clarifying these statistics prompted me to look into how many Jews were called up to the front and how many of them died. Hopefully, the provided information will shed additional light on the number of Jews who died directly at the hands of the Nazis and help future researchers. In order to find out the number of Jewish refugees in the USSR, I also had to look into the issue of the number of Jewish refugees from Poland. This chapter focuses more on the poorly studied refugee experiences of Soviet Jews before 1939, as well as new Soviet citizens from Latvia, Lithuania, Estonia, and Romania. As far as Polish Jews in the USSR are concerned, I tried not to bring in the specific issues they had to deal with. On the one hand, these issues have been studied to a greater or lesser extent already, but on the other, the history of Jewish refugees from Poland requires a separate in-depth study.[33] Therefore, the statistics of Polish Jews in this monograph are presented only briefly. Chapter 8 discusses the Kremlin's policy on refugee re-evacuation. It analyses how the approaches to this issue differed from region to region, as well as how the greater population reacted to the Jewish refugees' return and authorities' measures to reduce ethnic tensions in the Soviet Union's western territories.

In this current piece of research, I had difficulty balancing between the obvious tragedy of the Jewish refugees' situation and the danger of their victimization. To maintain this balance, I also tried to use documents indicating that their fate was not so dramatic. Most often, however, comparative analysis of these documents suggests that they were the result of the widespread Soviet practice of fraud and fabrication. It was more difficult to reveal the psychology of quite a few happy memories of Soviet witnesses. They can be attributed to childhood nostalgia, on the one hand, and, on the other, to poor knowledge of the everyday "adult" problems of those years. Most of all, as Nikolai Nikulin very correctly noted in his famous book *Memories of War*, in the postwar years the fear of "saying too much" was beaten into the consciousness of the Soviet people, who were traumatized by many years of fear.[34] This imperative—"not to say too much"—left its imprint on many testimonies and memories. It became an integral part of the collective memory.

Even though this work is devoted primarily to the research of the history of Jewish refugees, it also looks broadly at the attitudes toward non-Jewish refugees for a deeper understanding of the general state policy. An analysis of the situation in which Gentile refugees found themselves allows us to understand the extent to which Jewish identity influenced the attitudes of the local authorities and population toward various groups of refugees. From this retrospective examination, this study should contribute to our understanding of interethnic relations, as well as the nature of power in the USSR.

Considering the structure of power in the USSR, Gerald Easter and J. Arch Getty convincingly demonstrated how, in the 1920s and 1930s, Stalin consistently pursued the centralization of power at the expense of regional leaders. By the end of the 1930s, ambitious regional leaders who had a record of service to the party and used the "system of personal connections" with the Kremlin elite had been replaced by a new generation of party members or by leaders from other regions.[35] To add to this reduction in independent and local leadership, the prerogatives of regional leaders gradually began to narrow. Already by November 1923 the regional authorities had lost the leadership of the local structure of OGPU (Joint State Political Directorate, the name of the Soviet secret police between 1922 and 1934, when it was succeeded by NKVD), which was reassigned to the center. In March 1937, the department for "the fight against theft of socialist property and speculation" (OBKhSS) was established within the NKVD (People's Commissariat of Internal Affairs), putting party committees in a supervised situation, not only in the political but also in the economic sphere. Therefore, by the beginning of the war, the NKVD (after April 1943 the NKGB, People's Commissariat of State Security) represented the third parallel power structure, along with the Communist Party and the state (consisting of the Soviets and their executive committees). On the one hand, this new controlling power complicated management and further restricted the initiative of local officials, but on the other hand, being involved in the task of refugee absorption during the war, it also brought the benefits of encouraging local authorities to devote more attention to this sphere of activity. In this study I show how the centralized party and administrative authorities on the ground coped with the growing administrative and economic tasks.

In the course of this study, I have used most of all the archives available to me on the Chuvash ASSR and the Kazakh SSR. This is especially noticeable regarding the numerous negative examples cited in the work. The attitudes toward refugees in these two republics of the Soviet Union should by no means be regarded as exceptional. Reconstructing the situation in these republics is like looking through a keyhole, where you can easily see the overall picture of the refugees' situation in an area of tens of thousands of square kilometers from Turkmenistan in Central Asia to Kamchatka in the Far East. This is elegantly confirmed by, first of all, the numerous—both published and unpublished—interviews and, secondly, archival materials from GARF (State Archive of the Russian Federation) and other archives I was able to research.

CHAPTER ONE

Wartime Migration to the Eastern Regions of the USSR

Take a look around you
more attentively—
at the faces in the crowds,
stations, and marinas . . .
You see: spitting and swearing,
rushing about on sidewalks,
poorly dressed,
badly shod,
manly humanity!
It is torn, tormented, urinating,
bellowing with grief and pain,
wishing to live
by its own will . . .

—NIKOLAI ASEEV, "Town on Kama," 1942

FLIGHT AND THE AUTHORITIES

At the beginning of the German attack, the Soviet authorities still had no information about the brutal treatment of Jews, which was even worse in the occupied territory of the USSR (within borders on June 22, 1941) than in the countries previously conquered by the Wehrmacht. This information started to arrive a few weeks after the war began. A secret report written on August 3, 1941, on the activities of anti-German guerrilla and resistance groups operating in the Belorussian territory stated that the Jews in Minsk had been placed in a concentration camp and that on July 11 a large number of them were executed. The same report also mentions the execution of Jews in Slonim.[1] In a memorandum on the situation in the occupied territories of the republic, sent on August 19 to the Central Committee of the Soviet Communist Party's (TsK VKP(b)), the secretary of its Belorussian counterpart, Panteleimon Ponomarenko, emphasized that "the Jewish population is being exposed to ruthless annihilation." He listed examples of extermination of Jews in Brest, Logoshin, Pogost, and Shchedrin, reporting a large number of executions.[2] The August 25 report of Deputy People's Commissar for Internal Affairs of Belorussia A. Misiurev classified as "top secret," reported the murder of 10,000 Jews in Pinsk and an unknown number of Jews in Luninets, all within the same month.[3] About the same time, the head of the Sovinformburo (Soviet Information Bureau) Aleksandr Shcherbakov received a report from the People's Commissariat of Internal Affairs (NKVD) on the situation in Ukraine, according to which the killing of the Jews there was continuous.[4]

Some of the information obtained by the authorities appeared in the press. The July 13 issue of the newspaper *Sovetskaia Sibir'* published an article, "The Massacre of Women and Children," that related the shooting of the inhabitants of Lubaczów without specifying the ethnicity of the victims.[5] Those shot were Jews—before the war, they comprised about half of all residents of Lubaczów. The Soviet reader capable of reading between the lines could discern from the town's name "mestechko Liubachëv," given in the article, that the victims of the shooting were Jews. Almost a month later, on August 10, *Izvestia*, *Krasnaia Zvezda*, *Sovetskaia Sibir'*, and other newspapers published an article titled "The Nazi Atrocities in Brest and Minsk," which told of refugees captured on the road by the Germans and imprisoned in a camp in Minsk. The commandant of the camp forced forty-five Jews to dig a pit, into which they were then thrown by the Germans. Next, he demanded that thirty Belorussians bury them alive, and when they refused, the Germans shot them with the others. According to a witness, executions were held in this camp every day.[6] On August 12, *Pravda* reported that in Bel'tsy German and Romanian soldiers "shot about 200 old Jewish women."[7] The same newspaper, dated August 27, 1941, informed its readers that in one of the synagogues in Białystok, the Nazis burned 300 Jews in a synagogue.[8] On August 29, the writer Vsevolod Ivanov, from the words of a witness, wrote about the execution of three dozen Jews in a Belorussian towns.[9] At the very end of August, it also reported on the execution of 400 Jewish refugees in Kamenets-Podol'sk.[10]

The first time the authorities widely and publicly raised the issue of the genocide of the Jews was only at the end of August, when the Jews of Moldavia, Belorussia, and the Baltic republics—completely occupied—could not escape. On August 24, 1941, the Jewish anti-fascist rally took place in Moscow, with speeches by the People's Artist Solomon Mikhoels, the physicist and professor Pyotr Kapitsa, the film director Sergey Eisenstein, the poet and translator Samuil Marshak, the writer Ilya Ehrenburg, journalist and editor Shakhno Epshtein, and others. The very name of the rally, which, without doubt, was, if not initiated by Stalin, then organized with his approval, indicates that the leader temporarily abandoned his own definition of a nation, into which the Jewish people did not fit. Trying to mobilize "his own" Jews—but even more "foreign" Jews—in the struggle against Nazism, Stalin went even further the next day, authorizing an appeal in the press under the heading unthinkable in the prewar years, "Jewish brethren throughout the world!" The language was similar to the famous address "Brothers and sisters!" that he used at the beginning of the war. In an open letter to their fellow Jews abroad, the participants of the anti-fascist rally and other Jews well known in the country spoke not only about the heroism of Soviet Jewish soldiers, the need for aid to the Soviet Union, and the importance of the economic and political boycott of Germany, but also about the ongoing genocide against the Jews perpetrated by the German occupying forces.[11]

The publication of Tel Aviv's reaction to the rally, which made the front page of *Izvestiia*, also serves as evidence of an attempt to mobilize Jewish social circles abroad for the benefit of the Jews in the Soviet Union. The telegram sent on behalf of the Palestinian Socialist League (led by the pro-Soviet intellectuals Shlomo Kaplansky, Arnold Zweig, and Leiba Tarnopoler and renamed a short time later the League V) and the mass youth socialist organization Hashomer Hatzair reported readiness to fend off Germany's attack on Palestine and expressed solidarity with the Red Army and the Jews fighting within it.[12]

Despite the collected facts of the genocide and attempts to woo overseas Jewish communities, the GKO (State Defense Committee) gave no, not even secret, orders to evacuate the Jewish population from areas that were not yet occupied.[13] In light of the propaganda widely used by the Germans, such an order could indeed be evidence of the "Yid character of the Bolshevik regime" and cause an even worse attitude toward the Jews—and toward the authorities of the USSR. On the other hand, the Kremlin, no longer bound by the agreement with Germany, from the first days of the war resumed anti-fascist propaganda in the media, and the topic of antisemitism was widely used in it. Realizing that by doing so they brought grist to the German propaganda mill, the Soviet authorities still did not want to abandon the theme of the Holocaust, which they used to condemn the ideology of the enemy. The secretary of the TsK VKP(b) and head of Soviet propaganda, Alexander Shcherbakov, allowed authors, editors, and censors of articles and messages in newspapers a level of discretion in coverage of the Holocaust.[14]

Published somewhat late for objective reasons, newspaper coverage on the special persecution against Jews still had time to influence some Jewish families who had not yet been under occupation and were still solving a difficult dilemma: to flee or stay. Ania Maccabi-Iorsch recalls: "The newspapers began to report German atrocities against civilians, especially those of Jewish origin. And then we remembered the rumors that we had heard earlier from Polish refugees, but did not believe."[15] However, the readers' attitudes toward the state information about the Holocaust were ambiguous. During the years of Soviet rule, Jews, like other Soviet citizens, became accustomed not to trust the newspapers, seeing them primarily as a propaganda tool rather than a source of information.[16]

Many Jews in the western regions of the USSR also hoped that the enemy would not be allowed into their city. Konstantin Simonov would later write in his diary how he, along with Red Army officers, passed through the Belorussian town Shklov, headed east, and terrified Jewish women were standing in front of their homes, asking with their eyes whether they should leave or not. Near one of the homes, the military men stopped to have a drink, and there this question was voiced. His answer, which the women believed, was that the Germans were far away and would not be allowed into Shklov. And just a few days later, barely south of Shklov, the defensive line was broken.[17]

The elderly population especially did not want to leave their homes for fear of the difficulties of evacuation and arrangements in a new place. This was complicated by the fact that their sons had been drafted into the army, and some of their daughters lived in other places, communication with which, after the Wehrmacht attack, was difficult. Some of the elderly were seriously ill. Because of the categorical refusal of the elderly population to evacuate, daughters or daughters-in-law with their children often remained with them. A large percentage of the Jewish children who died in Rechitsa (BSSR) relative to the small percentage of Jewish women victims aged twenty-six to forty-five indicates that mothers with many children didn't leave, fearing, understandably, being left without homes and jobs. At the same time, many able-bodied women forty-six to fifty-five years old, without small children, left Rechitsa. Even more women aged sixteen to twenty-five, most of whom had no children or only one child, evacuated. The elderly population, justifying their unwillingness to leave, assumed that the Germans would not harm ordinary Jews—craftsmen and pensioners. This was based on the memories the German occupation in 1918, which, compared to the Polish occupation in 1920 and the subsequent Bolshevik control, was remembered as temperate. In addition, those who had been in Germany as prisoners of war in World War I remembered Germany relatively pleasantly.[18] In contrast, the Germans themselves in their propaganda aimed at the Slavic population of Belorussia insisted that they fought only Communists and Jews, whose obliteration would supposedly ease the situation of the general population. Leaflets with this content were scattered from aircraft, in particular over Bobruisk.[19]

Still, with the approach of the front line, many Jews tried to flee to the east. This decision was strongly influenced by the massive bombing and the wave of Jewish refugees from the west. A former resident of Rechitsa, Lev Dobrushkin, stated that the deluge of Jewish refugees (in trains, trucks, carts, on foot) contributed to the spread of panic throughout the town.[20] According to the memoirs of Maria Berlina, after the war began, many Jews came from western Belorussia came to Gomel in the southeast of the republic.[21] As Arkadii Gurevich also witnessed: "At the station in Gomel, a large number of people who had evacuated from the western regions of Belorussia had accumulated. To the 'accompaniment' of almost incessant bombings, the echelons formed which took these accumulated refugees, mostly women, children, and the elderly, to the east."[22] Vera Bel'skaia, who lived in Kiev at the time, recalls how in the city thousands of refugees gathered under open skies, speaking about the Nazis, and Kiev's Jews understood that it was necessary to escape.[23] But there were also those who did not trust the refugees from the west. A former resident of Shargorod, Arkadii Viner, states, "The stories of the refugees that the Germans were worse than the cruelest beasts were seen by some of the residents as part of official Soviet propaganda, which those older than us initially thought false."[24]

Refugees went to the east in an endless stream. Soviet documentary filmmaker Roman Karmen describes the movement from Latvia to the east, "Through the former front line, there was a continuous flow of refugees. Going on foot, by horse-drawn carts. A road cart on inflated tires, ten children in it, with adults walking alongside."[25] Journalist Konstantin Simonov recalls:

> There were especially a lot of Jewish refugees from Stolbtsy, Baranovichi, Molodcheno, and other towns of western Belorussia. Now, on the eighth day of the war, they were already past Borisov, which meant that they had been trekking for a long time, having set off already on the very first day. . . . Thousands of people traveled upon unimaginable wagons, droshkies, and carts, old men with sidelocks and beards and in the bowlers of the last century were traveling, exhausted Jewish women who had grown old early were traveling, children—six, eight, ten dark little kids with frightened eyes. But even more people walked alongside the carts. Among the ragged old men and women and the children, especially odd looking were the young women in their trendy coats, miserable and dusty, with fashionable side-parted hairstyles covered in dust. And in their hands, baggage, parcels, and things tied up in blankets, bedsheets, and handkerchiefs; their fingers clenched convulsively and trembling with fatigue and hunger.[26]

Leonid Sandalov, then chief of staff of the 4th Army of the Western Front, recalls the movement of people from Brest: "Along the forest roads and roadsides moved carts with safes and archives of the Party and Soviet institutions. From time to time one also encountered groups of newly mobilized citizens, accompanied by representatives of the military. But the refugees were far more numerous—men, women, children. All of them with baggage, wallets, bags. Dead tired, haggard with sorrowful faces, they moved silently to Kobrin, hiding from enemy aircraft under trees and in the bushes."[27]

Ilya Ehrenburg writes that "the evacuation of the western regions took place randomly and in difficult conditions."[28] In fact, the movement of refugees from the war zone was of little concern to the authorities there. Not only did they not provide transport, the authorities did not even think of a plan to guide the pedestrian flows of refugees to not-yet-occupied railway stations and assist them on the road with paramedic services.

The difficult situation in which the refugees found themselves only exacerbated the inclination of the authorities to contain the fleeing population. In Belorussia, the authorities of the republic, at the meeting on June 23, 1941, two days after the start of the war, decided to evacuate children from Minsk in two days, mainly due to the continuous bombing. At the same time, participants of the meeting discussed the prevention of panic. They resolved to create patrol barriers "for the dispersal of the human deluge," thus preventing the refugees from getting to the railway station in Minsk and interrupting their movement further east. Poorly grasping the magnitude of aggression and level of combat capability of the Red Army, the Belorussian authorities ordered the regional and district administrations to put the refugees to work and not to allow the use of vehicles for "personal evacuation."[29] In this regard, it is clear that Ivan Russiianov, then commander of the Minsk garrison, was disingenuous when he said in his memoirs that on the same day it was ordered to remove and transport out not only items of material and financial value, flour and meats, but also the population, which he allegedly saw as a major problem. Not embarrassed at all, he added, "the evacuation of the population and material goods was rather successful."[30]

Due to the large proportion of Jews among the refugees, this measure of the national authorities was directed primarily against them. We shall discuss the statistics in detail below, but shown here as evidence of this is a secret report to Stalin from the first secretary of the Belorussian Communist Party, Ponomarenko, composed at the beginning of July 1941. Written in a boastful manner, the report contained pronounced antisemitic undertones: "This conclusion should be emphasized—the exceptional courage, resistance to, and intolerance of the enemy by the kolkhozniks, in contrast to some of the military servicemen from cities, who think about nothing but saving their own skin. This can be explained to some extent by the large Jewish population in the cities. They were seized by an animal fear of Hitler and, instead of fighting, they fled."[31] Ponomarenko's statement shows his desire to force Jewish children, women, and elderly people to fight against the Wehrmacht. It corresponds to the Stalinist idea of creating urban militias, composed mainly of minors. I note in passing that this measure, taken from the experience of the Civil War, led to the almost total and nearly purposeless destruction of the poorly trained militias.[32]

Anxiety about calling down the wrath of Moscow curtailed the initiatives of the local administrators. They preferred to play it safe, coordinating the timing of the evacuation with the higher authorities. The authorities of the Krasnodar territory decided to submit to the commission for the priority evacuation under the jurisdiction of the GKO a request to allow the first stage of the evacuation (the Azov-Black Sea coast and the northern part of the territory), with the intention that it be finished by August 1, 1942. As for the other two parts of the territory, they planned to evacuate the population by turns at intervals of ten days. But a positive response from the Kremlin came only on August 3, when the Germans were already bombing with might and main the most important railway junctions of the territory.[33] Administrators had to choose between punishment for alarmism due to a hasty evacuation and punishment for leaving various assents and resources with the enemy due to delayed evacuation. The example of the Stalingrad region illustrates this conundrum. Because of the approaching front line, on July 13, 1942, the regional committee decided on the evacuation of the fifteen districts of the right bank of the Khopër and Don rivers. They began to evacuate hospitals and orphanages. A week later, however, came a menacing telephone call from Stalin: "Have you decided to hand the city over to the enemy?" Following were instructions to end the evacuation mood and deal with cowards and alarmists, according to the former secretary of the Stalingrad Party Committee Mikhail Vodolagin.[34]

Similar deterrent measures were taken by the authorities in Ukraine. When on September 1, 1941, several wives of servicemen in Mariupol' asked the military to evacuate them, they were told that this would be done in the spring. However, in a little over a month, the city surrendered, and they were shot.[35] As in Belorussia, authorities in Ukraine waged a propaganda war against the "evacuation mood." Because of this approach, an intolerant attitude toward people intending to go into the interior of the Soviet Union emerged. The recollections of Ania Makabi-Yoresh attest to the fact that in August 1941 in Zaporozh'e any talk about evacuation was officially classified as a "panic mood," and in the countryside at night neighbors shot at the wheels of carts of "cowards" who were going to be evacuated in the morning.[36] Most likely, Ania Makabi-Yoresh was describing one of the former Jewish kolkhozes—she was a native of one of them—which by the end of the 1930s had became international by ethnic composition. On October 12, 1941, in the courtyard of the military conscription office in Kalinin, Commander of the Western Front Ivan Konev calmed the crowd that demanded to be evacuated because of the threat of occupation. Believing this threat and the accompanying panic to be contrived, and to demonstrate his own calmness, he announced to the crowd that he was going to sleep. After that, as Konev writes in his memoirs, the crowd dispersed.[37] Describing it as an example of his ability to deal with the public, he does not mention that two days later the city was taken, and there was only time to evacuate material goods and archives. Among Kalinin Jews, the only ones who were saved were those who didn't wait for help from the authorities, having left for the rear on foot.

By July 6, 1941, the Presidium of the Supreme Soviet of the Soviet Union signed a decree about "spreading false wartime rumors that incite alarm among the population." The vague wording of penalties of two to five years in prison, "if this action does not by its nature involve harsher punishment,"[38] opened up opportunities for punitive measures. Reprisals against real or imaginary panic-mongers reached such a scale that the head of the UNKGB (Administration of the People's Commissariat of State Security) of the Kursk region, Pëtr Aksënov, was forced to restrain his own agency so that arrests of the "hostile" elements were made only with the sanction of the prosecutors, threatening violators with penalties.[39]

Before the Wehrmacht attack, the new Soviet citizens were not allowed into the Soviet Union past its summer 1939 border without special permits. In the first week of the war, this order remained in force.[40] Mikhail Chakhotskii vividly describes in his memoirs how their train, which left on the evening of July 23 from Pinsk to Gomel, was surrounded near Zhitkovichi by guards, who allowed only holders of "eastern" passports to go further.[41] Eliezer Bashan, a refugee from Vilnius, reports how thousands of refugees who were not allowed to flee to the east accumulated on the old border with Lithuania. Their group went south of the border station, and within five kilometers freely crossed the old border.[42] Aron Feigelovich's group of refugees perhaps went to the same border point. He states that having been ordered not to cross the border, one group of refugees turned back, while the other waited a day or two until the guards had left their post.[43] The same thing happened with the refugees at the old border with Latvia. Only after four days were J. C. and his wife able to stealthily cross it.[44] Meir Toker, a refugee from Lithuania, along with thousands of other refugees was also not allowed to pass through a Latvian border-crossing point to the east:

> People wandered in all directions, many families with children returned to their homes in Lithuania. And then there was a rumor that the crossing points at the

border were open, the detachments had fled, and we again moved eastward, there was no gate to block our path. Hungry and exhausted we reached Sebezh, here there was no delay, all were fed, and two days later a train arrived at the station intended for the evacuation of refugees. People were packed into the empty "freight train," and at the end of our journey we found ourselves in Mordovia.[45]

Due to the rapid German advance, the delay dramatically affected the fate of many Jewish refugees. It would be wrong to think that the prewar order was simply neglected to be rescinded. In fact, it was, on the one hand, a measure against the infiltration of saboteurs, but on the other, it fit well into the authorities' suppressive approach to suppress the problem of refugees. In addition, the authorities often suspected refugees from recently acquired territories of spying. The same Feigelovich recalls the immediate execution of a refugee who was found to have a camera in his bag. Konstantin Simonov recalls how near Borisov, in the same first days of the war, a detainee who did not have documents was shot. Simonov himself was mistaken for a disguised spy and arrested in July 1941.[46] The spread of "spy mania" was encouraged by the news of real German sabotage groups' actions, such as the capture of the bridges over the Northern Dvina and Berezina by the forces of the Brandenburg 800 regiment in the very beginning of the war. An NKVD directive issued on July 4, 1941, reported that spies and saboteurs, disguised as refugees, were infiltrating the rear.[47] A directive on combatting enemy signalmen in Moscow came out the following day.[48]

Greatly confused, the central authorities at first continued to overestimate their military strength. Therefore, instead of preparing new defensive lines, Stalin stubbornly gave orders to attack. This plans viewed the refugees only as an obstacle. Therefore, not planning to use the labor of more refugees in the rear, the authorities not only did little to evacuate the population, or at least to facilitate escape, but in many places even continued to obstruct it until the middle or even the end of July 1941. Following the decision of the central authorities on June 29, positions of army chiefs of the front line's rear protection services were formed. Each chief had a subdivision of the NKVD in disposal. In addition to providing communication, evacuation of the wounded, and fighting against saboteurs, their duties included "clearing the roads of refugees" and "rectification of the railways,"[49] which meant not only restoring the railway lines after the bombings but also removing refugees from trains.

Realizing the impossibility of completely halting the movement of people to the east, Chief of the Army General Staff Georgy Zhukov, on July 2, 1941, ordered that the refugees be sent only by dirt roads (an exception was made for family members of senior commanders and civilian top officials) and not by highway or the railway, which, according to his plan, had to be free for military maneuvering. According to the order, refugee movement outside of dirt roads should be immediately stopped, and, in general, they should be allowed into the rear no farther than 150 kilometers from the front line. At the same time, Zhukov ordered material goods to be transported into the rear by rail.[50] Due to the quickly approaching front line, as well as the panic, confusion, extraordinary efforts toward evacuation of material assets, and shortage of hands, the army chiefs of the front line's rear protection services often did not adhere to this order and other restrictive orders regarding refugees. In hundreds of recollections, Soviet war veterans describe how they retreated together with the refugees on the same road, often sympathizing with them and even helping them with problems on the road. Thus the soldiers tried to compensate as they could for a hasty retreat.

The refugees severely lacked help from the authorities. The family of Moisei Doman, living in Pervomaisk (Nikolaev region), wanted to leave immediately after the war began, but the town was not issuing permits for evacuation. Without permits, people rarely left, for fear of losing their rights to housing and being suspected of spying at their new place of residence. When the cherished permits to leave were issued in Pervomaisk, there were no train cars for the Domans: "They sent us everywhere, announcing that this train was exclusively for factory evacuees and that one was 'reserved,' to which the refugees had no access. . . . I and my elderly parents, younger brother and little sister, old grandmother, after each failure, worn out and exhausted, returned home, and the next morning went back to the station."[51] After a long ordeal, taking advantage of the fact that the last evacuation train leaving the town was not guarded against refugees and had open platforms with factory equipment, they boarded, unsupervised, with their belongings. Along the way, they were joined by other refugees.

Other refugees similarly "evacuated" from central Belorussia. Georgii Beregovoi, later a Soviet cosmonaut, recalls: "Platforms rolled on rails laboriously, slowly: originally they were for transporting coal or gravel, but now upon them sat and lay people who yesterday were residents of Bobruisk. Many were wounded. . . . On one of the platforms was a young woman in a knitted sweater torn from the shoulders to the shoulder blades. She sat with her back facing the movement of the train, holding to her chest with both hands a bloodied teddy bear. She was not crying; she was tense, unblinking, staring back—from whence the train came."[52] But in general, the situation in Belorussia was distinct. The administrators of the republic, finding out about the situation, fled with their families from Minsk by the evening of June 24 without notifying the central authorities in Moscow or the regional and district authorities in Belorussia about their departure, and some commissars did not even notify their own departments. After this, panic and anarchy broke out in Minsk and other cities of the republic.[53] Organizations seized each other's vehicles. There were situations when cars were taken away from kindergartens that were evacuating children.[54] On the same day, the army detained twenty-five cars on the outskirts of Minsk to be used for the purpose of the evacuation of officers' families. Although the former commander of the Minsk garrison notes in his memoirs that it was transport "without cargo or documents,"[55] it is hard to believe that only the drivers were being rescued from burning Minsk. Besides, amid the total panic and flight of the administration, it was only possible to obtain evacuation permits if the administrators themselves were riding in the car.

By July 7, 1941, most party and government leaders of Belorussia, altogether 171 people, and together with their families 466 people, made it to Moscow. The report of Moscow's police department about the arrival of the top Belorussian officials stated that "the families of certain republic's authorities carried with them a lot of different assets, even including carpets and so on, while a number of workers from the same institutions and their families (i.e., including children), who had asked to be taken by cars, but whose request was followed by denial, were walking to Moscow on foot."[56]

The panicked mood of the authorities of the republic was picked up by the administrations of several cities from parts of Belorussia that had not yet been occupied. In Rechitsa on June 28, just three hours after the regional authorities announced the order to evacuate the civilian population, state institutions were abandoned, secret documents were burned, and unclassified papers were thrown into the yard of the executive committee building. The first secretary of the Rechitsa Party Committee Aleksandr Kuteinikov and chair of the executive committee of the Town Council Vasilii Kostroma rushed to the rear with their families. Their actions, as well as the complete disorganization of the first wave of evacuations, strengthened the sense of panic among the population. Informing Moscow about this, the prosecutor of the Rechitsa district Trashchenko wrote, "Part of the population—women and children without food—went on foot in an unknown direction, and the other part, having remained at the marina, came back in the evening." Trashchenko himself stayed in place to prevent looting. The new prosecutor G. Safonov also reported about these events in Rechitsa to TsK VKP(b) in July 1941. He added that according to new information, on July 10 the Rechitsa executives returned to their area. The authorities in neighboring Mozyr' behaved even worse. Having commanded the population not to leave, in accordance with the above-mentioned outdated—but never called-off—order of June 23, the regional authorities themselves fled together with their families.[57]

In Moscow, the Belorussian authorities had to urgently correct the embarrassing situation in which they found themselves. Stalin at the time was quick to use violence. The members of the Central Committee of the Belorussian Communist Party and the BSSR Council of People's Commissars quickly returned to Belorussia in mid-July 1941, choosing Gomel as their base. There, led by Ponomarenko, they quite vigorously engaged in the organization of resistance and evacuation, for which a large part of the local authorities had also returned to eastern Belorussia. Fearing punishment for their escape and inaction, now the Belorussian authorities, on the contrary, were interested in increasing the number of evacuated people and, especially, in the removal of industrial plants and factories. Therefore, even such unimportant—from the point of view of defense—enterprises like glassworks, printing, plywood, and match factories were taken from the Gomel region to the east.[58]

The authorities of the republic had a harder time reporting on the evacuation of the population, as the majority preferred to remain under occupation. By that time, the Kremlin had begun to realize that the war would be protracted. Therefore, to increase the number of evacuees, the Belorussian authorities were already having information about the executions of Jews, likely giving verbal instructions to the local authorities to use it to persuade the Jewish population in the unoccupied territory to move east. There are multiple examples of the local authorities in southeast Belorussia alerting the Jews during the second half of July, although it is possible that they did it purely on their own initiative. According to Mordechai Altshuler, in El'sk one Belorussian Komsomol leader went from Jewish house to Jewish house persuading residents to leave. In nearby Kalinkovichi the local authorities were attentive to the request of the Jews for help with transport.[59] In neighboring Khoiniki, even on the train station radio somebody called for Jewish youth to leave because with the arrival of the Germans they would all be eliminated.[60] In Gomel the regional authorities dispatched train cars to the railway station for all who wished to leave. Moreover, the police went around apartment buildings daily and encouraged the people to leave.[61] Although most likely they did not target apartments of Jews, the topic of the Germans' attitudes toward the Jews came up during conversations with the Jewish residents. It is possible that this argument was also used by the regional leaders Turov and Zhlobin who, according to Ben-Tsion Pinchuk, also urged the Jews to evacuate.[62] The unprecedented efforts of the Belorussian authorities are illustrated by the actions of the Gomel police, who threatened severe punishments of those citizens who refused to send children under fifteen years of age to the rear. As a result, within five days of August, 250 children were sent with dedicated convoys from Gomel.[63]

We must also commend the returning Rechitsa authorities. They were visiting the houses of Jews and persuading them to leave. For the evacuation of the civilian population, the Rechitsa government organized heated freight train cars, in which, for the most part, populations from all regions left for the east. For boarding, it was necessary to produce a certified by the town authorities permit to evacuate. The issuance of permits, as a rule, was a trouble-free formality, whose purpose was only to document the fact of departure. The authorities did not control or regulate boarding, and the trains departed on a short notice. There was also a more organized evacuation of enterprises and their employees. They were sent by special cars or trains. From July 3 to July 11 the authorities evacuated from Rechitsa the nail factory equipment (six cars) and the match factory equipment (eight cars), together with the families of their employees.[64] Often during the journey the only stops the trains made were to change the locomotives, arriving to their destinations in the rear quickly. It was much more difficult to leave from the towns and villages that were far from the railway. The lucky ones were those who had procured carts or boarded passing vehicles—this allowed them to get to the train station.

Many of the refugees had to walk a long way on foot before they were able to get on the train. En route, whether on foot, in cars, but, especially, at railway stations or on trains, the refugees experienced bombings and machine-gun fire from German planes. Almost every one of the hundreds of memoirs and recollections about the evacuation contains references to fellow travelers falling victim to such attacks. Given this, and the fact that sometimes the bombs destroyed whole carts, cars, or wagons, it can be assumed that at least 2 percent of the refugees from western republics were killed by German planes. Although these victims were refugees, I do not include them in the refugee statistics (which I am yet to discuss), because most of them never managed to register as evacuees. They are direct victims of the war.

At that time, infantry regiment commander Amazasp Babadzhanian was shocked by what he saw in Belorussia. He recalls:

> We arrived in Liozno early in the surprisingly clear morning; the sky was cloudless. At the station on the tracks stood no fewer than ten echelons, crowded with evacuees. Inside the station, on the platforms, in boxcars, right on the railway tracks—everywhere there was a huge human swarm, mostly women and children—a real multicolored sea, pouring out over two to three kilometers. The sea moved, buzzed; through the rumble one could hear children's cries in different tones. . . . 27 Junkers appeared in the sky. . . . Bomb strikes aimed directly into the human mass, tearing out the bodies of their victims. I saw how the bodies of women and children flew into the air, bursting midair into pieces, and scattered

around. Even this turned out to be not enough for the vultures. Having dropped their stock of bombs, they regrouped and finished the people off by shooting machine guns from the low-flying planes. The planes left. Up until noon, in the whole area around the train station, you could hear the wounded groaning, the children crying, the women weeping. And at noon, tanks with a white cross on their armor came crashing into the station. The "Renowned" chariots of General Guderian. They descended upon the enemy. Only the enemies in this "battle" were women and children. But was that really so important. . . . The "glorious" chariots then went across the field of battle, finishing off the "enemy," those women and children who could not walk.[65]

The second secretary of the TsK KP(b) of Belorussia Pëtr Kalinin was amazed by what he saw on the road:

Along the Vitebsk-Velizh dirt road . . . day and night flowed crowds of refugees from Vilnius, Lepel', Polotsk, and Vitebsk, going east. There were hundreds of cars and carts carrying the wounded. Above the path hung clouds of dust. . . . Neither fatigue and hunger, nor bombing and machine-gun fire from the air—nothing could stop people rushing to get away from the roar of cannon fire, from the continuous drone of aircraft marked with sister crosses. The dead from the bombings were buried in the ground right beside the road without coffins, in silence, as if they were carrying a difficult, but an already familiar task.[66]

Commander of the 51st Tank Regiment Ivan Iakubovskii dramatically describes what he saw on these roads:

I will never forget the tragic roads of Belorussia and the Smolensk region, the downtrodden refugees. It seemed that from the front line flowed human sorrow itself. An endless stream of people moved to the east, in search of salvation from the impending disaster. Among them were women, children, and the elderly. But misfortune overtook them on the road. In the dark blue sky, which had become evil and strange, constantly circled the yellow-bellied planes with black crosses. The Nazi vultures with the equanimity of sadists shot at the defenseless crowd. . . . To speak frankly, as a soldier, I already had more than once come to look death in the face and say goodbye to friends fallen in battle. But to see in ditches and right on the road so many dead women and elderly people, mothers weeping over their bloody children, crying babies beside the corpses of their nursing mothers.[67]

According to the Chief of Staff Operations of the Southwestern Front Ivan Bagramian, the same thing happened in Ukraine: "The dramatic events played out at the crossings, where huge masses of people, machines, carts accumulated. Every fascist bomb hit its target. But even here there was no panic. Soldiers and commanders, having removed the dead bodies, broken machines and carts, rebuilt bridges, let through ferries. The refugees patiently waited for their turn."[68]

While the administrators in charge were threatened with harsh punishment for the failure to move away factory equipment, they carried almost no responsibility for the abandonment of the population wishing to go to the east. Stalin saw the people as merely appendages to the factories. There were about 200,000 refugees in Stalingrad at that time, whom the authorities were not able to accommodate and feed or to transport further east. As a result of the large concentrations and poor sanitary conditions, at the beginning of December 1941 an epidemic of typhus broke out.[69] Due to intensification of the Germans' bombings on the outskirts of the city in the summer of 1942 and the lack of regular evacuation opportunities for refugees, panic took hold. When the authorities still decided to take them by means of the Volga River, according to an eyewitness:

> On the pier something unimaginable was going on. When the boat approached the pier, huge crowds of desperate people took it by storm. Vouchers were supposed to limit the number of people on each boat, but restraining the crowd of refugees was a matter of great difficulty. Often the ships departed greatly overloaded. People, during beastly boardings, trampled the weak and the children. The last ship, the *Joseph Stalin*, departed on August 24 and was carrying 1,000–1,200 passengers, which was twice the regulated number. Their fate was tragic—German aircraft sank the ship and few escaped.[70]

Authorities gave a special place to the male population in their discussions of evacuation—the army needed soldiers, the factories needed workers, the kolkhozes needed tractor drivers. A telegram from Stalin to the first secretary of the Communist Party of Ukraine Nikita Khrushchev, dated July 10, 1941, along with criticism of Khrushchev's proposal to liquidate of all material goods and food remaining within 100–150 kilometers from the front line, gave instructions to send away the entire male population within 70 kilometers.[71]

Recruitment offices were obligated to evacuate from areas under threat those who were of premilitary age, born in 1922–1925.[72] Often this evacuation of premilitary aged youth was carried out late, and they were forced to trek out under bombardments or even during battles, sometimes crossing occupied territory. Often enough, these groups had to go to the east on their own—without money, possessions, or provisions. However, the recollections of former soldiers suggest that by this measure the authorities saved many Jewish boys from death.

There were several factors that negatively affected the evacuation of Jews from eastern Ukraine and the southwestern areas of Russia. The deportation of Soviet Germans from the Volga region and evacuation of millions of Moscow and Leningrad residents had a dramatic effect on it, leading to a shortage of rail cars and locomotives. It is not known to what extent, but the decree of the Supreme Soviet on February 16, 1942, also had a negative effect. According to the decree, the apartments left by the evacuated population were to be transferred to the urban authorities to be distributed for temporary use by the needy workers and employees who had remained in place. With regard to property that the refugees were leaving behind, although official rules gave them three options to choose from—transfer property to remaining relatives, sell it through thrift shops, or even have it delivered to the place of the evacuation,[73] during the war these options were impracticable. I have not found a single document confirming the use of even one of these options, and, given the large number of evacuees, such requests would have overwhelmed local administrative offices. After the decision was issued, the potential loss of homes was implied in the prospective refugees' question: "Should we leave, or should we stay?" After all, provisional measures in the USSR often became permanent.

The removal of the workers and employees of those companies that were subject to evacuation had several features. Due to transportation problems, people learned about the impending evacuation only the day before or even the day it was to happen. Each family made their own final decision to evacuate or remain. The local authorities, as a rule, did not insist upon evacuation. This could explain why only 40 percent of the former employees of even large industries and factories evacuated.[74] Such a low percentage of workers evacuating cannot be attributed to the summons to the army, because many of them were released from them.

Formally, each evacuated worker was allowed to take one hundred kilograms of cargo and forty extra kilos for each family member.[75] However, usually, there was no dedicated transport available for the delivery of luggage to the train station. Therefore, decisions what to bring depended on being able to find transportation and the strength of evacuees and their companions. At the same time, many of those who were leaving in the summer and autumn of 1941 did not want to burden themselves with a lot of possessions, in hopes that the war would end quickly.

In contrast to the evacuated factory and office workers, refugees decided on departure and its method entirely independently. Typically, for the refugees escaping dangerous regions, the authorities provided cars for the long road ahead, if such cars were available. However, compared to the workers and employees who were evacuated by their companies, especially those of important for the country's defense, the refugees were on the trains that moved more slowly. This was important considering the difficult situation on the railways, which we shall discuss below. Apart from this, there were no substantial differences between the evacuees' and refugees' conditions of migration to the east.[76] Much depended on the care and activity of the chief of the evacuation train. This is evidenced by the recollections of Grigorii Gogiberidze, who was the director of the Red Profintern Factory evacuated from the Iaroslavl' region:

> Some groceries were brought along with them, they bought some at station markets, and at major stations one could sometimes have dinner. We were traveling for the third week. . . . In one of the echelons, on the road, four were born, two died. As the head of the echelon, at each stop at any time of day or night, I would walk around the entire train. Once, in one of the heated freight cars, I found a fire burning right on the floor. Of course, the nights were cold, but people did not think about the consequences.[77]

The evacuated enterprises often quickly resumed their activities in the Urals, the Middle Volga area, and Western Siberia, and so many evacuated workers were welcomed there. Despite this, the authorities cared little about creating even tolerable living conditions for them. The memories of former migrants are at odds with the rosy descriptions of the evacuated workers being met by representatives of the local authorities, as presented by historian Viktor Fedotov. Based on evidence of questionable reliability, such overly sanguine reports usually describe the evacuated workers receiving apartment leases immediately after the official greeting ceremony and the subsequent disinfection procedures upon their arrival.[78]

In the eastern regions of the USSR, an evacuee arriving with their factory had only a theoretical possibility of resuming work soon. The fact is that, contrary to the fairy-tale assertions of the relevant Soviet historiography, the majority of the enterprises that were relocated with such difficulty to the east were not reconstructed at the new location, for various reasons, or it happened very slowly. Therefore, except for a small part of the evacuated workers who worked in important military factories, the evacuees found themselves in the same position as that of the refugees.

Jews made up a significant percentage of all the refugees to leave the territory of the former Pale of Settlement. Analysis of statistical data gives reason to believe that the proportion of Jews among all refugees from this area in the first three months of the war slightly exceeded one third. Here are the main points of this analysis. According to official statistics, on September 15, 1941, the proportion of the 486,906 Jews among all refugees registering at their places of arrival was 24.8 percent. Although the statistics covered only 1,962,207 refugees, and this was less than half of the actual number of the refugees at that time, the data on ethnicity have the character of a random sample, and therefore are perfectly acceptable for extrapolation. Of this (partial) number of refugees, 983,404 were from the territories that previously were not in the Pale of Settlement (including 76,375 from the Karelo-Finnish SSR; 548,225 from the Moscow region; 184,127 from the Leningrad region; 56,382 from the Murmansk region; 17,192 from the Kalinin region; 9,287 from the Orël region; and 91,786 from other regions of Russia). They constitute 50.1 percent of all accounted refugees.[79] The residences of most of these refugees were unoccupied throughout the war.

The official statistics of refugees are not broken down by nationality according to the place of previous permanent residence, while they are broken down in terms of the place of arrival. Nevertheless, we can assume that among the evacuated population of the RSFSR regions that were outside the former Pale of Settlement, Jews constituted 12 percent (118,000 people altogether). This was almost double their percentage, according to the 1939 census, in Moscow and Leningrad.[80] The twice-greater share of Jews among the refugees as compared to their proportion among these cities' inhabitants was due to very strong motivation to avoid German occupation. There is a variety of evidence for this. An inhabitant of Leningrad stated in August 1941, "The evacuation was thought up by the Jews. They themselves were frightened and ran away long ago, and we are not afraid and will not go anywhere."[81] The strong motivation of Jews to escape from Leningrad is conveyed, although in a highly exaggerated form, in a German report from October 2, 1941, based on the information of secret agents and prisoners of war.[82] Jews of Leningrad and Moscow were encouraged to leave by both the spreading German anti-Jewish propaganda and intensifying antisemitism.[83]

The estimation of 12 percent is also supported by other fragmentary statistical evidence. It is close to the statistics of Alatyr' (Chuvashia) at the end of 1941, which have a breakdown by refugees' nationality according to the place of their permanent residence. This breakdown shows that Jews made 14.2 percent of all refugees from the Moscow and Leningrad regions.[84] This assessment is confirmed by the statistics on the nationalities of the Leningrad children's homes in the Krasnodar territory. Among 124 children, 15 were Jewish (i.e., 12 percent).[85] They were mostly children who were taken out of blockaded Leningrad, while their parents were at the front or remained in the city. Although these statistics cannot serve as substantial evidence, as a random sample, it should still be considered.

Thus, among all the 978,803 refugees registered on September 15, 1941, that is, refugees from the former Pale of Settlement—Belorussia, Ukraine, Latvia, Lithuania, Estonia, Moldavia, and the Smolensk region (all within the administrative borders of June 22, 1941)—368,898 were Jews, which constituted 37.7 percent.

The obtained statistics allow us to estimate the number of Jewish refugees from Belorussia. To make this estimate, first, we shall determine the number of all refugees from Belorussia. The numbers cited in certain historiographical works on the evacuation from this republic—one to one and a half million evacuees[86]—are too high. The available archival statistics, dating December 1, 1941, state that from among the 2,559,853 of the total refugees who indicated their previous place of residence 262,769 were from Belorussia,[87] that is, 10.26 percent. If we use this figure to extrapolate the number of refugees from the Belorussian SSR among the 7.7 million total refugees in the USSR as of February 1, 1942, (the 7.7 million estimate will be addressed below), it appears then that there were 790,000 refugees from Belorussia. This figure is fully supported by Ponomarenko's annual report received by Stalin in 1942, in which he wrote that there were 780,000 natives of Belorussia in the evacuation.[88] The high mortality in 1942, to which we shall return, explains the difference of 10,000 refugees.

Given that the share of Jewish refugees was 37.7 percent of all who escaped from the former Pale of Settlement, it turns out that 300,000 Jews can be counted among the evacuees from Belorussian SSR. Of these, the number of former Polish citizens hardly exceeded 100,000, so the number of escaped Soviet Jews (as of summer 1939) amounted to 200,000. Therefore, the assumption by Mordechai Altshuler that only 132,900 Jews escaped from the territory of the Belorussian SSR (within the administrative borders of summer 1939),[89] should be considered undervalued. His calculations were based on the data from the 1939 census and the ChGK (Soviet Extraordinary State Commission) on the number of Jews killed in various cities. Meanwhile, the commission's statistics, compiled for the Nuremberg trials, were often exaggerated.[90] It should be noted that by June 1941 several thousands of Jews from western Belorussia (including the Białystok region) were living in the eastern regions of the BSSR, where they came for work or study.

It is somewhat more difficult to estimate the number of Jewish and other refugees from Ukraine. Unlike in Belorussia, the evacuation from this republic had still not been finished by December 1, 1941, although already by this date, using the method of extrapolation, we arrive at about 1.97 million total refugees from Ukraine.[91] This figure is largely confirmed by the April 23, 1946, report from the Statistical Office of the Ukrainian SSR, according to which

1.943 million people from Ukraine arrived to the places of evacuation in the USSR's eastern regions.[92] The difference between the two final figures can be explained by the executions of Jew among the refugees captured by the Germans in the North Caucasus.

Since the Germans focused initially on the offensive on Moscow, it was possible for a greater proportion of Jews to escape from Ukraine than from Belorussia. For example, 119,979 Jews were able to escape from Kharkov, or 92.1 percent of those recorded by the 1939 census.[93] At least 160,000 Jews were among the 400,000 evacuees from the Kiev region.[94] Therefore, for Ukraine it is more accepted to use the "subtraction from the remainder" approach. Of the total number of Jewish refugees in the Soviet Union (see table 10 in chapter 7) about 900,000–1,000,000 were from Ukraine (within the borders as of the summer of 1939).[95] This figure does not include Polish Jews who fled from Ukraine and numbered roughly 150,000 based on their total number in the USSR (we shall examine Polish Jews' statistics in detail later).

It should be noted that at the moment of the Wehrmacht invasion a portion of Polish Jews lived in eastern Ukraine, while a small portion of Jews in western Ukraine were originally from the east (the situation was the same in the BSSR). A native of the Kamenets-Podol'sk region in western Ukraine, Iosif Faigenboim recalls his escape from L'vov:

> The next day a wholesale flight of "easterners" from the city began, and we packed up and went to the station. However, the Central Station and all approaches to it were packed with people, approaches to the tracks were blocked by the army cordon, and on the platform only families of the commanders of the Red Army were allowed onto the trains. There was no way to leave. And we went to a secondary railway station in the city, Podzamche, and refugees there were fighting over every cattle car. Screams, a stampede, and the Germans were bombing as if on a schedule. The trains were boarded by turns, and our family was able to get on the last train departing from L'vov.[96]

An overwhelming majority of the Jewish refugees (85.5 percent in eastern Ukraine and 87.8 percent in eastern Belorussia[97]) lived in cities and towns that were connected by a railway line. Fewer Jews lived in villages and hamlets. Leaving from there was more difficult. They made their way to the station by foot, in passing-by cars, or carts that they were able to rent, buy from private owners, or obtain from the local authorities. In the best cases, the last-departing Jews were charged with taking to the rear state material goods, tractors, or cattle, which provided their families with transport and travel documents, both of which were very important in this situation. With regard to non-Jewish refugees in the east, among them, too, there were many people from the cities and towns, as rural residents were more strongly bound to their farms and private homes. They had more to lose from evacuation. Moreover, since the countryside wasn't heavily bombed, they had less incentive to leave their homes. Therefore, most kolkhozniks stayed put, hoping to sit out the war in their village or hiding from conscription with relatives in another village. Additionally, there were fewer Communists among kolkhozniks, which, on the one hand, did not require them to take an active part in the fight against the Germans, while, on the other hand, caused them to fear persecution by the Germans. The predominance of city dwellers among refugees is supported by some statistics. For example, of the 1,273 refugees who arrived in Kzyl-Orda (Kazakhstan) in September 1941 on the same train, only 92 people were villagers—7.15 percent.[98]

Distribution and Movement of Refugees

Although the Soviet authorities set up evacuation departments with a vast structure, which later underwent personnel and organizational changes,[99] immediately after Germany attacked, it was only on July 5, 1941, (two weeks after the start of the war) that they started making evacuation plans. According to these plans, the first priority in areas threatened by German occupation was to remove the valuable property of state institutions and enterprises, while the evacuation of children and the elderly was second and third, respectively.[100] Nevertheless, even these plans were more humane than Zhukov's orders mentioned above.

The evacuation authorities planned to send within only the first ten days of July 1941 150,000 refugees from Belorussia to the Tambov and Penza regions, 350,000 refugees from Ukraine to the Stalingrad and Saratov regions, and 350,000 refugees from Moldavia to Kazakhstan, while at that time not planning to direct refugees to other republics of Central Asia.[101] In practice, it was Kazakhstan that became the first place where the main flow of refugees was sent.[102] From there, some of the refugees redistributed to other Central Asian republics, as well as to Siberia and the Urals.

Initial plans for the placement of evacuees were based on the 1939 census data on population density. Although the desire to avoid a large percentage of refugees relative to the local residents was reasonable, the authorities ignored such important factors for the absorption of the recently arrived population as the availability of food supplies, jobs, and housing. Later, the central evacuation authorities had to correct their plans for the placement of evacuees.

In the new plans of the Governance of Evacuation, which reported to the Council of People's Commissars, alongside Kazakhstan, other republics of Central Asia also received priority status as final destinations for the evacuated population. The authorities chose Central Asia not only because of the low population density, particularly in Kazakhstan, but also because it was closest to the southern and southwestern regions of the USSR—Moldavia, Ukraine, and later the southern regions of Russia and the North Caucasus. Some cities and areas were closed to refugees because they were under martial law and authorities feared the penetration of spies in the guise of refugees. For evacuees who came "in an unorganized fashion" (i.e., not with the factories), the cities of Kemerovo, Novosibirsk, Prokop'evsk, Leninsk-Kuznetskii, Ufa, and other so-called "close cities of the first category" (the military production centers) were closed at the end of September 1941 by a special resolution of the State Defense Committee.[103] At this time the authorities were already not allowing refugees into Kuibyshev, where the Soviet government relocated. It was absolutely forbidden to quarter refugees in border areas.[104] Later, some restrictions were revised. We shall consider the restrictions that were in force in Central Asia below.

In practice, the distribution was largely dependent on situational decisions related to the railroad's capacity, the availability of train cars, and the number of refugees already placed in certain regions, territories, and republics. Besides, evacuation officials and the railroad administration, in consultation with the local authorities, sought to redirect the refugees to the neighboring region or republic in order to have less trouble with them. In September 1941, the chair of the Executive Committee of the Kurgan City Council, Mikhail Gevenov, asked that no more refugees be sent this city in the south Urals.[105] In November 1941 nine trains of evacuees were refused in Ufa, which led to a trial.[106] The railroad administration proceeded in the same manner in Penza. They did not want to host more refugees and redirected them to Sverdlovsk, Omsk, Novosibirsk, Georgia, and Turkmenistan.[107]

The secretary of the Makhachkala City Party Committee, G. A. Saenko, evicted from the city forty refugee families on August 9, 1942, due to food shortages and disease "among evacuated children." He again tried to send new arrivals (the front line was approaching) to Baku (Azerbaijan), but on August 15 the NKVD halted their further movement from Makhachkala.[108] As a result, as the former commander of the Transcaucasian Front Ivan Tiulenev recalls: "The whole railway line from Baku to Rostov was packed with trains carrying factory equipment and refugees. . . . With a heavy heart, we looked at the long mournful trains with thousands of women, children, and the elderly. The heated freight cars stood one after another from Nal'chik to Beslan, from Gudermes to Makhachkala, from Derbent to Baku."[109]

The central authorities and some republican authorities tried to fight such refusals of refugees. The redirection of refugees from the Alma-Ata evacuation center no. 1 in Kazakhstan to other republics of Central Asia caused a negative response from M. Iakovlev, Deputy Chief of the Evacuation Council of the Council of Kazakhstan People's Commissars, at the end of October 1941.[110] Discovering a similar practice in the actions of the Molotov evacuation point in January 1942, the head of the Governance of Evacuation and the deputy of the RSFSR Council of People's Commissars, Konstantin Pamfilov, expressed his indignation in an emergency telegram with a poorly concealed threat of punishment.[111]

Along with this conscious practice of reshipment of refugees, there were mistakes and confusion in the distribution of refugees. The ill-considered choice of the direction of trains carrying refugees or even an unclear destination, a congestion of railroad trains with evacuated equipment of factories and institutions, the priority of sending trains to the front, and the lack of train cars and locomotives led to many transfer points being congested with thousands of refugees. Often, local authorities and evacuation officials did not know what to do with them, as they were not used to making decisions independently.

This is how the famous pilot Sergei Luganskii describes what he saw at the train station of Rostov-on-Don in the middle of November 1941, on the eve of the German's first occupation of the city: "What was going on there! All the tracks were clogged with trains full of evacuated property. Those in the military were running around, demanding the immediate departure of troop trains. And thousands, many thousands of refugees who had completely lost their heads."[112] In late November 1941 at the Gor'kii junction, twelve trains with refugees accumulated,[113] in which there were presumably 22,000 to 24,000 people, given that, according to official data, about 1,800 to 2,000 people were placed in each train.[114] In those same days of November in Cheboksary, about 2,175 refugees collected in anticipation of further movement.[115]

Due to errors in the planning of the flow of trains full of refugees, many of them were "stuck" in Kazakhstan for weeks. Seeing the helplessness of the officials of the evacuation center in Alma-Ata, the People's Commissar for Internal Affairs of Kazakhstan Aleksei Babkin temporarily replaced them with his officers on October 22, 1941. According to his report, they could distribute several thousand refugees accumulated at the station in just three hours by sending them to regional centers. Redistribution was made by taking into account refugees' requests, which we can learn from the report's note on the resettlement in the suburbs of Alma-Ata mothers whose children were in the Alma-Ata hospital.[116]

There were more serious mistakes in the allocation of refugee flows. In July 1941 trains of refugees were sent back to Ukraine when they had already reached the Volga area. No fewer than nine trains with 8,450 refugees were sent back to Kharkov alone between July 8 and July 17.[117] In the same month some of the children taken out of Leningrad were placed in areas of the Leningrad region that had also been bombed and were under threat of occupation.[118]

Decisive measures to eliminate delays in the delivery of refugees were taken by the State Defense Committee on November 18, 1941. The committee issued instructions that trains with refugees be sent from stations immediately after military trains, with an assurance of a daily rate of travel of 500–600 kilometers.[119] But this measure did not produce the expected result since in addition to military trains to the east (carrying the wounded and materials for rebuilding) there was a great counterflow of military trains heading west. In addition, there was a great shortage of train cars due to evacuation trains' delays en route, as well as problems with unloading the evacuated cargo. In Saratov a hundred train cars with essential industrial equipment stood unloaded for an entire week.[120] On the approach to the Urals, especially crowded with train cars because of the slow unloading and distribution of the delivered equipment to enterprises, congestion was only eliminated in February 1942.[121]

At the beginning of December 1941, more than five hundred train cars of refugees accumulated at a half a dozen transfer stations in Kazakhstan.[122] Their total number can be estimated at 40,000 to 45,000 people, given that the refugees were often transported in train cars that were jammed with up to 80–100 people, but many more of them (90.4 percent) were sent in the so-called heated freight cars (*tepluskas*), which fit 50–80 people.[123] At the small junction of Dzhambul (Kazakhstan), whose own population was at 90,000, a third of these train cars—with 12,000 to 15,000 people—accumulated, and five more trains, carrying an estimated 9,000 to 10,000 people, were expected.[124]

During idle time, the refugees tried not to go too far, because the movement of the trains with refugees was often not announced in advance. According to numerous testimonies, at the time of such sudden resumption of movement, some refugees lost their loved ones, often children. Refugees also lost each other at train stations. Aleksandr Gusev writes in his memoirs: "In Batumi there were many refugees who had arrived on occasional ships from Odessa, Sevastopol, and other cities of the Black Sea coast. In a rush to evacuate, many parents lost their children, and children their parents. Now they were looking for each other. All the walls at the port, the railway station, the post office were covered with announcements [about about lost and found relatives], behind each of which was grief."[125] And Isak Kobylinskii described the refugees this way:

> They looked terrible: dirty clothes, unwashed, with dark wrinkled faces and unkempt hair. Many were lice ridden and sick. But to the Urals, Siberia, Central Asia, where the refugees were heading, it was still so far! With compassion we

looked on these poor families, languishing at the station for hours, not knowing the time of the departure of their train, which they boarded somewhere, not knowing the name of the next station. The trains left without notice. Because of this, time and again immediately after a stop, dozens of people emptied from the train cars, and here, right next to the train, in front of the eyes of many unwitting witnesses, quickly relieved themselves.[126]

Along the road refugees also lost those few possessions that they had taken with them. It was important to them considering the impending battle for survival. Their property was often stolen in the train or at the station while they were sleeping. This phenomenon was so common that in order to deal with it the Supreme Court increased the punishment, recognizing that the theft of evacuees' property in the train and at the station was an especially socially dangerous crime. Those found guilty were equated with bandits and could be executed and their property confiscated.[127]

In November 1941, the Commissar for Railways Lazar Kaganovich issued an order that evacuees' train cars had to be supplied with stoves.[128] However, the commissariat was unable to fulfill this order, as indicated by the numerous reports about cold cars. In December of the same year the railway administrators in Penza were convicted of sending refugees to unequipped trains, and the station officers were found guilty of extortion of bribes to equip these cars with stoves.[129]

Refugees were starving during transport. The officials at Tsentrosoiuz (the Central Union of Consumer Cooperative Societies) and People's Commissariat of Internal Trade, which was entrusted with feeding refugees in transit, had an extremely negligent attitude to this duty. The son of the poet Marina Tsvetaeva, Georgii Efron, wrote in his diary on his way from Moscow: "There is no food, that's the shittiest thing. And even then, most of the evacuees would be reconciled with this, if the train was going along fine. . . . I would be very happy to eat some bread, and all the others too, by the way."[130] A few days later, he wrote, "It has already been six days since one could obtain bread." However, on the evening of the same day, they were fed soup and given two hundred and fifty grams of bread on arrival in Syzran'.[131] Only after Kuibyshev (about one thousand kilometers from Moscow), those in the "writers' car" begun to be fed more regularly. Indeed, even in cases when evacuation centers distributed food to the travelers, the amount was extremely small. In Kurgan an entire train of refugees received only a total of 78 kilograms of bread, 102 breakfasts, 47 suppers, and 31 lunches.[132] Elena Sologub describes the road as follows: "It is impossible to understand how we traveled almost a month without food, often even without water. The first three days we held on as a family, eating only the single chicken that my mother had managed to cook on the road. Occasionally, locals approached the train, from whom several times we managed to buy clotted cream and berries, and once some kind of hand pies. At big stations it was possible to get hot water from special giant boilers."[133]

Sometimes mortality on the road reached enormous levels. Among the seventy-six people sent in December 1941 from the Kalinin region disabled home to the Urals, twenty-two died along the road. Of the 201 teenagers evacuated in January 1942 from a Leningrad vocational school, forty-two died on the way to Cheliabinsk. The authorities did not provide substantial assistance to the rest of the survivors, many of whom were ill. After three days of waiting in Cheliabinsk, they were finally sent to their destination in Kamensk, and seven more teenagers died along the way.[134] Among the 240 pupils of another Leningrad vocational school, during the journey to Stalinsk in the Novosibirsk region in February 1942, twenty-six children died due to poor nutrition, cold, unsanitary conditions, and lack of medical care.[135]

Especially difficult was the crossing of the Caspian Sea, and then the trek by river to Karakalpakiia in Uzbekistan. Boris Shnaider recalls:

> Enough bread for three days was handed out. This was the norm. And then the human tragedy began. Drifting on the barge without a motor for three weeks. Three weeks of daily deaths from hunger and the cold. . . . A few days before the end of the drifting, they hitched another barge to ours at night—with grain and onions. I decided to drag myself to the barge with the grain. But my legs, paralyzed from the cold and hunger, wouldn't hold me up. I crawled on my elbows, dragging the weight of my body on my hands. . . . First of all, I eagerly began to chew it. Then I gathered up my pants with a rope and stuffed wheat in my pants leg. I returned to my barge and crawled to the place where my mother, her sister Khasia, my sisters Roza, Ania, and Lida, my brother Sëma, and my grandmother were lying. My mother spread her lice-ridden shawl on the deck, untied the ropes on my pants and emptied the wheat. Everyone started to chew on the grain. . . . The entire stretch of the riverbank from Chardzhou to Urgench was strewn with the nameless graves of women and children. During the day they died, at night they came to rest on the bank and were buried. . . . Yes, it was a real "barge of death." Of the three hundred and fifty people sailing, not more than one hundred and fifty women and children disembarked.[136]

It is not surprising that many refugees arrived emaciated and ill. This is how an eyewitness described the first train of refugees arriving from Kharkov to Alma-Ata (at that time the capital of Kazakhstan): "The windows in the carriages were broken, patched with plywood and in some places with rags. There were gaping holes in the walls from bullets and shell fragments. And there were people in these cars. Dirty and rank, with yellowed, swollen faces, with husky, hoarse voices. And it was frightening to look upon the children. Emaciated by the long journey, they coughed, begged to eat. Life barely glimmered within them."[137]

Sending refugees to the east, the authorities were often aware that the long journeys would be detrimental to them. On their part, the refugees understood it even better. If they had a long journey ahead of them, they left their crowded and unheated freight cars that threatened them with infectious diseases. Of the nearly 3,000 evacuated by train from Leningrad to Aktiubinsk (Kazakhstan), only six reached their final destination, and among the almost 2,500 evacuees sent from there to Chimkent (Uzbekistan) by another train, only about eighty arrived. Most of the passengers from both trains chose to get off earlier: in Iaroslavl', Kuibyshev, or Tashkent.[138]

Although in July 1941 the authorities organized 120 evacuation centers (each center was designed to cater to at least one train at a time), 340 dining halls, and 57 health centers at the stations along the evacuation routes,[139] it was a drop in the ocean. Because of the small number of workers at railways stations' evacuation centers, there was objectively no time to help the hundreds arriving every day; in frontline areas, there were thousands of refugees. Sometimes, early in the war, those living in places very far from the front line, on their own initiative or at the direction of local administrators, brought food to the trains.[140]

The evacuation centers could not solve the many problems of refugees moving to the east, the majority of whom were people with disabilities, the elderly, women, and children. The strongly centralized, cumbersome bureaucratic mechanism did not have time to quickly help them with food, transportation, medical care, or money. Financial institutions were late with delivery of funds allocated for this purpose, as well as the resumption of payment of benefits, stipends, and pensions that refugees received at the place of their former residence.[141] Many officials were helpless, waiting for instructions and approvals for even the most minor issues. When the refugee Rabinovich's child fell ill along the way and was placed in the hospital at the Uglovaia station, the local evacuation authorities, when the child got better, could not independently organize even such a routine matter as his delivery to her in Semipalatinsk (both in Kazakhstan). The Deputy Chief of the Evacuation Council M. Iakovlev had to solve the problem.[142] Without his participation the officials also could not deal with the slightly more complex, but also requiring a responsible decision, issue of the provision of necessary facilities for the refugees arriving from the Baltic republics who did not know Russian.[143] The twelve-year-old girl Maria

Zaslavskaia, who had left the station in Aral'sk to buy food, managed to jump into the last car of the departing train. But it turned out that her mother had run off to look for her. Reaching Alma-Ata, the girl wandered the station for three months until her mother, who had endured a heart attack, came for her. An official at the evacuation center offered, instead of assistance in the search, to send Maria to the orphanage (with the result that she and her mother might have lost one another for good), but she was lucky—after two weeks of her train station life, a local family began to let her stay overnight.[144]

The conditions of transport of refugees to the east were no better, and often worse than the conditions of deportations of the so-called repressed peoples in 1941 and 1943–1944. Elza-Bair Guchinova in her work on the deportation of Kalmyks describes the same close and stifling railway cars, in which there was no water and no traces of any sanitation.[145] In contrast to the evacuated families, the expelled Soviet German families were allowed, in most places, to take with them one ton of household goods. In 1942 families from the North Caucasus were deported on the same conditions. Finns and Germans relocated from the Leningrad region, altogether about 90,000 people, had somewhat more strict weight limits. They were allowed to take with them not more than six hundred kilograms of cargo per household, which was associated with the greater challenges to ensure transportation because of the very quickly approaching front line in September 1941.[146] It is another matter that local NKVD commanders, often in a rush, did not give the evicted enough time to collect the allowable load.

In contrast to the departments responsible for the evacuation of refugees, the NKVD officers clearly knew where to send the deportees and to ensure a "green light" for the trains as much as was possible. Unlike the trains of deportees, the refugees' trains, as a rule, did not have headmen, which also slowed the trains' speed.[147] Due to the conditions on the trains described earlier, the transports' faster speed preserved many lives. Each train of deported Germans was accompanied by a doctor and two nurses with medical supplies[148]—something that the refugees severely lacked. The Germans were not transported in such cramped conditions as the evacuees.[149] According to Larisa Belkovets from Engels, the capital of the German autonomous republic on the Volga, the NKVD sent the Germans out with four to eight families in a car, at a rate of forty people per car.[150]

The food supply during the journey of deported Germans exceeded what the refugees received. Babkin, comparing the conditions of the movement of deportees and evacuees, in October 1941 noted that, unlike the evacuees' trains, the flat-bed cars of the trains with the Germans were filled with tables, and the staff managed to feed the whole train within thirty to forty minutes, as well as provided hot water for the journey.[151] Further, Babkin indicated that at the terminus trucks for transportation to kolkhozes were granted within five to ten hours, while the evacuees waited for five to six days.[152] But there were exceptional cases. From the station Zhangiztobe, also in Kazakhstan, 110 arriving refugees (among them 41 children) were not taken in by the kolkhoz for about a month, as a result of which they suffered from hunger and, later, from an outbreak of typhus.[153] Note that the terms and conditions of the deported Germans' transport, described by Babkin, were in line with the instructions and regulations developed by the leadership of the NKVD.[154] Due to the fact that most of the deported Germans arrived earlier in their places of resettlement, their living conditions were better than those of the refugees living in the same kolkhozes.

Unlike refugees, the deported Soviet Germans were even allowed to take out a five-year loan of up to two thousand rubles under 3 percent per annum for the construction of houses. It is unlikely, however, that many took advantage of this, as the local authorities often treated them with hostility. Additionally, in February 1942 the German men ages sixteen to fifty-five were drafted into the labor army (with its Gulag-like conditions). The refugees already had age limits: men aged eighteen to fifty-one were sent to the front. Moreover, in October 1942 the authorities summoned to the labor army those deported German women between sixteen and forty-five years of age who were not pregnant and had no children under the age of three (these summons did not apply to the refugees).[155] Since this cruel measure removed those who were at the most work-capable age, it had to affect the future mortality of the elderly and children, not to mention the women themselves. This order was carried out even though many of the deported Germans were already engaged in typical collective-farm labor at their places of resettlement. Into this labor army were drafted about seven or eight thousand men of the same age from nearly thirty thousand "socially unreliable elements" of the annexed Romanian territories, who had been deported to the east only a few days before the start of the war. Jews among them accounted for about one-third.[156]

Some researchers of the deported peoples frequently write about high mortality during transport, based not even on eyewitness testimony, but on rather relatively recently gathered family lore. In fact, the mortality rate among them was not so high. According to internal data of the NKGB, mortality during transport among deported Chechens and Ingush was 0.27 percent.[157] Their trains, like the trains with the deported Germans, were accompanied by medical staff, a total of 1,500 doctors and nurses, and en route medical isolation facilities were organized in order to prevent epidemics.[158] Similar NKGB reports on the Balkars suggest 0.1 percent mortality rate in transit.[159] According to Viktor

Zemskov, the number of deaths during the transport of Crimean Tatars was 191 persons (i.e., 0.13 percent).[160] The Kalmyks suffered the highest mortality rate among all the deported ethnic groups—1.14 percent.[161] The mortality rate among refugees during transport (not including deaths as a result of German bombings and shootings of the trains) was higher. The fragmentary statistics and numerous eyewitness accounts collected at various times allow to estimate their mortality rate at 1.3–1.8 percent.

Measures against the Concentration of Refugees in Cities of Central Asia

As we already know, in the new Soviet evacuation plans Central Asia was selected as one of the central places of distribution of refugees. At the beginning of October 1941, the People's Commissariat of Internal Affairs, on the orders of Lavrenty Beria, recommended sending to Uzbekistan former Polish citizens (including Jews) who were gradually being freed by the amnesty of August 12, 1941, from camps and prisons. In Uzbekistan alone the accommodation of a hundred thousand former Polish citizens was planned.[162] But even before the recommendation of Beria, Polish immigrants freed from camps flocked on their own accord to Central Asia. They sought to be in a region with a warm climate because they feared the harsh Russian winter. According to the reports for only one day, September 30, 1941, there were more than ten thousand liberated former Polish citizens on their way there.[163] Few of them had sufficiently warm clothing. In addition, when it became known that the Polish Army in the USSR, commanded by General Władysław Anders, would leave the Soviet Union, many Jewish men who had immigrated from Poland wanted to join it in Uzbekistan.

In anticipation of the cold weather, many other refugees placed in the Urals and the Volga area began to wonder how to survive the coming winter without warm clothing and firewood. Head of the Resettlement Department of Chuvashia Nikolai Zhukov reported in October 1941 to the Council of People's Commissars of the republic that he had been receiving piles of telegrams with requests to allow travel to Tashkent, Samarkand, and other cities of Central Asia.[164] Many refugees tried to get to the capital of Uzbekistan, inspired by Aleksandr Neverov's book *Tashkent—A Prosperous City*, published in 1923 and republished at least eighteen times. The references to this book that I have found in more than a dozen interviews and published memoirs speak to the refugees' broad familiarity with it, helped by its translation into Yiddish and Polish in 1924 and 1929, respectively.[165] The myth had been deeply entrenched.

Central Asia was not ready to receive them. Besides the overflow of refugees, the central authorities were still concerned about the loss of workers in the northern districts of the country: the autonomous republic of Komi and the Arkhangel'sk and Vologda regions.[166] In November 1941 the authorities tried to convince the Polish refugees to refrain from migrating to Central Asia through the Polish consulate's committees acting throughout the USSR,[167] but the consulate no longer could, or no longer wanted to, do anything. The second Soviet attempt to influence these refugees through the Polish consulate, launched in February 1942, also proved futile.[168]

Then in November 1941, the GKO issued a decree to evict from Uzbekistan former Polish citizens—Poles and Jews.[169] Within the framework of this decision, from November 25 to December 5, 1941, 36,500 Polish refugees were forcibly deported from Uzbekistan to kolkhozes in Kazakhstan,[170] making it their largest resettlement during the entire course of the German-Soviet war. To implement the plan, local executive authorities deported even those refugees who were already well situated in the Uzbek kolkhozes.[171] The deportation was carried out despite the protest of the Polish consulate, which rightly reasoned that the kolkhozes were not ready to accept the refugees and many of them would die due to the harsh climatic conditions.[172]

But the authorities did not want to hear it and, moreover, remained dissatisfied. For the second deportation on December 8, 1941, it was decided to send 21,500 former Polish refugees who accumulated at the railway stations of Kazakhstan to southern areas of Kirgizstan with subsequent employment in the kolkhozes.[173]

The worst fears of the Polish consulate came true. In some places in Kazakhstan and Kirgizstan the local authorities had great difficulty just placing the refugees,[174] not to mention supplying them with food. The measures undertaken to help the migrants[175] did not have tangible results, as they were inadequate and poorly thought out. Therefore, the majority of those deported to Kazakh kolkhozes who were able to survive the starvation and the harsh winter of 1941–1942 returned independently in the spring to warmer Uzbekistan. Many refugees who had settled in these kolkhozes on the orders of evacuation centers also moved to Uzbekistan. Stalin did not like the former Polish citizens leaving their jobs. Naively believing that the Polish consulate was behind everything, on January 24, 1942, he charged his cabinet to negotiate with the consulate the prohibition of such departures from the northern regions of the USSR, as well as from the Central Asian kolkhozes.[176]

At the same time, in organized raids the police were snatching up men and women at stations and markets, some of whom were sent to work in plants and factories. Among them were many Uzbeks from kolkhozes who were in the city to sell agricultural products and buy manufactured goods. According to Paul Stronski, and consistent with the statistical report from 1944, it was almost exclusively Uzbeks who were abandoning work in the cities, where they were sent from their rural homes.[177] Instead of admitting that such reallocation of labor was a mistake, the authorities engaged in tracing the fugitives, labeling them labor deserters. We shall focus below on labor deserters, criminals under Soviet wartime law.

A new migratory wave of Polish refugees to Central Asia followed in the summer of 1942.[178] They moved there even though they were relatively well situated in the Urals and Siberia and despite knowing about the problems with accommodations in Uzbekistan.[179] And while many of the Polish Jews doubted the possibility of departure from the USSR with the Anders's army, their move to Uzbekistan was also due to their fear of "breaking away from their own."

By this time, the deportations of refugees were on a smaller scale. They were mostly limited to the evictions of the homeless and "speculators," whom local authorities periodically caught in Tashkent, Alma-Ata, and other large cities.[180] At the same time the authorities had revised their policy of regional refugee accommodation, preferring to direct the newly arrived refugees not to Uzbekistan, but to the RSFSR, Turkmenistan, Kazakhstan, and Kirgizstan, and to facilitate this adjustment the People's Commissars of Uzbekistan even sent their representatives to Krasnovodsk in Turkmenistan, and Kuibyshev and Penza in Russia.[181] In addition, the authorities finally acknowledged that large numbers of Polish refugees, especially Polish Jews, had been urban residents who had no experience of farm work and came to the conclusion that using them in the Central Asian kolkhozes was simply impractical. The Polish refugees, for their part, were already trying not to be registered, to avoid contact with the authorities, whose credibility had already dried up.

The government especially tried to restrict the flow of refugees to Tashkent. According to the memoirs of David Salop, the clerk at the junction station in the Kuibyshev region asked them where they wanted to travel further. "We said, we want to go to Tashkent. No, they said, Tashkent is already full of people, epidemics are beginning." They were asked to go to Kazakhstan, and they agreed.[182] Rebecca Manley believes that the authorities' actions against the arrival of refugees in Tashkent were strict.[183] However, even though the authorities hindered their arrival not only to Tashkent, but also to Alma-Ata, starting in October 1941, and to Ashkhabad, from December of the same year, and then denied registration (*propiska*) there,[184] many persistent refugees managed to get into these cities, leaving their trains several stations before or past their desired destination.[185]

Therefore, despite the measures taken, these cities became overcrowded. The same happened in Samarkand and other cities in Uzbekistan. Not daring to apply to Soviet refugees strict measures like those applied to former Polish citizens (perhaps due to the fact that the former were more perceived as more loyal), the authorities tried to persuade them to leave on their own. In October 1941 Soviet refugees who had newly arrived in Alma-Ata were asked to move to Siberia or the North, to which the newcomers replied, "We cannot go there, because we do not have appropriate clothing, and if you do not leave us here, or in [other] warm regions, we would prefer to die."[186]

At the same time, many of the refugees themselves saw that Tashkent was overcrowded and that it was simply impossible to stay there. Leaving, however, was also not a simple matter. A witness to the situation, Anatolii Kotliar, describes it this way: "In the area near the train station . . . there was terrible pandemonium. Thousands of refugees, including a mass of screaming children wandering about as if in a dream, old men and women, sick patients lying on the ground, on suitcases, on pitiful rags. They all somehow inexplicably struggled for existence and the ability to move forward, because there was no possibility for many of them to settle in Tashkent. But the trains ran poorly. They froze in the near approaches to the train station, sagging under the weight of their bodies."[187]

∽

Thus, the hopes of the central authorities for a quick victory in the first months of the war affected their approach to the issue of evacuation of the population. Refugees were often hindered. It was only when the Kremlin realized that the war would be a protracted one and that it would need human resources to reestablish industrial and agricultural production, it began to value the refugees more. Faced with a dilemma whether to flee or stay immediately after the German attack on the USSR, many Jews decided not to leave their homes for three main reasons: lack of information about what awaited them under the German occupation, lack of or poor assistance from the authorities with evacuation transportation, and poor financial prospects for residing in the Soviet rear. For these reasons, families with many children and families with sick people often stayed at the home. Those who dared to flee to the east were subjected to heavy German bombardments on the road. The refugees suffered from a lack of food on the trains, as well as poorly organized movement of refugee trains and distribution to new places of residence. In the next chapter, we will see how the local authorities were coping with the unexpected task of absorbing the evacuees.

CHAPTER TWO

The Local Authorities Facing Refugees

Neglect of the Refugees' Needs

The local authorities' attitudes toward refugees clearly depended on their place in the power hierarchy. This hierarchy consisted of three tiers: higher level (regional, territorial, and republican administrations), middle level (district and city administrations), and lower level (management of large factories, village councils, kolkhozes, villages, and towns). All of them had the duty to care for the welfare of refugees. However, the lower their position, the fewer bureaucrats sought to adhere to the central government's line. Most in the lower and even some in the middle echelons of power were overburdened by the care for refugees. To some extent, this was due to their extreme busyness with a variety of other responsibilities, the most challenging of which was the acceleration of production in agriculture and industry, especially the defense industry. Therefore, assistance to the arriving population was for them only a secondary issue, which they often neglected. Moreover, a considerable number of them openly and brazenly oppressed refugees.

The chair of the Troitskoe Village Council in the Chkalov (Orenburg, after 1957) region said to his employees, "Throw them out, these evacuees."[1] The chair of Kolkhoz Shag Vperëd (Step Forward!) in the Telegino district of the Penza region, Grid'ko, responding to the refugees' legitimate requests for help, crudely suggested that they sell their clothes.[2] According to a prosecutor's report for the first four months of 1942, the head of the *raisobes* (department of social security) of the Mariinsk district in the Novosibirsk region (now the area included in the Kemerovo region) deprived refugee families of their allowances and pensions without any justification.[3]

In the Kabardino-Balkar ASSR, the director of the horse farm no. 94, on whose territory three dozen refugees from Leningrad were placed—half of them children—in response to a request for food aid made an obscene gesture and said, "Eat up your stash, and you won't get anything from me but the middle finger."[4] The chair of Kolkhoz Kommunary (Communards) in the Kustanai region of Kazakhstan, Usatenko, frightened the refugees by telling them, "Here we have cold winters, get out of here before the winter gets you."[5] A. N. Kusiakova wrote to her husband in 1942 from the Saratov region: "They pay no attention to us here. We've lived here for a month already, and no bread, no flour. . . . I left to save the children, not to have them die of cold and hunger. We shall be lost in the cold of winter. The chair of the village store said that they had received nothing for the evacuees, so they had nothing to give."[6] Her letter contrasts sharply with the glowing official report on the same Saratov region that formed the basis of the studies of Elena Krasnozhënova.[7]

The attitude was the same in the Chuvash ASSR. Avakumov, the chair of the kolkhoz in the village of Buinsk in the Urmary district called the refugees parasites and snakes, asking them, "Why did you come here?"[8] This did not prevent him from robbing them, to which we shall return below. The chair of the Kalaikasy Village Council, Toimasov, answered the requests of the refugees thus, "I shall not give you any bread, go to Moscow and get your bread there."[9] In the Ivanovo Village Council of the Tsivil'sk district, kolkhoz chair Zontov initially allocated to evacuees from the besieged Leningrad uninhabitable accommodations and then completely put them out on the street.[10] The chair of a kolkhoz in the Mariinskii Posad district, Trofimov, repeatedly said to a refugee from Moscow who asked for bread, "you came here to live off of us"; "you're bloodsuckers."[11] In the village of Akchi-Kasy, kolkhoz chair Nazarov jeered at the refugees: "Go to the *raikom*, they've got your tickets to Moscow there, and go to Moscow. Go home, I'll give you a horse and bread for the journey, just leave."[12] In the canteen of the Ishlei district center, the soup was sold to refugees for 10 rubles 30 kopecks and to the families local of officials for only 1 ruble 50 kopecks. When a refugee complained to the secretary of the Party district committee Sidorov, he asked her how she knew this confidential information. After hearing the answer, he kicked her and shouted at her, "You're nobody, you can leave!"[13]

Despite the extreme filth and lice-ridden condition of the refugees, the local administration in the village of Bol'shaia Sundyr' closed the public bath and for more than five months refused to give them soap.[14] The refugees in the Poretskoe district were similarly not issued soap, as a result of which and of a lot of weeding and planting they did on the collective farm, the skin on their hands often cracked because of the mud.[15] Chair Filipov of Kolkhoz KIM (Young Communist International) of the Kubassy Village Council converted a bath that had been designated for the use of the refugees into a pigsty.[16]

The attitude in Chuvashia to the children of the refugees was no better. According to the letter by the party activist Irina Lisanskaia, in the Sundyr' district the local retail workers and party and government officials refused to sell subsidized food for sick children, even despite medical prescriptions.[17] According to the report of the Commissioner for Evacuation Kuskova on the situation of evacuees in the Shumerlia district, children were not receiving rations of anything except bread.[18] The chair of the Executive Committee of the Pervomai district disallowed Mendel Guf to visit his nine-year-old son, who was in an orphanage in the neighboring district.[19] In the village of Maloe Shigarëvo, kolkhoz chair Vostrov refused to pane the window in a refugee's house, telling her, "If your child dies, I won't be responsible for it, but if the horse dies I will."[20] Common everywhere was the refusal to grant refugees horses, even when it came to sending children and the elderly to the doctor or hospital. One such refusal in Kolkhoz Bolshevik led to the death of a child from diphtheria.[21] On January 1, 1942, the party committee of the Sundyr' district organized a New Years' party for the children, where only children of the evacuees did not receive presents.[22]

Many lower-level administrators did not do anything to help provide refugees with warm clothing. An even bigger problem was footwear. As Nadezhda Mandel'shtam noted, shoes in the USSR were flimsy, and during the war the shoes that Soviet refugee wore would fall apart all at once, which could not be said about the shoes of Polish refugees.[23] The rapid wear and tear of shoes in the Soviet evacuation was due to the fact that many refugees, hoping that the war would end quickly, left not only without winter clothes and shoes but even without an extra pair of summer shoes. Because the refugees had to walk around all the time in the same pair of low-quality shoes, the shoes quickly fell into disrepair. The problem of footwear was so acute that kolkhozes tried to solve it by making braided bast shoes and selling the to the refugees at an affordable price.[24] In some areas, such as in Ishlei district of Chuvashia in 1943, refugees bought thousands of pairs of the bast shoes that had been made for them.[25]

The problem of children's winter shoes was especially hard to solve. According to the Kuskova' April 1942 report on the evacuation and resettlement of the evacuated population in the Shumerlia district in Chuvashia, forty-two children, that is, 18.6 percent of all the evacuees' children, did not attend school because of a lack of shoes.[26] In Shemursha (of the same republic), the seven-year-old son of Basia Shafran spent the whole winter in summer shoes, as a result of which he caught a cold and died in 1942.[27] The Leningrad refugee A. Epshtein, wrote to her cousin from Kirov, "Mara has no shoes, so she doesn't go to school, and they're very expensive at the market."[28] In the same place, the daughter of the refugee from Dnepropetrovsk Maria Amlinskaia, didn't have any shoes at all, and Amlinskaia herself had to walk to work barefoot before the frost until she found a pair of torn galoshes. In the Omutninsk district, also in the Kirov region, 45 out of 132 children did not attend school because of a lack of shoes and warm clothing.[29]

If the problem of footwear and warm clothing for the refugees required some effort of the lower authorities, the allotment of milk to children was easy enough for them to solve. Therefore, the fact that many kolkhozes refused to sell milk to refugees clearly demonstrates ill will toward them. Women with small children, in particular, complained about this problem. Feeding their children mainly bread, sometimes peas, mothers were particularly disappointed that the milk, needed for children's growth (and which was more available in villages than eggs, sour cream, and butter), was not being given to their children. In the Chkalov region the chair of the Michurin Kolkhoz Sidorenko refused to give half a liter of milk to a refugee woman even for a sick child, citing the fact that it was needed for the pigs, which were more important than refugees since the kolkhoz was liable for them. A few days later, the child died, and then his corpse lay in the closet for five days because the family had no money to bury him.[30]

There are many examples of the failure to give milk for the children of refugees in the archives of Chuvashia. In the village of Bol'shoe Shigaevo the kolkhoz board refused to give a daily glass of milk for the sick one-year-old child of a refugee woman, despite the doctor's prescription and the directive of the secretary of the district committee Moriakov.[31] The chair of Kolkhoz Serp (Sickle) in the Tsivilsk district, Danilov, refused to give milk to the sick child of the refugee woman Nikolaeva. To the criticism of the inspector of the Council of the People's Commissars of the republic, he said, "I am too sick, I also need a high-calorie diet." The investigation revealed that he took milk from the kolkhoz, even though he had his own cow.[32] The evacuation inspector A. Nikitina reported on similar situations in various locales of the Shumerlia district. She linked the death of twenty-four children in just a few months of 1942 to these conditions.[33]

Sometimes local authorities moved the refugees out of their jurisdictions so that they did not have to deal with them. The chair of the Elizavetino Village Council of the Mokshan district in the Penza region justified doing this by the impossibility to provide the refugees with fuel.[34] The chair of the Ermekeevo Executive Committee in the Bashkir ASSR, Sadykov, refused to accept refugees at all into his area, therefore they stayed at the railway station until he was put on trial.[35]

The practice of the lower authorities to ignore or mistreat refugees became such a widespread phenomenon in the Soviet rear that it prompted the central government to publicly call them out on this in an editorial in *Pravda* on December 18, 1941. This article was reprinted in many local newspapers and, in particular, in Siberia. Describing the involvement of the sisters of Sergei Kirov (the head of the Leningrad Communist Party assassinated in 1934) in the care for the refugees in their kolkhoz, the article concluded: "Only callous people, devoid the Soviet qualities, can be rude toward evacuees. Only hardened bureaucrats can treat the arriving Soviet people as outsiders. Meanwhile, there are signs that in some places the employees of local organizations consider caring for the needs of evacuees almost a burden.... Local party and government organizations and the natives of the rear areas should surround the evacuees with care and attention and make their new place of residence warm and home-like."[36]

However, as we have seen and will see further, the attitude toward refugees of the middle- and especially lower-level authorities did not changed.

Hostility at the Kolkhozes

Many chairs of kolkhozes and village councils were annoyed that the refugees did not want to work on kolkhozes. Indeed, some did avoid such work, as in some kolkhozes in Chuvashia.[37] Barbara Piotrowska-Dubik describes how in kolkhozes in Kazakhstan, natives of Moscow and Kaluga refused to work in a pigsty because of the stench.[38] Refusing kolkhoz work, these refugees lived off the sale of belongings brought with them, small informal earnings, salaries of relatives serving in the army, and government benefits to families of servicemen. A family with one working member and two children under the age of sixteen received from the government a monthly payment of fifty rubles in rural areas and hundred rubles in cities. If there were three or more dependents and one working member of the family, they received hundred and fifty rubles regardless of the place of residence. If there no family member was able to work, such a family received two hundred rubles.[39] Without extra help, it was very difficult for such families to survive.

In cases where refugees refused to work in the kolkhoz, higher- and middle-level administrators dispatched subordinates to conduct consciousness-raising among them, while many lower-level administrators took the practical path of educating refugees by hunger. In Tush-Kasinsk (Chuvashia), the chair of Kolkhoz Trud and the chair of the village council told Leningraders that if they did not go to work, then they wouldn't receive any food. However, not having completely recovered yet, the former residents of blockaded Leningrad were exhausted and could not work.[40] In fairness, it should be noted that this system of "education" of the population was not limited to the refugees. In the village of Soigino in the same republic, a local kolkhoznik, blind and unable to work, the wife of a Red Army soldier and mother of six minor children, was refused any help by the kolkhoz, because of which she hanged herself.[41]

Refugees had many reasons to refuse to work in the kolkhozes. Refugees from cities found the agricultural work to be a burden because they weren't used to it. Although Jews from villages and towns had experience in gardening, to which we shall return below, they were unfamiliar with complicated agricultural work. Some city dwellers also refused to work in the kolkhoz in the hopes that they would be sent to a city when it was discovered that they were of little use. Many of the refugees resented rural labor more because they were given the dirtiest work. This is the conclusion to which the inspector of employment Rudolf Elias arrived. In a memo, he describes how in Kolkhoz 13 Let Oktiabria (Thirteen Years of October Revolution) the refugees were sent to pick the straw out of the dirt with their bare hands, rather than with hayforks and rakes.[42] The chair of Kolkhoz Serp, Danilov, answering the evacuation inspector' question why he did not give equipment to evacuees, said, "Let them buy it themselves, then come to work."[43]

Meager pay was another reason for the refugees' refusal of the half-coerced work assigned to them. For instance, in Kolkhoz Novyi Put' (The New Way) in the Sterlitamak district of the Bashkir ASSR, only a few out of the fifty refugee women worked, because, unlike the kolkhozniks, they did not receive an extra ration of bread, which they already had the right to buy at a subsidized price through the public food distribution system. Besides that, the kolkhoz did not provide their families with fuel.[44]

Many refugees were not able to go to work during the winter because of a lack of warm shoes and clothing. According to the letter by the chair of the Supreme Soviet of the Estonian SSR, Johannes Vares, to the chair of the Evacuation Board, Nikolai Shvernik, this was the reason some refugees in Chuvashia stayed home and, therefore, did not receive food, allocated in accordance to the decision of the kolkhozes management.[45] Due to a lack of suitable footwear, Sara Murav'ëva was not able to work during the winter in Kolkhoz Bolshevik (village of Kokshanovo, Chuvashia). Because of her complaints about the lack of assistance from the kolkhoz, in February 1942 came auditors along with Nikolai Moiseev, Deputy People's Commissar for Social Welfare of the Autonomous Republic, who asked, "Why don't you wear bast shoes?"[46] This question came off mockingly, given that in January of the same year the temperature in Chuvashia reached a record low of minus forty-seven degrees Celsius.[47]

Some of the refugees could not go to work because they were sick themselves or had to care for sick family members. The chair of a kolkhoz in the Ordzhonikidze territory, Golub', according to a report, ordered to stop issuing food to a refugee, who had been working in the kolkhoz, as soon as she fell ill, saying that he was not obligated to feed bums and the sick.[48] In the village Iangireevo in the Chuvash ASSR, the kolkhoz did not give food to a refugee from Belorussia, Riva Kalvase, who could not work because of her two young children—eight months and four years old—and therefore they had only their bread rations to eat.[49] While Genia Asinovskaia from Vitebsk, mother of seven, was assisted by the local authorities, according to the report of the evacuation official, this aid was not enough and the family lived very poorly even by the standards of the time.[50]

Lower-level administrators often complained to higher authorities about the refusal of refugees to work. These complaints often concealed a reluctance to create the necessary conditions for such work. The Executive Committee of the Maiskii district of the Kabardino-Balkar ASSR stated that the wives of Red Army soldiers and officers did not want to work, but the audit showed that in reality they could not find jobs.[51] Everywhere the local lower-level administrations, in violation of the directives of the central authorities, were not helping refugees find even menial work, even if it was available.[52] This is especially clearly seen in several examples from Chuvashia. A statement by the mother of two young children, Abramovich, about help with her children and search for work to the Novo-Sheptekovskoe Village Council was not even read. After the evacuation inspector Larionova found a nanny for the children of Abramovich, she began to work on the farm the very next day.[53] In Kolkhoz Krasnaia Zvezda (Red Star) in the Shumerlia district, foreman Kozlov, even in the presence of the evacuation inspector, rudely cut off the refugee Baronenkov who was asking for employment: "Shut up, we're fed up, we've had enough of you."[54]

The chair of Kolkhoz Bronevik in the Ishlei district, Ershov, regarding a refugee woman's need for assistance with her three children and finding work, told her, "Go and die of hunger, it's no business of mine."[55] Refugees received a similar message from the chair of the Village Council Bychkov: "You should not have come here, get out of here as soon as possible."[56] Also in Chuvashia, Alma Lazdynsh from Latvia could not find work even in the kolkhoz, and its administration offered her no help. Brought to despair by bureaucratic callousness and lack of money, the woman, who had practically no knowledge of Russian, asked the local authorities to at least take her children, who were dying of hunger, to an orphanage, to which they replied that she was a bad mother.[57]

Indeed, some of the refugees could not return to work due to a lack of kindergartens, or, especially often before 1943, nurseries. Even in the places that had them, by October almost all in the villages and hamlets would close for winter.[58] The reason for this was the local authorities' unwillingness to heat them. The schools were better heated, but it was also cold there, and many students did not have winter clothing. When there was nobody to stay home with young children, some of the refugees, in order not to risk their children, were forced to stay home from work or skip part of the working days. On the other hand, mothers had to stay home when their children were ill, which happened frequently because of the wide spread of infectious diseases in schools and kindergartens.

At the same time, many refugees, including Jews, were successfully involved in various types of collective work. Some achieved quite a success. In the settlement of Khombus-Batyrevo in the Chuvash ASSR, Disman earned 246 workdays in the space of just four months, for which he was paid in grain; selling the excess of grain, he was able to buy piglets. Successes in labor could not but arouse the sympathy of the kolkhozniks. This in Disman's case. He was even given a good apartment.[59] Moisei Borukhovich, in Kurilovka in the Saratov region, earned 327 workdays, sowing, harvesting, and sorting grains and working as a wagoner in the winter.[60] Efim Kogan worked for 401 workdays in the Mariisnkii Posad district.[61] The Aibinder family in the village Russkie Nurvashi worked 358 workdays.[62] In the village council of Kul'uirisy, the families of Movsha Glozman and Lev Primak worked 325 and 267 workdays, respectively, just by November 1941.[63]

Jewish refugees achieved success in agriculture in other places as well. Liudmila Amromina was awarded a cow for her good tractor driving work in a Buriat kolkhoz.[64] Kogan, on the Voroshilov Kolkhoz in Kirgizstan, earned ninety workdays in a short period of time, for which he was mentioned in the newspaper *Pravda*.[65] Aleksandra Bril'man and Roza Bershader became prominent kolkhozniks in the Voroshilov Kolkhoz and Kolkhoz Rabotnik (Laborer) in Kazakhstam, respectively.[66] Emma Gutina was the best milkmaid in Kolkhoz Krasnyi Kut (The Beautiful Place) in the Kuibyshev region. In the Molotov Kolkhoz in the same region, Grinshtein was considered to be the best kolkhoznik.[67] Leia Mazur was in charge of the milk farm of the kolkhoz with the grotesque name Kzyl Koran (literally, Red Quran) in the Bashkir ASSR with 250 cows, 1,200 sheep, and other livestock. Her daughter Enia worked as a tractor driver of the local machine tractor station and was a Stakhanovite.[68]

However, in some places even a large number of workdays did not rescue refugees from the tyranny of the kolkhozes administration. For her 238 workdays in Kolkhoz Krasnaia Zvezda of the Shemursha district, Fania Feigina, whom we have already encountered, did not receive anything and experienced great difficulties trying to feed herself and her children.[69] M. Sosner found himself in the same situation, having worked sixty workdays during two months in Kolkhoz Kudeeevka; the kolkhoz chair even struck him from the list of recipients of bread.[70] The sisters Ester and Golda Katsman, who had two and four children, respectively, also received no bread in spite of the fact that they worked well. Bread was also withheld from Dvosia Golod, with three children, and Ida Minevich, with a child and a brother who had been wounded on the front. Having worked 120–200 workdays, they, like the Katsman sisters, managed to feed themselves only with potatoes grown in their own gardens.[71]

The situation in the Kabardino-Balkar ASSR was similar. Senior evacuation inspector Shklovskii was outraged by the administration of Kolkhoz Karagach, in the Primalkinskii district, which did not allocate the Tsikler family affordable housing; they slept on a dirt floor, despite the fact that they had worked a lot of workdays.[72] According to the same report, more than a dozen Jewish families also worked well in Kolkhoz Deia, but in spite of this the local store was forbidden from selling them bread if they were absent from work due to illness.[73]

The refugees in the kolkhozes were discriminated against not only in the calculation of workdays and in work assignments but also in food prices. In the village Soigino of the Chuvash ASSR, stale meat from the warehouse was sold to kolkhozniks for ten rubles per kilogram and to refugees for thirty—even though this meat was not produced by the kolkhoz itself but allocated to it by the government.[74] Moreover, in some cases kolkhoz administrations even fought against lowering the cost of groceries sold to refugees privately, by setting minimum prices for some products. A group of Muscovites from the village Ichikisy in the Chuvash ASSR complained to the authorities that the kolkhoz board set prices for potatoes for them at sixty rubles per pood (sixteen kilograms). What's worse, the cash price was only "on paper" and was applied only as an exchange equivalent to barter, and not for sale transactions.[75] The situation in the village of Kuvakino, in the same autonomous republic, was similar. Kolkhozniks did not sell potatoes and other food products to refugees but only exchanged them for clothes and other possessions. When the refugees complained to the kolkhoz chair Kuzin, he, instead of supporting them, said, "You've [already] given away two or three dresses, and if that's so bad—leave, nobody's making you stay here."[76] In the village Ryndino milk was not sold to refugees, only bartered.[77] In the village of Nizhnie Abakassy food products were exchanged for goods according to their nominal value—250 rubles for a kilogram of potatoes and 600 for a kilogram of flour, for example.[78]

The desire not to sell food to refugees but rather to barter for possessions, clothing, and shoes, was typical of many eastern regions and republics of the USSR.[79] This practice was the result of the depreciation of money. Another, even more striking manifestation of the depreciation of money was that in the summer of 1942 even in some rural state stores in the Chuvash ASSR goods could only be paid for with food products. This was facilitated in some places by good crops of vegetables that the refugees had from their allotted gardens. According to this practice, which was illegal under Soviet law, one box of matches cost refugees three kilograms of potatoes in the village of Bol'shoe Shigaevo and four kilograms in the village of Maklashkino. In the village of Shul'gino refugees needed to give the store sixteen kilograms of vegetables for two hundred grams of soap and ten kilograms of potatoes for a spool of thread.[80]

In some areas of the Chkalov region general stores did not sell a range of food products and soap for ration cards, demanding instead that the refugees pay their kolkhoz membership dues, from which they were actually released by special order of the central authorities.[81] This was also common in some areas of the Novosibirsk region.[82] The butter factory in the village of Ibresi (Chuvashia) sold their products only to local residents and not to refugees.[83]

The Housing Problem

Since there was little or no excess housing in the eastern regions of the USSR, the authorities forced the local population to share their housing with refugees, in accordance with the law of wartime (issued 1931). Records from Cheboksary, dated August 10, 1942, allow an overview of these policies. According to the documents, the upper limit of permitted living space was set in the city at 3.5 square meters per person. The rights to assign refugees to housing were granted to urban housing administration. It, along with the police, was supposed to enforce housing regulations. There were penalties for the violation of this order: a one-hundred-ruble fine or a month of hard labor, and imprisonment for the worst offenders.[84] Similar resolutions were adopted in all the eastern regions of the USSR,[85] but different limits were set. In Kirgizstan at the beginning of the war the housing limit was 8.25 square meters per person, but in September 1941 it was reduced by the decision of the People's Commissars of the republic to 5 square meters.[86]

Refugees, in turn, had to pay rent to the owners according to established standards. However, the standards were not universally respected because the authorities did not have enough power to enforce them. One of the refugees wrote in his diary about the situation in Krasnovodsk (Turkmenistan): "The little town was crowded with refugees, who were scattered in the streets. The local people here treat them with contempt, and with impunity fleeced them for permission to spend the night on the floor, for a glass of hot water, and so on."[87] In March 1942, the evacuation inspector of the Evacuation Council Khanin reported to the Bashkir ASSR authorities that the refugee tenants were usually placed in the corner of the kitchen or another room and charged exorbitant fees, approaching 150 rubles a month.[88] The living conditions and prices were similar in the Kabardino-Balkar ASSR and Kuibyshev region.[89] In the Krasnye Chetai district of Chuvashia rent reached 100 rubles, which was considered a very high price.[90]

In cities with a large number of refugees, it was very difficult to find an apartment, especially not shared with owners or with other refugee families. Aron Feigelovich, arriving in Tashkent, wrote: "It is pointless to think about any sort of help from the authorities. After an intensive search we finally found an apartment on the outskirts of the city, in Kuiliuk . . . in a clay hut."[91] The authorities, as a rule, offered assistance to famous figures of science and culture, important government officials and members of their families, who arrived in a separate evacuation. But even the poets Anna Akhmatova and Marina Tsvetaeva experienced big problems finding suitable housing.

Some recollections, of both refugees and of their host families, mention homeowners extending invitations to the refugees. However, these actions should only be considered as an attempt to prevent the forcible placement of unwanted refugees. Indeed, some refugee tenants could prove to be, for a variety of reasons, unpleasant or inconvenient for the home's regular occupants. A young woman, whose husband was in the army, was afraid to compromise herself by living under the same roof with a resettled man. Both refugees and locals feared to be under the same roof with alcoholics and criminals. On the other hand, many residents preferred to host doctors, teachers (if they had children), artisans, and members of other professions useful at that time. Of great importance to the decision to invite refugees to settle with them was the mutual liking that emerged in preliminary conversations with prospective housemates. This preliminary estimate of future relations often gave way to the disappointment of both parties during cohabitation.

Everywhere the refugees found themselves in very cramped conditions. In the Kabardino-Balkar ASSR each refugee often had only one square meter of housing.[92] In Cheboksary Gita Shrom from Latvia, along with six other family members, had to live in a kitchen with a total area of 7 square meters. In the same city, the families of Raukhman and Solovei, also composed of seven people each, had to live in the same amount of space.[93] In Alma-Ata there were cases of twelve refugees living in 9 square meters of space.[94] In Sorochinsk, in the Chkalov region, fourteen to sixteen refugees usually had 25–30 square meters of floor space.[95] In Tashkent Rakhel Rivkina settled in the eighteen-square-meter room of her uncle together with twenty-seven other relatives. They simply slept on the floor at night, and sometimes somebody would say—"I'm rolling over," when they all had to turn over.[96] But such conditions were the exception rather than the rule.

While in the Chkalov region 2.2 million rubles were allocated by the central authorities for the construction of housing, the local authorities only used 0.4 million to that end.[97] Besides, housing built for refugees often was also often not allocated to them, as happened in Sterlitamak. There the city officials took for themselves and their colleagues houses built for refugees with the use of the funds allocated by the central authorities.[98]

Given the shortage of housing in many regions and republics, barns and cellars were allocated for refugees, barracks were built, and dugouts dug.[99] The situation of the evacuated workers was no better. Even in places where they were welcome, the local authorities did not have suitable accommodations to house them.[100] Most of the 12,000 workers of the largest enterprise in the Cheliabinsk region, Magnitstroi, lived in dugouts that let water through during rains.[101] Near Berezniaki in the Molotov region tens of thousands of workers, recruited among refugees to work in factories, were living in the same conditions. The cold of winter, the crowdedness, and lack of air caused a high incidence of typhus and tuberculosis among them. The administration, however, was not worried. Although the ill were placed in separate dugouts, they did not even have toilets, did not receive sanitary assistance, and the food was very meager.[102]

The barracks of the Krasnoiarsk factory no. 4, where 882 people were living in March 1942, had no washbasins, ventilation, or hot water; the toilets were not cleaned; the garbage was not taken out. Everyone suffered from lice infestation.[103] The workers of factory no. 688, evacuated from Leningrad to Ufa, found themselves in a similar situation. They were taken to a school converted into a dormitory, were ten to fifteen families were settled in each classroom. All 322 people slept on the floor washed and cooked in the same place because there were no tables or chairs. The toilets were closed, and everybody relieved themselves in the schoolyard. Because of the unsanitary conditions, they fell ill with typhus and tuberculosis.[104] The situation was the same in the dormitory of factory no. 26, where workers evacuated to Ufa from Rybinsk and Leningrad lived. In addition to these diseases, the families of workers there fell ill with severe pneumonia; of the ten who fell ill in the beginning of 1942, four died.[105]

In the spring of 1943 People's Commissar of Armaments Dmitrii Ustinov for the first time drew attention to the difficult living conditions of factory workers. Having visited one of the workers' settlements, he was shocked by what he saw: "There was a so-called village of roofs—only an awning, and the living space itself in the ground." He demanded that the factory management provide the barracks with laundry, water, and firewood. After that Ustinov sent out a directive to all factories with a demand to regulate the living conditions of workers; in particular it stated: "There is no excuse for the fact that in a number of factories, the floors in the barracks are washed infrequently, the walls and ceilings are covered with dust, the same as the moment they were installed. The people sleep on dirty cots and bunks, for months they do not change the bedding because there is no place to wash it, and in various places lice infestation has become a daily phenomenon. It would seem that the simplest thing—boiled water—is not always available everywhere, and where it is, is often found in rusty, uncleaned cisterns."[106]

All refugees, both in towns and in kolkhozes, suffered from the cold. If they lived shared the quarters with landlords, they took the coldest parts of the premises and had to participate in the heating of the housing. We shall dwell more on the issue of these relationships below. Fuel problems were associated with the lack of workers to harvest firewood and transportation for its delivery. Because of this, in Ufa firewood was sold on the market at an inaccessibly high price—six hundred rubles per cubic meter.[107] This was several times higher than the average monthly salary of refugees.

In the kolkhozes of the Mari ASSR, refugees were forced to walk with their children five to ten kilometers to get firewood. They were not given horses on the pretext that they could not care for them.[108] The prospect of dispatching the kolkhoz cart and its driver for the delivery of firewood was not even considered. Refugees in the Kuibyshev region found themselves in the very same situation, having to travel long distances in winter to deliver firewood on children's sleds.[109] Such a situation with firewood, as interviews demonstrate, was widespread.

The results were tragic. In the Novodevich'e district of the Kuibyshev region three children of the refugee Shel'spud died from the cold.[110] At the beginning of 1942 in the village of Novyi Batoiurt in the North Ossetian ASSR, the children of the refugee Slomir were developing frostbite on their limbs due to the freezing temperature in the house.[111] The same happened to a child in the Soviet district of the Ordzhonikidze territory, where the refugees' homes in several kolkhozes were not heated for ten days.[112]

Disregard for the needs of refugees did not prevent district, village, and kolkhozes leaders from running laudatory articles in the local press about their concern for the evacuated population. In Nal'chik the above-mentioned inspector Shklovskii was so outraged by the articles that asserted that "in Kabardino-Balkar ASSR the conditions of the evacuated population close to paradise," that he found it necessary to specifically address this at a meeting of the republic's Council of People's Commissars in May 1942.[113] A similarly congratulatory article on the reception of refugees was published in Kirgizstan. Especially dubious is its claim that some children of the frontline soldiers were "sent to resorts."[114] The authorities of the Andizhan region of Uzbekistan also loved to organize such extolling press coverage.[115]

Attitudes toward the Families of Soldiers

The lower and middle echelons of the administrators made almost no difference in their approach to the families of refugees whose members served at the front and the rest, since there were so many of them. One Tashkent official responded to the complaints of the refugee Teplitskaiia, the wife of a frontline soldier, that no one was helping her, by stating bluntly: "We cannot help you all, and therefore it is better not to help anyone at all."[116] However, from time to time the authorities allocated additional food products and other goods to the families of frontline soldiers to show concern for them, but this meager aid had practically no effect on their plight. The Leningrad refugee A. Chepik wrote in November 1942 from the Saratov region: "Here comes a terrible winter. Last year, although it wasn't much, there was some care felt for the families of soldiers, while this year you're refused everywhere, and scolded for nothing. I despaired, I'm sick of everything. I would rather hang myself than live like this any longer."[117] Chepik's letter and the letter by Shliakina below strongly contrast with the rosy official reports from the Saratov region about assistance to families of serviceman, which Krasnozhënova uses in her work.[118]

From Kolkhoz Combine in Ishlei (Chuvashia) two Leningraders—wives of Red Army soldiers—complained to the chair of the Kalinin District Executive Committee Ivanov: "We are not given bread at the kolkhoz, we can't buy it at the market, and we have children to feed; after all, we didn't come here of our own free will." To which he replied, "And who the hell called you here? . . . It's not my problem, go and hang your children." After such an answer, one of the women, Bulanova, complained about him in a letter to her husband, which he gave to the command. The result was the intervention of the chief of the district NKVD and the military commissariat, thanks to which these refugees began to be provided with food.[119]

The kolkhoz chair Kornilov in the village of Egorkino (Chuvashia) refused to help wife and mother of soldiers M. Brodskaia, a refugee from Odessa and an invalid of third degree, with transportation and arrangements for easier work. Meanwhile, she was in charge of three more children and an elderly mother. To feed herself and her family without government's support, she was forced to sell almost all of her family's clothing and even bed sheets.[120]

Still, having a family member at the front, was helpful: on the one hand, it made any requests or complaints submitted to the authorities more powerful, creating some advantage over the others, and, on the other hand, relieved the suspicions of espionage, of which we have already spoken.

Regarding the very pressing issue of housing, the interests of the evacuated families of soldiers and officers were neglected not only by local lower-level officials but also by mid-level authorities. The chair of the Galkino District Executive Committee (in Zaural'e), Smetanin, demanded that Olga Elkina, the wife of a serviceman, move out of her apartment and hand it over to the secretary of the Executive Committee Grekhova. When she refused, the police searched her in the hopes of finding stolen food from the canteen where she worked. Although nothing was found, under the pressure from Smetanin Elkina was fired from her job. Only the intercession of the local military commissar helped her to keep the apartment. After that, Smetanin issued an order that Grekhova was to be given the apartment of R. Abramovich, whose husband was also at the front, whose pilot son was killed, and whose other son was recovering from wounds in a hospital. During the eviction by the police, Abramovich fainted, but the other wives of servicemen intervened on her behalf and, thus, prevented the eviction. In the end, Abramovich still lost the apartment and was assigned to another apartment, with a roommate.[121] Lieutenant Khazanovich's family of five lived in Ufa in an apartment that was considered bad even by comparison with the generally poor housing conditions. Despite the authorities' resolutions on the provision of other housing, it was not allocated; moreover, during the floods in the city, this family was altogether evicted and became homeless.[122]

There were quite a few cases when the heads of district offices appropriated, in part or in whole, several months-worth of cash benefits that frontline soldiers transferred to their evacuated families (officers, depending on their rank, could wire five hundred rubles or more). The prevalence of this practice is evidenced in the article "In the Prosecutor's Office of the USSR," printed simultaneously in several central newspapers on January 31, 1942.[123] This article, published during a difficult situation at the front, was designed to reassure the soldiers of the readiness of the authorities to help their families in the rear. From the correspondence, which went through the war censorship office, the authorities were aware that those at the front knew about the bureaucracy and officials' theft in the rear.

Evacuated families of Red Army soldiers and officers were discriminated against in the kolkhozes. Even though the economic situation of the refugees was worse than that of the local population, in the Poretskoe district they were completely deprived of their livestock and poultry, which were allocated to families of servicemen for their personal use in accordance with the April 16, 1943, decision of the Council of People's Commissars of Chuvashia.[124]

The attitude of the local administration to the families of junior and middle officers was only slightly better than to the families of the rank-and-file Red Army soldiers. Because of the indifferent attitude of local authorities and the poor work of evacuation services, they, like other refugees, also often suffered from unemployment, lack of food, clothing, footwear, essential goods, fuel, and lack of places in kindergartens.[125] The wife of the battalion commissar Shelepkov, having fled with two young children from the Smolensk region, was promised six times by the chair of the Regional Executive Committee of Rasskazovo (Tambov region) that he would help to buy shoes, underwear, and outwear, but he did nothing.[126] In the Kuibyshev region, the daughter of the pilot Khramov, deceased at the front, had frostbite on her legs due to lack of firewood.[127] In Alma-Ata the pregnant wife of Lieutenant Fen'ko, whose possessions had been stolen, lay hungry on the bare ground in a park with her baby, "exhausted, covered with lice, almost naked."[128]

In the Ishlei district of Chuvashia, the wife of the officer Feofilov sold off her personal belongings and was forced to beg with her four children, because the kolkhoz did not give her bread. The children of the officers, like other refugee children, did not receive milk at their new places of residence. A different attitude toward the families of officers was shown in the Kanash district of the same republic, where 391 officers' wives lived in 1942. Two hundred and fifty of them, depending on the military rank of their husbands, ate in the canteen of the military commissar. They were also separated by categories. Some received dinner only for themselves, and some for all members of their family. Such different treatment was determined not only by the ranks of their husbands but also by their personal ties.[129]

The fact that the attitude to families of officers in various places of the rear regions was not particularly warm is evident from the directive of the head of the Political Directorate of the Soviet Army and Soviet Navy, Aleksandr Shcherbakov, from July 10, 1942. It mentions a "haughty-disdainful, and sometimes mocking, attitude to the needs and demands of the wives of commanders, political workers, and frontline soldiers" in Samarkand and Frunze (Kirgizstan). He demanded from the military committees domestic assistance and aid with employment for such families.[130] Precisely this criticism, as well as the scandal due to the nonpayment of benefits, the lack of housing, the failure to provide ration cards and food to the families of commanders in the Osh region (and not a special concern for them, as believes Aganiyaz Annakurbanov), caused the adoption by the TsK KP(b) of Uzbekistan in the same month of a special decree "On evacuated families of the Red Army commanders."[131]

M. Sobolev, head of the department of the Council of People's Commissars of the RSFSR for the economic organization of the evacuated population, in January 1943 sent a letter to the regions condemning the poor care for the officers' families in the Sverdlovsk, Cheliabinsk, Chkalov, Kirov, and Tambov regions.[132] The newspaper *Krasnaia Zvezda* on February 28, 1942, published an editorial entitled "Assistance to the Families of Frontline Soldiers." The purpose of the publication was to show the care of the authorities in the rear about these families, but it was precisely this article that caused a flurry of complaints from the frontline soldiers to the newspaper's editor, David Ortenberg. They wrote about the poor treatment of their families in the Vologda,

Voronezh, Gor'kii, Kirov, Kuibyshev, Kurgan, Molotov, Novosibirsk, Saratov, and Chkalov regions, the Altai territory, the Bashkir and Tatar ASSRs. The frontline soldiers complained that their letters to the village soviets, district executive committees, military registration and enlistment offices, and district party committees of these regions and republics did not lead to anything. The memorandum on this issue contained almost four dozen examples of local authorities being rude to and ignoring the needs of the refugees. I will mention only one example, involving the mother of the Red Army soldier Zhukov. The mother of six soldiers called up to the front was evacuated to the Sandovo district of the Kalinin region, where she, not having received any shelter and or food rations to which she was entitled, had to resort to begging.[133] In the summer of 1942, the Briansk partisans wrote a series of complaints about the poor care of their evacuated families, in particular about the nonpayment of benefits and even the money from their salaries that they sent to them.[134]

The GlavPur (Main Political Administration of the Red Army) again tried to improve the situation of the soldiers' families. On April 4, 1944, Shcherbakov sent a directive to all rear military commissariats and political departments of the military districts, in which, assessing the situation of the military families in the Transcaucasian and Ural military districts as the worst, he demanded that appropriate measures be taken.[135]

Privileged Evacuees

The increased concern for evacuated families of nomenklatura officials and the commanding staff of the Red Army and the NKVD during the war was a continuation of the prewar practice of granting privileges to the elite.[136] This care was even legalized by a secret decree of the Council of People's Commissars of the USSR in July 1941. Families of party and state leaders, as well as military commanders, were fully guaranteed evacuation by transport, food, clothing, and medical care. Moreover, they could choose any place of residence except for Moscow and Leningrad.[137] The exception was the result of the already announced mass evacuation of the population from these places. These families were often allowed to take their property, including furniture.[138] For example, it took two whole train cars to evacuate the family of the chief of the Southern Railway and the family of his deputy to Kazakhstan.[139]

Already upon arrival, such families enjoyed the right of priority residence and work, as well as financial assistance—"lifting up."[140] In the year 1942–1943 the nomenklatura, in addition to wages and ration cards, received so-called limit books (or coupons books) for the purchase of discounted goods in special stores. Their monetary value reached one thousand rubles a year.[141] The top local administrators scrupulously checked how these elite families were accepted and settled in the new place. The deputy chair of the Evacuation Council of Council of People's Commissars of Kazakhstan, M. Iakovlev, in late August 1941 consulted the head of the evacuation department of the Semipalatinsk region, A. Kuznetsov, on the organized settlement of seventeen families of *otvetstvennye rabotniki* (responsible administrators, executives) from the Dnepropetrovsk region. He was informed that these families had arrived safely and were healthy and housed in apartments. Among them was the family of Leonid Brezhnev, the future General Secretary of the Soviet Communist Party. For the first weeks the Brezhnevs lived in the same house together with a family friend, Konstantin Grushevoi, the second secretary of the Dnepropetrovsk Regional Party Committee, who promoted Leonid in Ukraine. However, Grushevoi's wife did not like very provincial Semipalatinsk, neither did the wife of the first secretary of the same regional committee Semën Zadionchenko—they both thought that they should live in the republican capital, Alma-Ata, where they soon moved with their children.[142]

Alma-Ata was already closed to refugees, but this was not an obstacle for them. The Kazakh authorities reacted to such a move with understanding. Like the princess in Hans Andersen's tale "The Princess and the Pea," the wives of the Dnepropetrovsk's secretaries passed their test of belonging to the elite, claiming the best living conditions. The duties of the wives of the nomenklatura included upholding the unofficial privileges within the accepted bureaucratic hierarchy. It was not an easy duty, because increased demands could damage the career of their husbands, but lesser ones were fraught with a loss of authority, which could also affect, ultimately, one's position.

Unlike other refugees, families of nomenklatura workers had effective levers of influence upon careless local officials. Most often, the pressure was exercised through regional or republican authorities. Local administrators of different levels in many cases were themselves in a hurry to help these families because, on the one hand, they were afraid of punishments and, on the other, they were counting on assistance in career advancement. Besides, it was not a secret to anybody that the impression of a candidate's "readiness" for a new post was more often made based on personal contacts with him, and information from his service record was taken into account only when such contacts had not existed before.

However, a good attitude toward the families of the nomenklatura and other high-ranking officials was sometimes compensated not only by hypothetical reciprocal services in the future but also by practical help during the war. So, the remnants of food in four railway cars, received in one of the Ural regions for 170 families of NKVD officers, were given to the families of the district authorities.[143]

Several other pieces of evidence about care for the families of high-ranking and influential officials have survived. In Uly'ianovsk in August 1942, for the sake of their placement, five hundred apartments and rooms were vacated, former residents of which were deported to the countryside.¹⁴⁴ In July 1941, for the sake of the evacuated Moscow kindergarten no. 26 serving the children of the members of the local *raikom* and the executive committee of the Lenin district of Moscow, a teacher's vacation house near Cheboksary, in the Chuvash ASSR, was booked.¹⁴⁵

High-ranking officials were assigned to the special canteens closed to the public. As a result of the decision of the Krasnoiarsk Territory Council, the Minusinsk executive committee of the town council included sixty party and state apparatchiks on the list for preferential allocation of goods, including: the leadership of the town committee of the Communist Party, the town executive committee, the chair of the Komsomol committee, the head of the town commercial bureau, the head of the town office distributing ration cards, the editor of the radio station, the editor of the newspaper *Vlast' Truda*, the chair of the court and judges, the prosecutor and investigators, the police chief, and other *otvetstvennye rabotniki*. In August 1943, the list was expanded to ninety-four people, but they were broken into three categories in terms of supplies they received.¹⁴⁶

Because of the hardships of wartime, more than ever before, famous artists and writers were brought closer to the privileges of nomenklatura workers. This was a reflection of the increased need of the central authorities for the ideological support of the most authoritative cultural figures. Memoirs and diaries name three figures capable of lobbying for the interests of cultural workers in the evacuation: Aleksandr Fadeev, Aleksey Tolstoy, and Konstantin Fedin. But in several cases officials of the central administration were busying themselves for artists and writers. In September 1941, working in the secretariat of the Evacuation Council, Maria Kaganovich (Lazar Kaganovich's wife), asked the chair of the Council of People's Commissars of the Kazakh SSR, Nurtas Undasynov, to assist in arrangements for the poet Sergei Mikhalkov and his wife Natalia Konchalovskaia, who arrived in Alma-Ata with two children. Of course, local authorities took care of finding a good situation for Stalin's favorite.¹⁴⁷

High-ranking cultural producers themselves often could not defend, especially at the beginning of the war, their rights to special privileges. Sometimes the functions of the "nomenklatura wife" were taken on by acquaintances. A mediocre writer and military correspondent Nikolai Varta, on his way to Tashkent, would dress in a military uniform and appear to the station's superiors as the adjutant of his companion, author Kornei Chukovskii, who would go for a walk during the stops. Varta threatened them with an international scandal, and all sorts of food were rushed to the car, and they called to the next station saying that an "international person" was coming, and gifts needed to be prepared for him.[148] This story, preserved in the diary of the professor of literature Leonid Timofeev and somewhat comparable with Nikolay Gogol's "The Government Inspector," vividly testifies about the fears of provincial authorities.

Even the economic situation of elite members of the intelligentsia, if they did not belong to the most authoritative of its layers, left much to be desired. The same Timofeev, who was during the war the head of the Department of Soviet Literature of the Institute of World Literature of the USSR Academy of Sciences, noted in his diary in April 1943: "If we had no stocks that were still inexhaustible, and an income of 5,000–6,000 rubles a month, then it would have been quite difficult for us. But few [families] have it. And in fact, there was much that we lacked: there is almost never any meat and very little oil."[149] The truthfulness of this statement is not in doubt since the same diary entry describes in detail his wife and daughters' gardening.[150] The Latvian writers who appeared in Khalturin of the Kirov region were placed, altogether with their families, sixteen people altogether, in one room without furniture. They slept on the floor. The Penza City Council refused to register the Lithuanian poet Salomeia Neris with the words, "We do not need writers here." For her, as well as for the Lithuanian writers Liudas Gira and Petras Cvirka, the crude attitude of Soviet officials toward refugees was a real discovery of the USSR, deeply shocking them.[151] All these representatives of the Lithuanian intelligentsia, who were not yet elderly, undermined their health during the evacuation and they died after returning home, in 1945, 1946, and 1947, respectively.

It happened that families of high-ranking officials and army commanders experienced difficulties due to the faults of lower administrators. In Chkalov the local authorities did not take care of the provision of footwear for the children of the division commissar Vasilii Rudenko, as a result of which they did were not able to go to school.[152] In order to supply fuel to the families of workers in the Economic Department of the Council of People's Commissars of the USSR in February 1942, a personal intervention of the deputy chair of the Council of People's Commissars of the Chuvash ASSR and of the commissioner for the evacuation of the public, Vasilii Grigoriev, was required.[153] In April 1942 A. Vorob'ëv, authorized by the Council of People's Commissars of the RSFSR for the resettlement of kolkhozniks from the Tambov region to Saratov region, sought help from him for his evacuated family. The problem was caused by the negative attitude toward his family on the part of the owner of the house where they were settled. Because of the intervention, the family was resettled.[154] The family of the head of the 4th European Department of the People's Commissar for Foreign Affairs, Nikolai Novikov, starved and froze in the Verkhnii Uslon of the Tatar ASSR. His wife wrote to him in Moscow about this and the indifference of local authorities to the problems of refugees in October 1941. To save his family and his seriously ill son, Novikov had to go there himself with food. He demanded that the village soviet issue food to the evacuees following the norms. As Novikov later learned, their assurances that everything would be arranged were empty promises.[155]

This is not surprising; because of the significant expansion of tasks, the lower administrators ceased to feel any stability in their positions. They already lived with the idea that they could leave their office at any time for one reason or another, and if they were undesirably transferred, they would hardly be saved by services rendered to a high-ranking Moscow official or divisional commissar. Therefore, we can conclude that the well-established hierarchical mechanism or traditional informal "patron-client" interactions in the USSR, investigated by John Willerton, followed by Sheila Fitzpatrick,[156] was already undermined during the repressions of 1937–1938,[157] and during the war years was falling apart.

Novikov also found himself in a difficult situation in Kuibyshev, where he moved with his people's commissariat and to where, later, he summoned his family. He recalls:

> The food rations we received for our family were so meager that they did not allow even the children to eat enough. . . . The prices in the market, especially in the early spring of 1942, really jumped to the skies, and my salary and my wife's salary (she taught English to the staff of the NKVD) looked absolutely scanty. Then, in exchange for butter, meat, and milk for the children, all the things from our wardrobe which represented at least some exchange value were taken to the market, one after the other. . . . The matter could have become a catastrophe if I had not had from time to time "additional food"—at diplomatic banquets.[158]

The central administration was well aware of the crack in the management mechanism. At the end of the war, it attempted to improve the situation by, on the one hand, reinforcing the hopes of lower administrators to climb up vertically or diagonally and, on the other—increasing the privileges of the elite. The expansion of privileges affected even the non-party-administrative elite. In March 1944, the decision of the Council of People's Commissars of the USSR "On the organization of shops and restaurants in Moscow for the service of workers in science, technology, art, and literature, as well as the higher officers of the Red Army" was issued. A month later several dozen commercial stores were opened there, in which scarce food products and other goods could be bought at prices that exceeded those bought with ration cards but cheaper than market value and without quantitative restrictions. At the same time, the top officers received a 35 percent discount, while the remaining categories of employees received 25 percent. In the second half of 1944 similar stores were opened in several other large cities.[159] In these years, the central authorities also found other ways to support the intellectual elite.[160] According to the testimony of the same Timofeev in August 1944, "writers were given American clothes: a suit, underclothing, and so on."[161] Against the backdrop of the postwar famine, these measures contributed to the growth of the authority of the non-party-administrative elite in the eyes of lower administrators.

Local Officials and Refugees

General supervision of the actions of local authorities was to be carried out first by the evacuation centers and then by regional and republican departments for the economic organization of the evacuated population. They were also supposed to keep records, organize resettlements, and help with housing, facilitate the placement of refugees, and check on their living conditions. While the chiefs of these departments were interested in truthful and complete reports, some of the inspectors submitted rosy reports, which was the result of bribes they received. Such a report was compiled by David Valershtein on the results of his trip to Kolkhoz Arabusi in the Urmary district of Chuvashia in June 1942. He concluded, "I think it necessary to note that the leadership of the Urmary district is unremittingly engaged in the employment of evacuees."[162] Another inspector who visited this district at the same time, Larionova, concluded her report with the facts of poor care for refugees: "It is necessary to point out to the chair of the executive committee of the Urmary District Council, Iarandaikin, that he should pay more attention to the evacuees, engage in their employment and improve their lives, and get rid of the rude attitude toward them."[163] The refugee Parkhomenko in 1942 told to his son, a frontline soldier, in a letter confiscated by the NKVD about how, after a complaint of refugees to the Council of People's Commissars of Bashkir ASSR, the republican authorities sent an evacuation inspector into their Iglino district. He received butter and honey from them and then wrote a report in favor of the local administrators.[164]

The reason for the bribery of some evacuation inspectors was their low salaries. With a small salary of 200 to 300 rubles a month (with taxes and semi-compulsory donations deducted), they were allocated 400 grams per day of bread on ration cards, and the work was associated with frequent trips to various districts. Therefore, many bureaucrats, when presented with a choice, refused such work or later switched to another type of work. The authorities were forced to accept low-skilled workers as inspectors, which could not but affect the care of refugees.¹⁶⁵ Because of the staffing problem, sometimes people who did not have the opportunity to travel to the various districts because of health reason were taken on as inspectors.¹⁶⁶ In the department for the economic organization of the evacuated population under the Council of People's Commissariat of the Mari ASSR, according to a check, out of three inspectors, only one was suitable for the post, the other was illiterate, and the third could not travel around the districts because of his family situation.¹⁶⁷

The lack of evacuation officials was a factor everywhere. In the same Mari ASSR, one evacuation clerk was responsible for 2,800 refugees,¹⁶⁸ each family having many problems with housing, food, work, and medical treatment. The average situation in the country was only slightly better. By early 1942, there were 2,757 evacuation officials in the USSR.¹⁶⁹ Given the presence of seven million refugees (we will discuss this figure below), it turns out that each evacuation official was responsible for 2,539 refugees nationwide. This was too many. Nevertheless, in the spring of 1942 the authorities even decided to reduce evacuation officials working in employment and accounting.¹⁷⁰

As indicated, the local higher- and middle-level administrators adhered more to the central line in the reception of refugees than the lower-level authorities. However, among these administrators, there were officials who treated the refugee issue very negligently, such as the leaders of the Bashkir ASSR, the Kuibyshev region, the Mariinsk district of the Novosibirsk region, and the Glazov district of the Udmurt ASSR.¹⁷¹

The deputy chair of the Council of People's Commissars of Chuvashia, Vasilii Grigoriev, in his work records, under the heading "About work with evacuees," compiled the analysis of numerous complaints, grouped in detail the problems of the absorption of refugees, and outlined ways to eliminate them. In his conclusion, he wrote that "there is no connection with the evacuees, there is no real Soviet care," and that "it is necessary to gather those people who occupy the apartments [and] bring them to the understanding that they should help, show great magnanimity to the evacuees, that . . . helping evacuees is also helping the country against the enemy."¹⁷² Grigoriev himself showed concern for refugees. In particular, he granted requests of Leiba Golod to help with winter clothes and shoes and Tsilia Ister to help in heating her apartment and finding employment.¹⁷³

Chair of the Shemursha District Executive Committee, Nikolai Kosmovskii, was one of the few representatives of average administrators who sympathized with the problems of refugees, and in the winter of 1941–1942 he satisfied all of their requests for the issuance of feltboots.¹⁷⁴ And the footwear problem, as we recall, was vital. In August 1942 he compiled a note—"On the work with the evacuated population"—where he criticized the kolkhozes for the poor accounting of the workdays of the refugees, the high rent demanded from them, and their fuel insecurity.[175]

Another such leader was the chair of the executive committee of the Krasnye Chetai district of the same republic, I. Nikitin. In 1942 he sent letters to the chairs of the executive committees of village councils in his district with the stamp "top secret." In them, after describing the plight of the refugees and the negative attitude toward them, the main points of which we shall see below, he ordered eleven measures to be taken to correct the situation. Fearing the publicity of negative facts, Nikitin ordered these letters to be discussed with the chairs of the kolkhozes at meetings, so that only the secretaries of the local party committees could attend, and that these letters be returned in a day's time with the signatures of all those present attesting that they had read it.[176]

There were also lower administrators who actually took care of the refugees. The chair of the Kalinin kolkhoz in the Fergana Valley in Uzbekistan helped the refugees with everything he could.[177] Leningraders in the kolkhozes Almaz (Diamond), Partisan, Komintern, and the Michurin Kolkhoz of the Kalinino district of Chuvashia were relatively wellfed.[178] The chair of Kolkhoz Krasnyi Borets (Red Fighter) in Nizhnee Timercheevo of the same republic, Avdei Pavlov, provided his refugees with food and firewood for the winter. The refugees even promised to invite him to vacation with them after the war.[179] However, according to sources, such kinds of relations were rare.

The poor work of the administrative and party authorities regarding the absorption of refugees sometimes encouraged the third power structure—the People's Commissariat of Internal Affairs with its unit of the NKVD—to intervene in this process. At the end of October 1941 Aleksei Babkin proposed to the first secretary of the Central Committee of the Communist Party of Kazakhstan, Nikolai Skvortsov, a twelve-point plan aimed at improving the situation of refugees in the republic and improving the system of their distribution.[180] It is not known how the leader of Kazakhstan reacted to this plan, but in any case, the appeal of the People's Commissar for Internal Affairs of the republic, connected by a chain of direct administrative subordination to the then powerful Lavrenty Beria, was hardly ignored. In February 1942, the plight of refugees in the Penza region forced the regional NKVD to exert pressure on the other two local authorities to improve their work and the control of the funds allotted for the evacuees. At the same time, the deputy head of the Penza regional NKVD, Iakov Sinitsyn, warned the chiefs of the NKVD district departments subordinate to him that they would be punished for not taking measures to respond to the complaints of the evacuated population.[181] Thus, the People's Commissariat of Internal Affairs, during the war, was forced to move to a more active position in the sphere of absorption of refugees, which was the result of the poor functioning of the party and administrative verticals of power.

THE RESPONSE OF REFUGEES

The indignation of refugees at the indifferent attitude of the local authorities to them was often expressed in written complaints. Written complaints in the USSR even before the war were a particularly widespread form of discontent.[182] During the war years, with the growth of economic problems, their number particularly increased. Elena Khalantseva, on behalf of a group of Muscovites who found themselves in Chuvashia, asked Stalin to allow them to return to Moscow: "We agree to die under bombardment but not from hunger. The fathers of our children defend the fatherland, and they [the local authorities] starve us."[183] Mira Rapoport, in January 1942, from the village of Kalinino of the same republic, wrote to Mikhail Kalinin: "Our children are doomed to cold and hunger, solely due to an intolerant mocking attitude . . . on the part of the local leadership . . . and local residents who consider us to be the culprits of all evil. After the evacuees at the conference expressed their strong protest against the mockery of the local leadership, this attitude has worsened."[184] The special indignation of many refugees was caused by the publication on January 6, 1942, by the newspaper *Krasnaia Chuvashia* of a laudatory article on the local authorities—"Care for the Evacuated Population."[185]

An acute form of discontent with local officials is shown by their comparison with the Nazis. In Alma-Ata in the autumn of 1942, refugees often spoke of the authorities' callousness: "They're worse than the fascists."[186] At the same time, a group of Muscovites wrote to Stalin from the village of Sin'-Aldush of the Chuvash ASSR with a request to pay attention to the Hitler-like mockery of them and their children.[187] The refugees in Urmary, also in Chuvashia, called the secretary of the executive committee, Zhukovskii, "Hitler," for his rudeness to them.[188]

The refugee Parkhomenko wrote to his son, a Red Army soldier, that because of illness, the chair of the kolkhoz in the Iglino district of the Bashkir ASSR included him in the list of non-working people who were not to receive flour. In the end, Parkhomenko added: "Here is the real henchman of Hitler . . . I give my word, if I do not get any flour, I cannot vouch for myself, I'll die in any case, but we do not see the truth, and you will not find it."[189] The refugee R. Shliakina finished description of her economic conditions and the indifference of the Turki district of the Saratov region for *Pravda* with the conclusion "we are no better off here than under the Germans."[190]

It is worth noting that, unlike the local population, newcomers, especially from Moscow and Leningrad, were more educated and had a good command of Soviet epistolary rhetoric. They were more likely than local residents to appeal to higher-level organizations with complaints about local officials, to which the others were not accustomed. To some extent, the passive sabotage of state programs of assistance for evacuees by some officials was a kind of act of revenge for refugees' complaints.

If the complaints were addressed to the mid-level local administrators, they often did not lead to anything because of the practice of ignoring such criticism. Of the 781 refugee complaints received by the district authorities in the Altai territory in the first eight months of 1943, in 514 cases no measures were taken.[191] This was due to a weak pressure mechanism because of a lack of staff to replace lower administrators, and, in some cases, the involvement of district officials in the same corrupt network. As for the district prosecutors, they were sometimes themselves involved in the same networks, and sometimes they were under pressure from the district party apparatus, which wanted to retain the cadres. On the whole, however, the prosecutor's office more often influenced the lower administrators. When complaints did not concern the system of power, but rather petty officials or domestic disputes, they were most often ignored, since there were a lot of them and the authorities did not hurry to consider them. For example, in Sterlitamak, the city authorities and the prosecutor, to whom the refugees complained of the hostile attitudes of the homeowners, did not take any measures.[192]

The most effective were complaints to regional, territorial, and republican structures. Higher-level local administrators paid more attention to the rule of law, depended less on personal considerations in the field, and were less likely to be involved in corrupt groups. The same applies to the prosecutor's office at this level. This is well traced in the statistics of complaints in the Kemerovo region.[193] In Turkmenistan, the authorities of the Chardzhou region in November 1942 punished the officials of the Khodzhambas district for their "soulless treatment" of refugees.[194] In addition to restoring order in a specific administrative unit, such punishments were an educational tool for influencing other administrators.

Complaints to Stalin, Kalinin, Kaganovich, Molotov, newspapers, the Council of People's Commissars, and the Moscow City Council received most attention. After these complaints were received, they were dispatched by the secretaries to the higher and secondary local administrators for verification, and appropriate measures were taken, and reports made in a short time. They were afraid of suffering from inaction. However, the archival materials show that only a small portion of the complaints was confirmed by checks, which later found expression in the punishment of a low-ranking official (usually in the form of reprimand, severe reprimand, transfer to another job, and less often suspension with the initiation of criminal proceedings). Most of the accusations were classified as "not confirmed," since the recognition of the fairness of the complaints meant recognizing their management as ineffective. For this purpose, the use of slandering complainants was widely used, as in the case of a complaint against Notkina: "Even at home she does not work, she hasn't cleaned the floors since autumn, the mud all around the house has led to unsanitary conditions."[195] Whereas in reality, Notkina lived in a ruined house without floors, and we shall return to her.

An analysis of the address of complaints shows that officials were more likely to put themselves in the shoes of refugees if the complaints were accompanied by dramatically described details of everyday life. The Latvian refugee Maria Strauts complained to the republican representative about the problems that resulted her poor knowledge of the Chuvash and Russian languages. She finished her letter—translated with somebody's help—saying: "Help us, otherwise we'll die, and we will never see our homeland again. My little ones are very sick. They are good pioneers, but now they are abandoned without school, and the sick are lying on the bare floor. You have repeatedly helped us, please help us also now."[196]

Refugees complained especially often to their relatives. Only in one and a half months in autumn 1942, checking the correspondence by the military censorship of the NKVD in ten territorial-administrative units recorded 35,397 letters of complaint. Most of them were identified as being from the Kirov region—26,923.[197] This figure is especially impressive against the background of the total number of refugees there—73,904, including children.[198] The majority of the refugees were Leningraders. One letter from this region reports: "The canteen here is for the authorities, and we are the dregs. Sometimes it seems like you're not even living in the Soviet Union. The attitude toward the refugees—the devil knows. We are considered beasts."[199] From the Udmurt ASSR, C. Gugileva writes in 1942, "They don't like evacuees here, they ask why we came and made the prices soar. The local people are provided with everything, and we are doomed to starvation."[200]

Since the prewar system of repression suppressed even hints of collective forms of protest and created an atmosphere of suspicion and mistrust, there were few joint complaints. The materials of the Chuvash ASSR contain about a dozen such complaints. They, too, were mostly written by more active and educated Muscovites and Leningraders. In December 1941, a group of Muscovites who had been evacuated to Ichikisy and were suffering from hunger and cold sent a letter to the Moscow City Council, where in they complained about the local authorities. The authorities settled them in houses with broken glass, did not give them firewood or even transport for its delivery from the forest, located 13–15 kilometers away. They were not given food, and the things they had brought with them to barter had run out. The result was a high death rate of people weakened by hunger (especially children) from pneumonia.[201] A month later, in January 1942, a group of Muscovites from the village of Algashi in the Shumerlia district also complained. Addressing the complaint to the Supreme Council of the Chuvash ASSR, eighteen mothers on behalf of sixty-three family members wrote that they received only bread with their ration cards and no other food, including cereals, butter, and milk for their children, and that the kolkhoz did not pay them for their earned workdays. The women wrote that they were on the verge of suicide.[202]

Indeed, the discriminatory and disparaging attitude of the local administration, along with economic difficulties, drove the refugees to despair. In the autumn of 1941 refugees in Alma-Ata stated: "We have never met with such an inhuman and soulless attitude toward ourselves, and if we had known about it in advance, we would rather have perished from the bullets of the fascists, rather than die here by a slow death, while our husbands, fathers, brothers, and sons fight on the fronts."[203] From Baku, Gurzhii wrote at the beginning of 1942 to a relative: "We are on a pier, it was raining all night, and we've fallen ill. Nobody has any shoes. Thousands of people are sitting here, infested with lice, people get sick and die every day, and no attention is paid. We came here in vain, it would have been better to have been killed by the Germans than to be so tormented here."[204]

In general, refugees often wrote to relatives and authorities about their readiness for suicide. We have already seen a quotation from a letter by a refugee from Leningrad, Chepik, above. Also evacuated to Kirov from Leningrad, A. Epshtein, describing her serious economic situation to a relative, concluded: "I'm so upset that I do not know what to do. I may lay my hands on myself."[205] From the Molotov region, the refugee Volokhova wrote to her husband, a Red Army soldier in the Far East, in the autumn of 1942: "Send a call, or by the spring Tomka and I shall perish. Death awaits us here. The prices are such that it's terrible to write about them, everything is available by exchange only, but I have nothing to exchange. If you don't get us out of here, I will finish everything, so as not to torture myself and the child."[206] Vera Nikitina, the wife of a border guard officer, who in June 1941 may have been killed in the first German attack, wrote to the Soviet of Workers' Deputies of the RSFSR, "I'll kill myself so as not to see my child's torment." Escaping the front, she had no time to take anything with her, gave birth on the road, and it was difficult for her to get cow milk for the baby from the authorities, not having any of her own.[207]

It is difficult to say how serious these threats were. Even those who complained to relatives could have known that the letters were read by censorship officials (incidentally, in June 1942 their staff was increased by 3,800 new employees[208]). Therefore, the message in a letter about readiness for suicide could have been a channel for conveying this information to the authorities, especially since, as Fitzpatrick correctly writes, the authorities were very sensitive to such threats.[209]

In many cases these threats came of very real despair. Among a large number of archival materials I have examined, I never came across the statistics of suicides among refugees. It is not known whether such statistics were gathered at all, but if they were, they would hardly be complete, since everybody in the chain of power was interested in concealing them. After all, by pointing out a large number of suicides, the reporting official actually admitted his own poor work. One ought not to expect publicity about this issue at all. When in the autumn of 1941 the Molotov Medical Institute published an article with local statistics of suicides in trains and trams for 1927–1928, the collection was detained by the censor and the unsuitable statistics were deleted.[210] Some of the cases in the available archive materials suggest that suicide was not a rare occurrence. In the Chuvash ASSR, hounded by the negative attitude of the above-mentioned chair of the kolkhoz Trofimov, Pavlova tried to drown himself in the Volga River but was stopped by other refugees.[211] In the village of Kudeikha of the same republic a refugee hanged herself because of her inability to feed her three children.[212]

According to Podlivalov's information, in Kurgan the worker Tsukerman, due to endless insults and beatings—and this was the usual practice of treating factory workers at the mortar factory where he worked—threw himself under a train.[213] The author does not say whether these persecutions had an antisemitic character. In the Shabalino district of the Kirov region a refugee hanged herself—the wife of the officer Chuiko and the mother of three children, she was driven to despair by her inability to clothe and feed them.[214] The suicide of the poet Marina Tsvetaeva is indicative, motivated by the hopelessness of the situation in which she could not find work even as a dishwasher.[215]

∾

Different levels of power treated refugees in their own way. The refugees were treated the worst by the lower echelons of power, who did not see any significant benefit in refugees as necessary for the victory of the labor force. Local authorities considered that this was only a bad substitute for many of their "good" human resources who had gone to the front and "bad" outsiders. Chairs of kolkhozes and secretaries of village councils did not particularly like refugees, many of whom were urban residents. Even the successes of some refugees in agriculture often did not help to overcome the aversion of local administrators. The neediness of veterans' families did not encourage many lower-level administrators to help them as much as they could. The mid-level administrators were somewhat more benevolent toward refugees. Against the background of poor care for the majority of evacuees, the care provided to the privileged evacuees is remarkable. The forms of protest by refugees against the difficult economic situation in which they found themselves were numerous complaints and, in some cases, suicides. Often the reason or consequence of negligence toward the needs of refugees was the redistribution or theft of products and goods intended for them. We will see this in the next chapter. In these circumstances, finding well-paying jobs gave them a good chance of survival.

CHAPTER THREE

"He who does not work, does not eat"

The Employment Problem

As we have seen, the chairs of the kolkhozes widely used the slogan "He who does not work, does not eat," forcing refugees to work under any conditions. If work was a constant on the kolkhozes, there was not enough work in the cities, and, therefore, there was a lot of competition for jobs. Finding a well-paid job had a very direct impact on the survival of refugees. This was very hard for the unemployed, and in the first year of the war there were many of them. Official reports from that period testify to the high level of unemployment. For example, in 1942 17.6 percent and 26.8 percent of the able-bodied population were out of work in the Kuibyshev and Penza regions, respectively.[1] According to the official data provided by Marina Potëmkina, unemployment in the Urals among refugees was 35 percent in the years 1941 and 1942, 11.8 percent in 1943, and 9.8 percent in 1944.[2] Obviously, she meant the able-bodied population. Within the entire part of the RSFSR that remained unoccupied, unemployment among able-bodied evacuees was 20.1 percent at the end of 1942 and 14.6 percent by November 1943.[3]

However, all these official statistics elicit suspicion, based on detailed analysis of statistics from the Chuvash ASSR. According to the official report, on June 10, 1942, 30.8 percent of the republic's able-bodied population was unemployed,[4] and by October 1, 1942, that number dropped to 12.9 percent.[5] Within a month, unemployment fell again to 6.7 percent,[6] and by December 15 to 5 percent.[7] This were largely no evident reasons for such a rapid reduction in unemployment in just six months.

The manipulation of unemployment statistics to produce more positive reports was practiced by officials at different levels of Soviet government. Evacuation inspector Mikhail Kosolapov wrote about fraud in the Pervomaiskoe district of Chuvashia in his report to the head of the department for the economic structure of the evacuated population of Chuvashia, Nilolai Zhukov.[8] In June 1943 the head of the department of the Council of People's Commissars of the RSFSR for the economic organization of the evacuated population, L. Dmitriev, himself acknowledged to Zhukov that his report understated the number of the unemployed and that in reality their number was three times higher, no less than 5,000 instead of the reported 1,616.[9] It is difficult to say which source of information Dmitriev used; it is also possible that he suspected something was amiss with the rapid fall of unemployment. Perhaps, in some places the erroneous data on the percentage of refugees employed resulted in the misreporting of their numbers, which we will discuss in more detail below. In any case, compared to the unemployment statistics for Chuvashia, the Urals, and the RSFSR in general, the 28.5 percent unemployment rate among the able-bodied refugees in the Altai territory in April 1943 seems more accurate.[10]

Unemployment in Central Asia was even higher, as there were fewer industrial enterprises but a large number of refugees. In Pavlodar (Kazakhstan) in 1942, over 60 percent of former Polish citizens were unemployed.[11] Many refugees were unable to find work for months, and some searched for work for several years. Ruth Geht's parents could not find any work during their stay in Central Asia (1941–1944), and the family survived on food rations, by selling their clothes, and occasionally receiving parcels from abroad from foreign Jewish organizations.[12] In her interview, Geht compares the conditions of her stay in Central Asia and in a Siberian camp where her family of Polish citizens was exiled in 1940: "In Siberia, at least, there was work and people worked, albeit involuntarily, but they received some kind of food. In Uzbekistan there was no work, there was no food, there was nothing. We were not cared for, we were free, and everyone had to look after themselves."[13]

The experience of finding a job was different for different refugee groups. Those who had been Soviet citizens before 1939 found it easier than new citizens because they knew the Russian language and Soviet realities better.[14] If the Polish language made it easier for the natives of Poland to express themselves, to understand and read in Russian, the refugees from the Baltic states, Bukovina, and Bessarabia had more difficulties. Their situation was exacerbated by their total inability to write in Russian, which precluded the possibility of a written appeal to the authorities.

Having mastered the language (sometimes not only Russian, but, for example, even Uzbek[15]) and become acquainted with local realities, some of the Polish, Baltic, and Romanian Jews, being more enterprising and bold, unlike the Soviet Jews who had been intimidated by repressions, were able to organize either clandestine or official commercial ventures for the production or resale of products and goods. Often, they had to give bribes to officials. A native of

Romania, Moordekhai Liuksemburg, who one day successfully repaired his own pair of galoshes, went out the next day to the market in the mining town of Kyzyl-Kiia (Kirgizstan) to fix with his simple tools the galoshes for others: "People saw me and reached out with their worn-out footwear—holey, torn, tatty. . . . When I counted my earnings, I was stunned: four hundred rubles, a lot of money! During the war, incidentally, not a single factory in the Soviet Union produced galoshes, and the need for them was enormous. . . . For a pair of galoshes, I took twenty-five rubles, and it was paid on the spot. And if I had asked for more—they would have given more." He testifies to the fact that Polish Jews in this town were able to sew elegant and colorful clothes and headdresses for the Kyrgyz, which included jewelry made of precious stones and gold. With the money made they could buy vegetables, fruits, meat, and wool from the same Kyrgyz at the bazaar. For this commodity exchange Jews had to generously pay police officers and financial inspectors.[16]

The mother of Keila Fliker (Pruzanski), who, after deportation from Białystok, found herself in Pavlodar, was a model of entrepreneurship in these harsh conditions. She sold her clothes and possessions and bought a cow, the milk of which, together with the family's business—the production of skirts and gloves with the help of three adolescent children—saved them from hunger.[17] Dina Gabel deported from Lida, also a former Polish town, was resourceful as well. Being in a remote Ukrainian village in northern Kazakhstan, she established the manufacture of knitted socks and women's sweaters, which not only helped her to avoid being sent to work in the coal mines but also paid well.[18]

Such enterprising behavior often ran counter to the Soviet legal norm. Moshe Shtrasberg, his sister, and her husband, refugees from Poland in Uzbekistan, bought torn padded jackets (fufaikas) at the bazaars, repaired them if necessary, filled them with cotton, and then resold them. Once, on a train to Dzhizak, he was arrested on suspicion of speculation—he was wearing two padded jackets. Thanks to a bribe, the railway police let him go. At the bazaar in Dzhizak, a local police officer, threatening him with arrest, demanded a bribe. When Shtrasberg moved to Samarkand and was engaged in the textile trade, bribing the police at the bazaar became a regular practice, which allowed him to trade without hindrance.[19] The Polish Jewish cobbler Natan Brener, who found himself in Chimbai (Karakalpak ASSR in Uzbekistan), at first sewed shoes privately and his wife sold them. They earned a fair amount of money. Later, apparently because of fears of punishment, they joined an artel, which had been created in the town.[20] The Polish Jew Abram Zailbering, who was in Kanibadam (Tajikistan), quickly realized that in some cities of Central Asia food was very expensive, and in others, goods. He earned 12,000 rubles by taking just one trip to Tashkent and back.[21] At risk of finding himself in prison, he wondered why the communist authorities were fighting speculators who brought the population the benefit of reduced prices. On September 25, 1942, the State Defense Committee issued a resolution "On measures to combat profiteering." People were forbidden to transport more than sixteen kilograms of products on trains.[22] Even in the difficult conditions of the commodity and food deficit, protecting the principles was more important to the authorities than balancing the prices across the regions. Incidentally, refugees on the move suffered because of this resolution. Maria Zakharova was returning with her children to Moscow from Chuvashia when they were detained by the police, who confiscated all the food the family took with them and sent it back. Zakharova and her children were starving upon their return because the Dimitrov Kolkhoz, where they lived, refused to help them.[23]

Sometimes Soviet Jews also decided to engage in craftwork. The elderly Odessa cobbler Aron Meerovich, after a couple of months of a languishing existence in Alma-Ata, assembled several shoemakers and organized an artel to sew footwear for the Red Army. The local newspapers wrote enthusiastically about him.[24] Efim Iankelevich, who found himself in Kokand shortly after the outbreak of the war, recalls:

> In the evacuation I had to help my parents survive so that our family did not starve to death. My parents mastered illegal production at home. Women's bras and simple Uzbek dresses were sewn for sale at the market. The authorities severely punished such production, including with prison sentences. But there was a war going on, and the authorities closed their eyes to it. They sewed on a manual prerevolutionary Singer sewing machine. We sewed literally around the clock, taking turns—mom, grandmother Brana, and I. Mom also cut patterns, and my grandmother and dad carried the finished products to the market early in the morning. They were helped by my nine-year-old middle brother—Lënia.[25]

Anatolii Tiktiner recalls how his uncle Aron opened a workshop in Stalinabad (now Dushanbe, Tajikistan) to make galoshes, which were scarce, from old inner tubes. Polishing the rubber with sandpaper, fifteen-year-old Anatolii earned a nice amount of money there.[26]

Perhaps the greatest success was achieved by another artel in Kokand, founded by refugees from Kharkov. At the end of November 1941 nineteen artisans joined together to obtain permission to create a sewing artel. Like other artel workers, they had to face a shortage of raw materials, money, and premises. Because of this, they started with the simplest things—the knitting of women's hats, plaids, and handkerchiefs. Over time, the artel began to manufacture horse blankets for the cavalry and then to sew underwear for the Red Army and warm "helmet inserts" of their own design. Later, the production range of the artel grew even greater. Soon, its revenue stood at one million rubles. A year later seven hundred people worked in it, of which 15 percent were non-Jews: Uzbeks, Tatars, Russians, Ukrainians, Armenians, and others.[27]

Sometimes raw materials for artels were stolen from industrial enterprises where some of their members worked.[28] The struggle for survival pushed them to steal, although they could be caught and imprisoned at any time. The judicial system came down hard on small-scale entrepreneurs. In February 1942 in Novosibirsk, several people were tried for price gouging: they had been selling felt boots (*valenki*) at an inflated price—400–500 rubles each pair. Because at the time of the arrest the suspects had wool confiscated from them, it means that they did not actually resell the goods with profit but produced them themselves.[29] This indicates that even in difficult wartime conditions, the state was more concerned with preserving its commodity monopoly than with people having goods and earning a living. The publicity of such a case could not help but scare small producers from setting up production of highly scarce merchandise.

Therefore, many did not dare to engage in independent craft or entrepreneurship, although there were a fair number of businesspeople among the "western" refugees.[30] Most of them were forced to seize on any work. In Dzhambul Arie Katsav and several of his friends agreed to do heavy work in a dining hall all day—in particular, carrying water from the irrigation ditch—for only a bowl of soup and a *lepëshka* (flatbread) per day.[31] Hundreds of Polish Jews were forced to work for the Tashkent-Stalinougol' coal mines and the construction of the Farhad hydroelectric power station. About seventy Polish Jews worked at the Tashkent machine-building plant[32] (among the Polish refugees, there were many young men, which was important for taking on hard physical work). The authorities, to alleviate to some extent the problem of employment of former Polish citizens, organized for them several dozen craft enterprises in 1943.[33]

Refugees were often discriminated against during hiring. In Chimkent (Kazakhstan), the wife of an officer Likhtsner was denied the work as an accountant on the grounds that she was an evacuee. The refusal to hire the wife of the military doctor Grinshpan was justified similarly.[34] Instances in the Chuvash ASSR also serve as examples. A. Botvinova from Orël tried unsuccessfully for two months to find a job in Mariinskii Posad. When local bosses found out during interviews that she was a refugee, she was denied work.[35] Kheifits worked in the village of Akchi-Kasy for about a year as a bookkeeper, but then she was fired under the pretext of not knowing the Chuvash language.[36] According to the report of the evacuation inspector Anna Maznina in the spring of 1943, in the Chkalovskoe district of Chuvashia a refugee from Leningrad was not hired as a waitress, and later the position was given to a local woman. The evacuation inspector who reported about this incident claimed that local residents received preferential treatment at hiring.[37] Another evacuation inspector who visited the Alatyr' district in the summer of 1942 noted in his memorandum that the evacuees' complaints—that they were offered worse jobs than the local population—were confirmed.[38]

Demanding sexual favors as a condition of hiring or retaining employment was not a rare occurrence.[39] This situation put women in a difficult position, especially those who had many dependents. Complaints to superiors or local party bodies were often not filed because they treated such harassment with condescension.

The social status of many job-seeking refugees declined compared to prewar times. Klara Kamenskaia, who worked in Kiev as the head of the personnel department in a factory, was forced to work as a dressmaker in Tashkent. Aleksandr Fel'dman, the head of the zoological department of the medical institute in Stalino before the war, settled in 1942 for the post of laboratory assistant at the epidemiological station of Andizhan.[40]

As a result of unemployment, discrimination, and the decrease in job status, refugees had lower incomes, evidenced by the analysis of over five hundred questionnaires filled out by Jews in 1945 in the Belorussian town of Rechitsa, where they were repatriated after the war from the eastern regions of the USSR. According to the results of this survey, their salary fell from 350–400 rubles on average per month before the war to 150–250 during it, 60–70 percent of the prewar earnings.[41] It should be kept in mind that at the end of 1941 most of the refugees earned less than they did by 1945, because at the new place of residence and work it took them time to obtain useful connections, to advance in employment, and to subsequently move to other areas for better work. For example, according to the salary grades, nurse's aides, janitors, and yard keepers were paid only 115 rubles, nurses 205 rubles, pharmacists 225 rubles, and laborers 150–260 rubles. Doctors and accountants earned 350–450 rubles, depending on the position.[42]

Accounting was the most common profession among refugees. Of all refugees in the Alma-Ata region in October 1941 (and Jews accounted for 39.2 percent of them[43]), accountants comprised 5.9 percent. They were followed by actors (5 percent), tailors (4.8 percent), and teachers (4.3 percent).[44] Accountants were the most sought-after professionals in the rear. There were not enough accountants in the eastern regions of the USSR, especially in cities. The Novosibirsk newspapers ran several dozen "accountants wanted" ads in 1942, indicating a severe shortage.[45] The ads also spotlight a shortage of builders of all specializations, including engineers, as well as factory workers, drivers, and movers. Among the Jewish refugees, practitioners of these professions were few, but the need made them resort to factory work.

The artists were especially in demand. They were needed by the central government, both for direct agitation against the enemy and for demonstrating to the population the vitality of the country. Refugee teachers were also in demand, on the one hand because of the large number of children moving to the eastern parts of the USSR and, on the other, because of the number of teachers who had been called to the front. The authorities valued school education because it was the second most effective instrument of ideological influence on the Soviet family (the first was the mass media). Because of the acute shortage of clothing during the war, the tailors' artels were very much in demand, but the local authorities and tailors themselves did not always have the initiative to organize such artels. After all, it was necessary to find work space, equipment, raw materials, as well as organize sales, all of it in the face of bureaucracy barriers and caution.

Allowing the activities of one or another artel, local officials expected to receive some personal favors from them. In addition to the gift offerings for patronage, administrators who allowed the artels to produce scarce goods on their territory were encouraged by their superiors, as it was useful for good reporting to the government. On the other hand, the bankruptcy of an artel could cause its employees to complain to the law enforcement bodies, which promised if not punishment, then significant troubles for administrators. Complaints of certain categories of artel workers—the former deported, ex-convicts, those who had lost their documents, yeshiva pupils, and other persons with a "bad reputation" in the eyes of Soviet legal institutions—did not need to be feared. However, it was possible to run into accusations of indulging the "shady elements." After all, the years of repression were still very fresh in people's memory. To a large extent, security could be guaranteed by triumphant reports about the success of such an artel, especially if it were about its assistance to soldiers on the front. Newspaper coverage of their successes further reduced the likelihood of the artels' often illicit commercial activities—the ways of purchasing raw materials or selling finished products—being exposed.

Fearing criticism directed at them or institutions under their jurisdiction, lower-level and mid-level local authorities courted journalists, especially correspondents of central newspapers and radio stations, as well as inspectors of central and republican ministries. Visiting one of the Samarkand artels in 1942, the inspector of the Uzbek People's Commissariat on Light Industry accepted with pleasure from one of the artels two buckets of eggs, sugar, and butter. As a result, in the inspector's report this artel's output figures grew from 40 percent below the average level to 35 percent above it. The artel's achievement was announced on the radio to the pleasure of a local official who patronized it.[46]

Qualified tailors in the cities could earn money from "under the table work" for private clients, but the less skilled tailors, especially in rural areas, had fewer options to feed themselves. Shoemakers were somewhat better off because of the huge shoe deficit.[47]

In the USSR in general, but especially as a refugee status during the war, the ability to acquire useful connections was a very valuable quality. Connections were required everywhere: with the local authorities, in the military conscription office, with the police, at the store, at the hospital, at the pharmacy, and so on. In this regard, the choice of employment of family members was of great importance, since the connections provided mutual benefit. In addition to the work sites just listed, which affected the distribution of both people and goods, work in manufacturing was useful, for it was possible to pilfer something from such jobs for subsequent exchange for either goods or services. Employees, especially management, of canteens, meat-processing plants, dairies, soap makers, and so on were well positioned for this. These work places provided opportunities for participation in the shadow economy. In Tashkent, the General Public Food Trust used to give the canteen and restaurant managers a few months' illegal lease, after which replacements were made to write off the embezzlement on the "negligent" fired managers.[48]

Not everybody too advantage of the opportunity to steal foodstuffs or consumer goods. Some employees considered this behavior shameful. The head of the canteen in Ermoshkino (Chuvashia), Khana Rapoport, lived in poverty. According to the village council, she had almost no clothes and, most importantly, no winter clothes. Likewise, the waitress of the same canteen, Maria Grinshpon, and of another, Shiva Serebriannikova, did not have feltboots.[49]

It is worth adding that due to the influx of refugees, the peripheral regions acquired specialists, which they needed very much even before the war. However, the enmity toward refugees was so great that this fact did not receive due recognition, as we will see below. By 1943 the number of doctors in the Omsk region and the Altai territory increased by 60 percent compared to the prewar period and almost double in the Kemerovo region—from 898 to 1,780.[50] The fact that all 530 physicians who were evacuated to Alma-Ata by the beginning of 1942 worked in their specialty—even taking in account that some local doctors were called into the army—speaks of a large prewar shortage of doctors even in a republican capital. Incidentally, Kazakhstan suffered worse than other republics from an understaffing of doctors. In 1936 the need for doctors in this republic was met at 76.3 percent, and of all Soviet republics, the situation was worse only in Kirgizstan—73.5 percent.[51] Those who arrived in Alma-Ata

Table 1. The share of Jews among refugee doctors in several areas of Kazakhstan in January 1943[53]

Territorial-administrative unit	Number of all physicians	Number of Jews among them	Percentage of Jews among them
Alma-Ata	530	368	69.44
Remaining part of the Alma-Ata region	154	87	56.49
Aktiubinsk region	55	37	67.27
Western Kazakhstan region	123	46	37.40
Pavlodar region	41	17	41.46
Semipalatinsk region	163	84	51.53
South Kazakhstan region	265	180	67.93
Total	1,331	819	61.53

were more qualified than local doctors because they were educated in universities of Moscow, Leningrad, Vilnius, Warsaw, Bucharest, Iassy, and some even in Western European countries. A significant portion of these refugee doctors were Jews.[52]

It is unlikely that those few regions of Kazakhstan whose lists do not contain the column "nationality," but which contain many Jewish surnames, would change the statistics on the share of Jews among refugee doctors, 61.53 percent, presented in table 1. This was much higher than the prewar share of Jews among doctors in the entire USSR, which in 1939 was disproportionately high—23.5 percent.[54]

It seems that in other Central Asian republics the proportion of Jews among refugee doctors was at least over a half, while it was also significant in the Urals, Siberia, and other unoccupied parts of the USSR, although it was lower because of the smaller number of Jews among all refugees. It is worth noting that the proportion of doctors among all able-bodied refugees in the Semipalatinsk region in Kazakhstan, according to the available statistics, was very high—0.88 percent, while among able-bodied Jewish refugees (accounting for 45 percent of all refugees in this area) it was even higher—1.01 percent.[55]

Forced Labor

In need of labor, the central authorities on February 13, 1942, adopted a resolution to mobilize the able-bodied urban population to work in production and construction: men from sixteen to fifty-five years old and women from sixteen to forty-five. Exempted were women with children under eight and students.[56]

Although both refugees and local residents were mobilized, the refugees were more affected, since there were more unemployed people among them and refugees had fewer connections to activate to avoid mobilization. Guided by this decision, the Novosibirsk region party committee drafted a plan to mobilize 5,500 people for military factories.[57] With all the voluntarism of this resolution, the punishment for violating it was relatively mild—compulsory work at the place of residence for a year. Because of this, part of the population didn't show up to points of departure. There were particularly many evasions in Central Asia, whose vastness and a large number of refugees made it easy to get lost. Therefore, local authorities carried out roundups. David Bakas was caught up in one of them after his documents were stolen: "I bought a piece of bread and one cucumber at the market, but had only managed to chew the bread when the police raid caught all the passportless, homeless, and those suspected of draft evasion. I, without any documents, was immediately detained, and a large group of detainees was brought to the Tashkent prison."[58] Public campaigns for voluntary relocations to the Ural plants were also common in Central Asia. Travel costs—train fare and daily expenses—were covered for those wishing to go. Some refugees, having been disillusioned in Central Asia, preferred this way of leaving.[59] In this way, the authorities solved the issue of unemployment in these southern republics.

In addition to this countrywide mobilization of workers, local authorities also organized their own. In the Altai territory in June 1942, the authorities forcibly mobilized two hundred refugees to work at match factories in Barnaul and Biisk. In August they mobilized 150 to work at the Zmeinogorsk pig farm. In October–November of the same year, 1,300 refugees were mobilized to work in an ammunition factory in Barnaul.[60] In the Novosibirsk region in the first year of the war, there were four such compulsory mobilizations. Local defense factory Kombinat no. 179 had an increase of 12,407 forced laborers due to these measures. More than half of them were summoned in January 1942 in accordance with the decision of the regional committee. But even these measures did not eliminate the shortage of labor. Therefore, in May 1942 the NKVD Siblag (Siberian labor camp) was ordered to allocate another 3,000 workers to this plant.[61]

Forcibly drafted refugees could not help but be burdened by their new and unfamiliar work in production. Poor living and working conditions exacerbated this feeling. Therefore, the flight was a common phenomenon. By September 1942, 59.8 percent of the mobilized workers had fled from the defense enterprises in the Novosibirsk region.[62] To combat this phenomenon, the authorities employed the policy of "attaching" workers to defense enterprises. On December 26, 1941, the Presidium of the Supreme Soviet of the USSR issued a decree on the responsibility of laborers and employees of enterprises of the military industry for unauthorized abandonment of the workplace. Violation of it, though, was not equated with desertion from the army but, all the same, threatened a serious punishment—imprisonment for up to 8 years[63]—and this punishment was put into practice. In February 1942 workers Shapiro and Bogdanov received such a term for abandoning their work at the factory and returning to Moscow.[64] It should be noted that the January 3, 1942, decree of the Council of People's Commissars simplified the procedure for the punishment of such cases: complaint of the head of the enterprise was enough. This led to abuse. In the Ibresi district of Chuvashia, the refugee Ekaterina Ianchevskaia was arrested by the director of the forestry enterprise for just a one-day absence, which happened when she was called in by the military registration and enlistment office, and this was despite the fact, moreover, that typically she produced 150 percent of the norm.[65]

Harsh punishments did not prevent the escape of workers. In 1942 the number of wanted labor deserters reached one hundred thousand, both refugees and local residents. Authorities were able to detain about a fifth of these in the same year. In the Cheliabinsk region, eight hundred fugitives were used again at military enterprises but without pay, as they became prisoners.[66]

In the years 1942–1943 the number of laborers who were convicted by the tribunals was 500,833. Of these, 30 percent were adolescents under the age of eighteen. The majority of labor deserters were judged in absentia. For insufficient efforts to find and punish them, the authorities applied administrative measures against the chiefs of police and prosecutors. By 1946 the number of "runaways" convicted by the tribunals rose to 767,015. Unable to overcome the flight, the authorities issued an amnesty for workers of military plants at the very end of 1944, with the condition of their voluntary return by February 15, 1945. On June 7, 1945, this amnesty was extended to all convicted "labor deserters." Reporting on this, the prosecutor's office forbade the condemnation of fugitives in absentia. However, the tribunals continued to operate even a few years after the war. It was only in May 1948 that the "decree on fugitives" was abolished.[67]

At the same time, the authorities tightened penalties for violations of labor discipline, most often for absenteeism and tardiness. If, since the beginning of the war, in such cases the bread ration was reduced by a quarter, and some of the food ration cards were revoked, starting in August 1943 the Commissariat of Ammunition introduced a new type of punishment at its enterprises: arrest and dispatch to guardhouses that were specially organized at the factories. Those held in custody there were of two types: those continuing to work in their workplaces and those removed from their previous work. The latter were sent to other work. They did not keep the wages, and they lost food ration cards for this time, eating only at the guardhouse. Both categories returned to the guardhouse on their own at the end of every workday. There they were locked in cells and taken out for a walk or to the toilet under escort. Sleep lasted no more than six hours; at any other times they were forbidden to lie down. It was generally forbidden to sing or to read.[68]

In 1942–1943 the authorities organized population transfers to collective farms and fisheries, for which the *spetspereselentsy* (forced settlers) as well kolkhozniks were to be mobilized. They were sent to the Yakut ASSR, the Buriat-Mongolian ASSR, Khabarovsk territory, and the Irkutsk and Kamchatka regions to catch and preserve fish. On February 26, 1943, the Council of People's Commissars of the Chuvash ASSR, following the instructions of the central authorities, decided on the preferential voluntary transfer of the local population there, but only few volunteered. Even though the refugees were not attracted by the resettlement, in order to fulfill the plan, some of them were semi-compulsorily sent there by local authorities.[69] It is unlikely that benefits allocated to resettlers, like the forgiveness of state debt,[70] could attract refugees, who, as a rule, rarely received state loans.

It seems that the resettlement of refugees there was carried out without the consent of the central authorities, but rather only by agreement with the local offices of the NKVD. This conclusion follows from the letter by L. Dmitriev, sent on April 10, 1943, to the subordinate evacuation departments of the regions and autonomous republics of the RSFSR. In it, outlining the results of the mobilization, he reported that evacuated hairdressers, photographers, musicians, draftsmen, cashiers, typesetters, typists, and librarians, unable to work either in agriculture or at fisheries, were moved by local authorities from the Chuvash ASSR and the Penza region. At the same time, he complained that sending such workers only wasted the republic's resources.[71]

According to statistics, 541 Jews were among the "volunteers" sent from Chuvashia to the Buriat-Mongolian ASSR and the Irkutsk region in early 1943, 16 percent of the total.[72] The new conditions in which these refugee townspeople found themselves in the fish harvesting were very extreme, even compared to the difficult working and living conditions on the kolkhozes of Chuvashia. Although the mobilization of refugees for fish canning continued, due to Dmitriev's scolding, their number was greatly reduced. In the second and third quarters of 1943, only 32 Jews, or 2.2 percent of the total number of volunteers, left Chuvashia for these places and also the Khabarovsk territory.[73] Several dozen refugees were left behind at the last moment, due to the recognition of the unfitness for such work and harsh living conditions.[74]

The authorities were less ceremonious with the exiles than with the refugees. Seemingly, the exiles' status had significantly lost its peculiarity because

Jewish refugees, Irkutsk. USHMM, courtesy of Avram and Rina Romas.

the refugees also did not have the right to move, but, as it turned out, not completely. In addition, the exiled settlers continued to be subject to more strict registration rules. They were sent to fish harvesting in accordance with the decision of the Council of People's Commissars of the USSR on the delivery of additional 35,000 special settlers to the fishing industry, adopted in early 1942.[75] Unlike refugees, they were only relocated there forcibly, even in cases where the exiles were well settled and useful for local economy. This happened with the family of Rachel and Israel Rachlin, who were previously deported from Lithuania to the Altai territory. They were resettled in 1942 in Yakutia, on the coast of the Laptev Sea along with 170 other Lithuanian Jews, as well as Lithuanians, Karelians, and Soviet Germans previously expelled from the Leningrad region.[76]

In October 1944 the Council of People's Commissars of the RSFSR adopted a resolution on the strengthening of agriculture in the Saratov region by transferring there collective farmers from other regions.[77] This meant that the return home of the deported German population was not planned. Few refugees were resettled in this way, because, although they did work in kolkhozes, they were rarely accepted as their members, instead being low-wage workers. Among those refugees who arrived directly in the Saratov region in 1941–1942, Jews did not stand out as a large percentage of the population compared to other areas. This did not prevent the Soviet authorities from presenting the region, along with Kazakhstan and Uzbekistan, as an area of high concentration of Jewish refugees to the Joint Distribution Committee (JDC) in New York, as a result of which American goods and food were sent there.[78]

In the Chuvash ASSR itself, concerned with the large number of unemployed in the towns, the commissioner for the evacuation council in the Alatyr' district, Kizilov, recommended in January 1942 the resettlement of evacuated "disabled and elderly people without relatives" to the kolkhozes, while prohibiting the police from assigning these categories of the population to towns.[79] Based on his recommendation, by the decision of the Bureau of the Alatyr' District Party Committee, these categories of refugees were deported from the town of Alatyr' to the kolkhozes in March 1942. Moreover, only two days were given to the executive bodies to accomplish the resettlement.[80] The deportation was carried out, although such relocations were legitimized only by the decision of the Council of People's Commissars of the USSR of April 13, 1942, and even then only for the "most stressful periods of agricultural work." According to the resolution on labor mobilization, the unemployed urban population aged fourteen to fifty-five for men and fourteen to fifty for women were subject to being sent to kolkhozes. An exception was made only for students of the last two years of university, while schoolchildren in sixth through tenth grades were subject to this mobilization.[81] Despite the all-encompassing nature of the order, the deportations to the villages were not universal, because many kolkhozes, as noted, did not want to accept additional refugees and make living arrangements for them. The same resolution increased the mandatory minimum of workdays for kolkhozniks per year: 150 for cotton-growing areas and 100–120 for the rest of the USSR. In the framework of this total number of necessary workdays, even seasonal workday rates were spelled out, which made it impossible to compensate for a shortage of work at another time of the year. Even adolescents were not left out: from age twelve to sixteen, children were required to work 50 workdays a year.

Forced assignments to kolkhozes and manufacturing works, as well as the emergency nature of the work there, gave their directors exceptional opportunities to treat workers poorly, ignore safety rules,[82] introduce very long working days, and use child labor. Sometimes the living conditions of workers "at liberty" horrified even the officers of the NKVD whose forced laborers worked in the same plants. In February 1945 Fëdor Petrovskii ordered the Soviet German labor-army workers from the Novosibirsk military plant no. 65 to be transferred to another plant because, in the preceding six months, 7 percent of them and their family members had died because of malnutrition.[83] In fact, the annual average death rate of German labor-army workers in 1944 did not exceed 2 percent, reaching 6.1 percent only in the coal mines, and in 1943 these figures were even lower.[84]

The adopted resolutions sought to ensure the maximum labor supply for important objectives of the national economy. Given the lack of freedom of movement, the conscripted labor, the deportation of the civilian population, and official confiscation from those who had been evacuated along with enterprises of their abandoned housing, which we will discuss later, we can say that the whole country had become an enormous Gulag.

Provision of Food

One of the important problems that the Soviet authorities had to face during the war years was the issue of food supply for the population. It suffered from a shortage of food even before the war, and with its beginning, the situation deteriorated significantly. A reflection of this deterioration was the cancellation by the Council of People's Commissars of the USSR on February 11, 1942, of its own decree on the free provision of food for the evacuated population of July 16, 1941.

The main source of food for refugees was subsidized groceries issued by government distributors. The quality of the food—mostly it was bread—was not high. Nevertheless, even with these groceries, there were often interruptions.

Even procuring food with ration cards, as a rule, required standing in hours-long lines. The size of the ration was larger for workers and their directors, as well as engineers, technicians, teachers, doctors, students, and workers in communications, transport, and trade. They received 600–800 grams of bread per day. The second category was white-color employees, except those listed above. They were apportioned 500 grams of bread. Representatives of the third and fourth categories—dependents and children under twelve—were entitled to 400.[85] It should be borne in mind that in the rear areas embezzlement was widespread. In order to disguise it, the bread was soaked in water, which resulted in customers' smaller actual take-home amounts.[86] But even these small norms were reduced in November 1943 by an average of 100 grams as a result of the liberation of the occupied western regions of the USSR, where the population needed urgent food aid.[87] For the sake of this assistance, and also as a result of crop failure in 1943, kolkhozes in Kazakhstan ceased to issue groceries for dependents.[88]

The rations for meat or fish were very small: 1,800–2,200, 1,200, 500, and 400 grams per month, respectively, for each of the four population categories mentioned above. Rations for cereals or pasta were even less: 1,200–1,500, 800, 600, 800 grams per month, also respectively.[89] The difference in the rates may seem insignificant to us, but for people who were starving, it was very palpable. Sholom Omri noted that only when he was transferred to the first category because of a new work assignment in Fergana, he finally began to eat his fill.[90] For families with a large number of dependents the rations were not enough. Without additional food sources, it was very difficult to survive on ration cards.

Very few refugees could regularly buy something extra on the market. On average, in the unoccupied regions of the USSR, the following were the market prices per kilogram or liter: flour 80 rubles, beef 155, oil 578, and milk 44 rubles.[91] It should be noted that these prices fluctuated throughout the war years and varied depending on the region. In Chuvashia in 1942, the groceries on the market were somewhat cheaper: flour 20–25 rubles per kilogram, pork 80 rubles per kilogram, and milk 15 rubles per liter.[92] The prices were lower in Kazakhstan in early 1942: 8–10 rubles per kilogram of flour, 13–15 rubles per kilogram of rice, 20–25 rubles per kilogram of meat, and 8–10 rubles per liter of milk. But even these were perceived by the local authorities as "extremely high."[93] The shortages of food in early 1944 led to an increase in prices at the Sverdlovsk markets: potatoes from 50 to 75 rubles and meat from 200 to 350 rubles per kilogram.[94]

For many refugees, these groceries were not available. Bella Vladimirovskaia wrote from Samarkand, "One can get a lot of things on the market, especially for children, but I do not go there, and I am indifferent to the prices: I do not care if meat costs 60 rubles or 90 rubles, either way, it is not available to me."[95] Barber M. L. Cherniavskii, a refugee from Minsk who came to Syzran', and his wife, a seamstress, earned 141 and 175 rubles, respectively, in 1944. Because of low salaries and because the Cherniavskiis helped their daughter, a student, and as their sons were missing at the front, they lived in poverty.[96] Average salaries were not much higher, as we already saw above. It was especially difficult for families with dependents. They rarely had any money to buy additional food.

Since rations on cards had to be paid for, it often happened that a woman with two or more dependents who worked and had little earnings did not have enough money even to pay for ration cards. If she belonged to the second category and had three dependents, then the 1.7 kilograms of daily bread rations for everyone in the family cost her 1.7 rubles, which came to about 51–53 rubles per month. Mera Kaplan found herself in such a situation with three children and a salary of 150 rubles.[97] With this salary she had to pay 60–100 rubles for apartment rent and the military tax of 7.5 percent, buy other food, save money for shoes and clothes, and pay for utilities. It is not surprising that the refugee women in the village of Pandikovo (Chuvashia) declined coupons for clothing because, even in acute need, they could not pay 117 rubles for a dress or 94 for a skirt made by a state artel.[98] They dealt with the situation by selling their belongings, and when there was nothing left to sell, they sold a portion of their ration cards, because on the market a kilogram of bread cost eighty rubles.[99] The mother of two children, a refugee from Gomel, Fania Feigin had every reason to write in January 1943 to the local authorities, "You yourself know that you cannot live on a hundred rubles with children."[100] As Julie Hessler showed, given the wartime conditions, the authorities were sympathetic regarding the population selling their grocery cards.[101]

The situation was better for those refugee families who had several workers, including children aged thirteen to fifteen, who worked as much as they could. However, even the smaller children participated in the family economy. In Tomsk during the police raid on December 17, 1944, 117 "neglected" children were detained. Of these, thirty-three, at the age of eleven to thirteen, sold pies, saccharine, pancakes, paper, and so on.[102] It was worse for families with young children and sick elderly. If the old men fled to the east alone or later found themselves without children nearby, the chances of them surviving on a pension allowance of 80–100 rubles were low.

For survival and mutual support, some related families combined, especially since almost all families became incomplete. The refugee Mishket Liberman, having learned that her husband's parents and their three adult daughters were sleeping in the open air in Tashkent and that their mother-in-law had fallen ill with malaria, immediately invited them to join her in Novosibirsk, despite the fact that she had only half a room. They came and did not regret it—the city council soon gave this combined family a separate large room to live in.[103]

The above-mentioned state-mandated sizes of rations were, in many places, reduced by the local authorities. In some cases this was the result of theft, while in others it was due to disruption in supply. Due to the lack of food, in February 1943 in the Kurgan region, 300 grams of bread was given to workers and 200 grams to dependents (half the norm).[104] In the Troitskoe district of the Chkalov region, local authorities, without any justification, reduced the daily bread norm for refugees from 400 grams to 100 grams. In general, in many districts of the Chkalov region, according to the report of the deputy prosecutor, for a long time the refugees were not given bread at all.[105]

In the kolkhozes of the Frunze region of Kirgizstan (and in this region, 70–75 percent of all refugees lived on kolkhozes), refugees could not receive bread because of crop failure in 1942. In December 1942, the kolkhozes in this republic could not provide 57,000 refugees (i.e., 52.7 percent of all registered refugees in this republic[106]) with bread.[107]

In Sterlitamak in the Bashkir ASSR, bread was often delayed for five to seven days, and an inspection conducted in the Sterlitamak district revealed a delay of eighteen days in the delivery of food in one of the kolkhozes. In the neighboring Belebei district, the situation was even worse. The same inspection in several kolkhozes revealed two to three months delay in the bread supply.[108] In the Kozlovka district of the Chuvash ASSR, workers evacuated there in January 1942, did not receive bread with their ration cards or any other food for a whole week. The result was hunger and increased mortality.[109]

In these conditions workers, collective farmers and employees were particularly irritated by food inequality. Ivan Kharkevich, an engineer in Gor'kii wrote in his diary in the hunger-plagued April 1942:

> A striking characteristic of our meeting: there is a deputy commissar at the table—fat, albeit relatively young, with two medals—a well-fed factory director (Romanov), the chief engineer (rather fat), the secretary of the party committee (Novikov), pink as a pig, and a very well-fed secretary of the regional committee for industry (Kochetkov); on the contrary, across the table, the heads of workshops and departments: pale, with cheekbones showing and washed-out eyes. The bodies of this population were breaking down. It was difficult, very difficult, especially for certain workers. Nourishment was very, very poor. "Homestyle" noodles with water and without a sign of fats or vegetables—and bread. . . . Of course, from the same food with the additions of onions, you could significantly improve nutrition, but the cafeteria system did not work well, worked disgustingly, and

would continue to work poorly, on and on. Everything was founded on the lack of care and interest in improvements, on self-supply, theft, and the glaring abscess on the body of the USSR—*blat* [nepotism].[110]

"One man's war is another man's good fortune": Theft and Redistribution of Food

In many cases, the real reason for the delay in food supply and the reduction in portions was theft, since refugees were not able to get their missing rations retroactively. Avakumov, mentioned above, the chair of the kolkhoz in the village of Buinsk, was put on trial for issuing state-mandated bread rations to refugees as payment for workdays and also gave them a freeze-dried carrot, which comprised all the food of those who worked. When the refugees were allocated sugar from the state fund, Avakumov, along with the store's salesperson, took it.[111] Temetnikova wrote in 1942 from the Kirov region: "Our children do not hear [do not know] the smell of meat, but that pig of a district committee secretary is eating a separate meat dinner, I saw it myself. If a small amount of groceries arrives for the refugees, we look: this food will be eaten by someone who already has everything he needs. People drag everything through the back door for themselves or those close to them. This is being done by people who carry the name of our glorious Bolshevik Party."[112]

With the knowledge of and under protection from local administrators, salespeople in village shops used to steal groceries and other goods allocated to the refugees. In Iumanai in the Chuvash ASSR, the clerk Terent'ev gave evacuated Leningraders eighty grams of fish, instead of the two kilograms per month allocated to them, and sold the remainder illegally.[113] In the Tsivil'sk district of the same republic N. Kubeksi stole eighty kilograms of soap and twenty kilograms of semolina and rice, which she secretly traded at the black-market prices.[114]

The possibility of theft of funds from the state financial and trading system through the use of its multitiered and inadequate control was vividly presented in 1931 in Ilya Ilf and Yevgeny Petrov's *Zolotoi telënok* (The Little Golden Calf), which was still circulating in the first half of the 1940s. Sovietologist James Heinzen believes that, because of the moral and patriotic upsurge from the summer of 1941 to 1943, there were fewer bribes and less theft on the part of officials.[115] On the contrary, it is hard to imagine the first year and a half of the war to be any better. The wartime period, which produced, on the one hand, new defense structures and migrations that disrupted the prewar mechanism of financial control and, on the other hand, the acute shortage of products and goods, opened up new possibilities for the development of the shadow economy for corrupt officials. As before, the "disappearances" of groceries and other goods were covered up by their movement between departments, so that even the evacuation agencies had difficulty finding out where everything disappeared to.

Another way to hide the theft was the substitution of goods and food products. Even more often, theft was covered by mixing and diluting to conceal the goods' change in quality. The wartime evacuee to Kirov, Izolda Ivanova, recalls: "the bread rations we received were wet and heavy, blue-green from the grass mixed into the dough."[116]

All the existing Soviet literature on the war contains reports on the collection of food and other necessities for war veterans or refugees. Fudging the numbers, local authorities gladly reported on achievements of these drives to their superiors and to the press. Poor control of this aid allowed them to appropriate part of the collected goods for themselves or sell them on the black market. It is clear that the accompanying warm letters to veterans from the donating families, for many of which the donated products were not surpluses, ended up in trash. In the famine of 1942 dozens of tons of collected food gifts were not sent to the front but were put on sale in the military establishments of the Arkhangel'sk and Ural military districts.[117]

However, even what managed to escape the greedy hands of local business executives and military commissariats of the rear still rarely made it to the frontline soldiers. In April 1942 Deputy People's Commissar for Defense Lev Mekhlis drew attention to thefts in the army. Making an example of the Southern and Southwestern Fronts, whose supply officers handed over approximately two thousand care packages to the Donbas authorities and other individuals intended for the soldiers, Mekhlis ordered that their actions be brought to the attention of the prosecutor and that their commanders be informed as well. This was not enough, and a month later Stalin signed a GKO decree that gifts should be accounted for, that the GKOs should receive monthly reports from the fronts on the distribution of gifts, and that those responsible for their "squandering" would be subject to trial.[118] However, this measure did not help either. In the second half of 1942 and first half of 1943, according to a letter from the head of the Department of Agitation and Propaganda, Georgii Aleksandrov, to the secretary of the TsK VKP(b) Aleksandr Shcherbakov, the donations were rarely used as intended: the business executives of the Southwest and Leningrad Fronts used food gifts for to pay regular allowances; the Kalinin and Western Fronts allowed gifts to be sold to the military; of all thing collected for individual gifts, a little less than 15 percent went to the frontline soldiers, and the rest, instead of being distributed, sat in warehouses. Even out of the distributed food and other goods, most of them fell into the hands not of combat regiments and battalions, but of staff officers and servicemen. Various manipulations led to the large-scale embezzlement of gifts. Even according to incomplete inspections, a lot of "disappeared" personal belongings were found, along with 482 kilograms of oil, 110 kilograms of cheese, 1,210 kilograms of gingerbread and cookies, 1,844 kilograms of soap, and so on.[119]

Therefore, it is not surprising that the aid to refugees from UNRRA (the United Nations Relief and Rehabilitation Administration) was also stolen. According to the letter by the regional committee of the Communist Party, the commissar of the Tatyshly district of the Bashkir ASSR, Tukhvatulin, appropriated thirteen American gifts sent to the administration in May 1945 for the soldiers' families, replacing them with his own worn-out items. The chair of the Inspection Commission of the Tashla Village Council of the same republic, Dorofeev, similarly replaced twelve gifts. The same kind of theft was found in several other places in this republic.[120] At the Novosibirsk branch of the regional consumer association (Oblpotrbsoiuz) these gifts were also plundered by officials.[121] Tatiana Shapiro, a mendicant in liberated Odessa, responding in July 1944 to a letter from Ilya Ehrenburg about American gifts sent to the city, wrote that the former prisoners of the ghetto received nothing.[122]

A native of Poland, Larry Wenig, attests that officials were an important link in the system of getting food and other goods to the "black market."[123] The famous screenwriter Sergei Ermolinskii wrote even more vividly about this in his memoires: "An invisible chain was formed around those who stood at the helm of storage and distribution. All these terrible locusts, not trying too hard to hide it—people depended on them!—lived high on the hog. And around them people starved, struggled."[124]

A number of documented pieces of evidence of theft in the Chuvash ASSR have survived. In the Krasnye Chetai district the food and other goods allocated to the evacuated were appropriated by the local administration and retail workers.[125] In the Kalinino district the food products allocated by the authorities for those rescued out of besieged Leningrad were stolen.[126] In 1942 evacuees of the Shumerlia district of the same republic were given socks that had mysteriously disappeared, while the refugees were in great need of them.[127] In the Ishlei district, according to a letter from five officers' wives addressed to the chair of the Council of People's Commissars of the RSFSR, local authorities and trade organizations commandeer for themselves all or half of what the central authorities allocated for the evacuated.[128]

According to the memorandum of the inspector of the Presidium of the Supreme Council of the Chuvash ASSR of September 26, 1941, there were discrepancies between the food received and what was allocated. Chuvashia's People's Commissariat of Trade "for some reason kept to itself" five out of ten tons of butter and five out of fifteen tons of meat, allocated for evacuees from the besieged Leningrad.[129] An evacuee from Moscow, Irina Lisanskaia, reported in 1942 to the Council of People's Commissars of the Chuvash ASSR: "In the last days of September 1941 the last ration was given out: sweets, animal oil, cereal, and since then the evacuated population has received nothing [but bread], despite the fact that the local consumers' union (Raipotrebsoiuz) received and receives special funds . . . these funds are not being spent for their intended purpose."[130]

According to the report of the inspector of the department of the Council of People's Commissars of the RSFSR for the state of the labor system and household services for the evacuated population for November 1943 in Biisk (Altai territory), out of 1,011 rations allocated to the Leningrad blockade escapees living there, for some reason, one hundred were issued to local residents, and the rest allegedly to evacuees passing through the city.[131] Since it was impossible to check the list of rations for the passing-by refugees, it was difficult to prove the theft of rations.

The head of the state security department of the Chaadaevka district in the Penza region, Kondrat'ev, distributed bread to his relatives: his sister-in-law Saebekova and his uncle Kalapushkin received twenty kilograms of flour each. In the Podbel'sk and Pokhvistnevo districts of the Kuibyshev region, about 80 percent of the two-months reinforced ration intended for Leningrad children was plundered.[132] Investigations into the delayed sale of bread to refugees in a number of districts of the North Ossetian ASSR and the Gor'kii and Novosibirsk regions led to criminal penalties.[133] Theft and fraud were practiced by the low-level administration in the Kurgan region.[134] The already mentioned military commissar of the Tatyshly district of Bashkiria, Tukhvatulin, bought himself a cow for 1,500 rubles from a fund created by collective farmers for needy families.[135] In Leninabad the deputy director of the ice cream factory, which had been evacuated from Leningrad, did not add sugar to the ice cream. He gave half of the money to the deputy director and kept half for himself. They also gave a cut to the director of the factory and the NKVD leadership in the city.[136]

For 6,470 evacuees (mostly Leningraders) who were in the Tot'ma district of the Vologda region, special food and manufactured goods were allocated in 1942. However, as the inspection showed, they did not get a single kilogram of meat or butter, an item of warm clothing or a pair of shoes. In the city of Vologda in the same year, nineteen people were arrested in the hospital, having stolen food and other goods worth more than three hundred thousand rubles.[137]

Such thefts were so widespread in the USSR that the prosecutor's office could not eradicate them. The punishments applied to marauding officials were moderate: from dismissal to five years of imprisonment, less often ten. Sometimes they were even limited to stern reprimands, if there were mitigating circumstances, in particular if someone from the official's family served at the front. For example, the chair of the consumers association in the village Pandikovo in the Krasnye Chetai district of Chuvashia stole a ton of potatoes and a ton of flour. However, the prosecutor's office absolved him because he was drafted into the army.[138]

How mild the punishments for administrative officials were is especially evident in comparison to harsh measures against petty thieves who were not government officials. In January 1942 in Moscow, following the court's verdict, the clerk R. Akinina and her mother M. Kurochkina were shot because they had forged the signatures of the evacuated residents and received their food cards.[139] In Kuibyshev in July 1943, Remeniuk, But'ko, and Frank were sentenced to five years in prison for stealing potatoes from vegetable gardens, and Maslov was sentenced to two years for stealing onions.[140] In such cases, the prosecutor's offices applied punitive force to the full extent to intimidate and discipline the population.[141]

The theft of food intensified even more after the December 29, 1941, abolition of the order of the Commissariat of Trade on the sale of bread at commercial prices.[142] The order was revoked because of the reduction in state grain stocks. After all, there had not been enough time in many regions of Ukraine to harvest grain and transport it to the east. Due to the cancellation, dispatched refugees again began to receive so-called travel cards,[143] which allowed them to buy food, mainly bread, anywhere, unlike ordinary ration cards that worked only in a specific locality. However, given the short or unknown duration of stops that the trains with refugees would make, as well as long lines at bread stalls, it was unlikely that refugees could use them on the road.

Russian historian Aleksandr Shalak believes that among all thieving local government officials kolkhoz chairs were most notable, and they often became "whipping boys" because they were at the lowest level of government. Explaining their motives for stealing, he argues that the kolkhoz chairs were burdened by high official taxes and unofficial payments to their superiors.[144] Indeed, this practice did exist, but Shalak greatly exaggerates its scale. The evidence cited above indicates that the chairs of kolkhozes often channeled stolen food to their relatives. Besides, while openly hostile toward refugees, some of the kolkhoz leaders considered it unjust to steal the food and other goods allocated to them. Furthermore, kolkhoz chairs engaged in poaching even before the substantial increase in the agricultural tax in June 1943. It is unlikely that the local administrators from the middle echelons of power were in dire need of kolkhoz products for their families, since they were eating in special canteens and they were allocated good rations. The evacuation inspector Antonina Nikitina wrote to the authorities, "It is absolutely abnormal that in children's institutions they are fed [only] peas, and in the special canteens—rice, meat, eggs."[145]

In addition to theft, the redistribution of food and other goods allocated to refugees was widely practiced. They were redirected to the administration staff or used for other purposes. Authorities in the Yoshkar-Ola district of the Mari Autonomous Republic, having received three thousand meters of cloth from the central authorities for sewing warm blankets for refugees, distributed it to the local government employees, while refusing refugees' requests for clothing "due to lack of supply."[146] In the Kizner district of the Udmurt ASSR, officials had suits made for themselves from the cloth allocated by the central authorities for the evacuees.[147] The officials of the Sakmara district of the Chkalov region spent money that was allocated to buy consumer goods for refugees on their local employees' needs.[148] Authorities in the Gagino district of the Gor'kii region and the Darg-Kokh district of the North Ossetian Autonomous Republic did the same, for which they were later brought to trial.[149]

The chair of the Galkino District Executive Committee, Smetanin and the head of the trading department of the Galkino District Consumers Union of the Kurgan region Baltser distributed among their friends the textiles sent to the wives of war veterans.[150] As was discovered by the evacuation department, the authorities of the Krasnopartizansk district of the Chkalov region received from the central authorities four hundred kilograms of wool to make felt boots for the refugees, but instead they were later added to the collection of warm clothes for the Red Army.[151] Care for soldiers was more valued by the authorities. In the Sundyr' district of the Chuvash ASSR the vegetable oil that was allocated for the evacuated and the wheat flour and sugar meant for their children were instead used to make rolls, buns, and sweet beverages like *kissel'* for party meetings and gatherings of kolkhozniks in February and March 1942.[152]

The periphery of the Soviet republics was caught in a web of bribery, and not only the spheres of the distribution of food and other goods. A refugee from Lithuania, Shaul' Beilison, who worked as a well engineer in the Mary district of Turkmenistan, describes in detail how a state farm chair tried to bribe and intimidate him into signing a repair order worth a hundred thousand rubles while the real cost of the necessary work did not exceed a tenth of that amount. When Beilison refused, the kolkhoz chair complained to the prosecutor's office about his "careless attitude" toward work. To avoid arrest sanctioned by the bribed prosecutor, Beilison had to flee to another republic. However, he faced a similar situation in Stalinabad, working as an engineer on the construction of a creamery. Being a member of the trade union committee, he refused to sign a purchase order for cows for the construction workers' subsidiary farm, arguing that they were being overcharged. When they failed to bribe the obstinate engineer with money and good housing, the local party organizer and trade union leader obtained the cancellation of his exemption from the army.[153]

In Tashkent during the war all traders at the central bazaar paid bribes to its supervising police officer Rasulov. When this became known to the prosecutor's office, Rasulov was simply fined and not tried.[154] Most likely this mild punishment was the result of bribes. Many witnesses reported the need to bribe police officers at many markets of Central Asian cities in order to receive permission to sell things, even their own clothes, or face confiscation of the goods. When he was engaged in small business in Samarkand, Gedalia Goldberg testified, on several occasions he witnessed large black-market operations that involved high-ranking official.[155] In this connection, one cannot but agree with the conclusion of the wartime evacuee Eliazar Meletinskii that the shadow economy was particularly flourishing in Central Asia.[156]

The central authorities knew about the shadow economy and theft. They tried to fight it with more stringent measures than local prosecutor's offices. In 1942 the commandants and their deputies of the Tambov train station and one branch of the Iaroslavl' railroad were shot for the theft of parcels with gifts for frontline soldiers, as well as food products, that they covered up by issuing fictitious reports on the supplies for passing military units.[157] Worried about the colossal amount of bribery and theft, the People's Commissar for Internal Affairs Lavrenty Beria in April 1942 approved a plan to combat it. The new measures imposed the NKVD's control over the activities of the central and republican commissariats of trade, the Tsentrosoiuz, and the lower-level trade establishments. According to the directive, one of the means of achieving control was such an extraordinary method as the creation of a special agent network in these organizations.[158] In June 1942 the Supreme Court of the USSR adopted a decision to strengthen liability for the theft of ration cards, which also put under strict control all stages of printing and distribution of these cards.

Beria's plan bore some fruit. In 1943 in the Charyshskoe district of the Altai territory, the director of a dairy plant was arrested, together with accomplices, who managed to sell 3.1 tons of butter and 1.4 tons of cheese on the black market by deceiving the dealers and understating the percentage of the fat content of the milk and machinations involving receiving documents. In Barnaul in 1944, eight people were arrested who had been involved in the theft of a large number of ration cards, with which they received 76 tons of bread, 2.5 tons of sugar, 7 tons of meat and fish, and 140 kilograms of tea.[159] In Uzbekistan in the second half of 1942, the NKVD investigated 2,423 criminal cases against food thieves.[160] However, the main victims were petty "pilferers" who stole food or goods from their enterprises to feed their families. The regional organs of the

NKVD were afraid to touch corrupt officials because, on the one hand, this could cause trouble—the network of corruption sometimes reached high up—and, on the other hand, the NKVD officers themselves could be involved in this network.

Well aware of this, the leadership of Uzbekistan in March 1942 proposed to create a special "troika" to fight against the shadow economy. The troika it was planned to consist of the highest-ranking officials in the republic: the secretary of the TsK VKP(b) Usman Iusupov, People's Commissar for Internal Affairs Bogdan Kobulov, and Chief Prosecutor Beliaev. Fifty accused officials were to be punished by execution and confiscation of property. The troika wanted the verdict to be carried out "out of court" and then covered by the media on behalf of the prosecutor's office. The publicity around the planned verdict signaled that the republican leadership wanted to make an example of the disgraced officials, and the extrajudicial order of events that they wanted to apply this measure quickly. Members of the Communist Party's Politburo Vyacheslav Molotov and Anastas Mikoyan, who wrote to Stalin on this matter, tried to soften the prepared actions by, instead of creating a troika, accelerating the dispatch of cases through the prosecutor's office, having shot "only" twenty officials. But Stalin supported the Uzbek leadership, noting, "The robbers are not just thieves, but enemies of the state."[161]

In May of the same year, following in Uzbekistan's footsteps, the leadership of Kirgizstan decided to create a similar troika. It included the secretary of the Central Committee of the Communist Party of the republic, Aleksei Vagov, the People's Commissar for Internal Affairs Afanasii Pchëlkin, and the Chief Prosecutor Il'ia Komolov. On charges of banditry, robberies, malicious hooliganism, and theft of socialist property, the troika right away sentenced 150 people to execution. The Kremlin approved without delay the creation of the troika and its first sentence.[162] However, it is unlikely that the intimidation in Kirgizstan, Uzbekistan, and possibly in other republics, as well as the Beria plan, proved to be overall very effective. Observers do not see significant difference between 1942 and 1943 in illegal activities and black market dealings.

~

A well-chosen profession and entrepreneurial spirit increased the refugees' chances of finding a better place to settle in and to survive. Although the authorities were generally interested in saving the evacuated population, they did not count for much when it came to the question of state priorities.

In combating staff turnover, the authorities turned factory workers into state serfs who were prohibited from changing their jobs. This procedure allowed the directors of the enterprises not to improve the supply of food or working and living conditions of the workers. The provision of food and essentials was generally poor, often as a result of theft by leaders and officials. The central authorities struggled with this but were unable to remedy the situation. Everything stated above is in strong disagreement with the statements made in Soviet works, published in especially large numbers in the 1960s through the 1980s, about the great role of local authorities in food aid to the evacuated population (most often this aid appears to be mentioned next to the catch phrase "the evacuated families of frontline soldiers"). Their authors without any reason understand the words "funds are allocated and released" in a completely different way—as "received and delivered." Completing the image of the "empire of positive activity," these authors tried to represent the authorities most favorably, which was ideally served by party reports. In practice, the result of delayed deliveries, theft of food, as well as its objective shortage, was the spread of famine and death.

CHAPTER FOUR

Famine, Mortality, and Some Help

> Evacuation, evacuation,
> An inescapable evil affliction,
> It is clear that I can never
> Wait a bright time in life again.
>
> —ALEKSANDR GORODNITSKII, "Evacuation"

Famine

The widespread famine, whose wartime peak in the eastern regions of the USSR came in 1942, was the direct result of a shortage of food.[1] Testimonies from refugees who were based in different regions make this very clear. In the autumn of this year, the Leningrader A. Epshtein wrote from Kirov to her relatives:

> Things are very bad for me. Prices at the market are insane. I eat very poorly; in the dining hall there is only water with leaves [for soup]; they take a lot of coupons [for a meal], so there is not enough on the [ration] card for a month. I've sold almost all my clothes, I don't know what to do further.... It's cold as soon I come home, there's almost no firewood, there's nothing to eat, I feel as if I'm in Leningrad—except we're not being bombed, and there's no machine-gun fire. The room is cold, there is nothing to cook, there is no light, there is no kerosene, there is nothing to eat except four hundred grams of bread [per day].[2]

Izolda Ivanova, whom we have already encountered, recalls: "They did not starve in Kirov same as in the besieged Leningrad, but they were not well fed either. So as not to feel hunger, they chewed black viscous resin or stearin from melted candles. For children, dining halls were opened, where a bowl of soup or some *zavarukha* [porridge brewed with boiling water] was given out once a day according to [ration] coupons."[3] Another refugee from the same Kirov region wrote to a relative: "We have nothing, we are famished, and for the second time Kolia has been lying in bed and gradually starving to death. Here we will die of hunger, because there is absolutely nothing in Murashi, we haven't even had potatoes since spring. It would be better for us to die at home than to die here. How tired we are of starving in this world. How indifferently and with such disregard they treat us. They brought us here and abandoned us."[4] Muscovite families in the village of Nizhnie Abakassy in Chuvashia, after they had run out of things to barter, began begging food from the collective farmers and snatching frozen potatoes from their pigs.[5] In the Vologda region there were numerous cases of refugees consuming corpses of dead animals, grass, and even straw.[6]

A refugee from L'vov who was working in Novokuznetsk (southwest Siberia) as an aircraft equipment technician, Iosif Faigenboim was eager to serve at the front because of the cold and hunger in the rear. They wouldn't let him leave, giving him a *bron'* (a status that forbids an employee from being drafted). He began to work incompetently and achieved his goal: "I went happily [to the front] because I had long ago decided for myself that it's better to die in a battlefield than to die from hunger in the rear."[7]

Perhaps even worse than in the Volga area, the Urals, and Siberia was the situation in Central Asia. Although, as was shown above, the economic situation of a family depended on its composition, the professions of able-bodied members, the ability to acquire useful connections, and personal initiative, their well-being was no less affected by where they stayed. Even before the war, it was common for industrial centers to receive better food supplied than the outlying areas of the Caucasus and Central Asia.[8] Obviously, due to smaller number of industrial enterprises in Central Asia, this practice continued during the war. Iaffa Kolinski, Fraida Celnikier, Zeev Frenkel, and Nota Berman testify themselves, and the Polish writer Henryk Grynberg cites somebody else's testimony, that it was impossible to get bread in Samarkand, which caused many refugees to die in the streets.[9] They are echoed by Rabbi Nakhum-Shmeriiagu Sasonkin, who described the situation in Samarkand: "Going out into the cold streets in the morning, we stumbled upon the swollen bodies [of the refugees], deceased from exhaustion. They lay about on the streets, and no one was in a hurry to bury them."[10] This is also evidenced by another former refugee, Joseph Barten.[11]

The situation was similar elsewhere in Uzbekistan: in Bukhara, Kokand, and the "bread-rich" Tashkent, as well as in many small towns.[12] Irina Rovinskaia recalls how in Tashkent they slept on the street near the railway station and were very hungry. Her mother died there, her brother fell ill—he was taken to the hospital and she did not see him again. She and her sister engaged in begging and rummaging through garbage dumps in search of food.[13] Nadezhda Mandel'stam believed that she survived in Tashkent thanks to Anna Akhmatova: "While we lived apart, she always saved for me a piece of bread or a bunch of pasta from dinner, and later when we lived together, we lived on her ration.

I worked, but my earnings would be enough only for starvation. What saved one was not money, but rations, that is, the ability to procure groceries at state, rather than market prices."[14]

Abraham Zylbering describes how in Kanibadam (Tajikistan) he bought a flatbread on the street and, as he was just preparing to eat it, a man suddenly jumped out of the bushes, grabbed it, and immediately swallowed it.[15] Inna Gaister recalls, "There, in Fergana, the value of human life was negligible. The men especially were dying."[16] Only by the summer of 1944 did the food situation in Central Asia improve somewhat. Dov Dunaevskii testifies that sour cream and butter, which had not been seen at the markets of Tashkent since the late autumn of 1941, appeared again only in 1944.[17]

Many of those refugees who arrived from Moscow or changed their place of stay from the Volga area or Siberia to Central Asia bitterly regretted it. Inna Gaister reports that when in the spring of 1943 they had the first opportunity to return to Moscow, they immediately left Uzbekistan.[18] Tatiana Goikhman, who moved to the town of Buston (Bukhara region, Uzbekistan) from the Middle Volga area in October 1942 wrote to her husband Meir a week later, "Life here is difficult, of course, more difficult than in Ul'ianovsk."[19] Anatolii Kotliar, whose family had also been in the Middle Volga area, moved to Tashkent and then, seeing that the refugees there were starving, settled in one of the Kyrgyz kolkhozes, later asking in his memoirs the rhetorical question: "Why did we not stay in Kuibyshev?"[20] Anna Bruell, who moved to Kazakhstan during the war, writes in her memoirs, "When I think about it, I don't understand, it was worse for me than in Siberia."[21] Bernard Dov Weinryb cites the testimony of a Polish Jew who came to Samarkand after being released from a special camp in Siberia: "It was worse here than in exile. After a short time my father and mother died of hunger."[22] The same opinion was held by Mosheh Atsmon, who noted that in Samarkand, where his father died, the hunger was much worse than in the Urals.[23] The Polish refugee Jadwiga Ihnatowicz-Suszynski and her six children, left a kolkhoz in the Urals for Samarkand, but were immediately deported to the Kazakh kolkhoz, and were even hungrier there.[24]

Having arrived in Samarkand, Max Komito and his comrades—other Jewish refugees from Poland—were starving because they could not find work. They took to heart the advice of Soviet soldiers—to move to Sverdlovsk—and were not disappointed.[25] In general, according to statistics, starting in 1943, the number of immigrants from Central Asia to Sverdlovsk began to grow.[26] Other statistics show a large flow of refugees in May 1943 from Uzbekistan to another region of the Urals—Chkalov—also for same reason, to settle in better.[27]

In conditions of famine, it was very difficult to keep kosher, and most of the observant Jewish refugees were forced to abandon kashrut.[28] Not being able to feed themselves, some refugees, children and adults, were begging for food, despite the authorities' attempts to fight it.[29] Jewish refugees were no exception.[30] Some Jewish refugees, former Polish citizens, were even forced to engage in prostitution for food.[31] This fact itself speaks of a particularly difficult situation. Although those of them who were deported to the east in 1939–1940 could bring with them some of their possessions, by 1942, having been through multiple transfer points and camps or having used it to barter on the market, they had hardly anything of value.

The severity of the problem of nutrition in the eastern regions of the USSR is indicated by cannibalism in Siberia and the Urals.[32] Some facts of cannibalism were also documented in Central Asia, but it was the so-called market cannibalism, when people were killed for the purpose of subsequent sale of their flesh at the market to inexperienced buyers.[33]

Disease

The eastern regions of the USSR in particular suffered from infectious diseases even before the war,[34] but with its beginning these diseases spread much more forcefully, especially starting in the autumn of 1941.[35] The testimony and memoirs show that there was no refugee who did not fall ill with a life-threatening disease at least once. According to a report by Natalia Danilova in Kanash (Chuvashia), because of a lack of hospital beds, typhoid patients remained at home.[36] In the orphanage of the Privolzh'e district of the Saratov region, 103 out of 320 children (about 32 percent) were ill with tuberculosis.[37]

The high mortality was due to many doctors being sent to the front and an acute shortage of medicines (especially aspirin, petrolatum, calcex, streptocide, sulfide, quinine) in hospitals and pharmacies.[38] According to the memoirs of Anatole Konstantin, in one of the villages of the Dzhambul region in Kazakhstan—where they were during the war—although there was a doctor among the refugees, she had no medications besides aspirin. As a result, many children died there, both refugees and local residents.[39]

The hotbeds of epidemics were the railway stations, where refugees spent long hours and even days waiting for the possibility to move somewhere or in the hopes of meeting relatives and acquaintances among those arriving, from whom they could learn about the fate of their relatives. For many homeless people, the stations were places of residence.[40] The People's Commissar for Internal Affairs of Kazakhstan reported in October 1941 that in Alma-Ata many refugees with children were staying in the open air in public gardens and on the train platforms for five to seven days, without warm clothes or regular meals and being severely lice infested.[41] In Tashkent, even in mid-January 1942, homeless refugees continued to spend the nights on the city streets, including the railway station square, which therefore was ironically nicknamed "waiting hall no. 3." Despite the onset of cold weather, in which viruses are known to spread less rapidly than in summer, in Central Asia, infectious diseases, especially raging typhus and typhoid fever, spread even more during the beginning of 1942.[42] By then, in Samarkand there were 918 typhoid cases (counting only those that were recorded), while in November 1941 there were only two cases.[43] One of the important reasons for the spread of diseases in Central Asia was the dirty water from irrigation canals and *howzes* (ponds) that the refugees had to drink.

Lice spread epidemics, but there were not enough hygienic means to remove them, on the one hand, and, on the other hand, little effort was exerted, either by public health officials or by local administrators. In March 1942, the military tribunal sentenced the head of the sanitation section of the Tashkent railway, Senin, to five years in prison for sending in an "unsanitary state" a train from Samarkand with patients who needed urgent hospitalization. At the same time, the station commandant Kusanov was sentenced to eight years for the "unsanitary" evacuation in Gur'ev.[44] Against the backdrop of total unsanitary conditions in public places in the rear, these measures were indicative of officials who accidentally "got in the way of the flame."

Many chairs of kolkhozes and village councils not only did not organize bathing locally but also did not provide transport for refugees to visit the bathhouse in neighboring settlements. According to testimony, in one of the kolkhozes of the Dzhambul region refugees had to walk ten kilometers to get to the bathhouse, which was possible only in the summer when the road there was dry.[45] There was a lack of change of clothes. According to the report of the evacuation inspector Natal'ia Danilova of February 5, 1942, on the state of medical care in Chuvashia, 80 percent of refugees suffered from lice, and the public health officials believed that the responsibility of care for the evacuated population lay with the doctor at the evacuation center and not them.[46] In Central Asia, because of the warm climate, the spread of lice among refugees may have been even more widespread.[47]

In addition to lice spreading epidemic diseases, the cramped housing conditions also played a part. Refugees were often housed in barracks where, due to overcrowding, poor heating and ventilation, as well as generally poor hygienic conditions, epidemics often spread quickly. Out of the eight Jews in a one-room barrack of the Akhun Babaev Kolkhoz in Uzbekistan in 1942, after less than a year, only three remained alive.[48] The situation in kolkhozes was similar in the Chkalov region. In its Tashla district in May 1942, there were ten cases of typhus, and those were only the registered cases. All of those who took ill with typhus were evacuees. In another district of this region, Sakmara, in the

Molotov Kolkhoz, ten cases of infant mortality as a result of the same disease were recorded.[49] Besides, overcrowding also created multiple sociopsychological problems, intensifying depression, which we will return to in our consideration of the causes of death among the refugees.

Many refugees who arrived in Central Asia from the Caucasus were infected with malaria during the passage across the Caspian Sea.[50] According to the recollections of Nakhum-Shmeriiagu Sasonkin, in the spring of 1942 in Turkmenistan, in the city of Krasnovodsk, even cholera appeared, spreading from there to Uzbekistan.[51] However, additional data on this could not be found, so it is possible that we are talking about rumors caused by some other infectious disease. The Soviet historian Aganiiaz Annakurbanov portrays in rosy terms the activities of the Turkmen authorities on the prevention of diseases. Without mentioning the epidemics that spread in the republic, he cheerfully describes how the evacuated population was completely disinfected, supplied with first-aid kits, hospital beds, and was treated by teams of skilled epidemiologists.[52] In fact, the situation there was catastrophic. Rita Fainer testifies about malaria in Chardzhou, where there were no doctors at all.[53] According to the memoirs of Anatole Konstantin, there was not a single doctor at the train stations, not even at the railway station in Ashkhabad, where they arrived from Krasnovodsk sick with dysentery.[54]

According to the memoirs of Bina Grantserska-Kadari, who worked at the time as a nurse in the neighboring Urgench district of Uzbekistan, the population of the entire district was served by only two nurses. The whole district had only one syringe, despite the huge number of patients suffering from malaria or other diseases. Whole kolkhozes perished at that time because of the malaria epidemics.[55] Bella Vladimirovskaia wrote from Samarkand to her brother's wife, "We have not suffered from the climate, but most of the evacuees have been ill, especially with malaria, which knocks them off their feet; there is ordinary and tropical [malaria]."[56] Malaria outbreaks also occurred in Kazakhstan and Tajikistan.[57] Malaria raged throughout the war years not only in Central Asia but also in other eastern regions of the USSR, for example, in the Urals.[58] Central Asian hospitals, most of them poorly equipped, could not cope with a large number of affected refugees, especially since priority was given to wounded soldiers, who were often sent there for aftercare.

Noticing the rising wave of mortality, in February 1942 the authorities decided to prevent epidemics in the country by improving the hygienic condition of refugees.[59] Throughout Central Asia, during February–March 1942 public-health improvements for refugees were carried out.[60] In Kazakhstan, as part of these measures, a secret order was given to sell six tons soap, very scarce at the time, to Polish refugees.[61]

However, locally, the authorities reacted carelessly to the decision to improve diseases prevention. Public baths still worked irregularly, most often due to lack of fuel. Having studied the sanitary conditions in the USSR, Donald Filtzer elaborates on the frequency of visits by the population to bathhouses. In 1944 Cheliabinsk provided for each resident one wash every two and a half weeks. In Iaroslavl' in 1943 every inhabitant on average washed eight times a year. Other cities, as Filtzer reported, were not much better.[62] Given that the refugees were in the worse situation compared to the local population, it can be assumed that many refugees washed not more than once per month. In the Aktiubinsk region for their inattention to the populations' sanitary condition the chair of the executive committee of the Kliuchevoi District Council Kulmukhamedova received severe reprimands, and the head of the area's health department, Shramko, and the head of the health department of the Chelkar district, Gorelova, were dismissed.[63] Certainly, less visible lower administrative and medical officials treated public health even more negligently. Many memoirists and interviewees note that lice accompanied them throughout the entire war. Mendel Vensober recalls that lice reappeared three days after disinfection.[64] Therefore, despite the sanitary measures taken, in 1942 saw the largest typhus outbreak in the USSR of the entire war period—there were 363,000 of only recorded cases.[65]

In addition to data on epidemic diseases, archival materials indicate the prevalence of scurvy. Even according to official information, it affected about ten thousand people annually in the Urals during the war.[66] Many believed that salt could cure scurvy, resulting in government vendors selling it illegally through the back door at an exorbitant price. In the village of Soigino in the Chuvash ASSR, a food stall manager told the evacuation inspector, "There is salt in stock, but this is supply the second quarter [of the year], and we are not allowed to sell it now."[67]

Children very often suffered from diseases. Bella Vladimirovskaia reported to relatives in December 1942 from Samarkand: "Last year, a lot of children suffered from dysentery, scarlet fever, and diphtheria, along with pneumonia."[68]

Death from Famine and Banditry

Between January 1941 and January 1942, the death rate in in the Altai territory increased by 18 percent, which was, according to the demographer Vladimir Isupov, because of the evacuated population. Mortality in Western Siberia overall grew by 25 percent from 1941 to 1942.[69] According to the historian Vladislav Kruglikov, in the Sverdlovsk region, the death rate in 1942 was higher by 35.8 percent in rural areas and by 44.8 percent in the cities in comparison with the previous year.[70] According to Gennadii Kornilov, during that period the annual death rate also increased throughout the Urals (comprised of the Molotov, Sverdlovsk, Cheliabinsk, and Chkalov regions, as well as the Bashkir and Udmurt ASSRs) by 3.2 percent in rural areas and in cities by 43.8 percent.[71] Donald Filtzer provides similar statistics of the growth of mortality in industrial rear cities, but from about 1940 to 1943.[72]

Most likely the situation was actually worse because the local administration and, especially, party leaders tried to play down the death rate in official reports. After all, deaths tarnished the data and showed their own negligence. The concealment of mortality is easy to trace in Bashkiria. At a meeting of the regional committee in May 1944, the mass outbreaks of septic tonsillitis were discussed. The meeting's minutes indicated not the actual number of deaths of 1,510 (about them below) but only 19.[73] The authors of the book *Bashkiriia during the Great Patriotic War: A Compendium of Documents and Materials* (1995) selected a document with the lower figure for publication because it showed the concern of the party for lowering mortality. Official documents now kept in archives cannot be considered as reliable sources. Unfortunately, there is no alternative to them. The numbers was fabricated even at the level of registration of deaths by registry offices (ZAGS). Elena Gribanova gives an example of one district center in Kazakhstan where the local ZAGS office registered only ten deaths in ten days in the entire township, but the visiting inspector of the republican party commission personally counted forty corpses of people who died during that day in one local hospital alone.[74]

As was mentioned, no demographer has studied the deaths of the refugees separately. It is logical to assume that the mortality among them was higher than that of the local population, if only because the latter had better housing, living conditions, and material resources. An official investigation by the government of the Chuvash ASSR in February 1942 concluded that refugee children in the town of Ichikisy died more often than local children.[75] Of the Muscovites who arrived there, fourteen people died in five months.[76] In the Kozlovka district of the same republic, according to a "top secret" report dated February 9, 1942, by the train traffic inspector Mikhail Kosolapov, the evacuees working at the plant no. 494 were starving along with their children. The death rate increased, especially during the week of January 23 to January 29, when food, including bread, was not issued to them at all.[77]

As we already know, fearing the cold, many refugees assumed that in the warm climate of Central Asia they would have a better chance of survival. However, mortality there, apparently, was higher than in other eastern regions of the Soviet Union. During the war years, about three thousand refugees from Poland were buried in just one Jewish cemetery in Bukhara. David Azrieli, who lived in Bukhara, remembers: "Hundreds of people, exhausted to the extreme, were loitering around the city. Often they fell asleep on park benches and did not wake up anymore. Every morning workers with carts went around the city. The carts would be loaded with hundreds of corpses that appeared overnight."[78] In nearby Kagan, just in December 1941, 280 children of Jewish refugees died.[79] Sarra Shpitalnik, who worked during the war as a statistician, abandoned her profession because she could not remain indifferent to the daily reports of the numerous deceased in the city.[80] Leonid Shmurak said in an interview: "We came to the town of Osh, Andizhan was nearby. They placed us, we worked in kolkhozes, and we were given food for this. Mostly we picked cotton in the fields. There, too, it was unbearable, two brothers and a sister, still little, died . . . and we survived somehow."[81]

Joseph Geller vividly describes the dramatic events that happened to him in the Uzbek kolkhoz in just a few months: "At that time my grandmother, Roza Shpaikhler, died. On Saturday my father died, then my mother, and then my uncle Moshe Weicenblum, and his wife, who had barely turned 23. Out of our relatives, who had numbered 11 people, 4 were left. Two aunts, myself, and a three-year-old cousin."[82] Arkadii Dael' talks about the life of his family in the village in the Kokand region: "In 1942 my mother died in my arms, and in 1945, when I was in the army, my sister died in Kudash. In general, for our family this Kudash became a tragic place; here, during the evacuation, eight of our relatives died. We lived in a small mud hut made from adobe. The hunger was terrible, it reached the point that you had to steal fruit from the orchards and hide grain in your bosom."[83] Polina Rivkina testifies: "On the other side of the Caspian we were loaded into a train and we went to Tashkent. Already in Makhachkala, children were ill with measles, and, as we rode to Tashkent, the whole road was strewn with corpses of children, who were being removed from the train."[84] Almost immediately after the arrival from the Caspian Sea to an Uzbek kolkhoz in 1942, the parents (also former Polish citizens) of Lea Rubin died. She herself became ill with malaria and barely survived.[85]

According to the available statistics for 1942 and the first month and a half of 1943, in just one old non-Jewish cemetery in Samarkand, 1,063 Jews were buried.[86] Numerous simple tombstones at the Bukharan-Jewish cemetery (also in Samarkand) also testify to the high mortality among refugees in these and subsequent years. The situation in Tashkent was no better. Aron Feigelovich describes his arrival there: "The train stops, and we do not believe our eyes—the platform is full of refugees, there are thousands of them, there is no place to step foot. Many lie directly on the platform and the adjoining square—are they sleeping or sick? Then we were told that many were sick with typhus, that there were many deaths."[87] As a result of the high mortality in Tashkent, the Ashkenazi Jewish cemetery was overcrowded, and so in late 1943, the authorities agreed to organize one more.[88]

Hospitals in the Volga area and Uzbekistan, where deaths occurred because of infectious diseases, did not send bodies away to relatives, preferring to bury their dead centrally in common mass graves.[89] To facilitate the funeral procedure and to lessen their own burden, the hospital administration rarely notified relatives about deaths. Many learned about the death of their close ones and the already completed burial during a routine visit to the hospital. The refugees who died in kolkhozes were buried not even in cemeteries, but in wastelands beyond the aul or village. Only in rare cases were special plots of land assigned for such burial places.

Mortality among refugees was even higher than in forced labor camps and colonies. There they were under the care of the NKVD, which was in great need of the labor force. As Andrei Suslov argues, in 1942–1943 Lavrenty Beria made significant efforts to provide food, preserve health, and improve the lives of these prisoners. As a result, their mortality from 1942 to 1944 decreased from 2.1 percent to 0.8 percent.[90] Against the background of these statistics, the assumption of the Polish historian Piotr Zaron that in the summer months in some parts of Central Asia 10 percent of Polish citizens died every month is striking.[91] Although this figure is clearly exaggerated, since most of these former Polish citizens managed to somehow survive for about six years, it is still a reflection of the increased mortality among this category of refugees.

It is somewhat easier to find out the causes of increased mortality than the statistics. To identify the diseases that led to death, I looked through three hundred records (*dapey 'ed*) on relatives and acquaintances—refugees, who had died in Central Asia, which had been filled out for the Holocaust museum Yad Vashem in Jerusalem. The causes of death, recorded in these logs, can in no way be equated with medical conclusions. These records allow to understand only the general situation.

According to these records, in 36 percent of cases death occurred as a result of starvation, and in 15 percent it was due to starvation plus illness (without specifying which one). In the remaining 49 percent of cases, death occurred as a result of diseases:

1. typhus and typhoid fever—13 percent
2. mental disorder because of depression—8 percent
3. dysentery—4 percent
4. tropical malaria—4 percent
5. meningitis—3 percent
6. tuberculosis—3 percent

7. diphtheria—2 percent
8. inflammation of the lungs (pneumonia)—2 percent
9. name of disease not specified—10 percent

Numerous and more detailed testimonies, also kept in the Yad Vashem archive, together with the published memoirs of former refugees, point to the same diseases as the causes that led to the death of their relatives and acquaintances.

Weakness, resulted from chronic malnutrition, caused low resistance of the organism to diseases. Low resistance was also caused by severe depression and nervous disorders that followed after receiving the sad news about loved ones, with the refugees suffering from anxiety about them and their fate.[92] The German socialist and publicist Mishket Liberman, who came to Novosibirsk during the war, testifies: "People died of horrors, of longing, of ordeals. The trouble fell on them so suddenly."[93] As can be seen from the list above, from depression alone, even without an infectious disease, quite a lot of refugees died—8 percent. Nervous disorders were without a doubt a factor contributing to high mortality from exhaustion as well.

Most of the deaths (56 percent) in Central Asia occurred in 1942, in accordance with the records of the Yad Vashem Museum. Analysis of the death dates of Polish citizens who were parents of the children in the Namangan orphanage in Uzbekistan shows that most of them died in 1942 as well.[94] In 1942 was the year when the majority of the 17,000 refugees who perished in the Vologda region during the war died.[95] Kyrgyz demographer Shaiyrkul Batyrbaeva, comparing the number of evacuees in Kirgizstan at the beginning of 1942 and the beginning of 1943, established that their number decreased by 36,438 people. She suggested that the decrease was due to re-evacuation.[96] However, there was nowhere to return to, and, on the contrary, in 1942 new waves of refugees arrived in Central Asia. Therefore, allowing for a small migration of refugees to neighboring republics, as well as the mobilization of draft-age people into the army, the overwhelming majority in this number should be considered dead.

The numerous above-cited evidence for the especially high mortality rate among refugees and the entire rear population in 1942 is supported by archival sources (see table 2).

A comparison of 1942 with the prewar 1940, when the death toll for the entire USSR was 1,124,567, is hardly justified, since the population of the territory under control of the Soviet government was several times larger. For the same reason, a comparison with 1941 is also not entirely relevant. As for the comparison with 1944 and especially with 1945, the reduction in mortality (as

Table 2. Mortality and its most common causes in unoccupied urban settlements of the USSR in 1941–1945 (based on materials from the declassified table of the Central Statistical Administration of the USSR)[97]

	1941	1942	1943	1944	1945
Mortality	702,200 (100)	1,158,926 (100)	878,640 (100)	664,871 (100)	619,538 (100)
		Causes of death (% of total)			
Heart diseases	57,187 (8.14)	139,637 (12.04)	140,923 (16.04)	103,188 (15.52)	93,628 (15.11)
Pneumonia	119,177 (16.97)	163,830 (14.14)	95,875 (10.91)	66,900 (10.06)	63,201 (10.20)
Pulmonary tuberculosis	64,458 (9.18)	104,864 (9.04)	102,927 (11.71)	80,537 (12.11)	84,242 (13.6)
Dysentery	19,098 (2.71)	44,435 (3.83)	23,167 (2.64)	11,556 (1.74)	6,559 (1.06)

shown in table 2) is especially impressive given the increase in population due to the liberated areas.

The table of the Central Statistical Administration of the USSR (on which table 2 is based) contains 83 causes of death, however there is no "hunger" or "exhaustion" among them. Most likely, "hunger" fell mainly into the following categories: "other causes of death" and "inaccurately identified causes"—in 1942, 95,999 (8.28 percent of the total) and 113,717 (9.81 percent of the total), respectively.[98] Given these large numbers, it difficult to argue that these sections actually contain only "hunger."

Vladimir Isupov, on the basis of demographic analysis of the entire Soviet territory, also notes 1942 as a record death rate.[99] Another demographer, Leonid Rybakovskii, singles out this same year as having the most extraordinary death rate during the entire war. He noted that among the urban population, it increased by 50 percent since 1941.[100] In Tashkent mortality in 1942 was twice the death rate in 1941. Considering the growth of the city's population due to migration, mortality there increased by 65 percent in 1942 compared to 1941, according to the analysis of Rebecca Manley.[101]

Although in 1943 the situation in the USSR, in terms of food supply and disease incidence, improved slightly, nevertheless, refugees' mortality in this year, according to the Namangan source mentioned above, remained quite high—over a quarter of all deaths during the war years, and according to the

Yad Vashem records, exactly a quarter. According to statistics on the Urals, mortality there decreased by 34.8 percent compared to 1942, including 37.7 percent in cities and 32.2 percent in rural areas.[102]

In 1944 the unoccupied part of the USSR was swept up in an epidemic of alimentary toxic aleukia (aeptic angina), from which 28,000 people died, according to official data. Almost half the deaths occurred in the RSFSR. Mortality was particularly large in Bashkiria, where in only five days of May, 1,510 people died from it. In the Chkalov region, 1,980 people died from the disease in the same month. As it turned out, the disease was caused by the consumption of overwintered millet and wheat. Hospitals rarely could save these patients.[103] Therefore, overall in the Urals mortality was slightly lower in 1944 than 1943—by 5.1 percent, which includes a 16.4 percent decrease in cities, whereas in the villages mortality, in fact, rose by 4.6 percent. While the mortality rate in the villages of Bashkiria actually increased by 42.4 percent, in the villages of the Kurgan and Cheliabinsk regions it decreased by 30.9 percent and 20.2 percent, respectively.[104] The continuing high mortality was due to prolonged malnutrition. In the Sverdlovsk and Cheliabinsk regions, respectively, 34 percent and 27.4 percent of all deaths in 1944 were identified as directly caused by dystrophy and avitaminosis. In the Udmurt ASSR these were the main causes of death.[105] In many other places as well refugees suffered from avitaminosis, which sometimes led to death.[106]

In Kazakhstan, the epidemics also continued. Former Polish judge Itskhak Rozanskii (Ignats Rozenblit), who worked in Dzhambul for various Polish organizations for the settlement of refugees, reports that in the winter 1944–1945 about two thousand Jewish refugees died from the typhus epidemic in that town.[107] In the same winter 120 former Polish citizens died of starvation in the Dzhurun district of the Aktiubinsk region.[108] And in Alma-Ata many lives were swept away in 1944 by an outbreak of typhoid fever.[109]

Against the backdrop of Piotr Zaron's assessment, the estimation by Yosef Litvak, according to which the mortality rate among Jewish refugees, former Polish citizens, for the entire period of their stay in the USSR (i.e., for seven years—from autumn 1939 to autumn 1946) totaled 35–40 percent, looks moderate. Here he included the deaths of those who were mobilized in the army.[110] Given the difference in timing, Litvak's assessment is confirmed by a request filed in February 1944 by the Soviet Jewish Anti-Fascist Committee (JAC) to Stalin for the establishment of the Jewish Republic in the Crimea. It reported that about one and a half million Jews had evacuated to Central Asia, who for months were lying around the railway station areas, bare and hungry; their mortality rate was 25–30 percent.[111]

In a small part of the records at Yad Vashem (2 percent), the cause of death was banditry. The famine, the weakening of the police forces due to lack of personnel, and the influx of a large number of newcomers contributed to its spread. Most of the bandits (56 percent in 1943), who were of various ethnic backgrounds, were army deserters or were hiding from conscription into the army.[112] In Central Asia attacks on passersby happened mostly in the evenings and at night but sometimes in the daytime.[113] According to Miriam Aharonson's testimony, a Russian deserter, dressed in a soldier's uniform, one day tried to attack her mother in Samarkand in broad daylight. Bina Grantserska-Kadari also recalls that in Samarkand in the evening one could get stabbed in the back. Moshe Grosman writes in his memoirs about such attacks in Samarkand as a common practice.[114]

In small settlements bandits even attacked houses. During a robbery in a village near Tashkent, the parents and younger brother of Hillel Livshits were killed. Lea Lerer was a witness to a similar robbery, also in a village near Tashkent, during which the whole Jewish family was killed at home.[115] Perhaps this is the case that Moshe Grosman mentions.[116] Two bandits attacked the house where the Glikman refugee family lived in Kolkhoz Sovetskaia Karakalpakiia. They were lightly strangled, and then robbed; even their outerwear was taken.[117] There is more evidence of the lootings of Jewish families in Uzbekistan and Turkmenistan.[118] Although Jews were more often the targets of robbery, they were not the only victims. As one Polish boy testified during the war, in one of the kolkhozes of Central Asia his father left the house, and "Uzbeks killed him just because he had new Polish shoes."[119] The spread of banditry in Central Asia is underscored by a decree of the State Defense Committee in November 1942 on combating hooliganism and banditry in Uzbekistan.[120] During just the years of 1943–1944, the authorities liquidated 1,100 gangs with more than seven thousand members in Central Asia. By 1945, there were at least thirty-four other gangs in Central Asia that were known to the authorities, but which could not be liquidated.[121]

To an even larger extent than in Central Asia, banditry spread in another marginal area of the USSR, the North Caucasus. During the war 4,523 bandits were liquidated by the authorities in the Chechen-Ingush ASSR alone.[122] Alexander Statiev, who provided the figure, calls them insurgents or participants in armed resistance to the Soviet regime. It is difficult to agree with this, since they attacked only the civilian population, always with the aim to rob. In the spread of banditry, Central Asia was different from other unoccupied Soviet regions, in that the bandits were more organized, while in the RSFSR attacks were carried more often by individual robbers.

According to the statistics given in 1944 in Beria's report on the Sverdlovsk region, 95 percent of murders there were committed with a goal of seizing food cards, food, and personal items.[123] In the Kurgan region during five months of the same year, bandits killed twenty-five people, according to the recorded statistics only. At the same time, according to the information provided by Valerii Polivalov, who supplied these statistics, the police kept silent in order to improve crime indicators.[124] According to the testimony of Stanislav Postnikov, in his native Kineshma in the Ivanovo region, some of the wounded Red Army soldiers who were there to convalesce "united with the local punks, formed gangs, and tried to steal and rob."[125] In total, according to official data, in the rear regions of the USSR 192 civilians were killed by deserters in 1942.[126]

Perhaps Jews more often than others were objects of robbery due to the widely held opinion of their wealth. In Kuibyshev in 1945, several Jewish refugees were murdered in the course of robbery and looting. Because the proportion of Jews among the victims of such robberies was disproportionately large, in Kuibyshev, as elsewhere, such attacks were treated by Jewish refugees as acts of antisemitism.[127]

Gardening

Due to the worsening of the famine in early 1942, on April 7 the central authorities decided to develop gardening in the country. In May of the same year, the Council of People's Commissars of the Chuvash ASSR issued an order to provide evacuated families with plots for planting potatoes and vegetables and to allocate seeds for this purpose.[128] As a result, by autumn 1942, 74 percent of all refugee families began to cultivate plots in twenty-eight districts of this republic.[129] Similar orders were adopted everywhere in the rear areas. They were accompanied by a well-organized campaign in the press.[130]

This measure produced positive results. Gardening saved many refugee families from death. Jacob Sosniak who lived in Frunze during the war testifies: "The authorities gave out vegetable gardens. . . . We planted corn, melons, and potatoes. Without this, we would not have survived."[131] Tsilia Goikhshtein, who was starving in Alma-Ata, remembers that her mother did not get to them from Talgar, twenty-five kilometers away, because she couldn't abandon her garden. In the autumn, her mother brought back a few sacks of potatoes and cooked some, which was remembered as a holiday. The hungry daughter asked how much she could take and received the answer: "Take as much as you want!"[132]

It should be noted that gardening for many refugees was something they were used to. An analysis of the records of Rechitsa Jews shows that on the eve of the war, 41 percent of them were engaged in gardening. Moreover, by 1931 agriculture was the main occupation for a quarter of a million Jews, accounting for 10 percent of the entire Jewish population of the USSR.[133] The overwhelming majority of them lived in those areas that later occupied by the Wehrmacht, which means that some of them could have fled to the eastern regions of the USSR. Itska Kopel'man, a worker from Kolkhoz Ukraina, located in the former Jewish agricultural colony Romanovka, along with his entire family worked in the Papanin Kolkhoz in the Samarkand region during the war. Therefore, the good results in horticulture, which some Jewish refugees obtained, are not surprising. The family of Dina Gabel, who came to a Ukrainian village in Northern Kazakhstan, achieved a yield of vegetables the size of which the locals had never experienced themselves.[134] Gita Levitan from the Chuvash TsIK Kolkhoz collected 720 kilogram of potatoes from his garden comprised of only 0.04 hectares of land.[135] A former refugee from Moldavian SSR, Liana Degtiar, who was in the valley of the Kurgan-Tiube region (Tajikistan), recalls: "We also received a very small piece of land for a garden. We got crops twice a year. The climate was hot, and there was irrigation there: all vegetable gardens had several irrigation ditches. Every evening people made clay dams to hold water for kitchen gardens. We grew carrots, potatoes, corn, lentils, beans, eggplants, paprika, and melons. We had a lot of vegetables. I could eat as much as my heart desired. Each of us ate melon three times a day. We dried the melons on the roof and got a melon marmalade, unusually tasty."[136] Such abundance, however, was the exception.

Although the refugees, where they could, started gardening even before the 1942 decree was issued, it was greatly expanded by the authorities. Whereas in 1941 gardening in the rear areas of the USSR involved 4.5 million people, in 1942 it was 6.5 million, then in 1943 already 9.2 million, and in 1945 in the same regions—10.4 million. At the beginning of the war, 89 percent of the vegetable gardens were planted with potatoes, and by the end of the war somewhat less—86 percent.[137] According to the data for the Sverdlovsk region for 1942, almost 40 percent of all potatoes eaten by the population were potatoes grown in their own gardens.[138] The role of potatoes in the diet of the rear's population is difficult to overestimate. Considering the important place of gardening in providing food for refugees, theft of food from the plots became a serious problem for them. The refugees expressed their indignation about the thefts both to local authorities and judicial officials, as well as in letters to newspapers. In response, the prosecutor's office severely punished the captured thieves, sentencing them to imprisonment from one to five years.

The fact of the allocation of land to refugees could not but inspire the collective farmers with the hope of liberalization of the Soviet agricultural system through expansion of personal plots. With the refugees' re-evacuation, the allocated land to them often fell to the hands of farmers and did not return to the kolkhozes. However, the central authorities saw the allocation of land to refugees only as the forced measure necessary to save them. In September 1946, a sharply titled resolution "On measures to protect public lands of collective farms from misappropriation" was issued. The central authorities threatened collective farmers and kolkhoz boards with judicial sanctions and obliged them to establish the use of land following the prewar rules.[139]

Jewish Aid from Abroad and the Soviet Government

It should be noted that the Jewish Anti-Fascist Committee was an obedient instrument of Stalinist propaganda in the West, primarily among American Jewry. And it was quite successful. The Jewish population of the United States donated $20 million to the Aid to Russia Fund. The American Committee for the Settlement of Jews in Birobidjan (Ambidjan) collected money for the purchase of medicines (primarily penicillin) and 100,000 wrist watches. Having taken patronage of Orphanage Serebrianye Prudy (the Silver Lakes) near Stalingrad with five hundred children of different ethnicities, Ambidjan brought them food, clothing, bedding, medicines, workshop equipment, and an electric generator. The Society for Settling Toiling Jews on the Land (OZET) gave the JAC a printing press worth $100,000 and raised money to build hospitals in Leningrad and Stalingrad. The World ORT (Association for the Promotion of Skilled Trades) sent machinery to the artels of Ukraine and Belorussia immediately after the liberation of those territories. The British Jews donated $10 million to the Aid to Russia Fund, and the British Jewish Fund for Assistance to Soviet Russia sent ambulances and X-ray units worth $0.2 million to the USSR. The pro-Communist Palestinian League V, led by Shlomo Kaplansky, Arnold Zweig, and Leib Tarnopoler, sent $0.8 million to the USSR, as well as ambulances and medicines. The Jewish organizations of Argentina and other countries of Latin America, Canada, and Australia collected $1 million for the USSR. General assistance to the USSR by foreign Jews (through organizations or directly) through the JAC was estimated at $45 million.[140] Nikolai Terenchenko remembers his studies in the Suvorov Military School: "American stew, bacon, condensed milk, egg powder, even dates that ended up in the rice porridge were excellent. . . . Once, for some reason, we were given a piece of chocolate each, and on the wrapper was this inscription: 'A small present for the Soviet children from the Jews of Mexico.'"[141]

American Jewish Joint Distribution Committee (AJJDC) and Jewish religious organizations in the US also assisted to the USSR.[142] During the visit of JAC's Solomon Mikhoels and Itzik Fefer to the United States in October 1943, the AJJDC collected $0.5 million for the USSR.[143] Unlike many of the foreign

Jewish organizations cooperating with the JAC, the AJJDC sought to help refugees specifically, even regardless of their nationality. The USSR's reluctance to allow the arrival of the AJJDC envoy to verify the distribution of aid raised the suspicion that it did not reach the refugees at all. Therefore, by the end of the war and immediately thereafter, the AJJDC and some other Jewish organizations had stopped transferring money to the USSR, preferring to send parcels to available addresses, mostly Polish and Baltic Jews. According to Soviet official data, in 1943 over 30,000 parcels were sent, about 90,000 in 1946, and over 180,000 in 1947. In Minsk 1,050 parcels were received just from the United States in 1946, 1,924 in 1947, and 1,405 in the first quarter of 1948.[144] Sometimes the parcels were addressed to the synagogue and were then distributed to the hungry families, as was done in the liberated L'vov. Over a thousand parcels were distributed there to invalids of war and labor, to orphans and families of the dead, to former prisoners of war and demobilized soldiers, to students, and those in severe need. Besides, 244,000 rubles were distributed to the same categories of the Jewish population.[145]

The Soviet authorities were very displeased by this practice since it was accompanied by complaints about poverty and the lists of suffering Jews being sent to the US. The secretary of the TsK KP(b) of the Belorussian republic, Gusarov, who informed Moscow about this aid, reported that private letters "about the alleged hunger and poverty in the Soviet Union, about prohibitively high prices [and] low salaries were sent abroad."[146] In L'vov the authorities reacted to the distribution of food and other goods more radically, arresting and denouncing the chair of the Jewish community Lev Serebriannyi.[147] In an attempt to bring the AJJDC aid back into the Soviet distribution system, the JAC informed to the United States that the refugees were allegedly complaining about parcels of "worthless junk" sent through Tehran.[148]

A few years earlier, feeling the moral responsibility for distributing the aid received by the central government, the chair of the JAC, Mikhoels, and the executive secretary of the committee, Epshtein, in in a May 1944 letter to Vyacheslav Molotov, not only lamented that in the liberated Ukrainian regions the surviving and mendicant Jews did not receive any of the foreign aid, but also asked to create within the committee a commission for aid's distribution.[149]

Stalin did not appreciate the complaints of the committee and the above-mentioned letter about the establishment of Jewish autonomy in the Crimea.[150] After all, he posed purely propagandistic tasks to the committee within the country. The committee coped well with them, adhering to the position of the Evsektsiia (Jewish section of the Soviet Communist Party) with its Bundist idea of cultural autonomy and a negative attitude toward the Zionists. Unlike the main central newspapers, and sometimes even local ones, *Eynikayt*, the

Yiddish-language mouthpiece of the committee, never allowed itself to criticize local governments.[151] In its pages one could only read about the support of Jewish refugees in the rear by other Soviet peoples and the good attitude of the administration toward them.

Stalin's support for the creation of Israel in the discussions at the UN, the permission given to Polish and Romanian Jews to return to their countries for subsequent migration to Palestine, as well as some other indulgences designed to arouse the sympathy of Western Jews, gave the committee the illusion that they could reach an agreement with Stalin. Encouraged by the purportedly improving prospects, the committee's leadership began to behave incautiously. In the light of the murder of Mikhoels in 1948, Epshtein—who unexpectedly was found dead at home on July 27, 1945—could also be a victim of Stalin's reaction to the behavior of the "brazen" leaders of the JAC.

∽

In the new places of their residence, refugees faced two main problems—starvation and disease. Although the central authorities wanted to help them, they did too little to do so. The most notable achievement of the authorities was the expansion of vegetable gardens, which helped hundreds of thousands of refugees to overcome hunger and related diseases. However, late involvement in horticulture did not save most refugees. Mortality took on unprecedented proportions, especially in 1942. Later on, the situation was better for those Jews and others who, until the autumn of 1939, had no Soviet citizenship and were, therefore, more closely associated with the Jews of the United States and Palestine. Since the middle of the war, they were receiving charity packages of basic necessities from abroad. Foreign Jewish organizations had sent parcels for refugees to the USSR before, but these were sent through official channels and therefore there is no evidence that this assistance reached the refugees.

Even worse off than refugee families were the underage refugees in orphanages. The next chapter will demonstrate that the propaganda slogan "All the best—for the children" had nothing to do with the Soviet reality. Orphans suffered from all the same problems of the Soviet rear, but unlike children in families, they could not count on the support and sympathy of their relatives. Because of antisemitism, the situation of Jewish children in orphanages was particularly tragic, and therefore, it is important to explore this subject.

CHAPTER FIVE

Orphanages, Adoption, and Jewish Children

We started one more thing here.
It will be clear to you from the letter:
Your children have not fallen into enemy claws.
They arrived to us safely.
In a fatherly way, we, like their own relatives,
Caressed them and wiped away their tears.
We each took one of the children
Without sorrow, let them grow up in our home.
We swear to you that we will save the children!
We will raise swashbucklers, we shall set them upon steeds.
Do not let your heart ache for the children,
We will protect them like the apple of our eye.
We shall provide them with every needed thing.
As in the spring a crowd of young lambs,—
As if never having experienced a disaster,—
In joy they grow up surrounded by amusements.

March 1942[1]

Categories of Orphanages

During the war, tens of thousands of Jewish children found themselves in orphanages and boarding schools across the USSR. Their fate was tragic. To the suffering due to the difficult economic situation in these institutions, antisemitism and general xenophobia, with which broad sections of the Soviet population were infected, were often added. All orphanages, where children from the western regions of the USSR ended up, can be divided into four categories: (a) evacuated, (b) old local orphanages, (c) new orphanages specially created for refugee children, and (d) new orphanages shared by local and refugee children.

Many evacuated orphanages came from Leningrad and, especially, Moscow. Most of the children in them had a father at the front and a mother who either remained working in the hometown or was also evacuated but gave the child to an orphanage because she could not feed them, be responsible for their health care, and provide other necessities. According to official figures, in 1943–1946, an average of 3,000–3,300 rubles a year was allowed for one child in these orphanages.[2] This equaled approximately 250–260 rubles per month, which was slightly higher than the average Central Asian salary of 150–250 during the war. The following evidence fully refutes the official figures.

If one parent (usually it was a mother) had more than one child under the age of fourteen, they often could not provide any the children with living better than those they would receive in the orphanage. The transfer of the child to the orphanage was dictated by the uncertainty on the mother's part that she could feed both herself and the child.[3] Mothers preferred to send her children to orphanages so that their relatives could find the children in the case of mothers' death. The situation in which the Liuksemburgs, refugees from Zhitomir, found themselves in Uzbekistan was quite typical. When Mikhlia Liuksemburg's husband Moisei was called up to the front, she could not feed their three children, and, keeping only the one-year-old Polia, she sent the elder children, aged ten and twelve, to a quarantine orphanage in Tashkent. For some reason, the administration separated the children, and they then found themselves in different orphanages—Sonia in the Iangiiul' district, and Boris in the Tashkent district. Dorit Bader-Whiteman cites the dramatic story of a ten-kilometer journey in Uzbekistan of a mother with a child to an orphanage, who was not accepted there because of overcrowding and, obviously, because of the mother's presence. Believing the orphanage to be the best option for saving the child, she left the child at the doors of the orphanage and left (this episode resulted in a years-long psychological trauma for the child).[4]

Some orphanages from the western republics of the USSR were also evacuated. The Riga orphanage was relocated to the Chkalovskoe district of the Chuvash ASSR.[5] Twelve orphanages from Ukraine moved to the Andizhan region of Uzbekistan. Overall, seventy-eight orphanages arrived in Uzbekistan.[6] Forty-three orphanages were evacuated to the Altai territory from Kiev, Dnepropetrovsk, and other cities in Ukraine.[7] In Turkmenistan, there were forty-five evacuated orphanages.[8] In the summer and autumn of 1941, ninety orphanages with 10,208 children, which arrived mainly from Ukraine and central Russia (not including Moscow), were placed in Kazakhstan. In total, on July 1, 1942, 111 evacuated orphanages were placed in Kazakhstan, accounting for 65.7 percent of all 169 orphanages in this area.[9] In total, according to official figures for 1941–1942, 976 orphanages were evacuated to the east of the USSR with 107,223 children.[10] These statistics included those children's homes and summer camps that in June 1941 took the children to the countryside for the summer; with the outbreak of the war, they were evacuated directly to the east, turning into orphanages.

The situation in the evacuated orphanages was similar to the situation in local orphanages. For example, in the Kharkov orphanage now housed in Kazalinsk (Kazakhstan), theft and beatings were common.[11] The proportion of Jews in evacuated orphanages was higher, since the percentage of Jews among the general population of the western regions was higher. Before the war, Jewish children found themselves in orphanages mainly because of the repressions of the late 1930s.

In addition, refugee children were housed in the orphanages created for local orphans before the war. These orphanages were mostly comprised of children who arrived there shortly after birth. They had never known parental care and often were, therefore, embittered toward society. Many negative phenomena of Soviet society found a fertile ground here. These orphanages were especially difficult for the children of refugees. There was still a great deal of power hierarchy, a system of patronage and theft, which were often exemplified by the behavior of the orphanages' directorate and the staff. For example, in Frunze, seven hundred children who arrived from Odessa and Leningrad in the summer of 1942 were assigned to the old local orphanages.[12] Irina Rodshtein and other children from Belorussia found themselves in such an orphanage in Gur'ev. She remembers how the old-timers beat them and took away their food, clothes, and possessions. The staff did not pay any attention to this.[13]

In the Belozërskoe district of the Kurgan region, children from orphanages engaged in theft from the gardens of collective farmers.[14] In the Tashkent orphanage on Sundays and holidays, when it was possible to leave the premises, most of the children stole in the streets, on public transport, and in the bazaar.[15] When, in the winter of 1942, Nadezhda Mandel'shtam was carrying a packet of salted herrings, received as part of her rations, most of them were snatched away by a group of teenagers who attacked her.[16] However, the children were guided by their own moral principles. When, in the Alaiskii market in Tashkent, a boy in rags tried to cut the pocket of Anna Akhmatova with a razor but was caught by the hand of her companion and then released with the reproach that he was stealing from a hungry Leningrader, he soon returned with a pie that he stole for her.[17]

Among the new orphanages for refugees, orphanages created for the former Polish citizens prevailed. There were also orphanages organized for children from the Baltic republics, among them were five Estonian orphanages that, by 1944, housed six hundred children.[18] They were created on the initiative of the evacuated leadership of these republics, which sought to maintain contact with their countrymen. As part of this aspiration, the republican authorities also defended the interests of "their" refugees to local and central authorities. This was a big part of their official activities. The creation of such orphanages was motivated by the need to teach Soviet patriotism in the children's native languages. The Belorussian authorities lobbied for the introduction of the Belorussian language of instruction in the new orphanages from Belorussia.[19]

Among the evacuated pioneer camps that received the status of orphanages, many were from Belorussia (especially from the Minsk region), and fewer from other western Soviet republics. Sometimes teachers and management remained the same, but more often not, the leadership changed. Compared with other orphanages, children assembled in the new orphanages were from well-off families. But even here children created their own hierarchy.

New orphanages and boarding schools to house both the local and refugee children were created because the other three categories of orphanages could not provide places for the huge number of parentless and homeless children that appeared during the war. The number of orphans increased as a result of the death of parents from disease or hunger and also because of the fathers' departure to the front. In Kazakhstan alone in 1943, 29,350 street children were detained by the police.[20] And in the first two and a half months of 1944, 2,566 street children were caught in Tashkent.[21] Orphans from the liberated western regions of the USSR were placed in boarding schools, new common orphanages, and, when spaces were available, in other orphanages, according to a special resolution of the Council of People's Commissars, dated May 25, 1943, on the removal of the orphans to the east.[22] The authorities were not in a hurry to return the evacuees or create new orphanages in the liberated areas. It was justly believed that the conditions for the normal functioning of orphanages in the newly liberated regions were unsatisfactory because of economic breakdown, problems with the cadres, and shortage of large buildings that remained intact.

Because of the opening of new orphanages for refugees and new joint orphanages, the number of orphanages in the USSR increased during the first year of the war from 2,100 to 3,400. The number of children in them increased during this time from 280,000 to 366,000. All in all, during the war the number of orphanages grew to almost 6,000.[23]

Material Conditions of Children's Stays in Orphanages and Boarding Schools

For decades, Soviet historiography showed how well children lived in orphanages and boarding schools during the war. Rosy and boastful reports were made about providing children with high-calorie and fortified food, clothing, and footwear. Following are some typical examples. In the Pakhta-Abad district of Uzbekistan, for children's needs kolkhozniks collected three tons of *shala* (raw rice), two and a half tons of wheat, two cows, four sheep, and two pigs. In the Namangan district of the same republic, according to the official reports, the children of one of the orphanages were fed four times a day.[24] The local youth of the Chardzhou and Ashkhabad regions (Turkmenistan) provided shoes for 1,979 and 3,850 evacuated children, respectively.[25] The youth of the Issyk-Kul region (Kirgizstan) donated to orphanages 1,712 units of shoes and other goods, 4,479 kilograms of flour, 2,720 kilograms of dried fruits, 85 kilograms of confectionary products, and 1,270 kilograms of other assorted food products.[26]

Celebratory reports were accompanied by enthusiastic press campaigns. In the newspaper *Krasnoe Predural'e*, in March 1944 an article by E. Zharkov, "We Shall Not Have Orphans," was published, where the author drew a rosy picture of what he allegedly saw in the Taush orphanage: "Warm and cozy . . . cheerful voices. . . . The older children lovingly care for their younger brothers and sisters, telling them fairy tales, taking them on walks, making toys. . . . They are dressed in new felt boots; clean and ruddy, the boys have found a new family here. . . . The children of the orphanage help the families of the soldiers. For Nikiforova, the mother of two frontline soldiers, they collected five hundred rubles. . . . The children of the orphanages were surrounded by the care and attention of the community."[27] This is a typical example of the false representations and fraud of the Soviet era.

In reality, many food products and other goods for the children either did not reach them at all or arrived in a much smaller quantity than was officially allocated. According to the memorandum on the Chuvash ASSR (written no later than September 26, 1941), a 365 kg allotment of meat was issued to the Kogiz orphanage, but in reality nothing was delivered. Evacuated children's institutions in the same republic were formally allocated 287 kilograms of fish but received only 30.[28] As indicated in one report, the People's Commissariat of Trade "issued allotments, but no one was concerned with the extent to which these foodstuffs were actually distributed to the relevant organizations."[29] To central authorities' recommendations, resulting from the investigations they conducted, about the need to ensure the correct distribution of food and other goods, the Narkomtorg officials replied that it was impossible to do so because of a very limited number of officials.[30]

All this proves that orphanages had become the object of a shadowy seizure of food and other goods allocated to them by the state. The evacuation inspector A. Nikitina reported to the authorities in 1942 that the district officials ate in a restricted-access dining hall where there were meat dishes, eggs, and tea with sugar, and "all these products are taken from children's institutions and the hospital."[31] It is not known whether the head of the department of the Council of People's Commissars of the RSFSR for the economic organization of the evacuated population, L. Dmitriev, had any information about the embezzlement of this aid in Chuvashia or knew that this practice existed everywhere, when in June 1943 he demanded that his counterpart in the Chuvash ASSR, Nikolai Zhukov, establish control over aid to children's institutions.[32]

Aleksandr Shalak also writes that children's institutions and hospitals suffered from theft of food and other goods. The only dubious part of his account is his explanation that this behavior was caused by the underfunding of local governments.[33] In reality, salaries of the local administration were several times higher than average salaries, and their personal plentiful supply of food did not necessitate stealing food products. They came by it easily. For example, in the Cheboksary district, the evacuated wife of the secretary of the Moscow's Leningrad District Party Committee, the wife of the chair of the local district executive committee, and the head of the district committee for education took their meal at a kindergarten.[34] Therefore, most likely, in addition to the fact that seized food products were delivered to the canteens catering exclusively to the state and party officials, these goods were also illegally siphoned off to the black market.

Donations of food and other goods to orphanages, kindergartens, and schools were frequently embezzled as well. After laudatory reports about collection these donations, because of poor control over the subsequent distribution, the families of local officials, partially or completely, took control over them.[35]

Not infrequently directors of orphanages personally participated in the theft of food and property. A. Nikolaev, head assistant of the Novosibirsk regional department of public education, wrote about this practice in July 1944.[36] The director of the international orphanage in Ivanovo, T. Makarov, stole meat and butter from the children.[37] Lidia Chukovskaia, who worked for the public commission for assistance to evacuated children in Uzbekistan, recalls: "Theft during the war took monstrous, exponential dimensions in Tashkent. I remember an incident when a one-and-a-half-ton truck, loaded with little coats, passed by the gates of the orphanage, went to the market. I remember how the building materials sent for the winter repair of the children's bedrooms all, entirely, went to the construction of a new house: in the yard, a house for the director for personnel was built. The thieves quickly closed ranks with the prosecutor's office, and there were practically no police after them." She adds that they stole from more than one orphanage.[38] During the inspection of the Tashkent orphanage no. 25, the children complained to the inspectorate: "In the winter we received wool, but this wool all went to the administration for blouses, hats, gloves.... Everything is taken out of the orphanage and sold."[39]

As a result, the situation in the orphanages became very nasty. According to the recollections of the former residents, they were half-clothed and half-starved.

When, one day, Dov Dunaevskii's sister brought him food to an orphanage in Tashkent, he tried to eat as much as he could right away because he knew very well that whatever was left for later would be taken away from him by the other children.[40] Perhaps in this or another Tashkent orphanage, according to the official report, the children ate only 400 grams of bread and a bowl of soup daily.[41] There is no doubt that it was a thin soup without meat. Danielle Bell recalls that she was always very hungry in an orphanage in Siberia in 1942.[42] In the orphanage near Dzhelalabad (Kirgizstan), there were no sheets, pillowcases, beds; children slept on mattresses in pairs.[43] According to the survey, the courtyard of Tashkent's orphanage no. 25 was contaminated with feces, and the children were malnourished due to the theft of food by the director.[44]

The lack of food in all orphanages and the lack of heating in some of them, as well as the unsanitary conditions, contributed to the spread of diseases among children. Critical of this situation, Lidia Chukovskaia wrote, "It was believed that orphanages were well supplied, but there were cases of scurvy and pellagra [a type of avitaminosis]."[45] In the orphanage in Ibresi (Chuvashia), according to the medical examination conducted there in 1942, only half of the children were completely healthy, and among the rest the most common diseases were: tuberculosis (30 cases), bronchadenitis (20), relapses of trachoma (15), impetigo (11), and malaria (9).[46]

Internal reports from that period, written not to drum up the next great achievement but to address existing problems, testify to the ubiquitously difficult situation in orphanages. In December 1942 the director of the orphanage in the town of Olonki in the Irkutsk region complained to the TsK VKP(b): "The children are ragged; even linens, blankets, mattresses, and towels are lacking.[47] In Mordovian ASSR over half of the children did not have winter shoes.[48] In one of the coldest regions of Siberia, the Krasnoiarsk territory, in 1944, there were 1,246 coats, 2,273 felt boots, and only 839 hats for 5,683 children living in orphanages.[49] However, even what was available was in very poor condition: only a third of the total was not torn or rotten, according inspections.

In one orphanage in Idrin (Krasnoiarsk territory), none of the children had a spare change of underwear or coats.[50] An inspection of the orphanages in the Udmurt ASSR, carried out in 1944, revealed that some of them had no bed linens whatsoever, while other had no more than 20 percent of what was necessary for the children's beds. The children's nutrition was also poor.[51] It was no better in the Cheliabinsk region: in some orphanages only one-third of children had warm clothes, and none of them had any spoons at all. The situation an orphanage in Kynov (in the Molotov region) was especially bad. There, half of the children suffered from dystrophy due to hunger; they did not have underclothes. In the winter of 1943–1944, these children walked to school in the snow wearing only socks wrapped in rags, which resulted in twenty-eight cases of frost-bitten feet.[52]

In the Skorobogatovo children's home in the Kurgan region, thirty-two children did not go to school because they did not have a coat or winter shoes. In the Vargashi orphanage of the same region, sixty children without coats were sent to school wrapped in blankets, and in the Korkino orphanage, forty-nine children had fourteen beds and thirty-nine blankets for all of them and there were no washbasins whatsoever. Also in the same region, in the Chashi orphanage, there were only ten plates for sixty-eight.[53] Gita Blium, who lost her children during the flight to the east, found them eleven months later in an orphanage (she does not specify which) without clothes and shoes.[54]

The difficult situation in the evacuated orphanage in Poretskoe, in the Chuvash ASSR, is confirmed by the results of an inspection carried out in February 1942 by the superintendent of the Council of People's Commissars of the RSFSR P. Panteleev. More than half the children were lacking not only beds but also mattresses, and they slept on bare bunks. Besides, there were only a few dishes. There were no washbasins or washbowls. The children, however, could not go to the bathhouse because they did not have a change of underclothes and soap. Once the first-graders returned to the orphanage in tears because the teacher of the local school called them "smelly goats." Due to the lack of indoor plumbing, the children used an outhouse even at night in the winter. The children had no coats. It took until the end of January 1942 for fifteen coats to be made, and twenty-seven of the children never received one. Nobody had felt boots. The orphanage had no electricity, only one kerosene lamp. Because of the lack of food, children from the orphanage in autumn 1941 went door-to-door asking for bread, but later they stopped because they began to receive more food in the orphanage; this was mainly bread and pea soup.[55]

The boarding school in the village of Sin'ialy in the same republic, where all sixteen children were evacuees and mostly orphans, had, in 1942, no bed linens, mattresses, blankets, or pillows. Nobody had shoes, and only a few of the children had threadbare coats. The girls from the boarding school enrolled in a pharmaceutical school in Cheboksary also had no clothes and no shoes. The boarding school had no dishes, soap, or matches, and there was not enough food, as a result of which the children were emaciated, which was documented by the inspection of the resettlement superintendent A. Maznina.[56]

Igor' Zolotusskii recalls: "In Siberia, to where we were evacuated, we quickly began to starve. The supplies that were evacuated from Moscow ended, and the orphans had to venture out to make money. We sold random junk, wheat, threadbare sheets that were coming apart at the seams. These had been taken off the clothes lines and were traded for a cup of tea and a cube of saccharin.

We also sold cylinders of frozen milk and half-cooked wheat from the pigsty."[57] The former head of the district health department E. V. Loshkova describes how children in all three orphanages of the Sorochinsk district of the Chkalov region did not see bread for months, eating frozen potatoes and cabbage: "Malnourished to such an extent that they look like skeletons, nervous because of the horrors of the war, covered with sores, dressed in rags, practically barefoot, they are huddled around a barely warm stove and are silent."[58]

In the years 1944–1945 the food situation in some orphanages in the USSR got even worse. As was explained to the children, this was a consequence of the need to feed the residents of the liberated territories in the west.[59] Considering the difficult economic situation in orphanages, the practice by some directors of arranging the writing of thankful meeting resolutions or letters from parents and relatives seems cynical. For example, in February 1942 in one of the hungriest months of the war, a meeting of 250 parents of the Soviet district of Moscow was organized, where, after a speech by a representative of the boarding schools in the Alma-Ata region, they, in writing, thanked the authorities for the "normal conditions" enjoyed by their children.[60] However, not all officials could turn a blind eye to the difficult situation in children's institutions. This is what caused the resignation of Maria Milovidova in July 1942 from the position of inspector of such institutions in the Chuvash ASSR, as is indicated in her notice: "My health does not allow me to continue in this work."[61]

The high mortality rate in orphanages was a consequence of the poor conditions therein. According to the interdepartmental report obtained by Rebecca Manley, in the first quarter of 1943, 130 children died in orphanages in Uzbekistan and 1,258 were sick,[62] apparently severely, otherwise they would hardly have been noted in the report.

Labor and Punishment in Orphanages

Caught in a difficult economic situation, the management of orphanages sought additional funds for their institutions. One of the means of replenishing the budget was the use of children in various production jobs. Nadezhda Paletsikh, who researched the situation in the Urals, writes that the orphans as young as twelve years old were employed.[63] At the age of thirteen to fourteen, many already worked a full day in production. In Tashkent these children worked at a shoe factory or the Kliment Voroshilov Metallurgical Plant.[64] In Vasiugansk, in the Narym district, they worked on the shop floor of the industrial complex.[65] Since the use of adolescents of this age was contrary to Soviet legislation, the authorities circumvented the law by forming so-called schools of factory training—FZO (until 1940 they were called schools of factory apprenticeship, FZU).

Antonina Komarova, who worked in Chkalov at Leningrad's Kliment Voroshilov Plant no. 147 recalls: "Once in the winter of 1942 the shop manager and I were invited to the personnel department. We went into the room and saw an unusual picture. Squatting, huddled against the wall, sat about twenty-five boys and girls aged about thirteen to fourteen. They were poorly dressed, and in the yard it was minus forty Celsius. It turns out that these were children evacuated from Ukraine. . . . I took patronage over the arrivals. Somehow we got to the shop. So as not to freeze, we ran rather than walked to the dining room."[66]

An even more widespread means of replenishing the budget, as well as feeding children and educators, was the use of children in agricultural work on kolkhozes and in their subsidiary farms.[67] If the management of the orphanage did not steal and could skillfully perform such work, this helped to overcome famine. Pëtr Valetskii, who found himself in the Sverdlovsk orphanage no. 1, remembers with gratitude its director, thanks to whose efforts in agricultural work the children did not starve.[68] Sometimes children not only provided for themselves but also sent agricultural products to the front. This was possible for the orphanage of Minsk children who found themselves in a wealthy, formerly German kolkhoz in the Saratov region. A former resident of the orphanage Sergei Goldin recalls:

> I mastered all agricultural work: plowing, harrowing, cultivation of fields, harvesting. We mastered everything when it came to caring for horses: feeding, cleaning the horses and their pens. We even became good riders, and sometimes after the bathing of the horses, we arranged big races, which were strictly forbidden because they were working horses. In autumn we harvested the crops and harvested hay for the livestock. After the end of the autumn works, we shepherded herds of cows, and at night—herds of horses. It was unsafe because in the late autumn there were many wolves in the steppe, and running into them was not uncommon.[69]

Children were often used in hazardous work. In July 1943, the Novosibirsk regional department for public education banned the involvement of children in the cutting of trees and grasses as the result of an accident in the Maslianino orphanage, which ended in the amputation of a child's arm. At the same time, mowing grass was allowed from the age of fourteen.[70] It is unlikely that orphanages stopped the practice of using even younger children at these jobs, as kolkhozes and local authorities very rarely supplied them with firewood, and educators consisted mainly of women, often from urban areas.

In general, the authorities welcomed the involvement of children in the work, since, on the one hand, this lightened the burden of financing these institutions, and, on the other hand, they always considered labor as one of the most important means of raising children. However, in 1943 there was still an acute shortage of workers, because of continual call-ups to the front and a high number of adult deaths in the rear. Although by this time the German army under General Guderian was captured at Stalingrad and German prisoners became an important source of labor, they were still not enough. As a consequence, in September 1943 the government issued a directive to send all teenagers over the age of fourteen who were at the time at juvenile correctional labor colonies to FZOs, as well as manufacturing and railway vocational schools.[71]

The approach of the authorities to child labor was reflected in a curious way in the work of Andrei Sinitsyn in 1985. Reporting that during the war the authorities recruited 52,000 adolescents over the age of fourteen, he presents this information not as a forced measure but as an achievement by placing it in the section "Nationwide Care for Children Left without Parents" of a book published for the fortieth anniversary of the end of World War II.[72] Moreover, the adolescents' work on the home front during the war has been even more often portrayed in the patriotic literature in the USSR and later in Russia as an ideologically based impulse to help the country. Not disregarding the patriotic feelings of these adolescents, one should nevertheless recognize that their main motive to work was hunger. Postnikov recalls how at the age of fourteen or fifteen he was ready to take any job because the family started starving after the death of their father. Postnikov moonlighted where he could: he pulled barrels of tomatoes out of the frozen pond for the Oblpotrebsoiuz, cleared the snow off the roads, unloaded salt from the barges, and sawed and chopped firewood.[73] Fifteen-year-old at the beginning of the war, Arkadii Dael' recalls his life on his arrival in Uzbekistan: "I worked collecting cotton and on a farm, herding sheep, undertaking any work to bring food to my family."[74]

Immediately after reaching the age of sixteen, children were released from orphanages, and places were arranged for them on kolkhozes, on state farms, in factories, and vocational schools.[75] However, even children over the age of fourteen who escaped from an orphanage or who remained without parents after being detained by the police were no longer taken to orphanages but were employed, that is, they "plunged into society."[76] Orphaned children who were newly arrived in the eastern regions of the USSR, starting at the age of fifteen, were also sent to work on the state farms and kolkhozes.[77]

For orphans such "starting out in life" was very difficult, since they were usually sent off without any kind of household property, having only their shoes and clothes, and even then, they had to pass on some of their clothing to the children who remained in the orphanage. Unlike other children, upon leaving these institutions they could not count on material support from their families; and the family in the USSR was a survival unit because it was hard for an adult alone person to feed themselves. In this situation, those leaving the institutions had almost no choice but to cooperate with each other.

The situation in each orphanage strongly depended on the director. Some of them were poor business executives and organizers, and some even suffered from alcoholism. The director of the Leningrad orphanage located in the village of Ishani in Chuvashia, according to the probe of the evacuation inspector, was an alcoholic: "Andreev does not deny that he drinks, and he does not intend to quit."[78] There were also some good directors. Liubov' Potashnikova, the director of the Leningrad Young Patriots Boarding School, which had been evacuated to Shadrinsk in the Kurgan region, was well regarded. An energetic woman, she cared with love for the children, among whom there were many orphans; she was a diligent manager and skillfully selected staff for the school.[79]

More often than not, the management of orphanages punished children by giving them extra duties, prohibiting visits from relatives, and not permitting to leave the orphanage. In a number of orphanages, if the misbehavior was more serious in the eyes of the administration, at its instigation, the violators were beaten by older, thuggish residents. Such cooperation with administrators rested on their willingness to turn a blind eye when orphanages' tough guys commandeered from weak children or in other ways violated daily routines and house rules. Sometimes the caregivers and directors relied on such cooperation because of the fear of revenge or threats on the part of those students who were involved in criminal activities. In some orphanages the administration itself used corporal punishment. In the Chimkent orphanage the headmistress beat fifteen-year-old Daniil Iushkovskii with a belt because he left the orphanage grounds without permission.[80] A director of one new orphanage, who found himself on the territory of the liquidated German Autonomous Region, also beat children, who came from the former Minsk pioneer camp.[81]

Not uncommon was the transfer of adolescents from orphanages to the so-called correctional labor colonies for minors under the administration of the NKVD. Such a measure gave the administration of orphanages an additional instrument of punishment.

Adoption

A vivid proof of the confusion and helplessness of the authorities in the face of a large number of orphans and homeless children that had appeared during the war was an attempt to shift care for them to the population. This attempt was formalized in a special resolution of the Council of People's Commissars of the USSR of January 23, 1942, on the organization of children left without parents[82]. The decision was accompanied by a powerful campaign in the press.

On January 31, *Pravda* published an article "You Are Not an Orphan, Young One!," which told about the tragic circumstances in which parents of several children had died and how several workers at the Moscow Krasnyi Bogatyr' Rubber Shoes Factory took them into their care.[83] A month later the same newspaper published a long article "We Save Children," with excerpts from letters from across Russia in support of the Muscovites' initiative.[84] Dozens of similar articles were published in the central and local press.[85]

Starting in the mid-1930s there were three forms of private assistance to children in the USSR—guardianship, custody of relatives, and adoption. In the first option, the state provided financial support for children through their guardians. Very often witness testimonies and even archival documents confuse guardianship with adoption. And since there is no way to clarify which form of aid is really meant in each case, we will keep to the language of the sources. To encourage adoption, in September 1943 the Supreme Soviet of the USSR issued a decree allowing the use of the adoptive parents' names and last times as children's patronymics and surnames. Although the decree stipulated that children ten years old and older had to be asked for their consent, it is clear that it was difficult for children to resist the will of their adoptive parents.

In Uzbekistan an immediate response to the 1942 resolution was the adoption of children by collective farmers of the Iangi-Iul' district. The Stakhanov Agricultural Artel of this district took on the full support of an entire evacuated orphanage.[86] Next, a women's organization in Tashkent issued an appeal to the women of Uzbekistan with the call to adopt evacuated children: "We will fulfill our fraternal duty to the Russian people, to the peoples of Ukraine and Belorussia."[87] Similar appeals were soon issued throughout the republic.[88]

In the context of tense ethnic relations in Uzbekistan, the republican authorities supported, and perhaps even initiated, the adoptions carried out by the Shamakhmudovs, mentioned in the introduction to the book. For the sake of this version of the Stakhanovite experiment, another discourse of the Soviet era—the happy life of orphans in the system of orphanages—was sacrificed. Although during the war years the situation in orphanages, as we saw, was especially bad, at that time family conditions were not often preferable for fostering children. This was the case if the adoptive parents were poor or did not receive sufficient assistance from the authorities. Sometimes this care took the form of an organizations' supervision over the adopted children in their new families. Patronage decisions were made at workers' assemblies or assemblies of military units.

According to official information, 2,500 children were adopted in Uzbekistan during the war.[89] Of these, about 47 percent were in Tashkent, and among the rest, families from kolkhozes prevailed.[90] In Andizhan and Samarkand, local families, both Uzbek and others, also took many orphans in their care—one or two at a time.[91] Children were adopted by representatives of different ethnic groups, and often by government officials; the adoption of orphans by Iulia, the Russian wife of Usman Iusupov, the first secretary of the Central Committee of the Communist Party of Uzbekistan, served as an example. The orphaned Genia Rabina was adopted by a Tajik family in a kolkhoz near Samarkand. She grew used to the family, and her aunt had to make a serious effort to take her from there. It is estimated that at least one hundred Jewish children were adopted by Tajik and Uzbek families.[92]

Some Uzbek families adopted refugee children to compensate for the loss of their own. Child mortality in Central Asia in these and subsequent years was the highest among the republics of the USSR. Sometimes there were abductions of children of refugees. Moshe Levertov describes how several Uzbeks from the aul near Samarkand captured a three-year-old Jewish boy and carried him to their home. The child was rescued.[93] I learned in 1991 about the successful abduction of a Jewish boy in Tashkent during the war from Anvar B., his Uzbek relative.

Jewish refugees also adopted children. The physician Ven'iamin Faibushevich adopted in Tashkent two orphans who arrived there from Ukraine.[94] Doctor Abram Korsunskii and his wife, living at that time in the Saratov region, adopted Asia and Viktor, whose parents, refugees from Lodz (Poland), died of hunger and disease.[95] In Kokand Il'ia and Vera Rovinskiis adopted a four-year-old Jewish girl, Irina.[96] In Alma-Ata the cashier of the Confectionary Factory Siderman took on a girl who unexpectedly rushed to her during a visit to an orphanage with the words: "Mama, where have you been for so long?"[97] In Chimkent, also in Kazakhstan, the family of Genia Belkovskaia adopted a Jewish boy from Poland, Boria; after the war his sister took him.[98] In Shemursha in the Chuvash ASSR, a refugee from Gomel, Basia Shafran—after her elder seven-year-old son died—took on the girl Maria Vinnik in 1942.[99] In Orsk, in the Chkalov region, another refugee from Gomel and a mother of two children, Raia Fradkina, after learning about the death of two women in Bukhara who left behind four children, went there and took them into her care.[100] The refugee Liza Bodinovskaia in Kuibyshev adopted an orphan from Leningrad, Nina.[101]

In February 1942 the women of the military garrison stationed in Frunze came up with the initiative of adoption. The families of six commanders adopted orphans.[102] The case of the family of the Osh gardener Imin-akhun Akhmedov and his wife Mairamkhana, who adopted a total of thirteen children, was a continuation of the Stakhanovite initiative of the Shamakhmudovs from Tashkent. Perhaps because there were no local journalists in Osh, this case was not widely publicized in the press. In total, 944 children were adopted in Kirgizstan.[103]

In Kazakhstan, the assembly of the female activists of Alma-Ata also appealed for the adoption of orphans. By the summer of 1942 the total of 507 children were adopted in Kazakhstan.[104] In Tajikistan in January 1942, a decision was made to eliminate "child neglect,"[105] although it is not known what was done in the framework of this campaign. A similar decision to assist children left without parents in order to eradicate homelessness was taken by authorities in Turkmenistan in March 1942. However, just the problem of children's homelessness and the lack of orphanages in 1942–1943 were not possible to solve there.[106]

In Russia, too, adoption was common. In its first nine months of the initiative, 4,500 children were adopted in Moscow.[107] By the end of the war, 565 children had been adopted in the Kuibyshev region and 197 in the Chuvash ASSR.[108] Altogether in the RSFSR by January 1943, according to official information, 13,922 children were adopted.[109] Even here, however, it was not possible to solve the problem of homelessness. In just the third quarter of 1944, about 4,000 homeless children were detained in the Kemerovo region.[110] In the first half of the same year, 686 were detained in Omsk.[111]

In some cases, the goals of adoption were to force the children into hard labor, coerce them to engage in theft or even prostitution. In situations like these, adolescents tried to escape from foster families or guardians. Edna Eizenstein was adopted by a Jewish woman named Enta. She forced Edna to work for her and did not let her go to school. When, on one occasion, the authorities gave sweets to Edna, the adoptive mother took them away. After the war, the girl was taken away by her brother and brought to Poland.[112] In two known cases in Uzbek and Turkmen kolkhozes, the goal of adoption of girls was to obtain a *kalym* (Turkic for "bride price") as a result of marrying her off later. In both of these cases, the girls were well kept and treated well. Despite this, during one of the holidays, the two sisters, from an Uzbek kolkhoz, fled the house where they were held. In the district center, they could not find their elder brother who was staying there, and they were taken into the orphanage for Polish children. According to the story of Mina Ben-Zion, her younger sister had a fever that evening, and she was placed in a local hospital. In the morning, when Mina came to visit her sister, she was told that her sister was dead, but none of her belongings were returned, nor was she told where she was buried. Years later, Mina continues to believe that her beautiful sister was abducted.[113]

In all, about twenty thousand children were adopted in the mentioned republics by 1943. Therefore, even taking into account the adoption of a certain number of children in the Transcaucasian republics (Armenia, Georgia, and Azerbaijan) and those adopted in the USSR in 1944–1945, the official information that by the end of the war 350,000 refugees and children who had lost their parents had been adopted was false.[114]

Meanwhile, the Uzbek poet Gafur Guliam, being touched by adoptions, in 1942 wrote the poem "You Are Not an Orphan," slightly altering the title of the above-mentioned *Pravda* article from earlier that year. I quote here a passage translated into Russian by Anna Akhmatova:

> Here you are at home. Here I guard your peace.
> Sleep, O piece of my soul, my little one! I am your father!
> Whatever you want, I shall give to you,
> My cares shall become my happiness . . .

Although the majority of orphans lost their families before the war or already as refugees during it, Gafur Guliam underscores the severity of orphaned children's experience of the executions, hinting at the Jewish origin of the poem's hero:

> Why did you tremble? Whence your fright?
> Perhaps the grief of Odessa has come in a flood?
> Or the tragedy of Kerch? And in a child's mind
> Rushed, rumbling in the blazing darkness,
> Bloodthirsty barbarians, those who, while destroying
> All living things almost killed you!

Like another Guliam poem, "I Am a Jew" (1941), the poem about the orphan made a strong impression in Uzbekistan on the local and visiting intelligentsia. As for the central authorities, because of the growing accusations of pandering to Jews, which we will address below, their reception of the poem "You Are Not an Orphan" was very restrained.

The state adoption campaign only slightly improved the situation of homelessness and neglected children. Many of them continued to engage in petty theft and sometimes robbery. Therefore, the authorities resorted to punitive measures. On June 15, 1943, the Council of People's Commissars of the USSR issued a decision—"On Strengthening the Struggle against Child Homelessness, Neglect, and Hooliganism"—prescribing the establishment of juvenile correctional labor colonies even for children aged eleven to fourteen years old, living for long periods without parents and detained for theft and hooliganism, and violators of discipline in orphanages.[115] The directors of the factories where there was a shortage of workers greeted this decision with enthusiasm. The director of the evacuated defense plant no. 188, V. K. L'vov, suggested that the Novosibirsk Regional Party Committee organize such a labor colony at his plant. To house the children, he found five abandoned barracks.[116]

Jewish Children in Orphanages

As was already mentioned, in the eastern regions of the Soviet Union there were entire pioneer camps and kindergartens on summer vacation that were urgently removed from territories under threat of occupation. There were many Jews among their children.[117] In particular, children from Minsk arrived in the Chuvash ASSR and the Kuibyshev region. The Minsk nurseries no. 19 and no. 41, the kindergarten no. 15 from Orsha, and the Białystok sanitarium camp ended up there.[118] Many of these evacuated children's institutions found themselves in the Mordovian ASSR: 560 in the Ichalki district and 220 in the Atiashevo district. The Ardatov district of the same ASSR housed 154 such children from Brest, 50 from Baranovichi, and some number from the orphanage in Orsha.[119] Children and institutions also arrived from other places—from Narva (Estonia), Bobruisk (Belorussia), and Druskininkai (Lithuania).[120] However, according to numerous sources, a large number of such children remained in the occupied territory since the parents and relatives of many of them have never been found.[121]

In addition, Jewish children whose parents were killed during the bombings of trains that took the population to the east often ended up in orphanages, as did Jewish children who were separated from their families either during the same bombings or because of the sudden departure of the train after a long stopover.[122] In some cases, Jewish children were lost and then found in orphanages, due to the fact that the war began in the summer when many of them were staying with relatives in the western Soviet republics without parents.[123]

The available statistics on the Chuvash ASSR confirm that a large proportion of Jews in some orphanages resulted mainly from the arrival of pioneer houses and summer camps from the western regions in 1941. However, the later arrival of Jewish children to orphanages cannot be ruled out entirely.

Children who came from the western regions of the USSR arrived at orphanages often without documents, and therefore their nationality was recorded from their own words, or they were registered as Russian, "to make it easier to live." Older children could hide their Jewishness, fearing antisemitism, and the younger children did not always know their ethnicity. By October 1941 in the Chuvash ASSR, among the 343 evacuated children under the age of sixteen without parents, the percentage of children under seven was 52.5 percent.[125] Their share changed by the beginning of 1942 when young children accounted for 44.3 percent of the 458 children who arrived without parents.[126] Therefore, it can be assumed that the actual share of Jews in orphanages was at least several percentage points higher.

Table 3. Orphanages in the Chuvash ASSR with a large proportion of Jews, September 19, 1941[124]

Location of the Orphanage	Total number of children	Number of Jews	Percentage of Jews
Alatyr'	285	71	24.9
Ibresi district	166	32	13.7
Kalinino district	83	26	43.4
Pervomaiskoe district	95	68	71.6
Poretskoe district	239	68	28.5
Sovetskoe district	165	24	14.6
Chkalovskoe district	50	29	58
Shumerlia	109	37	34
Ial'chiki district	218	50	22.9
For all orphanages (including those not listed here)	5,578	524	9.4

Some Jewish children avoided orphanages. The twelve-year-old Shura Budman, who was one of such children in Tashkent, told the commission attempting to place him in an orphanage: "Do you not see, I work . . . I live with good people . . . I sleep under the table, nobody bothers me, I do not bother anyone—I only need shoes." Working as an assistant in a studio, he earned 105 rubles. The commission found for him only girls shoes with rubber soles and some coupons for dinners. Six months later the Uzbek public commission sent him to Novosibirsk, where his mother finally found him.[127]

A Jewish child in the evacuation was often under more severe pressure than an adult. There was less open antisemitism in the workplace than in the school, because schoolchildren were not as heavily constrained by the rules of social behavior as adults. Children had to go to school every day, where they often faced more antisemitism than they had experienced in their prewar school. It was difficult to change schools, but in rural areas it was impossible. However, it was many times harder for Jewish children in orphanages. Mockeries were mixed with feelings of loss of loved ones, loneliness, lack of emotional attachments, and anxiety for their future. Unlike children living at home, they could not "rest" from antisemitism after school. Even leaving the orphanage premises was prohibited. In Tashkent, only on Sundays adolescents were released until nine in the evening.[128] Children suffered especially from antisemitism in new joint and old local orphanages, where Jews were often few. Dov Dunaevskii and Alter Zaidman testify about how they were beaten and called names in Tashkent because they were Jews.[129]

Because of antisemitism, some of the children tried to hide their Jewishness. Ten-year-old Semën Vaksman learned in an orphanage in Uzbekistan that it was a shameful thing to be weak and to be a Jew. He internalized this so deeply that he could not part with his antisemitism even after his father took him from the orphanage in 1944.[130] Dov Dunaevskii also tried to hide his nationality.[131] For many children, this was impossible because of their appearance, visiting relatives, Jewish names, and the fact that Russian was not the native language for some of them. Some of the children sought to preserve their Jewish names, not without reason, hoping that their relatives would find them. Some children tried not to forget Yiddish because they considered it an important element of their Jewish self-identification. This was dangerous. Lev Levin, when he was in the village of Borodaevka in the Saratov region, accidentally betrayed his Jewishness with his knowledge of Yiddish, for which he was often beaten, usually at night.[132] One of the refugee, unable to withstand antisemitic persecution and beatings in old local orphanages, fled to a Polish orphanage.[133]

However, in Polish orphanages antisemitism was not uncommon. Many of those who spent time there testified that they were beaten, mocked, and mistreated in every possible way.[134] As Ruth Cohen attests, Jewish children were deprived of food and clothing in Polish orphanages.[135] According to other testimonies, Jewish children were given smaller portions of food compared to Catholics, an injustice that children were especially acutely aware of.[136] One of the manifestations of the negative attitude of Polish education authorities in the USSR was the removal of many Jews during the evacuation of Polish orphanages with the Polish army of Anders to Iran in 1942.[137] Many of the former residents of these orphanages remember bitterly ethnic separation that took place bore the departure for Iran. Leia Lerer spoke with gratitude about an unknown Polish captain, who during this process said that she was his daughter and not Jewish at all.[138] In some orphanages relations among children of different nationalities, include Jewish children, were normal, which hinged on the position of the educators and management.[139] Yaffa Iras, Joseph Barten, and Fraida Celnikier testify that while the Polish children mocked them, the teachers defended them.[140]

Starved and struggling for survival, orphan children often started on the path of crime. As Dov Dunaevskii writes in his memoirs, their Tashkent orphanage was an incubator for criminals.[141] Indeed, Semën Vaksman, who spent several years there or in another orphanage in Uzbekistan, by the age of fourteen so firmly adopted the criminal model of thinking that his parents, having found him, could not set him straight, and after the war he associated with criminals and along them was sent to prison, where he died.[142]

After the start of the German invasion, more than a hundred thousand children left for the east with their orphanages or pioneer camps. Tens of thousands of refugee children found themselves in orphanages after losing one or both of their parents while fleeing or upon arrival to the east. The situation in Soviet orphanages before the war was already inadequate, and during the war it deteriorated even further. Due to shortage of trained personnel, orphanages were often headed by administrators who had no pedagogical experience and were corrupt. Hunger and a severe scarcity of all goods in orphanages led to theft. It was especially difficult for Jewish children in orphanages. They suffered from antisemitism of both staff and peers. The children were starving and sick. Many of them had resort to theft to get something to eat. Violence was widespread among children. To supplement the orphanages' budget, it was common to send children as young as twelve years of age to work, most often in factories and collective farms. Children worked there for long hours and were sometimes seriously injured. The central authorities, understanding the bad situation in orphanages, launched an adoption campaign.

In the next chapter, we will see how the local residents met the refugee families.

CHAPTER SIX

Culture Clashes

The Predominance of Hostility

Despite some successes of refugees in farming and, in general, in adaptation to a new place, including joint work with local residents, study, living, mastering new traditions and rules, this did not always lead to a rapprochement. The presence among the refugees of a large number of better educated and better dressed Leningraders, Muscovites, natives of the western regions of the USSR, and also former Polish citizens irritated the local population. It was a meeting of the rich, by Soviet standards, of the West and the poor of the East. Siberia, Kazakhstan, and to some extent the Urals were the traditional places of exile in the Russian Empire and then in the USSR. In the Stalin era expulsions and deportations were often preceded by confiscation of property. Moreover, in comparison with the European part of the USSR, its Asian part was more poorly supplied with goods that did not constitute a basket of "essential goods," and one needn't even speak of the sale of luxury goods.

Rachel Glikman was strongly impressed by how the local women of fashion in a Siberian town literally snatched the beautiful Polish dresses she was selling to support herself.[1] In the village of Tokushi (northern Kazakhstan), a Jewish refugee from Lida exchanged her prewar winter coat and a few other items of clothing with a young local Ukrainian woman for an entire house.[2] Sergei Ermolinskii, whom we have already encountered, was surprised at the vitality of the bazaar in provincial Kazakhstan after the arrival of the refugees: "What could you not find in Chili: crepe de chine, fashionable shoes, antique veils, exceptional underwear, razors, portraits of Kachalov, and various seductive trinkets. At first, the collective farmers were especially fond of these unprecedented miracles. The goods [meaning food brought with the intent of exchanging it for these things] were brought personally by kolkhoz kings, chairs, noble brigadiers, wealthy socialists."[3] Further, Ermolinskii describes the decisive role that chocolate truffles, which they had never tried, played during his exchange with local boys.⁴

In general, in the situation of a total deficit of food and other goods, the bazaar (or market) occupied an important place both in the life of refugees and local residents of towns and villages. Expansion of market trade during the war made it possible for the latter to buy inexpensively the personal belongings of refugees: jewelry, watches, cameras, elegant utensils, sheets, clothes, underwear, and so on. In the USSR many of these items, especially in the provinces, had long been difficult or even impossible to buy. However, by no means all locals could offer money or food in exchange for these goods. Food manufacturers, town dealers (speculators in Soviet terminology), and well-paid officials were the ones who were able to participate in such exchanges. By the way, the bazaar served not only as a place of purchase and sale but also as the largest information and social center. In addition to exchanging news and rumors, here people sought out acquaintances in order to learn something about their relatives.

Among adult refugees the majority were women between sixteen and fifty-five years of age, as many men of the same age were in the army and many older women and men did not dare to evacuate. Since the conscription of men from the frontline regions was more complete than that of men from the eastern regions, where they were needed by the authorities to maintain the previous industrial production and agriculture,⁵ many of the refugees quickly became widows. This and their economic need gave local men, including family men, the hope of intimate relations. With better manners and behavior, refugees were more attractive than local women. Therefore, and especially given the prevailing deficit of men, the presence of refugees could not but irritate the local women. This irritation found an outlet in a bad attitude toward all refugees and the spreading of unflattering rumors about them.

Without trying to understand their circumstances, the local residents were negative about the unwillingness of some refugees to work in the kolkhoz. A local resident of Shadrinsk (Cheliabinsk region) wrote in September 1941 in his diary about his lodgers: "Lidia Andreevna and Nadezhda Alekseevna went to the town council this morning, or rather to the town agricultural council, where they showed certificates about their illnesses and refused to go to the kolkhoz to work. This caused an energetic remark from the head of the town agricultural council, A. G.: 'It's amazing how all these evacuated people are all sick and do not want to work in the kolkhozes!' What do they care about work, the evacuees, especially the Muscovites? In the queues they say that some evacuees brought a lot of money with them."⁶

The negative perception of refugees was also greatly affected by the general decline in the standard of living in the eastern regions of the USSR, which was due to food shortages and the growth of queues. The arrival in 1941–1942 of a large wave of refugees, although it lowered the prices of clothes and other goods, led to a significant rise in the cost of food, to the joy of the collective farmers and the discontent of local townspeople. Expressing his displeasure with this, the chair of the city executive committee of Kurgan, Gevenov, connected the price increase in the city of more than ten times with the arrival of refugees.[7] In Sterlitomak locals openly told the refugees, "We do not need you, go back where you came from, because of you everything became expensive."[8]

Marina Potëmkina, a researcher of the Ural regions, writes that the locals were irritated by the arrogant attitude of the arriving population who referred to them as provincials.[9] It is true that some of the refugees looked down on the local population; however, it is difficult to believe that this outlook was very widespread, since the former were so much dependent on the latter. In any case, the archival materials I have examined for this study do not contain complaints to the authorities about this behavior of refugees, even if quarrels between them and the owners of apartments were frequent. However, in the memoirs and diaries of refugees, the backwardness of the local population of Siberia and the Urals and the indigenous people of Central Asia is sometimes mentioned. Incidentally, the early migrants from Eastern Europe who had lived there since prerevolutionary times also considered the indigenous Central Asians as backward. Refugees, for example, were bewildered by polygamy and early marriages in Kazakh kolkhozes.[10] David Azrieli was shocked by the fact that a girl's life seemed to hold less value than a horse in the eyes of the Uzbek collective farmers. He learned this when the collective farmers became very angry over the fact that he almost drove a horse to death saving the life of an Uzbek girl.[11] Even in these cases, though, there are no hints of arrogance; on the contrary, all the authors talk about their attempts to establish contacts with the local population, adhere to local rules, and in some cases learn the local language or dialect.

The desire to assimilate local behavioral norms did not come immediately, and it did not come to everyone. Anatole Konstantin tells of the killing of a large grass snake by one refugee, which he mistook for a poisonous snake. The local Kazakhs, upon learning about this, were very upset—they considered the killing of harmless snakes a bad sign. They buried the snake and began to treat all refugees worse.[12] In general, the arrival of a large number of strangers was perceived as a threat to the existing habitual way of life. Therefore, the local population, especially relatively ethnically homogeneous populations, tried to protect their world from the aliens, ignoring the agitational efforts of the central authorities to unite different population groups in the rear. These efforts, widely reflected in the Soviet press of those years, influenced the studies of many

Soviet and post-Soviet researcher, like Potëmkina. Adhering to the concept of brotherly mutual assistance of the Soviet peoples during the war years, modeled on the official historiography and the media, and following regional patriotism, she asserts that "in most cases evacuees were perceived by the residents of the rear areas as people in trouble and need of help."[13]

Another opinion was held by the representative of the Evacuation Council in the Alatyr' district of Chuvashia, Kizilov. In his memo of January 1942, he wrote: "There is growing discontent between the evacuees and non-evacuees. Some of the evacuees have morbid moods because of their material insecurity, which adversely affects those around them."[14] Rebecca Manley, who studied the situation in Tashkent, gives examples of good relations, but on the whole she believes that the relations between refugees and the local population were tense.[15]

The position of the local population toward refugees is difficult to assess objectively because it's located in the sphere of human relations, which is difficult for statistical research and often ambivalent and not fitting into simple logical models. In any case, when analyzing sources, priority should be given not to ostentatious public statements of wartime but to reports made by evacuation officials for their departments. However, such reports are also not free from subjectivity because when reporting on the poor situation of evacuees, the officials actually wrote about missteps in the areas for which they themselves were responsible, and therefore such reports should be analyzed and compared with other types of sources.

In this regard, particular attention should be paid to the results given by Potëmkina herself, an inspection carried out in Votkinsk (Udmurt ASSR) in the winter of 1941–1942. She showed that about 60 percent of evacuees' families housed in private homes experienced unfriendly relationships with the homeowners.[16] This percentage, as it seems to me on the basis of many other reports and testimonies, very closely reflects the ratio of hostile to friendly or neutral relations of local residents to refugees.

Indeed, regardless of nationality, refugees were perceived most often as alien outsiders. T. V. Mishina wrote in 1942 from Chkalov region to a relative: "A complete ugliness is in the Department for Evacuation. The population is benighted; they look at us like dogs. They put us in a room where there are only rats and mice; there is no stove. And the floors are as dirty as the ground. We sleep on the floor. We wanted to wash [them], but there are no rags and no buckets. The people are harmful."[17] An employee of the Molotov Kolkhoz in the Sakmara district of the same region refused to give milk to a sick child, despite the orders of the authorities to do so.[18] I. Massol wrote from Pervouralsk to a relative: "Ellochka, get us out of here, we've run out of strength. You've probably seen the movie *Prisoners* [1936]—we look just like them, a precise copy. They don't consider us human."¹⁹ A. F. Pavlova wrote from Erevan: "I feel here that I am not in a Soviet country, but somewhere abroad, in a capitalist country. They look at us not as if we were evacuated away from the beastly Nazis, but as refugees who flee not knowing from what. People here lack awareness and do not feel the position of the Soviet people."²⁰

In many places refugees were perceived negatively from the very moment of their arrival, and therefore attempts on the part of the arriving refugees themselves to explain their nasty reception are inconclusive. Mikhail Mishnaev remembers what he had seen in one of the villages of the Krasnodar territory: "A huge number of evacuees have accumulated here in Slavinskaia. I remember an old man walking with a dead child in his arms, crying . . . These unfortunate refugees were mercilessly plundered by the locals who took their possessions; a piece of bread cost an arm and a leg."²¹

In the Volga area, which had a very high concentration of non-Russians, ethnic Russian refugees were often poorly treated. In 1942, an evacuated Russian boy was tormented in the Mari village, and in another village a Tatar would not give water to a female Russian worker in the field, stating, "I would rather die than give a Russian to drink."²² In the Krasno-Oktiabrskii district of the Gor'kii region, according to the prosecutor's report, the local Tatar population was also hostile to Russian refugees who had arrived there. In the village of Krasnyi Ostrov, even the chair of the village council answered numerous requests for help from refugees thusly: "Uruss ["Russian," in Tatar] refugee, why did you run away, you are a burden to us."²³

The poor attitude toward the refugees was manifested everywhere, including the Chuvash ASSR, for which plentiful evidence exists. In the Tsivil'sk district of the republic refugees and local residents, according to the survey of the labor inspector of the evacuated population Maria Shapiro, clearly distinguished between each other using the pronouns "we" and "they." The refugees said, "We cannot live with them; they hate us; they want to get rid of us as soon as possible; they laugh at us when we work."²⁴ According to the chair of the executive committee of the Krasnye Chetai district of the same republic, I. Nikitin, the chairs of the kolkhozes Krasnyi Maiak (the Red Beacon), Krasnaia Zvezda (the Red Star), Krasnye Togonashi, Bud' Gotov (Be Prepared!), Stal' (Steel), and the Budenny Kolkhoz in his district scoffed at the evacuees, considering them "some sort of strangers." He went on to describe how they were particularly rude to refugees—they did not give them jobs and did not arrange nursery placements for the children, the refugees were expelled from their homes and their children were beaten²⁵(we will see other examples below). When in the village of Bol'shoe Shigaevo (Chuvashia) wanted to hire the refugee Zhurakhova, the secretary of the village council Morozova said,

"We cannot entrust this work to her, she will assign [extra] workdays to the *mairas* ["non-Chuvash women" in Chuvash language]."[26]

In July 1942 thirty collective farmers of Kolkhoz Dvigatel' Revoliutsii (the Engine of Revolution) refused to deliver the exhausted Leningrad blockage evacuees from the Kanash railway station to various locations around the area.[27] In the village of Trekh-Boltaevo of the Shemursha district, in the same year, children threw sand at the refugees. In the same place, the children threw sand in a bucket of soup that the refugee Konoplianskaia was carrying home.[28] In Kolkhoz Krasnaia Zvezda of the Shumerlia district, the saleswoman Abramova regularly cheated the refugees while issuing groceries. She also at one point closed the store for ten days and left for Cheboksary; as a result, the refugees went hungry for that entire time.[29] In Kolkhoz 13 Let Oktiabria (Thirteen Years of October Revolution) the farmers mocked and laughed at the refugees, whom the kolkhoz chair sent to pull the straw from the mud with their bare hands.[30] In the village of Novo-Larionovo, according to the report of the evacuation inspector, Kirilova, the house's owner, spoke to the tenant Anna Bezrukova and her family, "Why'd you have to come here? They should have killed you all there."[31] According to Liudmila Gavrilova, in a Chuvash kolkhoz where they stayed during the war, the attitude toward the refugees was hostile.[32]

A seller who ran a state stall in the village of Bol'shoe Shigaevo, Kuznetsov, deliberately delayed the issuance to the refugees of ration cards for flour, matches, soap, and salt. He took for himself the sheepskin coat intended for the evacuees at his stall. He replied to the complaints of the refugees, "Complain even to the prosecutor himself, I still will not be punished, I am the chair of the Audit Commission, and the prosecutor is my relative." The sympathy for the refugees exhibited by the agronomist Ofitserov aroused the irritation of Kuznetsov and the accountant Mironov, who told him that he was reporting the workdays of the evacuees in vain because they would cut them short anyway. Behind his back, they accused the agronomist of bad management and told the collective farmers that the kolkhoz did not need him.[33] In general, kolkhoz management itself often manipulated the workday records, which was clearly confirmed by Nikolai Zhukov in December 1941 in his memorandum on the situation of evacuees in the Mariinskii Posad district of the same republic.[34]

Refugees often met a negative attitude toward themselves in Central Asia as well. At the state farm of the village of Fëdorovo in the Kustanai region of Kazakhstan, refugees were not even sold eggs and dairy products, although they fed cottage cheese to pigs and chickens. The workers of the farm refused to share their utensils with the refugees.[35] According to the information on the arrival and arrangement of evacuees in Kazakhstan dated September 5, 1941, members of the Lenin Kolkhoz of the same district received the refugees in an unfriendly manner, seeing them as spongers.³⁶ Anatole Konstantin, who was in the Kazakh aul at the same time, noted that traditional eastern hospitality did not apply to refugees, and only one Uzbek family living there shod sympathy for him and his mother.³⁷

One of the manifestations of the negative attitude toward the refugees was the beating of their children, which was very common throughout the eastern regions of the USSR. In the Chuvash ASSR, in the village of Buinsk of the Urmary district, local children, and sometimes even adults, threw sticks and stones at the children of the evacuees (among them the overwhelming majority were ethnic Russian). The chair of the Izhekei Regional Council of the same republic urged local adolescents to throw sticks and stones even at adult evacuated Russian women who expressed dissatisfaction with his attitude at a meeting. The foreman of Kolkhoz KIM (Young Communist International) of the Kubasy Village Soviet, Longin Dement'ev, himself beat up evacuated women, for which he was convicted.³⁸

In Kirov a xenophobic attitude toward the arriving Muscovites and Leningraders was also passed on to the children. Izolda Ivanova recalls how after school, local boys ambushed them and shouted, "Beat the evacuees!" pelting them with snowballs.³⁹ In Uzbekistan the reaction of the local children to the negative perception of refugees by adults was more pronounced. Lidia Chukoskaia, describing in her diary the evacuation along with Anna Akhmatova to Central Asia, made the following entry: "I pushed Anna Andeevna away from the window—the Uzbek boys were throwing stones at our train, shouting 'Here's a bombing!' A stone hit the wall of the car. We were somewhere very near Tashkent."⁴⁰ This record was made in November 1941, when hunger felt yet little in Uzbekistan. The theme of the beating of evacuated children by local schoolchildren in the village of Malaia Tomylovka in the Kuibyshev region⁴¹ was called upon in the report of the director of the Governance of Evacuation of the Council of People's Commissars of the USSR, Konstantin Pamfilov, to draw the attention of the republican and regional leaders to this phenomenon and emphasize the need to actively engage in ideological work in the system of public education.

In Central Asia cruel treatment of refugees was especially evident if one of them was caught stealing fruits and vegetables from private gardens. Not infrequently, one so discovered was brutally beaten. In Stalinabad Anatolii Tiktiner, along with friends, stole eggplants from Tajiks' gardens. When he was caught, he was flogged with a camel thorn, so that almost all the skin on his back was ripped off. According to his recollection, he barely survived.⁴² An extraordinary case occurred in 1943 in Tashkent, where a ten-year-old Russian boy from an orphanage was caught, raped, and then killed. This murder caused serious frictions between the Uzbeks and the teenagers of the orphanage, who tried to avenge their friend.[43] Similarly, dramatic events occurred in the same year in Samarkand. Several cadets of a pilot school, caught pilfering cherries, were beaten with sticks by the owners, which led to a fight; other cadets came running to the fight, and residents of the neighborhood joined in on the other side. The authorities sent an armed detachment of the NKGB to suppress the fighting. The unarmed cadets, in response to the shooting, threw stones. During the encounter, two cadets and a soldier were killed.[44]

By the 1970s, several theories about the origins of theft circulated in Uzbekistan. The theft was allegedly brought there by migrants from the starving Volga area in the 1920s, refugees during the war of 1941–1945, or visiting workers restoring Tashkent after the earthquake in 1966. It is difficult to say whether any of these are correct and, if so, to what extent. In any case, theft was encountered in the Bukhara Emirate before Russia conquered it, and during World War II, it was also not considered blameworthy on the part of some Muslim teenagers (and sometimes even adults) to take away food, shoes, and clothing from a refugee, especially a teenage refugee. In Samarkand two Uzbek teenagers attacked the thirteen-year-old Moshe Levertov, beat him, and then took from his pocket ninety rubles and fled. Similar events took place in other cities of Central Asia.[45]

Refugees faced a negative or indifferent attitude in the local academic environment. The evaluated Odessan historian Saul Borovoi in 1942 complained in a letter to Vladimir Picheta about the indifferent attitude toward his everyday problems on the part of his local colleagues in the Samarkand Pedagogical Institute.[46] From the letter, one gets the sense that the author chose cautious expressions and did not want to overload the famous professor with his problems.

As shown by the secret report of the RSFSR Prosecutor's Office for April 1942, a sufficient number of facts indicating a disparaging attitude toward the medical and sanitary services for refugees were recorded in a number of districts of the Ordzhonikidze territory, the North Ossetian ASSR, and in the Novosibirsk region and some other regions.[47] According to the report of the deputy regional prosecutor for December 1941 for the Chkalov region, the only nurse in the Sakmara district treated the refugees very rudely and did not provide them with any medical assistance.[48] When in January 1942 four elderly refugees with frostbitten legs arrived in the Tatarsk district of the Novosibirsk region unable to move without help, they were denied, despite insistent requests, medical assistance.[49] In the village of Kumashki (Chuvashia), Terent'eva, a midwife, refused to accept a birthing refugee, arguing that her maternity home was not for the evacuees and that the woman should go to the city. As a result, the refugee gave birth on the way there. Terent'eva's position found sympathy even among mid-level administrators. The regional Medical Union of the Shumerlia district punished Terent'eva with only a reprimand, while the executive committee did not punish her at all.[50] The issue was dealt with otherwise in Kabardino-Balkaria. In the Leksinskii district of this autonomous republic, for failure to come to the aid of a woman in labor, the midwife Knaeva was punished with a year of correctional labor.[51]

The situation was aggravated by the fact that, as we saw above, the authorities forced the local residents to crowd together and "make room," and certificates for the resulting "surplus" housing were issued to refugees who were supposed to live there, paying the owners a standardized price. On August 7, 1941, the Bashkir Regional Committee of the Communist Party reported that in the village of Teroshlia (Sterlitamak district) and the kolkhoz with the symbolic name Dobroe Nachalo (A Good Start; Ulu-Teliak district), "there were isolated cases of collective farmers' refusal to provide apartments to evacuees."[52] Khanin's report also noted that in Sterlitamak, "a significant part of the householders show a clearly mocking attitude toward the evacuees who live with them. They apply any measures to evict them from the apartments, stopping at nothing. They bring livestock into living rooms, deprive them of the opportunity to use the stove (even when they provide the owner with fuel). They forbid them to pass through the common room, they don't open the doors to the evacuees returning from work and . . . in the tenants' absence they throw their things out on the street, they even erase them from the house registration book in absentia."[53] The owner of an apartment in Sterlitamak told the refugees, "Go away, I don't need you, get the hell back to your Odessa."[54] According to the report of the evacuation department of the Council of People's Commissars of the RSFSR in the same city, in order to drive out a family of refugees, they put a goat into their room and put their things in front of the entrance, saying "by tomorrow, you'd better not be here."[55]

A resident of the Dubovyi Umët district in the Kuibyshev region, with the purpose of evicting the refugee Iurevich and his three children from the apartment, washed the floor with urine and forced her tenants to sleep only on the floor. A sheep was also placed in the house. The hostess put a dead crow or felt boots for drying on the food of the evacuated family.[56] Similar methods were also used by some householders in the Tatar, Mari, and Kabardino-Balkar ASSRs, and the Penza, Cheliabinsk, Chkalov, and other regions.[57]

In the Stalin Kolkhoz in the Samarskoe district of Kazakhstan, some homeowners did not allow the refugees to use the stove for cooking.[58] Although the official who reported this to the regional committee pointed out that almost all the refugees in the kolkhoz were Jews, yet there are not sufficient grounds for considering this case, and the cases below, as manifestations of antisemitism.

The Goldshtein family was kicked out of the house they resided in Rembaza, in the Prokhladnyi district of Kabardino-Balkaria.[59] In the Novosibirsk region the housewife Leshchova, who wanted to evict refugees, took the window frames and the stove dampers out of their room.[60] According to the evacuation department of the Council of People's Commissars of the RSFSR, in Karagai (Molotov region), Karagaeva, the mistress of the house, wishing to evict refugees, deliberately did not start the fire in the winter, and if she did start it, she opened the door to the street. At the same time, she forced the refugee Kamenskaia's son to walk barefoot in the house, "so as not to spoil the floor," as a result of which the boy fell ill and died.[61] In the Gvardeiskoe (Kuibyshev region), a landlord, in the absence of their parents, drove the children of the evacuated Kremenkova into the street when it was thirty degrees below zero.[62]

Many examples of bullying are contained in the more accessible archives of the Chuvash ASSR. In the Vurnary and Kanash districts evacuation inspectors recorded several cases of the destruction of stoves in houses where refugees lived by the houses' owners.[63] The Muliar family of refugees from Moscow living in Cheboksary was forbidden by their landlords to use the stove, even for heating water and food.[64] In the village of Bol'shoe Shigaevo, the owner of the house did not allow the refugee Shapiro, who was living with her, to use the stove for cooking. As a result, according to the evacuation inspector Nikitina, the refugee went around the village asking everyone to let her bake potatoes. In the village of Ichikisy, the local population would not loan the refugees dishes, buckets, and irons even temporarily.[65] As a result, refugees lived in unsanitary conditions and often suffered from lice. In the village of Zavodskaia, also in the Chuvash ASSR, the owner Vasina, despite having a five-walled house (a house divided in half by a bearing wall), while preparing for Easter, expelled the refugee Ivanova and her son, who had settled with her, to live in the kitchen where a calf lived.[66]

In the same republic, a woman of the house also treated poorly the wife and young son (they rented only corner of two square meters) of Lev Maizel, a quartermaster in the army. Attempts by the refugee to obtain something from the authorities were not successful, and only her husband's letter to the Moscow City Council led to the receiving alternative housing.[67] According to the report of Rudolf Latsis, the accountant of the military registration and enlistment office, Dem'ianov, broke the door to the room of the refugee Sara Blium who had lodged with him under the order of the local authorities and threw out her things into the street, for which he did not bear any punishment. According to the same Latsis report, in the village of Chkalovo, a refugee from Latvia, Khava Irs, had to give birth on the street in negative forty-degree weather, because no one wanted to let her into the house. After returning home from the hospital, due to the lack of a bed, she had to sleep with the child on the floor, as a result of which the child fell ill.[68] In the village of Nizhnie Kumashki, due to the fact that she was also forced by out of the house by the owners in wintertime, the refugee Bukhanova gave birth to a child in a stable.[69] In the village of Pikhtulino, in the Cheboksary district, Anastasiia Danilova tossed Fruma Belinson and her four children out on the street.[70]

At first glance, these instances of a negative attitude correlate poorly with reliable information from the report of A. Somov, head of the Chuvash ASSR, to Aleksandr Pekshev, deputy chair of the Council of People's Commissars of the RSFSR, that the collective farmers of the Shikhazy district of this republic collected 149 poods of bread, 3,000 poods potatoes, 720 poods of vegetables, 139 kilograms of wool for felt boots, and so on.[71] In reality, such duties were imposed on the collective farmers by the administration. They were perceived as an additional tax and caused even greater hostility toward refugees because the economic situation of the collective farmers left much to be desired.

The reaction of refugees to the hostile attitude of the local population was similar to the attitude of local administrators. This is evidenced by letters preserved in the archives of the NKVD military censorship department of letters. In one of them A. Feonova of Molotov wrote in 1942 to the front: "The people here do not like the evacuees; we are like beasts to them. Instead of helping us, they try at every step to harm us. One ought to take such people and hang them along with Hitler. Then the front would benefit more."[72] In the same year, Romanchuk wrote to a relative on the front from the Riazan' region: "The people here are not kind, they are difficult. They look at us evacuees like beasts. They hate us very much and are even overjoyed when we are hungry. They say, that's enough out of you, you ate your sausages, you'll live now without."[73] Another woman, Selina, wrote from the same Riazan' region: "Here we are not even allowed into the barn to get out of the rain. We live under a bush. We have no bread; I walk, I beg, but no one gives us any. . . . We steal carrots for the child, he is alive, barely; what to do, where to get something? It's very difficult. I think perhaps we shall die soon. Vania, it's terrible to look at my child, how he suffers."[74]

A native of the L'vov region, Adam R., testified right after the war: "The attitude of the local population (Uzbeks) was very hostile. They did not make any distinction between us [the Poles] and the Russians."[75] Obviously, he believed that the attitude of Muslims toward the colonizing Russians in Central Asia should have been worse. Another Pole, also a native of the L'vov region, Mechislav S., attested to the brutal attitude toward his family on the part of the Uzbek population.[76] In one way or another, to the Muslim population as a whole, all refugees were, to varying degrees, unwanted aliens. Ania Makabi-Yoresh, who moved with her family in 1945 from the Volga area to Tashkent, noted with surprise that the Uzbeks look with hatred at the evacuees and were waiting with impatience for them to get out.[77] We shall become acquainted with other examples of xenophobia in Central Asia in the next chapter.

On the other hand, there was often a tolerant or even warm attitude toward refugees among the locals, examples of which will be seen below. To some extent, propaganda about assistance to the evacuees played a positive role in this. In addition to compassion for the problems of refugees, some local residents positively assessed the arrival of writers, artists, and also qualified doctors, teachers, and artisans. Local media often drew the readers' attention to the improvement of their cultural and consumer services as a result of the arrival of the evacuated population.

"The Jews should have been abandoned to Hitler": Antisemitism in the Rear

Attitudes toward Jews were often worse than the general attitude toward refugees. For the Slavic and other populations of the eastern regions of the USSR, they were even more alien by tradition and mentality than most other refugees. Although, according to the 1939 census, 55 percent of Jews of eastern Belorussia still considered Yiddish their mother tongue, many of them spoke Russian well or passable.[78] Most often they did not have a language barrier, but in the Russian outback, a specific pronunciation made itself felt.

Although most residents of the eastern regions had never seen Jews, through rumors the population was deeply infected with prejudices that are correctly classified as *primitive antisemitism* rather than nebulous *domestic antisemitism*. In remote places these prejudices sometimes assumed extremely exaggerated forms. Aleksandr Shakhmeister remembers: "The town of Ochër is a small town in the north of the Urals. Before us, they had never seen any Jews. The drivers of the carts that drove our family said they were told that the Jews were not people, but monsters with horns on their heads and big fangs in their mouths. Imagine their surprise when they met us: 'Look,' they shouted to each other, struggling to cope with the shock of recognition, 'they are quite like us! Ordinary people!'"[79] In the Russian kolkhoz village of Kuzhnur in the Mari ASSR, the girl Khana Davidson was shocked by the local children when, after her affirmative answer to the question "Are you Jewish?" she was asked to show her tail and horns, and then they unceremoniously began to feel her head.[80] Many other refugees speak in interviews and memoirs of different versions of such prejudices.

More sophisticated prewar antisemitism included two main charges. Some accused the Jews of being disloyal to the USSR and lacking patriotism, while others accused them of broad participation in the institutions of power and shifted responsibility for all the failures of domestic politics to them. Although the use of either of these two charges was determined by a different attitude to Soviet power, there were many individuals who operated on both accusations. Due to the difficult situation in which the USSR found itself at the beginning of the war, these accusations even intensified. The first group began to blame the Jews for not fighting a common enemy, but "hiding in Tashkent." For this pseudo-patriotic accusation they were not usually punished. The second group hoped that, after the conquest, the Germans would crack down on the Jews, who were allegedly guilty of collectivization, famine, repression, and the crusade against the church. Behind these accusations was a poorly hidden critique of the Soviet system.[81] Such accusations were widespread throughout the territory of the USSR, albeit unevenly. Joon Seo Song suggests that there was much less antisemitism in Siberia than in Ukraine due to the lack of antisemitic tradition there.[82] One could agree with this statement if described the prerevolutionary situation only. In wartime Siberia, however, after millions of refugees and deportees arrived there—even earlier dispossessed and also repressed "socially hostile elements"—as well as laborers arriving to work, these two types of antisemitic accusations already had a wide circulation.

Even though it is sometimes difficult to distinguish antisemitism from widespread xenophobia in the USSR, there are pieces of evidence that point to the presence of antisemitic underpinnings in many incidents. In one of the villages of the Belebei district of the Bashkir ASSR the residents refused to resettle the refugee Jews. In 1942 engineer Boris Kopman wrote to the first secretary of this republic that two sixteen to seventeen year olds had come to his mother and threateningly asked her, "Are you a *zhidovka* (Yid) or a Russian?" Only her threat to deliver them to the NKVD forced the teenagers to back down. When a widow of a soldier deceased on the front appealed to one of the leaders of Ufa to help improve her housing conditions, he began with clarifying whether she was Jewish or not. Learning that she was, he refused to help. Kopman also wrote that during the beginning of their first night in Ufa, a group of teenagers approached the house on Pushkin Street, where evacuees from Kiev and state and party workers had been settled, and began knocking at the windows shouting, "Beat the Yids, save Russia!" Not limiting themselves just to this, they tried for an hour to rip out the front door, continuing to shout pogrom phrases. The lecturer Lev Iakobson reported about the blood libel to the same committee of the party. According to him, rumors were circulating in Birsk that a missing Russian boy had been killed on Easter for Jewish ritual purposes. In mid-May the corpse of the missing boy was found intact in one of the wells in Birsk, and only then did the rumors stop.[83]

In the village of Trekh-Boltaevo in the Chuvash ASSR the children ran over the Jewish boy Zlotnikov on horseback and severely injured him, according to Kosmovskii's note. The next phrase of this note indirectly indicates that this was done on antisemitic grounds: "There are often cases where the national feeling of chauvinistic elements offends the personal dignity of the evacuated."[84] Evacuation inspector David Valershtein wrote about this case in a report ten days later. He wrote in the same report that the caretaker of a local cattle trading company burst into the house of an employee of this organization and beat him.[85] Kosmovskii pointed out in a note to schoolteachers that they bore full responsibility for the "Soviet education of the children" and were obliged to respond to every such incident, whether it happened at school or on the street.[86] There are other examples of antisemitism in Chuvashia. In the village of Pervomaiskoe, according to the report of Latsis, children, chanting the words "Rip out all the Jewish cucumbers," ruined the kitchen garden of the refugee Chernia from Latvia.[87] Iakov Karasin spoke of a warm attitude toward him and his family coming from their landlady in Cheboksary and, at the same time, gave an example of regular beatings in school of his friend Revik Abramian, an evacuee from Moscow, who merely looked like "a Yid."[88] In the village of Pikhtulino storekeeper Filip Andreev in 1942 liked to say, "Stalin gave the order to kill the Jews, not to feed them milk."[89] In the village of Novo-Larionovo Antonina Nikitina, with whom Abram Kantor and his family had been settled, said to them: "Do you think you are hidden? Soon the day will come, do not think you will not be found. You Jews sold out for power, because of you, the whole Russian race suffers."[90]

Marina Potëmkina cites almost a dozen officially recorded examples of antisemitic attitudes toward Jewish refugees in the Urals.[91] There are also other examples. The nine-year-old Mikhail Khefets, who was in Irbit, was caught by a company of local boys and, having twisted his arms and tied a noose around his neck, they led him somewhere, explaining to the curious and uninterested adults they met, "We are hanging the Yid."[92] To these incidences in the Urals should be added the anti-Jewish pogrom in the Sverdlovsk region. According to Rebecca Manley's collected information, the pogrom-makers shouted, "Here's your second front—kill the Yids!"[93] Volf Gutman testifies:

> We ended up in Zlatoust of the Cheliabinsk region without any clothes, without money, without anything. We were settled with a Uralian family. We were in the front room with a large Russian stove that was not lit, they were in the second, and they had a stove. In the evening the family gathered, and only "Yids, Yids" was heard. Mom could not stand it, she complained to the executive committee, [and] they were clearly given a dressing-down. And they took a door and hung

it between the rooms. And that was it, we were screwed. The walls were covered with ice, you could practically ride a sled on them.[94]

According to the testimony of K. Red, in one kolkhoz in the Kirov region, where he was sent along with other deported Polish Jews, at first, they were mistaken for Poles. However, when the locals found out that the new arrivals were Jews, "who crucified Christ," the attitude toward them worsened. When one witness asked for a horse to take his pregnant wife to the doctor forty kilometers away from the village, he was refused. They had to go on foot. But in the middle of the journey, his wife could no longer walk, and the peasants who passed by did not give her a lift, despite her pleas. The man had to carry his wife.[95] Waldemar T. in his testimony particularly emphasizes the hatred of local authorities for refugees—both Poles and Jews.[96]

Having researched the situation in the Middle Volga area, Viktor Fedotov also asserts that Jewish refugees often faced domestic antisemitism, including its extreme forms.[97] Vladimir Barsukov, who believes that various local populations treated refugees differently, gives several examples of a sympathetic attitude toward them, describing how hard it was to find a residence for his family in Ul'ianovsk; he also recalls cases of antisemitism. When they almost agreed on a rental with hosts, their twenty-five-year-old daughter appeared with a hysterical cry: "Yids, get out of here!" This shocked the author, who grew up in a mixed Jewish-Russian family.[98] In Chapaevsk, Kuibyshev region, a doctor, Kalistova, who was Jewish, was insulted and groundlessly accused of treating only Jews; shoes and pillows were thrown at her. Local authorities did not react to complaints.[99] In the Mari ASSR in December 1941, according to the report of the inspector for the evacuation of the population P. Radionenko under the Council of People's Commissars of the RSFSR, there were instances of antisemitism toward refugees by a number of kolkhoz chairs.[100] In the Russian village Tetvel in the Tatar ASSR, the Vaksman family was at first tolerantly received, but when they brought from Uzbekistan a son who had been lost during the evacuation and who had a pronounced Semitic appearance, the attitude toward them immediately worsened, and the children began to be called "little Yids."[101] In the village of Arkadak in the Saratov region local youth stopped children (who had been evacuated from a pioneer camp near Minsk) on the street. There was an "exam" on the pronunciation of the letter *r*. If the children did not roll their *r*, they were brutally beaten.[102]

In South Siberian Rubtsovsk (Altai territory) according to the written notice sent by G. M. Malenkov and N. M. Shvernik, a local resident of Gazizov in July 1945 insulted "with words and actions" the Jewish refugee I. G. L'vovskaia and hit another "old woman who fell from the blow, but when upon learning that she was Russian, apologized, adding at the same time—I thought you were Jewish." After that, he beat the local Jewish woman Patukhova and the Polish Jew D. Lazarskii, who covered for her. In the same months in Rubtsovsk, the war veteran Markov beat several Jews during a football game.[103] Leonid Vaksman, who was studying in an industrial school of Sibsel'mash Plant, was beaten by his classmates, and to the question "What are you beating me for?" they answered "For being a Yid."[104] In the autumn of 1942, Jewish children were periodically beaten in schools and pioneer camps in the Cheliabinsk region.[105]

Elia Gekhtman, who found herself along with thirty-five other Jewish refugees in the hamlet Malogolovskii in the Stalingrad region, testifies:

> The Cossacks didn't even understand what "Jews" were, and at first, they treated us in a brotherly way, like family. But there was an old man in the hamlet, a veterinary assistant, and he began to go from house to house and agitate the Cossacks, saying the Jews were "Christ-sellers, they crucified Christ, and they drink our blood." And within a few days, the attitude toward us changed dramatically for the worse, as if a wall of alienation had grown between the local horsemen and us. And when two months later the front line began to approach us, the Cossacks no longer stinted on the threats, the horsemen spoke openly: "Soon the Germans will come, we'll hang all the Yids!"[106]

The director of a secondary school in the Poltavskii hamlet in the Briukhovets district of the Krasnodar territory refused to hire Maria Rubinchik because of her ethnicity.[107] According to one diary from the Platnirovskaia village of the Krasnodar territory, as the front line approached, rumors spread that many Jews and Communists had been sent to Kuban' to poison all the Cossacks and take possession of their goods. The evacuees were openly threatened: "The Nazis will come, and we will get rid of all of you."[108] Before the occupation of Piatigorsk by the Germans, several representatives of the Leningrad Polytechnic Institute (including Jews) tried to explore the opportunities for students and teachers to move to Georgievsk (about fifty kilometers away). However, they were forced to return because of the hostile attitude of the local population, who refused refugees not only lodging but drinking water.[109]

According to the report of Shklovskii, the senior inspector of the evacuation department, on May 5, 1942, in the village of Kotliarevskaia in the Maiskii district of the Kabardino-Balkar ASSR, the collective farmer Andreeva tried to evict the refugee Sheinergain from her apartment, falsely accusing her of stealing lard. In the same village the collective farmer Moiseev removed the roof and windows of a house, leaving the refugee Krongauz in a cold building. The Jewish refugees complained to the authorities that, according to residents of the villages of Kotliarevskaia and Novoivanovskaia, also in the Maiskii district, it was the Red Army soldiers, who had passed through, who instructed the locals: "Expel the Jews, otherwise Hitler will come, they will hang you and they will not be gracious."[110] In the Cossack village of Novoivanovskaia residents generally declared, "we will allow Russians, but not Jews."[111] The Cossacks in the village of Sovetskaia (in the Ordzhonikidze territory) wanted to slaughter the Marshak family, refugees from Krivoi Rog, when they learned that they were Jews. They were rescued by the mistress of the house where they were staying. Her son, wrapping up the hooves of the horses in rags "so they did not clop," secretly took them to the station.[112]

The refusal of assistance forced some refugees to steal kolkhoz food products, which in turn provoked the wrath of the collective farmers. Although all refugees preferred theft to death by starvation, due to particular bias against them, Jews were especially disadvantaged. Having a hostile attitude toward all refugees, the local historian of Shadrinsk Vladimir Biriukov conveyed these sentiments in his diary: "I have heard a lot of complaints about the Jewish refugees who have settled in both the city and the village. In the latter, new residents feel free to behave themselves however they want: they take (steal) potatoes, they milk cows in the absence of the cows' owners . . . The chair of the village council, knowing that it is impossible to take stringent measures, has only advised that everything be locked more tightly."[113]

The increase in prices in the bazaars of the North Caucasus led to an increase in the hostility of the Slavic population toward Jewish refugees. In this regard, it is difficult to overestimate the testimony of Pëtr Poluian, who lived at that time in Makhachkala:

> On the following Sunday . . . it was necessary to pass through the territory of the bazaar. It was literally packed with evacuees. Passing through the bazaar, we saw empty counters. The market was unrecognizable. Here and there, smoked fish were sold under the table and expensive caviar. The city was filled with evacuees from Odessa. Within just a day, all the food had disappeared, down to the cookies. In the stores the shelves were bare; prices had jumped so high that you couldn't buy anything with our pennies. They, the residents of Makhachkala say, have whole suitcases of money. Without waiting for Sunday, they went to the auls, and, like locusts, began to buy everything in bulk, without bargaining. So, suddenly, the inhabitants of the city found themselves in a situation of hardship with regard to food; beggars appeared. Those same people from Odessa did not want to defend their city, they [i.e., women, old people, and children], they simply threw it at the mercy of the Germans and Romanians, not forgetting to take money and jewelry with them. But not everybody had them. . . . The

evacuees began to appear on almost every street begging for anything that would help them survive. Our dining hall was near the road leading to the city. People began to walk to us daily, asking for at least something: the remains of lunch or dinner. They held tins in their hands, offered their things in exchange. The people were thin, poorly clothed. Their appearance showed that they had experienced much grief.[114]

These contradictory memories of the refugees are confirmed in the more tolerant diary entries of Zinovii Miller, who also ended up in Makhachkala: "These people, who lived at home as honest, well-to-do workers, languished in this barn in need, in the cold, surrounded by the contempt and even hatred of the local population."[115]

The Moscow intelligentsia also encountered antisemitism. Leonid Timofeev in the middle of October 1941 wrote in his diary, "They say that in some places where there were evacuees there were hints of pogroms against Jews. The children of writers who were evacuated were in a very bad situation. The Il'ia Sel'vinskii family lives in a hut where through the wall people are constantly talking about how they will soon be beating the Jews."[116]

The Central Asian Case

A similar attitude—that they were a priori guilty—Jews found among a part of the population of Central Asia. During the dispatch of conscripts in 1942 to the military unit from Tashkent, an unknown person cried out, "Why are they the Jews not summoned to the army and sent to the front?" The cry was accompanied by a call for an anti-Jewish pogrom.[117] To some extent, the spread of a rumor that instead of fighting with the Nazis, the Jews fled to "fight" in Tashkent was facilitated by the arrival in Central Asia of a large number of Jewish men of draft age; one part of them were refugees who did not have time to be summoned to the army while at their previous place of residence but would be summoned later (in this connection it is significant that two of the three heroes of the Soviet Union drafted into the army in Samarkand were Jewish refugees), and the other part was from territories annexed in 1939–1940. The latter were not mobilized to the front line by the authorities from July 1941 until mid-1943.

Incidentally, I'd like note that in Central Asia, as well as in the Caucasian republics, in comparison with Russia, visitors were generally struck by the presence on the streets of a large number of men. This was largely because the native ethnic groups of the outlying republics had more privileges to free themselves from conscription to the front. For example, in Uzbekistan, Uzbek students were released from service, including first-year students entering university.[118]

In July 1943 the Council of People's Commissars of the USSR issued a decree on the training of cadres of national teachers in Uzbekistan; the return from the front line and the "labor army" of teachers who were *korennye zhiteli* (native population) of Central Asia was part of this plan.[119] A part of the Slavic population who migrated during the war to these republics, who lacked experience of Eastern ethnic groups, mistook the indigenous youths for Jews.

In Central Asia, as we shall see, the Jews made up almost half of the refugee population, which was much higher than the average for the USSR. Therefore, the "Jewish question," in the context of the arrival of a large number of newcomers, stood here more sharply than in the Urals or Siberia. Many sources indicate that in Central Asia, the spread of antisemitic sentiments came from Slavic refugees from the western regions of the USSR, as well as from local Slavs and Tatars.[120] Although the Tatars and Slavs began to settle in Central Asia starting in the last third of the nineteenth century, the majority of them (about two hundred thousand) arrived in 1921–1922, during the famine in the Volga area.[121] These migrants, who settled in towns and villages, usually had only small gardens or had no gardens at all. The arrival of a large number of refugees, and in particular the Jews, led to a rise in the cost of food at the market, where, incidentally, during nearly the entire war, almost any kind of food could be purchased.[122] The reaction to price inflation was discontent with Jewish refugees. Zinovii Miller described the attitude of Slavic townspeople toward them in his diary entry for December 1941:

> The population of Chardzhou, like the local population of other cities, treated the refugees with hatred, especially the Jews. For the first time during our evacuation, we came across a kind of brutish antisemitism that was nurtured here. Many local residents refused to even rent out their apartments to the hated Jews. They came to us—I even overheard the conversation of a prominent local leader—with tightly packed purses. To them nothing is expensive; they tear our last morsel away from us. There will soon be a famine in Chardzhou, and the Jewish refugees who are buying up everything here will be guilty. And why put up with them? After all, they cannot even be called Soviet citizens: they allegedly flee from the Germans, but in essence, they are driven by fear of war. Many of them under the guise of evacuees simply shy away from participating in the war: the Jews have long been distinguished by their cowardice.[123]

Rachel Rivkina recalls that it was local Russian who during the war taught the Uzbeks to taunt the Jews and call them Yids.[124]

The authorities recorded numerous cases of antisemitism in Central Asia. There are especially many sources about its manifestation in Kazakhstan. A secret report of the Central Committee of the Communist Party of this republic from June 1942 noted, without giving full details, that the engineer Startseva, who was evacuated to Chimkent together with the Kiev chemical and pharmaceutical plant, "carried out an antisemitic attack." Further, the report spoke of the lack of political work at the plant, whose leadership was limited Startseva's punishment to strict reprimand, and that antisemitic talk was widespread in the city; a worker was beaten at the market on antisemitic motives.[125] According to the secret report of the chief prosecutor of Kazakhstan dated September 1942, antisemitism in three regions was widespread in the form of public insults, the approval of Hitler's actions against Jews, beatings, property damage, refusal to hire, distribution of leaflets with a call not to sell food to Jews, and the spreading of rumors about the murder of children by Jews. For these actions in Kazakhstan from January to September 1942, sixty-two people were brought to trial.[126] In Dzhambul Russian invalids even attempted to organize an anti-Jewish pogrom.[127] It is not clear how it was suppressed. There was at least one dead—the melamed (the teacher of the ḥeder) Moshe.[128] Vladimir Petrov, appearing in Alma-Ata, described how evacuated students from Moscow pushed a Jew out of a restaurant when they needed a place there. When Petrov asked them about the reason, one of them replied that the Jews had stolen money in Moscow, evaded the army, and lived like kings. Petrov thought to himself that, judging by the poor figure cut by the Polish and Bessarabian Jews in the streets, they did not have even a few rubles.[129]

The attitude was similar deep in provincial Kazakhstan. A fifth-grade student, Ioann Tselnik, wrote in August 1942 to *Kazakhstanskaia Pravda* from the Belousovka settlement in the East Kazakhstan region: "I am a Jews, and everywhere I go I hear the word 'Yid.' Beatings have become more frequent. Recently my mother (she works in the store) was almost killed. One antisemite, shouting "beat the Yids!" burst into the store and, grabbing the scale weight, swung it at my mother. But mom had time to duck . . . Besides, wherever I am, toward me are flung cigarette butts, dirt, stones . . ."[130] An eighth-grade pupil G. Sorokin wrote to Stalin from Leninogorsk: "The Jew is a second-class citizen. You cannot walk down the street—there are exclamations: 'Here comes the kike,' or 'Beat the Yids, save Russia!' You can't go to the movies if you try you'll be beaten."[131] In the village Grebenshchik in the Gur'ev region, Lev Mistetskii, who had been orphaned and was starving, heard in the bread line: "The Yids came here, and life got difficult for us—they took everything."[132]

The situation in neighboring Uzbekistan was no better. In August 1942, Beria's People's Commissariat for Internal Affairs was presented with a report on the spread of antisemitism there:

In connection with the arrival in the republic of a significant number of Soviet citizens of Jewish nationality, anti-Soviet elements, using the dissatisfaction of certain local residents with the crowding of housing, the increase in market prices, and the desire of some evacuees to get into the system of trading, procurement and supply organizations, counterrevolutionary work has intensified in the direction of inciting antisemitism. As a result, in Uzbekistan there have been three cases of Jews being beaten, accompanied by antisemitic cries. . . . I. I. Deriugin, having arrived to Samarkand from the front on the occasion of injury, and his wife, A. I. Soldatenkova, while drunk, beat the actor of the Kharkov Jewish Theater Landau and his wife, the actress Lev. During the beating, Deriugin and Soldatenkova shouted antisemitic pogrom slogans in the presence of a crowd of up to two hundred people. Deriugin and Soldatenkova were arrested.[133]

The same report also informs of the arrest of A. Dudarova, the head of the medical unit, who had been found to have leaflets calling for the killing of Communists and Jews, as well as the nurse M. Svistukhina, who was engaged in antisemitic propaganda in the tram in the form of promises that with the arrival of Hitler, all the Jews would be slaughtered. According to the NKVD, a worker at the Tashkent plant no. 84, Avdeeva, in 1942, with her friends, declared that when Hitler came she would hang all the Jews in her apartment.[134]

In practice, there were many more manifestations of antisemitism unregistered by the authorities. In March 1942 in the Fergana region, Sima Zelikman's four-year-old child died after he was refused admission to the hospital because "the Jews do not protect their homeland, and they [the personnel] save [only] the children of the soldiers."[135] At the same time in Fergana, Menachem Begin heard a drunk screaming in the street: "Get rid of all the Yids!"[136] In Samarkand, during a documentary film about Ukrainian partisans shown in the city garden, an appeal to the audience was heard: "Do not be afraid of the Germans, they are our liberators, they only kill commissars, Communists, and Jews." Nobody rebuffed the speaker or called the police. In the same city Russian invalids wrote on the walls of the synagogue, "Beat the Yids, save Russia!"[137] In Tashkent and Alma-Ata the disabled people "welcomed" the passing Jews with cries of "Abrasha."[138] In Tashkent this nickname was given to many passersby by invalids, when they blocked off the pavement at the entrance to the bazaar and demanded money for vodka. Meletinskii writes that their words 'Do not pass, comrade!' sounded rather menacing."[139]

Antisemitic incidences were also noted in Kirgizstan. Russian workers sometimes directly told their Jewish colleagues, "We will soon kill all of you."[140] In the town of Tokmak, in the presence of a policeman, a woman told a Polish

Jew, "Just wait, Hitler will come soon and you'll all get it."[141] Alice Vinik had to face antisemitism in one of the Ukrainian villages of Kirgizstan.[142] Stefa Bloch met with the same in another Ukrainian kolkhoz. Once, when she was not at home, the owner threw her baby and all her things out onto the street and did not let them into the house anymore. After that, only the poorest Ukrainian woman in the village agreed to let them in. When Stefa, on her way home from work, once ripped a few apricots off of a branch hanging over the fence, the owner of the garden sicced a dog on her.[143]

Open manifestations of antisemitism irritated many members of the intelligentsia. In Tashkent in August 1942, writer Vladimir Lugovskoi struck a passerby who shouted, "Beat the Yids!"[144] Also in Tashkent, Orientalist and archaeologist Sergei Tolstov beat a passerby who had taken his Uzbek companion and colleague Iakhia Guliamov for a Jew, and began to scold him and all Jews.[145] When Lidia Chukovskaia told Anna Akhmatova about the statement she heard on the train that the Jews should have been left to Hitler, she firmly declared about the one who had said it: "These people must be killed."[146]

But not all cultural figures sympathized with Jewish refugees. The writer and film director Aleksandr Dovzhenko, who was in Ashkhabad during the occupation of Ukraine, was annoyed by them. In April 1942, in his diary addressed to the Ukrainians of the occupied territories, he wrote, "You didn't have suitcases, protected with covers and forged with brass nails, to flee to the east to placate Jewish fears,"[147] even though the information about the genocide of the Jewish population was available by then. Even more angrily, he commented on the toast "to life" (the translation of the traditional Yiddish toast "*le khaim*") made by Mikhoels at some celebration in Tashkent: "In your love of life, here in this pious panegyric, I see an ordinary fear of death. Because of it you do not fight, because of it you run to Tashkent."[148]

As has already been seen in the examples, and as we shall see further, the invalids often acted as the initiators of antisemitic actions. There were several reasons for their aggression. The authorities often sent them to be treated medically in Central Asia, as a result of which there was a large concentration of them. Since there was also a large concentration of Jewish refugees, not only from Poland, the disabled had a feeling that the Jews did not fight the Germans. Given that in Hitler's propaganda (distributed over the radio and especially on leaflets dropped from the planes over the front line),[149] the Jews were called the main enemy, some invalids believed that they suffered for the sake of defending the Jews. Mark Edele believes that war veterans were an opposition group after the war because of unrealistic hopes for a change in society.[150] In the disabled war veterans, this disappointment was stronger; it came before victory, and the "guilty" Jews were an easily accessible target to take out their discontent with the regime.

However, another important reason for this hatred was economic competition. The fact is that disabled people often organized illegal commercial structures in Central Asia, trying to force Jews out of a trade. Georgii Efron wrote in his diary in Tashkent: "Disabled people are a problem. Ninety-nine percent have privileged access [to goods] and resell at inflated prices what they receive everywhere—in the bazaars and on the streets. All the invalids drink. A lot of soldiers are depraved—mostly the wounded."[151] In Stalinabad, invalids monopolized the trade in alcohol.[152] The same Mark Edele reports on the organization and functioning of such clandestine networks of war invalids in Siberia and the Urals.[153] L. L. testifies that in Andizhan invalids controlled the trade in tobacco and alcohol. Once he was sitting in a restaurant under their control with an old Jewish man whose two sons were killed at the battlefield. There were drunken invalids at a nearby table, and one of them loudly told about how, under Rzhev, all the Jews fled from the Germans, and generally liked to be commissars and staff officers. After these words L. L.'s companion burst into tears.[154] To this, we should add that some invalids hated the Jewish commissars who raised soldiers from the trenches to attack.

Antisemitism was a widespread phenomenon among schoolchildren of Russian-speaking classes in Central Asia. The well-known historian Yuri Bregel spoke in interviews of the beating and name-calling of Jews in one of the schools of Fergana, where he then studied, trend and not one-off incidents.[155] The Jewish children in the Russian school of Stalinabad were also collectively beaten and taunted for their ethnicity.[156] In the schools of Kzyl-Orda (Kazakhstan), according to the testimony of Iakov Eshkol, Jewish boys were stripped of their pants—to check if they were circumcised—or had their lips smeared with lard. Moreover, often the Slavic children did not want to sit next to the Jewish children at the desks, and the teachers lowered the Jewish children's marks and treated them poorly in every possible way.[157] Jewish children were also beaten in the Russian school of the village Ushtobe (Uzbekistan), because of which the Polish Jews tried to transfer their children to a Polish school.[158] In the Osh region (Kirgizstan), according to Khaim Kats, Jewish children were mocked by their Ukrainian peers (exiled there with their parents after de-kulakization), who also set the Kyrgyz children against them.[159]

As for the native Muslim population of Central Asia, initially many of them, especially in small towns and villages, did not distinguish between the refugees, considering them all Russian.[160] Later, some of the Muslims began to consider the Jews separately. However, this was not followed by a change in attitude toward them in one direction or another among most of the population. Many

Muslims continued to help the Jewish refugees with food, clothing, medicine, work, and also supported them psychologically, which was no less important.[161] Bina Boiman has written in her memoirs about the kolkhoz in the Fergana Valley: "The Uzbeks provided us with food, from everything they themselves had: hot cakes, straight from the oven, dried fruit, rice, and so on."[162] When her brother fell ill and their father left with him for a week to the hospital (their mother died in the first year of her stay in the USSR), two Uzbek women took the thirteen-year-old into their house (all residents lived in *kibitka*, a kind of yurt), fearing for her safety. Alexander Masiewicki noted that in their area in Kirgizstan, where about five hundred Polish Jews lived, antisemitism was not felt.[163] The happy attitude of the Uzbek population toward refugees in Tashkent was remembered by Sophia Abidor.[164] Michael Garber testifies to the lack of antisemitism and the good attitude toward refugees in the Uzbek kolkhoz where he stayed during the war.[165] Some of the Central Asian Muslims treated Jews better than they treated the Slavs, who were often considered to be colonialists.[166]

At the same time, part of the indigenous Muslim population perceived all refugees in general, including Jews, negatively, seeing them as parasites and strangers.[167] Several sources indicate that the attitude of Muslims toward refugees worsened in the second half of 1942 in connection with the Wehrmacht's attempts to conquer Stalingrad.[168] According to the testimony of Roman Weiss, the Uzbeks hated the Russians and waited for the arrival of the Germans.[169] Paul Stronski quotes an Uzbek Komsomol member as saying to his Russian colleague, "If Hitler or Germany invades Russia, then we will crush everything of yours here and we will talk with you differently." In the same place, Stronski cites another, a more aggressive statement by one Uzbek to his Russian colleague: "Soon we will get rid of all of you."[170]

Possibly it was such threats that led to the spread of rumors in Uzbekistan that Muslims were preparing for anti-Jewish and anti-Russian pogroms in the event of the Wehrmacht approaching. The Polish writer Aleksander Wat wrote that Russians, Jews, and, in general, all refugees fearfully awaited pogroms by Uzbeks.[171] Anatolii Krasnov-Levitin recalls: "Many Uzbeks hated Russians as much as Jews. In the days of Hitler's victories, among some Uzbeks there was a phrase in circulation: 'When the Germans will come, we will smear the roofs with Jewish blood, and the doorsteps with Russian blood.'"[172] Georgii Efron writes about the same thing in the summer of 1942 in his diary.[173] L. L. testifies that on the eve of the Battle of Stalingrad, rumors circulated that Uzbeks and Russians were preparing to organize an anti-Jewish pogrom in Andizhan.[174] The aforementioned Leonid Timofeev also noted in his diary: "Uzbeks were going to go after the Jews first, then the Russians, but they gradually calmed down."[175]

It is not surprising that in this connection, the Russian and Jewish populations of Central Asia resented the manifestations of public disloyalty to the central authorities on the part of the local Muslim population and the granting to it of broader exemption from conscription into the army. They were particularly outraged by desertion. Despite the fact that the number of persons who had not arrived at the military registration and enlistment office to be sent to the front, as well as deserters, were large among the Slavic population,[176] during the war years the opinion spread that Caucasians and Muslim men from Central Asia deserted most often.[177] This opinion was fueled by not unfounded view that prospects of being exempt from military service for a bribe were better in the republics of Central Asia.[178]

Often Jewish refugees, especially teenagers, were driven out of bread lines.[179] Henryk Grynberg, referring to the queues in stores, recalls, "We stood for days and nights for 400 grams of clay-like bread. The Uzbeks went out of turn and still scolded the Jews."[180] Rabbi Sasonkin describes how in Samarkand the Uzbeks beat to death a yeshiva student who had shamed them for cutting in line to buy bread and immediately selling it at exorbitant price to the refugees.[181] Gorkov possibly had the same case in mind when he recalled the beating of a religious Jew by Uzbeks in a bread line in Samarkand.[182] Saul Borovoi describes in his memoirs how during the long waits in lines in Samarkand, locals called refugees "parasites" and demanded that they receive food last.[183]

The above-mentioned letter of the JAC to Stalin also said that the attitude of the native population toward Jewish refugees was very unfriendly.[184] According to Maria Beizer's testimony, in the Uzbek kolkhoz where she lived during the war, the refugees were treated very badly. Her father, brother, and little nephew died from hunger and disease there; the collective farmers did not want to sell milk for them.[185] Chaim Cymmerman, who also lived in a kolkhoz, testified in 1943 that the Uzbeks hated the Jewish refugees and often attacked their children.[186] Jakub Rosenblum also spoke of the hatred of the Uzbeks for the Jewish refugees in their kolkhoz.[187]

In the second half of 1942 the number of cases of bullying and beating of Jewish refugees in general increased in Central Asia. According to a secret report received by Beria in 1942, Jews throughout Central Asia feared for their safety.[188] The report, mentioned above, of the prosecutor of Kazakhstan also reported that of all sixty-two judicable antisemitic incidents in the republic in the first nine months of 1942, forty-two (67.7 percent) occurred from August 1 to September 4.[189] Iakov Eshkol testifies that in Kzyl-Orda (Kazakhstan), under the influence of the local Slavic population, the Kazakhs, who had previously treated the Jewish refugees well, began to treat them poorly.[190] An incidence of an antisemitic pogrom occurred on Kolkhoz Kazakhstanskaia Pravda in the Iliiskii district of this republic. The head of the kolkhoz, Turapov, promised the Kazakh collective farmers that he would "clear the collective farm from the evacuees and first of all from the Jews." He was supported by the chair of the village council, Pavlova, and the kolkhoz activists. It was decided to evict ten families of Jewish refugees, and leave the Russians. On November 3, 1942, kolkhozniks under the leadership of the Communist Dzhemgul pulled the windows along with the frames out of the houses of the evicted families and threw their things into the street. Pillow feathers flew in the air. Some of the property was plundered and destroyed. The evicted tried to resistance, but the forces were unequal. Families along with their things were loaded on carts and, accompanied by collective farmers, sent to the village council. Pavlova, seeing this from the porch, was frightened by the consequences and ordered the refugees to go back. Nevertheless, after the investigation of this case she was dismissed, and the deputy of the village council Olzhabai Uskenbaev, for the mockery and beating of evacuees, as well as the illegal eviction from the kolkhoz, was expelled from the party and put on trial. Apparently, the rest of the organizers were not severely punished.[191]

The unfavorable situation in Kyzyl-Kiia (Kirgizstan) in 1942 forced the mother of Sara Garber to change her surname to Garbenko, to impersonate a Ukrainian woman.[192] Mikhail Raitzin testified that Uzbek and Russian children in Tashkent beat him for being a Jew.[193] The Soviet writer Vsevolod Ivanov, who was in Tashkent at the time, wrote in his diary that the wife of the Yiddish poet Peretz Markish, Esfir, after learning that her children living in a children's sanatorium in Chimgan (Uzbekistan) were bullied by other children, walked the ninety-five kilometers there on foot. On the way, she did not manage to buy even bread crusts or a cup of milk in the villages. The locals told her, "We do not sell to Jews; this war is because of you."[194] The inhabitants guessed about her nationality because of rumors about a large proportion of Jews among the refugees.

In Kanibadam (Tajikistan) in September 1942, Abraham Zylbering witnessed the Tajiks beating two Jewish refugees.[195] According to the testimony of the Polish Jew E. G., in Leninabad, also a Tajik city, disabled Russian invalids incited Muslims against Jews. He even reports on individual cases of murder there, as a result of which Jews in 1942 tried not to go out in the evening. One day E. G. put on his suit, which he had bought back in Poland. His appearance in a good suit on the street caused the negative reaction of a Russian passerby who declared, "You are drinking our blood." Tajik children threw stones at refugees there. The Polish Jews complained in Yiddish to the head of the local NKVD, Shneider, but according to the testimony, this did not lead to anything.[196]

Another witness points to Russian invalids as spreaders of antisemitic sentiments among the Slavic and Muslim populations in Stalinabad.[197]

As already mentioned, the police often did not arrest the instigators, preferring not to interfere. Shlomo Leizer mentions a case in Osh (Kirgizstan) where young Uzbeks attacked a Jew in front of two police officers.[198] After the case described above, when in Alma-Ata students pushed a Jew out of a restaurant, he complained to a policeman, but the policeman waved him off.[199] In general, many Jewish refugees witnessed the noninterference of police officers who were present at the scene of such antisemitic insults and even physical attacks.[200]

Therefore, the diary entry of Vsevolod Ivanov from July 25, 1942, deserves attention: "M. Golodnyi said yesterday that several nationalist organizations have been uncovered here, even among policemen who intentionally held back information about cases of antisemitism."[201] Most likely, the local prosecutor's office, having learned about the facts of the informal practice of ignoring antisemitic cases by police officers, presented this as an activity of an anti-Soviet organization. This was perhaps a manifestation of the inconsistency of the Soviet law enforcement agencies. It was difficult for the central authorities to give informal instructions to the prosecutor's office. It was much easier to do this through the NKVD. Since at that time antisemitism was widespread, because of the spread of propaganda about the privilege of Jews in the USSR and the significant deterioration of the economic situation in the country, the central authorities began to dissociate themselves from the Jews. Within the framework of this relatively sharp turn, which fit well into Stalin's new internal political discourse of 1942 that was aimed at developing Russian chauvinism,[202] the authorities began to avoid publicizing scandalous "Jewish" cases. Court cases involving antisemitic incidents could be regarded as protection for Jews. Vladimir Petrov, who was thrown into a camp on political charges in 1935, was stunned by the rampant antisemitism and its impunity, which he discovered after his release in late 1941.[203]

From 1943 began the silencing of the merits of the frontline Jews in the press. The head of Agitprop, Aleksandr Shcherbakov, reprimanded Ilya Ehrenburg for frequent descriptions of the heroism of Jews at the front.[204] The pivot to silence on the Jewish theme prevented the managing editor of the newspaper *Krasnaia Zvezda*, David Ortenberg, from publishing in May of that year a letter from the Soviet writer Aleksandr Stepanov, the author of the famous novel *Port Arthur*. Strongly shocked by what he saw in Frunze, he wrote: "On antisemitism. Demobilized from the army, the wounded are its main distributors. They openly say that the Jews evade the war, sit in warm places in the rear, and they conduct real pogrom agitation. I witnessed how the Jews were driven out of the queues, even the women were beaten by the same legless cripples. . . .

On the part of the police, in relation to such misconduct, criminal softness appears, bordering on direct connivance."[205]

The deterioration of the attitude of Muslims toward refugees was not only due to the approach of the front line but also as a result of German propaganda spreading in Central Asia. In this propaganda the Soviet government was portrayed as Jewish.[206] The Germans even hoped to cause an uprising in Central Asia, for the organization of which in May 1944 the sabotage group of Ageev, made up of fourteen former Kazakh prisoners of war, was dropped into Kazakhstan by parachute.[207] In 1942 a rumor even spread among the refugees that near Tashkent, Uzbeks had killed several Jews.[208] Most likely, this did take place, but they were killed not because of their ethnicity, but because of robbery. It is possible that they were referring to the several cases of robbery mentioned above. Nevertheless, the dissemination of this information with a nationalistic explanation was a reflection of the escalating ethnic relations.

There was another reason for the increasing antisemitism among the Muslim population in 1942. During the end of the nineteenth century, a superstition spread that Jews use the blood of gentiles to make matzah. In the 1920s through the first half of the 1930s, the spread of blood libel increased.[209] At that time the authorities managed to stop these rumors, but during the war they broke out again. The same rumors circulated at that time in Kirgizstan.[210] They were no less prevalent in Uzbekistan. During the war, this libel was spread by the director of one of the Uzbek schools.[211] In one Turkmen kolkhoz near Bukhara, they believed that only Bukharan Jews used blood for cooking matzah, whereas Ashkenazi Jews did not.[212]

Some Poles contributed to the further spread of superstition about the use of gentile blood for matzah. Samuel Honig writes in his memoirs about how before Passover in 1942 local residents of one of the settlements in the Mari ASSR began to hide children from the Polish Jews who had been sent there, having heard the blood libel spread by the Poles. He complained to a local NKVD representative who, although he did not find those spreading the rumor, conducted an outreach conversation with the local population.[213] It is unknown whether this talk achieved its purpose. In January 1945, the secretary of the TsK VKP(b) Georgii Malenkov was informed that in the Volzhsk district of Mari SSR, schoolchildren believed that Jews have a custom of consuming the blood of Christian children.[214]

A number of other sources also point to the Poles as propagators of antisemitism in Central Asia.[215] Avraham Klevan gives an example of how in a kolkhoz in Kirgizstan, under the influence of the antisemitic propaganda of the Poles, Muslims began to feel worse toward Jews, which led to open clashes. Only the intervention of the NKVD prevented a more serious conflict between

Jewish refugees and Muslims.[216] Shlomo Leizer testifies that in those kolkhozes in Kirgizstan where the Poles lived alongside Polish Jews, the attitude toward the Jews was worse than in those places where they did not.[217] In August 1943 representative of the Union of Polish Patriots, Boleslav Drobner, even spoke against the spread of antisemitism at a meeting of Polish refugees.[218]

Good Memories

It would be wrong to believe that the entire population of the rear regions had a negative attitude toward Jewish refugees. Memoirs and interviews of former refugees contain many mentions of individuals who helped them during the war. Inessa Livshits writes about the hospitality of the mixed Uzbek-Russian family in Samarkand with whom they were settled in 1941.[219] Toby Klodawski-Flam in her memoirs tells how neighborly women fed her and her friend at an Uzbek kolkhoz near Dzhuma. When the girls were at work, the women brought potatoes, tomatoes, or onions into their hut that had been left open, explaining to each other that "the girls have nothing."[220] The twenty-year-old Ida Kaminska-Miron, hiding her ethnicity, in a Turkmen kolkhoz near Bukhara, was welcomed into the family of the kolkhoz chair, where she learned the Turkmen language, learned to observe the local customs and prepare local dishes; she grew so accustomed to living there that she felt almost as if she were with her own family.[221]

Dina Gabel several times encountered local residents who treated her very well in the villages of northern Kazakhstan.[222] Doba Belozërkina remembers the positive attitude of the local population in Alma-Ata.[223] Liana Degtiar points out the absence of antisemitism in the village of Vashstroi in the Vakhsh valley in the Kurgan-Tiube region (Tajikistan); the majority of the population was Russian.[224] Daniil Iushkovskii describes a warm attitude toward the refugees in a Cossack kolkhoz of the Rostov region.[225] Khaim Kats was pleased with the reception in another Cossack collective farm in the same region.[226] Roza Bazylianskaia (Amromina) testifies to the positive attitude toward the refugees in the Buriat kolkhoz where she was placed.[227] Itskhak Shteingart was very pleased with the attitude of local residents to refugees in Ioshkar-Ola (Mari ASSR) and Urgench (Uzbekistan).[228] Polina Rivkina testifies: "In Aktiubinsk with a sick child, no one would take us into an apartment. But, in the end, my mom made an arrangement with Katia Aslanova, a kind Tatar woman, and she took us into her apartment, which was practically just outside the garden, near the cemetery and the airfield. It was one big room, which my mother divided into two. We built an oven there and settled in."[229]

Grigorii Refas, who lost his parents during the flight to the east, testifies: "The Bashkirs treated the children from the Baltic states very well. I ended up in a small village; they gave me bast shoes, and the old man in whose home I was placed accepted me as a family member.[230] The positive attitude of the inhabitants of the same Chuvash ASSR is evidenced by Anna Solovëva, Anna Tolochinskaia (Beilinson), Gutia Turk, and Nina Notkina.[231] However, it should be kept in mind that these testimonies from Chuvashia are from childhood or adolescence, in which memories of the everyday negative moments are usually mitigated by more vivid impressions. This is evident from the response of Anna Tolochinskaia. To the direct question of nutrition, she replied that the kolkhoz administration gave out little food, and in her first year there she had no proper clothes, so she did not go to school. It also came to light that they did not have a garden, unlike many other refugees.[232]

We have a wonderful opportunity to observe an even sharper level of dissonance between childhood memories and the real situation in the example of the Notkin family, who found themselves in the Chuvash ASSR. Nina Notkin recalls that while living in the village Parkhi-kasy, in the Ishlei district, when all the members of the family were in the hospital, she begged and collected crusts of bread door to door. One person didn't give anything, another person reacted warmly. Several people wanted to adopt her. What she collected she ate herself and also gave to her hungry family members at the hospital.[233] Unlike her—on the whole positive—memories of the evacuation, archival documents speak of the extremely difficult situation in which the Notkin family— the mother and her four children—in fact, were. According to the report of the inspector Larionova, the chair of the collective farm, Surkov, treated the Notkin family mockingly. He placed them in a house with half-ruined walls, without a floor and a stove. Despite the fact that the eldest seventeen-year-old son worked in the kolkhoz, they were not given even bread and resorted to eating grass. The situation was aggravated by the fact that the mother and one of the sons were very weak after suffering typhus and pneumonia. Larionova herself arranged a one-time delivery of bread to them and found an empty house in the village, where the kolkhoz chair reluctantly agreed to resettle the Notkins. When she then complained to the chair of the executive committee, Khersonov, he started to cover for Surkov. Together they went to the kolkhoz for an inspection, but they could not solve the problem, because all the local leadership was drunk, "from the chair of the village council to the brigadier."[234]

In all probability Larionova's efforts helped the Notkin family; after all, Nina survived the evacuation. However, as we already know, the conscientious inspectors of the evacuation department were few, and one met with Surkov types much more often. Nina's memories of her evacuation experience were overall positive. Such an assessment was the result of corrections and self-censorship, formed under the influence of the myth—which was successfully absorbed into the mass consciousness—about the successful absorption of the evacuees, which we discussed in the beginning of the book. French sociologist Maurice Halbwachs termed the repression—and even replacement—of individual experience with collective experience "social memory."[235]

ANTISEMITIC OFFICIALS AND THE POSITION OF THE CENTRAL AUTHORITIES

Administrators were not supposed to take into account the ethnicity of refugees when it came to moving them, housing them, and providing food for them. In practice, however, the disposition of a particular official to each refugee was of great importance. Some administrators, especially in the lower echelons of power, were not free from the antisemitism that existed before the war and which spread even more during the war under the influence of German propaganda.[236]

Making decisions about general issues, officials with a prejudiced attitude toward the Jews could not but believe that they constituted a large percentage of refugees. And although they understood that far from all of them were Jews, they still treated all refugees as unwanted aliens who violated local norms of behavior and customs. Therefore, negative attitude of local officials to refugees, discussed above, should be viewed as a manifestation of not only their reluctance to spend time on them but also of antisemitism. The relatively few officially recorded cases of antisemitism openly expressed by administrators do not necessarily reflect the entirety of the attitudes toward Jewish refugees. According to the complaint of Boris Kopman to the regional party authorities, one of the city chiefs in Ufa, dealing with a request for better housing from an applicant whose husband had been killed at the front, asked about her nationality and refused her upon learning that she was Jewish.[237] The evacuation inspector's review showed that in the Mari ASSR the kolkhoz chair Strel'nikov intentionally gave refugee Berlin extra work, called him names, and mocked him because of his Jewish nationality. This despite the fact that the Berlin family did impeccable work for the kolkhoz and performed four hundred workdays in a year.[238]

Paul Stronski quotes a kolkhoz chair in Uzbekistan who said that it was time to drive out the Jews and suggested that all problems were due to their lack of agricultural knowledge.[239] This stereotypical view that Jews, being townspeople, had little knowledge of agriculture, was not based on reality. As we already know, many Jews in the cities of the former Pale of Settlement had, on the eve of the war, garden plots and were actively engaged in gardening. Animal husbandry was also not foreign to Jewish refugees. In Rechitsa on the eve of the war about a third of Jewish families kept a cow or a bull, while 30–40 percent even raised pigs, mainly for sale.[240] As for Jews evacuated from Moscow and Leningrad, the overwhelming majority of them moved to these cities from the same Pale of Settlement during the 1920s–1930s and were therefore also familiar with gardening.

These instances of the officials' prejudiced attitude toward Jews can in no way be called state antisemitism. The central authorities regarded antisemitic actions or statements as manifestations of disloyalty to the regime: they were well informed about the widespread popular opinion that Jews dominated the country's government. NKVD reports classified manifestations of antisemitism under a general heading of anti-Soviet sentiments.[241]

In early October 1941 Mikhail Shamberg, deputy head of the organizational department of the TsK VKP(b), reported to the secretaries of the Central Committee about the rise of antisemitism in Moscow and the Stalino, Gor'kii, Ivanovo, Kuibyshev, and Penza regions. He lamented the lack of push back against this phenomenon.[242] At that time this signal did result in the desired change, but starting in 1942, influenced by the ever-growing manifestations of domestic antisemitism, the central and republican authorities, although reluctantly, started to fight against it, even though some higher-level officials were themselves prejudiced against Jews, as we saw in the case of the Belorussian Communist Party leader Ponomarenko. According to the prosecutor's report on the situation in the RSFSR during the first four months of 1942, S. Sturov, chair of the village council of Suslov (Mariinsk district in the Novosibirsk region), was convicted of antisemitic actions and statements against refugees. According to the same report, Golovatin, chair of Kolkhoz Vperëd (Forward!) in the Circassian autonomous region, was convicted of antisemitic statements and general harassment of refugees. Zakharchenko, the chair of a kolkhoz in the Kizliar district of the Ordzhonikidze territory, was also brought to trial for saying: "An order has been issued to build a ship the size of a farm, to put all the Jews in it, take them out to the middle of the sea, and sink them."[243]

On September 30, 1942, the Party regional committee of East Kazakhstan adopted a resolution to begin a propaganda campaign against antisemitism.[244] The committee made a reference to the well-known statement that Stalin made in 1931 that antisemitism led working people into the jungle and that active antisemites were to be punished by death. Over the first half of 1942, twenty people were convicted of antisemitic actions, and an additional forty-two were convicted just in the Alma-Ata and Semipalatinsk regions of the republic in August of that year.[245] Apparently, no fewer people were convicted at the time in Kirgizstan.[246] E. G. testifies that in the summer of 1943, the authorities, at first, tried to hush up the murder of a Jewish refugee and her child in Leninabad, but at the request of Ashkenazi Jews the perpetrators were caught, and the three murderers—two Tajiks and a Russian—were publicly tried in a city park. All were sentenced to death. After this trial, the city police began to arrest people for aggressive manifestations of antisemitism, which led to an improvement in the situation.[247] In the Lebiazh'e district of the Cheliabinsk region in July 1942, the former chair of the district Consumers Union, Kol'ev, was expelled from the party and apparently dismissed from his position for manifestations of antisemitism.[248]

As already mentioned, starting in 1943 the central authorities preferred not to have cases of antisemitism and the struggle against it to be reported in the press. However, this does not mean that antisemitism was ignored. In June 1943, a member of the Communist Party from Ukraine, Akim Koshman, was expelled from the party and dismissed from his post as the head of the NKGB detention facility in Uzbekistan for systematic beatings of the imprisoned Jews. His case was considered at the highest level of the republic.[249]

In only a few cases of the activities of the republican and central authorities of this time have I discovered anti-Jewish discriminatory behavior toward refugees. Most of them involved Ponomarenko. At the end of May 1942, the evacuated Belorussian authorities, through party organizations of the rear regions, collected lists of Belorussian refugees only.[250] Although the archival records that I had at my disposal did not indicate for what purposes these lists were needed, the answer was found in a published volume on the activities of the Belorussian Communist Party in 1941–1942. According to the documents, the Council for People's Commissars of the BSSR distributed 140,000 rubles to 664 Belorussian families.[251] In another case, the department for the employment of the evacuated population, under the auspices to the Council of People's Commissars of the BSSR, lobbied to facilitate reunification of Belorussian evacuee families,[252] while Jewish refugees from this republic, as evidenced by numerous archival documents, did not receive this support. Such a policy was discordant with the prewar nonethnic approach in dealing with the people's everyday issues.

Unlike the Belorussian authorities, the evacuated authorities of the Baltic republics cared for all their refugees. When in October 1941 the representative of the Latvian government in Chuvashia and deputy of the Supreme Soviet of the USSR M. Khorunzhii asked the local authorities to send lists of evacuees from Latvia and help them with clothes and shoes, he did not single out ethnic Latvians.[253] Assistant Permanent Representative of the Latvian SSR to the Council of People's Commissars of the USSR Rudolf Latsis, examining the situation of the Latvian immigrants in Chuvashia, did not exclude the Jews from the inspection.[254] The chair of the Supreme Soviet of the Estonian SSR Johannes Vares in the autumn of 1941 asked the chair of the USSR Evacuation

Council Nikolai Shvernik to send warm clothes and shoes to five thousand people from the Estonian SSR, regardless of their nationality.²⁵⁵

Local Jews and the Refugees

The spread of antisemitism among the local population compromised in the eyes of the Jews the government-propagated discourse of the "friendship of peoples." This, as well as the Nazi genocide and the high mortality rate among Jewish refugees, caused an unprecedented rise in national self-awareness among the Jewish population of the USSR. The struggle for the return of their property in the liberated cities and the state antisemitism that had spread at the end of the war further intensified this process. One of the manifestations of the increased national consciousness was the widespread participation in religious observances during and, especially, after the war.

In Central Asia participation in religion increased among Jewish refugees as early as 1942–1943.²⁵⁶ In those years, in Kyzyl-Kiia (Kirghiz SSR) Romanian and Polish Jews, including those who had been relatively nonobservant before, organized an underground minyan. For tens of thousands of rubles they bought a Torah scroll from the Fergana Museum of Local History, which had it in the warehouse. When in 1944 five boys were born in Kyzyl-Kiia, the organizer of the minyan, Mordekhai Liuksemburg, brought a Bukharan-Jewish mohel to perform circumcisions.²⁵⁷ An article written by Isaac Sheinman for the *Eynikayt* newspaper testifies to the religious "awakening" in Kirgizstan. According to the article, the Jewish religious community was officially organized in Frunze in early 1942; initially, its membership stood at several hundred, but it declined to 115 as a result of the re-evacuation of 1944–1945. In 1944 the local authorities even allowed the community to buy a house in the city center for organized prayers. Perhaps the authorities' amenability was due to the community's donation that year of 10,000 rubles for to build a tank unit and 4,000 rubles for the support of military families.²⁵⁸ In any case, the establishment of the minyan was part of the ongoing state campaign for some liberalization of religious life in the USSR.

In general, the conditions for initiation into the Jewish religion in Central Asia can be assessed as very favorable. Anticlericalism in Central Asian and North Caucasian regions of the USSR had not been as ruthless as in the European part. During the war years, this it receded everywhere because, on the one hand, the authorities had many more important tasks and, on the other, they deliberately weakened the antireligious pressure to lessen the discontent of the population already suffering from a multitude of hardships. Although in some cases the authorities at that time resorted to repressive measures, in general, they were more inclined to "intimidation by warning." Their goal was not to eradicate underground religious activities but only to fight against "too open" manifestations of religion. This was done so that the population did not have a feeling that state power was weakening, something the state could not admit. In 1946 the head of the Misnagid yeshiva, Itskhak Kopelman, was arrested in broad daylight in the Bukharan-Jewish bazaar in Samarkand. He was interrogated in the local branch of the MGB and was suddenly released at night, with orders to leave the city immediately.[259]

During the war not only a lot of believers were concentrated in Central Asia, but so were most of the religious authorities that existed on the territory of the USSR. In a very short time they managed to establish connections with each other and organize themselves. The Chabad especially succeeded in the revival of religious life, quickly establishing the illegal work of synagogues, yeshivas, ḥeders, and organizing the shehitah (the slaughtering of animals for food in accordance with rabbinic law). In 1942 Rabbi Eliahu Roitblat opened an underground Chabad yeshiva in Samarkand. Due to the high mortality from epidemics and famine, it soon ceased to exist but resumed in 1943 under the guidance of Mendel Futerfas (1907–1995) and the administration of Nison Nemanov (1904–1984). Among the teachers were Mikhail Tetelboim, Nakhum-Shmeriiagu Sasonkin, Shmuel Notik, Moshe Rubin, Avraam Eli Plotkin, and Zalman-Shimon Dvorkin. Aba Pliskin and Israel Leibov taught in the ḥeders. According to memoirs, up to 150 young people were trained in the ḥeders and the Chabad yeshiva of Samarkand.[260] The Braslav Hasids also established their own center there. The most active among them was Levi Itskhak Bender (1897–1989).

In Tashkent, the Chabad movement headed by Rabbi Shneur-Zalman Gorelik also founded an underground yeshiva, in which up to sixty pupils were trained.[261] The rabbi of Nevel Israel Levin and the rabbi of Riga Mordekhai Nurok taught the children in the Tashkent ḥeders. Besides, in Tashkent during the war, the leadership of the religious community of Moscow and several other cities could be found.[262] A small yeshiva for twenty students was also opened in Dzhambul. Under the leadership of Rabbi Moshe Rubin, Talmud-and-Torah for seventy children was organized, as well as many minyans and a rabbinical court. Just as in Samarkand, religious Jews here built a mikvah with their own money.[263] A lot of moral support for the Chabad refugees with regard to these activities was provided by letters from New York from the sixth Chabad tsaddik, Yosef Yitzchak Schneersohn (1880–1950), sent by different routes.[264]

Researcher Irina Osipova, referring to the Hasidim's stay in Central Asia during the war years, idealizes their organization and secrecy.[265] The point of view of Avraham Gershuni and Nakhum-Shmeriiagu Sasonkin, who were there at that time, that the authorities had detailed information about their religion activity but turned a blind eye to it, seems more precise.²⁶⁶ The NKVD-NKGB received such information from informers they recruited primarily from among Polish Jews, who "worked" with them more often.²⁶⁷

Stalin at that time had to demonstrate to Jewish organizations in the West that he had, to a certain extent, softened the formerly rigid attitude toward Jewish culture and religion. Already by 1942, the *Chicago Sentinel* published, with reference to an official Moscow note, that in Samarkand, Tashkent, Alma-Ata, and other cities of Central Asia, tens of thousands of Jews, including Polish Jews, were celebrating Passover. The same article mentioned a certain rabbi from a Ukrainian town who, being wounded, fled from the Nazis and was saved by Soviet soldiers; now in Uzbekistan, he praised the Soviet Constitution for the freedom of religion.²⁶⁸ In an article in *Eynikayt*, which was focused primarily on the West, its editor Shakhno Epshtein wrote that Jewish workers from Poland in Andizhan had organized a study group for Bukharan Jews who were unfamiliar with Hebrew so that they could get acquainted with Jewish literature. Epshtein also noted that such study groups were going to open in other cities of Uzbekistan, including Bukhara.²⁶⁹ It is clear that what was being discussed was the teaching of religious literature.

Polish Jewish refugees bake matzah for the Passover holiday, Samarkand. USHMM, courtesy of Hynda (Szczukowski) Halpren.

For the sake of survival, Jewish religious movements organized their artels, which allowed them to earn good wages and not work on Saturdays and holidays. The Hasidim Chabad homeworkers set up a knitting artel in Tashkent. Similar artels were later established in Samarkand and Dzhambul. The artel in Samarkand made yarn from local cotton, stained it, and then made cloth. Everyone was trained by two families of experienced weavers from Lodz—Wiesbauers and Turkins. Based on the name of a neighborhood in Lodz—Bałuty—they named their artel the New Balut. In addition to the Jews (and among them were the famous Rabbi Alter Vagshol, timber merchant Iosif Ekersfeld, and businessman Faibush Rozenberg), other refugees, as well as local Uzbeks, worked in the artel. The artel sewed clothes for the army and for the local population.[270] In Dzhambul, the Jewish artel Birlik ("unity" in Uzbek) in 1944 alone processed 4,500 square meters of sheepskin for sewing fur coats, manufactured 1,650 pairs of felt boots, sewed 6,000 sets of underwear for the Red Army, and so on.[271]

The growth of national and religious self-awareness among Jews, who had earlier departed from Judaism, was influenced, in part, by wounded Jewish soldiers, convalescing in Central Asia, who witnessed the Holocaust in the west of the country.[272] In 1942–1943 some Jews, who had received information about the death of relatives and friends, began to find psychological comfort in religion.[273] E. G. reports that in Leninabad even members of families of senior administrative and party officials visited the synagogue and circumcised their children.[274] Aron Feigenblum recalls how much he was surprised to see the NKVD officer loudly reading Kaddish in the Khatyrchi synagogue.[275] Even those who had not known how to pray before began to attend minyans and synagogues.[276] Yosef Litvak describes how on Yom Kippur (he assumes that this was in 1943, but could be in 1944), at the Polish hospital in Samarkand, all the Jews who could walk enthusiastically gathered for a memorial prayer. However, it turned out that no one had a prayer book, and no one remembered the prayers by heart.[277] Therefore, one can hardly agree with Yaacov Ro'i, who claims that the growth of Jewish self-awareness during the war did not affect the growth of the number of believers.[278]

The story of the funeral of Avraham Iuditskii, historian and publicist, clearly shows the strengthening of Jewish self-awareness. He came to Tashkent in 1942 and, suffering, like many others, from hunger, waited in a long line in the dining hall to get a bowl of watery soup. Once at a common table, he got into a conversation with Ehezkiel Keitelman, then a beginning writer from Poland. Introducing himself, Iuditskii said that he probably not heard of him. Annoyed, Keitelman answered, "How could one not have heard of you," recalling Iuditskii's articles in Soviet newspapers on the eve of every Jewish holiday, "filled with antisemitic poison against everything Jewish." Then, forgetting about caution, Keitelman talked for a long time and ended his speech with the words: "You took our holidays from us, replacing them with camps." Coming to his senses, Keitelman was frightened of denunciation, but everything turned out okay, and he every felt sympathy for Iuditskii—they continued to converse in the dining hall and were already talking calmly about life. When Iuditskii died in September 1943 of hunger and depression in the hospital, a group of writers gathered informally to discuss the organization of a funeral for their colleague. At that point, the writer Der Nister (Pinkhas Kaganovich) unexpectedly offered to bury the deceased "warrior against the Jewish religion" in the Jewish cemetery according to the rite. When these dozen writers came to the hospital with an Uzbek wagon, officials refused to issue the body on the pretext that they could not find Iuditskii's unused ration cards. Then, according to Keitelman, writers, who themselves were undernourished, sacrificed their cards for a colleague, for the sake of the mitzvah (commandment) of the redemption of a dead Jew. This act and the ensuing funeral rite not only rallied these writers from different countries but also accorded them solidarity with the deceased, not as a colleague, but as a Jew.[279]

The growth of national identity and involvement in religion in 1943–1947 are demonstrated by the requests of Jewish groups for the opening of synagogues in fifty-three different cities of the USSR.[280] These cities were not under German occupation, so it was not a question of recovery of destroyed property or the return of confiscated by Germans religious premises. Jews in Central Asia were no exception. In 1943 Bukharan Jews were successful in the opening of a synagogue in Stalinabad.[281] Because of a petition in 1945, a synagogue was opened in Bukhara as well.[282] In the same year, the authorities were ready to legalize one of the underground prayer houses operating in Alma-Ata, but Jewish believers were afraid to officially become members of the religious community.[283] In Frunze the Jewish religious community, officially established in 1944, was registered in June 1945.[284] The Ashkenazi Jews of Tashkent unsuccessfully sought for seven years—from 1943 to 1949—the return and opening of the synagogue that was taken from them in 1942 and turned into an officers' hotel.[285] The authorities had initially intended to return the building, despite the resistance of the military authorities, but in the second half of the 1940s, it was decided not to, the decision affected by the rise of the antisemitic state discourse.

Increased national self-consciousness found expression not only in increasing attention to Judaism but also in the growing interest in Jewish history and culture. In 1943 a small underground circle of Russian Jews formed in Samarkand to study Jewish history.[286] The hall of the Kharkov Jewish Theater, located at that time in Samarkand was completely filled during the performances; the performances were attended by teenagers as well, many of whom did not even know Yiddish.[287]

The growth of national self-consciousness raised, in turn, the level of solidarity among the Jews. Jewish refugees often found among local Ashkenazi Jews, including those who were completely assimilated, various forms of support: housing, food, clothing, and work. Particularly important was the assistance of doctors, officials, and administrators, of which there are many examples.[288] Here are just a few of them. Moshe Grosman describes the case of a visit to the administrator of the Samarkand Gorkombinat by the members of the funeral society Chevra Kadisha with a request for financial support. Fearing provocation, he drove them out, then immediately called Grosman and gave him three hundred rubles for them. At the same time, he warned Grosman not to include his name on the lists of donors. Moreover, the administrator promised to donate money every month,[289] which he did as, otherwise, the author would have noted it. According to the testimony of Kh., there were about two hundred Jews together with him in his working battalion, mainly from Bessarabia. The battalion was erecting a storage facility for oil near Krasnovodsk. The Soviet engineer Rabkin was a supervisor. At the risk of causing complaints about patronage of the Jews, he tried to find easier work for them.[290] Many Jewish refugees from Poland and Romania recall the special warm support of Soviet Jewish doctors.[291]

There were many cases of mutual assistance amongst the Jewish refugees themselves, both among Soviet Jews and within the informal communities of Polish, Lithuanian, Moldavian, and other Jews. More often, Soviet refugee Jews helped the other communities because of their better circumstances. It also happened that Polish Jews helped the Soviets. Vladimir Vaisberg recalls how in Dzhambul their family (three children without a father) was guarded by an informal community of Polish Jews.[292]

The attitude of Bukharan Jews to Jewish refugees from European Russia was ambiguous. Most often they supported the Hasidim; they had an especially warm attitude toward the Chabad movement. A certain segment of Bukharan Jews joined this branch of Judaism even before the war, under the influence of its representatives in Central Asia—in 1896–1920 (with interruptions), Rabbi Shlomo Eliezerov (Kazarnovskii), and throughout 1923–1930s, Rabbi Simkha Gorodetskii. In the mid-1920s, five or six Bukharan Jews were trained in the Chabad yeshiva in Leningrad.[293] One of them created the Chabad minyan in Samarkand, which was in operation during the war.[294] In the war years, the connection of Bukharan Jews with Chabad was strengthened. Many Bukharan-Jewish teenagers began to visit the Chabad yeshiva with great enthusiasm.[295] In the courtyard of Avraam Aminov, eight families of Chabad Jewish refugees were located. Even more Jewish refugees lived in the courtyard of Rafael Khudaidatov, also in Samarkand. Despite the great risk, he even agreed to build a mikvah in his yard, an idea initiated by Rabbi Sasonkin.[296]

Inasmuch as the authorities ordered local residents to rent part of their housing to refugees, the Bukharan Jews preferred to provide rooms in their homes to religious Jews. On the one hand, they feared the appearance of non-kosher products in their homes, and, on the other hand, they feared denunciations for adherence to Jewish rites. Besides, such a settlement created a unique learning opportunity about religious subjects for their children. The abandonment in 1942 by many of the Bukharan-Jewish pupils of public schools was the result of the sharp spread of religious education at home or in underground ḥeders.[297]

The well-known Bratslav Hasid Mordekhai Lesker formed friendly relations with the Bukharan Jews of Samarkand. He was impressed when, in conditions of almost total hunger, a wealthy Bukharan Jew arranged a wedding for a pair of refugees from Poland. The pilaf that the guests ate was unforgettable for them.[298] The Chabad Hasid Natan Barkan mentions in his memoirs the assistance to the poor refugees on the part of the wealthy Bukharan Jews of Samarkand.[299] Another Chabad Hasid, Israel-Yehuda Levin, speaks well of the Bukharan Jew from whom he rented a room.[300] Etia Lekakh recalled how in Bukhara, the Bukharan Jews helped them with food.[301] A Bukharan Jew—a distributor of bread in Kermine—apparently taking Menachem Begin for a religious Jew after he asked in Hebrew where the synagogue was located, began to supply him well with bread.[302] Aron Feigenblum recalls that the prosecutor in Khatyrchi was a Bukharan Jews, because of which Jewish refugees were not beaten in the nearby tungsten mines. Moreover, the prosecutor told them, "I will not try you for refusing to work on such a day (Yom Kippur)."[303]

Evidence suggests that Bukharan Jews in some cases also helped nonreligious Jewish refugees. A resident of the orphanage in Tashkent, Dov Dunaevskii, testifies that during the war the family of Mani Danielova fed him. He, who did not receive even enough bread, was treated to special pleasures—pilaf with raisins and sandwiches with pork fat.[304] Dorothy Abend was helped by a family of Bukharan Jews in Kermine, renting a room from them.[305] The Samarkand family of Il'ia Khudaidatov sheltered the orphaned Genia Rabin, taking her from the kolkhoz.[306] More former refugees witnessed the help of Bukharan Jews in yet other cities.[307] In autumn 1941 a group of Jewish refugees from Lithuania was detained in Tashkent on suspicion of espionage. Their case was handled by Bukharan Jewish investigator. Realizing that they are "Israelim," he immediately let them go with a recommendation to leave the city for three days, for example, to go to Samarkand. They did this.[308]

Jewish refugees celebrate a wedding, Bukhara. USHMM, courtesy of Pessia Polak.

These examples testify to the solidarity of some of the Bukharan Jews with the Ashkenazi Jews. Shakhno Epshtein cites in an article for *Eynikayt* the words of the former shoe shiner Khamid Abramov: "Hitler does not distinguish between Jews of one kind or another. He wants to exterminate the entire Jewish people." Further, the author tells that Abramov and his friends traveled from Kokand to Tashkent to see the premiere of Yiddish performance of *Tevye the Milkman* at the Moscow Theater. Despite the fact that they did not understand the words, they were happy with the number of Jews who came to see the performance.[309] Although *Eynikayt* was an ideologically slanted newspaper and was an official intermediary between the authorities and the Soviet Jewish readers, this article seemed to reflect the true feelings of some of the Bukharan Jews.

Even though the Bukharan Jews helped mainly the Hasidim, their collective memory firmly remains convinced that they helped all Ashkenazi refugees during the war.[310] In contrast, former Ashkenazi refugees preserved more evidence of denied assistance. Rakhel Noiman reports that Bukharan Jews did not help Jewish refugees in Bukhara.[311] A similar situation was witnessed by Henrik

Rubinshtein in Kokand, Mikhail Margolin in Shakhrisiabz, and Beniamin Cherpichnik in Tashkent. Iafa Dolinskaia, Gedalia Goldberg, and Rut Gekht say the same thing about Samarkand.[312] Moshe Levertov, a student of the Chabad Yeshiva in Samarkand, emphasizes the hostility of the Bukharan Jews toward them, the Ashkenazi Hasidim. According to his story, a Bukharan Jewish policeman demanded the highest bribe from their shochet for ritual circumcision. Levertov singles out only Iurii Niiazov, whose home was always open to Hasidim, including those with typhus. Niiazov got infected from them and died.[313] E. G. testifies that in Leninabad the Bukharan Jews treated refugees with the same indifference as did the rest of the population.[314] Henryk Grynberg, in his collection of testimonies, concludes that the Bukharan Jews in Uzbekistan initially helped the Jewish refugees, but then gradually stopped.[315]

Although Bukharan Jews had housing, permanent work, connections, and established living conditions, compared to the refugees, and they understood the local realities well, which helped them to survive the hard times, one cannot ignore the plight of some of them. These were families that had not yet fully recovered from the severe economic crisis experienced by the community in the late 1920s and early 1930s.[316] Most of these families were in economically backward Bukhara. Rojza Lauterbach testifies that the Bukharan Jews lived very poorly, not having "anything to cover their backs with," and therefore their help could not be counted on.[317] Nakhum Teper reports that the rich among Bukharan Jews were deported, and the poor in Bukhara had nothing to eat, but their attitude toward the Polish Jews was cordial, and they prayed together.[318] According to the testimony of Bukharan Jewess Berta Guliamova, her mother, thirty years old, died in 1942 in Bukhara from hunger.[319]

Dov Levin believes that the cause of tensions between the Bukharan and Ashkenazi Jews in Samarkand was in an attempt to prevent the burial of refugees in the Bukharan Jews' cemetery in 1942.[320] There was a quarrel on similar grounds in Tashkent as well. In 1942 Bukharan Jews refused to help one Ashkenazi family in organizing the funeral of a deceased relative.[321] Sasonkin explains the reason for the conflict as the reluctance of religious Ashkenazi Jews to trust the burial ceremony of Bukharan Jews. Being in the center of these contacts, he also testifies that the Chevra Kadisha of Bukharan Jews in Tashkent and Samarkand could not cope with the volume of funerals it had to perform. To help meet the need, Chabad opened their own Chevra Kadisha there. They began to identify the Jews among the deceased and keep a record of them.[322] The creation of these organizations caused a temporary quarrel with Bukharan Jews. They saw this as a manifestation of mistrust and, indeed, for a time resisted burial at their cemetery in Samarkand, and possibly in Tashkent, of Ashkenazi Jews through the Chabad Chevra Kadisha.

Without loosing sight of the importance of the Chevra Kadisha for the burial of deceased refugees, it should be noted that in cases where the deceased did not have relatives (and this happened often), the burial provided the opportunity to dispose of clothing, valuables, unused bread, and other types of ration cards. This was important in the conditions of continuing hunger. In some cases documents that did not feature photographs of the deceased who were officially unregistered granted the possibility of receiving further ration cards for hungry members of the religious community. It should also be noted that in the cities of Uzbekistan there were many Jews who did not receive food cards, for various reasons—being afraid to register (for example, because of leaving their former residence without permission) or having been denied a residence permit. More often, however, documents and especially food cards were taken from the deceased earlier: by medical personnel, if the refugee died in the hospital, neighbors if it happened at home, or by passersby if death came on the street. After the Soviet authorities began to allow the departure of Polish Jews to Poland in 1944–1945, the value of documents found on the deceased refugees who were Polish citizens before 1939 particularly increased. These documents presented an opportunity to leave the USSR. The situation was similar in other eastern regions.[323]

In fact, the change in the attitude of Bukharan Jews toward the Ashkenazi refugees for the worse was due to the strengthening of negative attitudes toward them from the surrounding population of Central Asia. Many Bukharan Jews found it "proper" to distance themselves from refugees. This change is very remarkable. It shows the spread of a danger signal among Bukharan Jews, who knew well the mood of the indigenous Muslim population, having lived among them for a long time and knowing well their psychosocial behavior. According to Nakhum Teper, Bukharan Jews were very concerned about the high cost of living caused by refugees and the negative attitude of the local population toward them.[324] The former director of the Soviet branch of the Joint Distribution Committee, probably based on testimonies of those Polish Jews who left the USSR with the Anders's army, wrote in December 1943 to the chair of the JDC advisory council James Rosenberg that although the Bukharan Jews recognized some Ashkenazim as rabbis and teachers, nevertheless, even Russian Jews were considered outsiders, which caused the deteriorating relations with the indigenous population.[325] This point of view is confirmed in the testimony of E. G., according to which because of the deterioration of the attitude of Tajiks toward refugees in 1942, Bukharan Jews began to avoid close relations with Polish Jews.[326]

According to the Polish writer and journalist Moshe Grosman, this distance on the part of some Bukharan Jews even grew into a hatred for Russian and

Polish Jews. He gives an example: in Samarkand, he was passing near the market in the Bukharan Jewish quarter at night with a friend, when an unfamiliar Bukharan Jew came up to them and with the words "Here's a gift for you, Polish Jew!" hit him in the face.[327] In an interview, Gedalia Goldberg spoke about an event in which the head of the Bukharan Jewish quarter took Goldberg's documents and documents of another Polish Jew and then brought them to the military enlistment office to draft them into the army.[328] Such an act was a reaction to the widely spread stereotypical opinion that "the Jews do not fight."

The unfriendliness of some of the Bukharan Jews toward the Ashkenazi refugee Jews was sometimes manifested even in relation toward the religious among them. In Kzyl-Orda, recalls Iakov Eshkol, Bukharan Jews didn't help the Ashkenazi Jews, saying "If it's so bad for you here, why did you come here?" Even during the *iamim noraim* ("days of awe," the ten days from Rosh Hashanah to Yom Kippur) the Ashkenazim were not allowed to pray in their synagogue and had to do it in the courtyard.[329] In Tashkent, according to Beniamin Cherpichnik's testimony, Bukharan Jews allowed the Ashkenazim to pray in their synagogues only on Saturdays and on holidays, not on weekdays.[330]

There was another reason for this attitude. The fact is that some Bukharan Jews were afraid of denunciations by unfamiliar Jewish refugees.[331] Frightened by the repressions of 1937–1939, which had hit the community extremely hard, these Bukharan Jews were particularly afraid of coming in contact with people who belonged to Zionist parties or who did not register with the police. Myriam Bar, in her autobiographical book, relates how a young civil servant, a Bukharan Jew, who had been courting her, broke off the relationship with her after learning that she did not have any documents. At the same time, he did not give her over to the executive authorities.[332] According to Kh., in a Bukharan Jewish kolkhoz near Tashkent, Polish Jewish refugees were involved in a discussion about Zionism and Bundism, which led to their arrest.[333] Perhaps the Bukharan Jews considered this discussion a provocation and decided to inform the law enforcement about it first.

∽

The majority of the local population disliked the refugees, as they were seen as a force rapidly destroying the habitual local way of life. The situation was aggravated by the measures the authorities took to compel the local to share housing, as well as by skyrocketed prices caused by the arrival of refugees. Negative attitudes toward refugees were also amplified by their higher prewar economic and cultural status and, in many cases, ethnic differences. Although some local population of non-Russian regions didn't like the Russian refugees, the attitude toward Jews in all regions of the rear was generally worse. In addition to experiencing primitive antisemitism, Jewish refugees were accused of disloyalty to the Soviet Union and lack of patriotism, on the one hand, and, on the other, of dominating of Soviet institutions of power. Antisemitism was particularly acute in Central Asia, where Jews made up almost half of the refugee population.

The attitude of the officials was ambiguous. Nevertheless, there is a general trend. The lower the position, the less tolerant the attitude toward refugees was due to the fact that the local officials adhered less to the general state policy and were more influenced by the surrounding population. In turn, the increase in antisemitism, along with the spread of information about the numerous victims among Jews, both in the occupied territory and behind the front line, contributed to the growth of Jewish identity. It facilitated the spread of religion among the Jewish population, the growth of mutual support, and, especially, the mutual assistance among relatives. For this purpose, relatives tried to settle together, which was reflected in the migration flows. Migration and refugee statistics will be discussed in the next chapter.

CHAPTER SEVEN

Statistics on Refugees and Their Migration

Communication and Migration of Jewish Refugees in the Rear

The receipt of grocery ration cards at evacuation centers (they were often located at railway police stations) and recruitment to work were enabled by the registration of a residence permit with the police. Living more than a month without registration could result in a prison sentence for violation of the passport regime. In practice, a large number of refugees violated it by bribing landlords or officials, and the state structures responsible for overseeing the passport regime often did not have sufficient staff for comprehensive oversight. Those who wished to avoid being registered as Jewish refugees can be divided into four main groups: (a) religious or Zionist activists who feared arrest for their activities; (b) those evading conscription into the labor army; (c) those who were distrustful of the authorities; and (d) those who had lost their documents.

The last group was probably the most numerous, since thefts of clothing, purses, men's briefcases, and ladies' handbags—and the documents along with them—flourished everywhere. The theft of documents was practiced in order to hide from a search using somebody else's name (documents at that time did not have photos), to acquire any documents at all, if they had lost their own, and to receive additional ration cards using other people's documents. Those hiding from search with other people's documents included exiles, persons who had evaded military service or left work without permission, and in general all those who had reason to fear arrest and trial. In Novosibirsk someone else's passport could be bought for three thousand rubles[1] (about ten months pay). The refugees who lost their documents were afraid to report this to the authorities because of the fear of being sent to work in kolkhozes or in the plants, whose poor working and living conditions have already been described.

During the deportation campaigns, local authorities also expelled refugees from the cities, which caused many of them to be afraid to register. The majority of the unregistered refugees were those who had been foreign citizens before 1939, as Soviet refugees were more law abiding. Refugees from those regions of Poland that had become part of Germany under the 1939 treaty between Germany and the USSR had special reasons not to trust the Soviet authorities. After all, many of them were deported to work camps in 1940 after they stated that they preferred to remain Polish citizens during a special survey conducted by the Soviet authorities, the text of which contained no warnings of reprimands. Even more disappointed were the former Romanian citizens, because until 1940, due to successful propaganda, they were more likely to believe in Soviet internationalism and social justice.

Rebecca Manley argues that refugees and evacuees were reduced almost to the state of deportees because of restrictions on movement and the general attitude of the authorities. As proof, she cites the fact that Soviet Germans were included in the statistics of the evacuated population.[2] It was not by chance that Andrei Vyshinskii, who was then the first chair of the legal commission of the Council of People's Commissars of the USSR, proposed to completely equate these two categories, combining them in one category—"exiles."[3] Gennadii Kornilov, on the other hand, believes that the deportees (Soviet Germans, Poles, and others) were never counted as evacuees.[4] In reality, local officials sometimes combined the deported Germans and refugees under the general heading "Information on evacuated citizens."[5]

In some cases, they were later listed separately as "Germans" and "evacuees" in official report, as was done in December 1941 by the chair of the executive committee of the Alma-Ata regional council, Sharipov.[6] But in some other cases, these same groups were combined in "factsheets on the total number of the arriving population."[7] Meanwhile, the central authorities tried to remove the deported Soviet citizens from the statistics of the evacuated population. When compiling a summary of the number of evacuated people on January 1, 1942, the deputy chief of the CSA (Central Statistical Administration) S. Morozov explained its reduction —in comparison with the previous report—as due to the removal of 168,656 deported Germans who had mistakenly been placed in list of one of the regions.[8]

The deported Soviet Germans were more often called *nemtsy-pereselentsy* (German settlers) but the (also, in fact, deported) residents of the Karelo-Finnish SSR were called evacuees. Before the arrival of the Wehrmacht, the authorities managed to relocate almost 90 percent of the population of Karelo-Finnish SSR.[9] Having no information on such a total evacuation, Vadim Dubson doubted the number of migrants from Karelo-Finnish SSR, led by

Kumanëv.[10] Meanwhile, this was the most significant percentage of the evacuated population among all administrative-territorial units of the USSR during the war years. Fearing that the mass migration of Karelians, Vepsians, and Finns would be perceived as ethnic deportation, the authorities evacuated Russians and representatives of other groups form the autonomous republic as well. Once settled in their new places of residence, "evacuees" from this autonomous republic were subject to a special, so-called personal supervision,[11] which indicates the special circumstances of their resettlement. The special status of the Finns who were resettled from the Leningrad region, as well as of the Germans, is further indicated by the explanation of the deputy People's Commissar for Internal Affairs, Vsevolod Merkulov, that they were not administratively deported but forcibly evacuated.[12] The difference is that the transfer was not preceded by arrest. Only those who refused to leave were to be arrested. As for the deported Jews (former Polish citizens), they, as well as former Romanian and Baltic citizens, appear in the reports not as deported but as evacuated, as mentioned at the introduction.

In the regions, territories, and republics, the authorities were interested in "unloading" refugees from the cities and sending them to rural areas, solving simultaneously the problem of unemployment and the housing shortage in the cities, where, as we already know, as a result of crowding, the townspeople lived in very cramped conditions. In addition to the above-mentioned local deportations in Ul'ianovsk and Uzbekistan, such evictions also occurred in Kuibyshev and Penza, where in the autumn of 1941 artisans, the unemployed, and some other categories of residents were deported to small regional centers.[13] As a result of this policy, at the end of 1943, 52 percent of all refugees in the Ural regions and republics found themselves in the countryside, while at the end of 1941 only 43 percent lived there.[14] At the same time, in the regions with large industrial centers, such as Sverdlovsk and Cheliabinsk, only 22.8 percent and 37.5 percent were in rural areas, respectively.[15]

Practicing organized labor migration themselves, the authorities tried to prevent individual travel and to attach the arriving population to defined places of residence. This was done with the following intentions: to reduce the traffic along railroads that were teeming with military transports, to prevent turnover of workers, to facilitate the registration of evacuees, and to prevent their concentration in certain regions. Therefore, to move from one area to another, refugees had to seek permission, which could not be granted even by local executive authorities. According to the instructions, for each case, the refugees had to contact the head of the local NKVD office. Naturally, considering and responding to these inquiries added to the already heavy workload of local officials.

At first, local authorities addressed the issues of uniting close relatives rather liberally. For receive permission to move, the relative planning to leave had to provide two pieces of proof—evidence that their relatives really lived in the place to which they were traveling and that they had additional living space. An analysis of almost a hundred Jewish refugees' requests for departure of from Alatyr' (Chuvashia) for 1942 shows that in 56.7 percent of cases the authorities, allowed relatives to reunite.[16] Local administrators were agreeable in cases of the requests from the unemployed, who argued for approval of their requests by citing better opportunities in a new place. At the same time, the authorities did not require assurances from potential employers regarding the applicants' immediate employment. Those who wanted to leave in order to continue their education often received similarly positive responses.

According to the practice established in Chuvashia, requests to leave for Central Asia were unequivocally denied if the request was formulated off the need for better housing conditions and lack of warm winter clothing.[17] Additionally, moving to "close cities of the first category" was also forbidden.[18]

The central authorities made efforts to suppress these individual movements. On May 12, 1943, the deputy head of the department for the economic organization of the evacuated population of the Council of People's Commissars of the RSFSR sent a letter to authorities in Chuvashia urging them to limit permits for change of residence and demanding that they not allow unauthorized movements. He was indignant that at some train stations in the republic the police daily detained up to thirty refugees without permits.[19] Perhaps this letter seemed too soft to the head of this department of the Council of People's Commissars of the RSFSR, L. Dmitriev, but it is also possible that the higher authorities demanded that he completely stop the movement of refugees. Therefore, just two weeks later, on May 29, 1943, he sent a letter to his subordinates at local evacuation departments, demanding a tougher approach to issuing permission to move in order to end the "aimless movement of evacuated citizens on the country's railways." Calling for an end to the existing practice, he ordered them to give permits only with the consent of the regional executive committees of locales where the refugees intended to settle.[20] Making this new rule, Dmitriev could not help but know that it would greatly complicate any move, given the heavy workload of the local administrators. At the same time, he made it known that anybody who departed without proper authorization would be sent back. As a result of this letter, the chairs of the district executive committees of Chuvashia in July 1942 were criticized by the deputy head of the Council of People's Commissars department for the development of the evacuated population of this republic, Zhukov, for being too soft when considering such requests.[21]

With the hardening of the authorities' attitude toward the resettlement of refugees, some women began to seek support from drafted husbands. In January 1944, from the territory occupied by the Germans, the partisan Moshe Pikman appealed to the headquarters of partisan detachments with a request to allow his family, long sick with malaria, to move from Central Asia to another place.[22]

An analysis of refugees' requests to move shows that the Jews among them were more mobile and made more efforts to reunite in places that they considered offering better economic conditions. Correspondence was the instrument by which refugees identified such places and found relatives. Since the nineteenth century in Russia, exchanging letters had occupied a more important place in the life of Jews than in the life of the Slavs.[23] During the Second World War, correspondence became more important than ever. The writer and journalist Arkadii Perventsev, at the end of 1941 in Gor'kii, wrote in his diary: "It is empty in the stores, empty in the markets, empty everywhere. There is a gray mass in the post office and at the telegraph office. Communications are choked with the flow of telegrams and letters. The country is on the move, family-oriented ethnicities like the Jews are leaving their homes. After all, a Jew can seek out his or her Rebekah or Samuel with millions of telegrams, requests, and statements, and will find them."[24]

In this connection, the letter of Matvei Paperna, written at the end of July 1941, is noteworthy. He left Leningrad for the front in the first days of the war; a month later he was able to make a quick return into his already empty apartment. In the mailbox he found a letter and telegrams from different places from his evacuated wife and her five brothers. After that, he sent them each other's contacts and put them in touch with his brother and sister.[25] Escaping from the ghetto in Mikulino (Smolensk region) to Soviet territory in 1942 and arriving in Chuvashia, Galina Stivenzet immediately began to look for relatives through correspondence with their common acquaintances. Having found them, she traveled to the Iaroslavl' region.[26] The mother of Anna Tolochinskaia (their family fled to Soviet territory from the ghetto in Kolyshki, Vitebsk region) also immediately began corresponding with her relatives in Saratov.[27] Gita Bliumberg, who was in Ibresi (Chuvashia), received a registered letter from her niece in Cheliabinsk, wherein she was advised to move, along with her family, to live with them.[28] Evgeniia Ioffe was evacuated along with her mother and sister from Leningrad to the Kirov region. Having corresponded from there with relatives in Tashkent and having compared their situations, they went to Uzbekistan three months later.[29]

Great efforts to restore communication were made by the Gol'dberg family from Leningrad, as can be seen from Girsh's letter on September 15, 1942. I will give its beginning in full:

Dear Sonia! This entire time we have received from you three postcards from the road and a fourth, finally, from a place with an address. The last brought us much joy. Yesterday I wanted to send you a telegram, but they would not take it without indicating the post office number. Mom wrote a telegram. Today I'll try to. Be sure to tell the post office your number and in general your telegraph address. Yesterday we remembered the birthday of Allochka, but there were nobody and nothing to celebrate it with. We regret that we did not go with you; now we have to wait. Let's hope that you can settle in there a little bit, and the time will come when we will be together again. The main thing I'm wondering is whether you have a connection with Lëva. During the entire time of your absence, we did not receive any letters for him, and nothing came to the apartment in Lesnoe. Our request to you is to write to us often and about everything in detail, especially how Allochka is behaving. We—in turn—will not skimp on letters either. We receive letters from Abrasha often. The other day we sent him a parcel: a shaving kit, cologne, collars, handkerchiefs, pencils, and so on. He and Boria are alive and well. Boria does not write often.[30]

In the same envelope was a letter from his wife Tauba Gol'dberg. It also contains evidence of high communicative activity, but pays even more attention to clarifying the economic conditions of the respondents:

Dear Sonia and Allochka! First of all, happy birthday to Allochka. May everything be the way I wish for her. . . . Write in detail how things are arranged, the attractions of the area, how thing are at the grocery store, and how much you can get. The main thing—about Allochka, about her health, and about your own. We also do not get anything from Moscow from Lëva's relatives. Rakhil' often stops by and often calls; they have received a letter from Mania's sister, they do not know anything about the others. The day before yesterday they received a detailed letter from the Dukors. Little by little, they are settling in, they are better off now than us. The Dukors' address: . . . Abram is very interested in your resources in terms of money. We told him that you are in need until you are able to establish contact with Lëvushka.[31]

Intensive efforts to restore communication sometimes produced fantastic results. Mordekhai Liuksemburg, who had been sent from Bessarabia to perform defense labor along with hundreds of other men, whom, as foreigners, the authorities feared to mobilize in the army, ran into a fellow from Bendery—Avrom. Six months later, with the front line approaching, they decided to go to Nikolaev together, where Avrom had a sister whom he had not seen for about twenty years. Upon arrival, they unexpectedly discovered that Mordekhai's wife Rivka had sent a postcard to Avrom's sister, where she indicated her new address—a village in the North Caucasus. This calmed Mordekhai, who was very worried about the fate of her, her children, and other relatives, with whom he had parted in Chisinau, to which the Germans were approaching at that time.[32]

The role of the organized reference section of the resettlement department was extremely important in helping refugees and their relatives in restoring communications. In the autumn of 1941 the department was evacuated from Moscow to Buguruslan. With the move, the departmental staff decreased from 704 to 113 employees by the end of 1941 but was expanded by sixty employees in 1942.[33] Overwhelmed with many millions of inquiries, the department could not process all of them, especially since it did not have complete lists of refugees. As a result, by December 1941 the department was able to identify the place of residence of only 5–7 percent of all searched-for persons.[34] However, by February of the next year 11 percent (166,964 people) had been found.[35] In addition to the reference section, local public commissions for assisting evacuated children were involved in the search. During the first eight months of the war, 300 children were found by such commissions in Uzbekistan out of 3,700 search requests.[36]

Without relying on the reference section and the commissions, refugees everywhere left notes on the walls of railway stations. Emmanuel Karp recalls:

> Alma-Ata was packed with evacuees from the west of the country. I went to the train station. There, all the walls were covered with names and addresses of refugees; this was a way of searching for relatives in the war. And then I noticed, among other inscriptions—a note from my mother!, which read—"The family of Karp from Crimea is leaving for the Saryozek station." This was in the direction of present-day Baikonur. And I went in search of them. I found my mother and three younger brothers and sisters in Kolkhoz 10 Years of the Kazakh SSR.[37]

Another way to restore connections was to exchange lists of inquiries with fellow countrymen or acquaintances. Although such practice cannot be ruled out among non-Jews, this was probably the invention of Jewish refugees. The results were sometimes impressive. Lev Stel'man remembers: "If you were very lucky and found a friend, you would exchange lists with addresses. In this way my uncle Fima met with a fellow worker who, along with his young wife, was heading south. They talked, and uncle Fima gave them his list." Later this list made its way from Chuvashia to the hands of his sister in the Voronezh region. The lists, however, were not always at hand, and more often acquaintances simply exchanged information. The same author testifies: "My father, still on the way to Alatyr', met a man who had talked with uncle Zakhar; he had seen Izia and even knew where he was being taken. Also, through a chain of acquaintances, the first of whom had read the message of my cousin Klara; my aunt Sonia learned where her daughter was."[38]

Good communication through letters and oral contacts between acquaintances contributed to the concentration of Jews in various localities in the second year of the war. Among the 161 requests from different refugees for travel outside the republic from the Pervomaiskoe district of the Chuvash ASSR from July 17, 1941, to January 22, 1942, the requests of Jews amounted to 65.8 percent.[39] And this despite the fact that Jews in this district accounted for 43.5 percent of all refugees, according to the information from January 30, 1942.[40] It was much easier to change one's place of residence within one region, province, or republic, than to leave it altogether. Partly as a result of local migration within the Chuvash ASSR, Jews were particularly concentrated—in addition to the Pervomaiskoe—in the Kanash district. By 1943 Jews numbered 27.6 percent of all refugees in the town of Kanash. Even though Jewish refugees moved to other regions, territories, or republics in 1943, accounting for 59 percent of all refugees who left Chuvashia, they continued to concentrate in this district. Their share in the town of Kanash increased to 44 percent by March 1944, and in the Kanash district, not including the district center, the proportion of Jews among refugees was even higher—52.9 percent.[41]

In the Chkalovskoe district of Chuvashia in early 1944 the proportion of Jews among refugees was also large—46.7 percent.[42] By July of the same year, because of re-evacuation into the liberated areas, their share fell to 38.7 percent.[43] The available data on the Shemursha district of the same autonomous republic shows that Jews there also constituted a large proportion of refugees (see table 4). Such a large concentration of Jews in this area can be explained by the tolerant attitude toward refugees from the local chair of the district executive committee Kosmovskii, who was mentioned in this connection above. It follows that the reason for the concentration of Jewish refugees in some places within the same region was the sympathetic attitude of local authorities.

Table 4. Changes in the number of Jews among refugees in the Shemursha district of the Chuvash ASSR, 1941–1943[44]

Date	Number of all refugees	Number of Jews	Percentage of Jews
October 1, 1941	1,370	220	16
February 1, 1942	965	506	52.4
June 15, 1942	959	471	49.1
December 15, 1942	959	471	49.1
July 1, 1943	1,032	423	41

As a result of the centralized distribution of the refugee train traffic early on and subsequent local resettlements to be closer to family, it appears that Jewish communities were often formed around the place of origin. This is well traced in the Chkalovskoe district of Chuvashia, where among the 356 Jewish refugees the Gomel region's residents prevailed—61.2 percent; and among the others, natives of Latvia were 21.9 percent, and those from the Polesye region numbered 12 percent.[45]

In several areas of Chuvashia, there were few Jewish refugees. In the Ishlei district, Jews accounted for only 4 percent of all refugees in March 1944.[46] In Alatyr' at the time they numbered 18.7 percent (26.46 percent at the end of 1941), and in the Alatyr' district (not including the district center), their share barely reached 3.6 percent.[47] There were few Jews in the Kuvakino district—only 7 percent of all refugees in 1943.[48]

In Cheboksary, the capital of the Chuvash ASSR, the proportion of Jews among refugees was quite large (see table 5). This is not surprising, since they were representatives of, mainly, "urban professions."

The evacuees from the Moscow and Leningrad regions were most concentrated in the areas adjacent to the Upper and Middle Volga and from the river further east to the Urals. In November 1941 together they accounted for 72 percent of all refugees in Tatarstan, 73 percent in the Iaroslavl' region, and 43 percent in the Sverdlovsk region.[50] They were also quite numerous in southwestern Siberia. According to the report of the local authorities of the Omsk region, in April 1942 refugees from the Moscow and Leningrad regions accounted for 48 percent.[51] They were far fewer in Central Asia and the North Caucasus. In North Ossetia they, respectively, were 4.3 percent and 1.9 percent.[52] In Kirgizstan in 1942, refugees from the Moscow and Leningrad regions accounted, respectively, for 4.7 percent and 11.9 percent.[53] Since those evacuated from the Moscow, Leningrad, and other northwestern regions

Table 5. Changes in the number of Jews among refugees in Cheboksary, Chuvash ASSR, 1941–1942[49]

Date	Number of all refugees	Number of Jews	Percentage of Jews
October 1, 1941	3,324	907	27.3
January 1, 1942	5,846	1,632	27.9
February 1, 1942	7,444	2,343	31.5
June 15, 1942	6,216	1,750	28.2
September 15, 1942	6,615	1,814	27.4
December 15, 1942	6,734	1,836	27.3

prevailed in the Urals, in the Volga area, and in Siberia,[54] initially the share of Jews there was lower than in the southern Soviet republics, where the authorities sent more refugees from Ukraine, Moldavia, Crimea, and the North Caucasus.

Most refugees from Belorussia and the Baltic states were sent to northern and central Kazakhstan and some to the middle and southern Volga areas. In this regard, the data on one of the many trains arriving in the autumn of 1941 in Kzyl-Orda (Kazakhstan) is notable in that it contains information on the refugees' place of residence before the war (see table 6).

Comparison of the share of refugees from territories acquired by the USSR in 1939–1940 with the eastern Belorussian regions shows that the share of "westerners" was not small. As can be seen from table 6, some managed to escape even from the most western areas of the USSR—Brest and Białystok regions. Sometimes many people from the same locality could be found together. Valentin Smolentsev, a native of the village of Kuzhener of the Mari ASSR, testifies: "Evacuees from the western regions of Ukraine arrived in our district. . . . In general, mainly young people came, and they were maybe exclusively of Jewish nationality."[56]

As for refugees from eastern Ukraine, the Crimea, the North Caucasus, Bessarabia, and Northern Bukovina, they often ended up in Central Asia. This is confirmed by the analysis of the lists of refugees in two Turkmen cities—Tedzhen and Krasnovodsk—and also in Kazakhstan's Akmolinsk and one of the districts of the Akmolinsk region (see table 7).

Table 6. Distribution of refugees arriving in Kzyl-Orda in September 1941, according to their place of origin[55]

Area	Number of arrivals	Their share in relation to all arrivals in %
Minsk region	371	29.2
Mogilëv region	220	17.3
Estonian SSR	156	12.3
Vitebsk region	143	11.2
Białystok region	131	10.3
Latvian SSR	84	6.6
Lithuanian SSR	60	4.7
Western Ukraine	58	4.6
Brest region	50	3.9
Total	1,273	100

Table 7. Distribution of Jewish refugees in several places in Turkmenistan and Kazakhstan according to a place of departure by summer 1942[57]

Place of exit	Tedzhen	Krasnovodsk	Akmolinsk	Atabasar district of Akmolinsk region
Eastern Ukraine[58]	49.3	46.8	61.3	78.5
Western Ukraine	5.8	2	4.2	0.5
Eastern Belorussia	3.9	2.9	9.6	12.2
Western Belorussia	—	0.5	0.5	—
Poland	1.3	—	1	—
Bessarabia and Northern Bukovina	21.4	22	4.8	3.9
Northern Caucasus	3.9	14.6	2.6	0.2
Crimea	5.2	7.3	—	0.1
Moscow and Leningrad regions	5.2	1.5	13.4	0.9
Other[59]	3.9	2.4	2.6	3.7
Total	100	100	100	100

The low number of Polish immigrants shown in table 7 can be explained by their reluctance to register, as already mentioned. It does not in any way reflect the real situation.

The highest ratio of (all) refugees to the local population was in Uzbekistan. According to the central evacuation authorities, in Uzbekistan for every 1,000 local residents, there were on average 115 refugees, while in Russia 70, in Kirgizstan 68, in Kazakhstan 63, and in Georgia only 5. The distribution of refugees within the republics was also disproportionate. In Kazakhstan, in the Alma-Ata region, there were 88,400 refugees, while in the Gur'ev region only 8,900. The placement of refugees in the RSFSR was also disproportionate. In particular, there were many refugees in the Cheliabinsk region, 425,000, while another Siberian region—Irkutsk—with hasher weather conditions, housed only 19,500 refugees.[60]

The Total Number of Refugees

Determining the number of refugees who found themselves in the Soviet rear remains one of the most problematic issues in the history of this war. Official statistics compiled by the CSA included in the category of the "evacuated" all citizens who used any transport to move to the east. This is also true for the ten million people whose movement to the east was recorded the railway department by December 1941.[61] The problematic nature of these statistics lies, for one thing, in the fact that it includes the movement of the deported Germans (there were 942,927 of them),[62] the Ingrian Finns, Romanians, and Romanian Jews. Nevertheless, Georgii Kumanëv, more than others in Russia who have investigated the issue of the evacuation, unconditionally accepted the official CSA data that by the end of February 1942 there were seventeen million evacuees in the eastern regions of the USSR.[63] Mark Harrison believes that the refugees numbered between fourteen and nineteen million.[64] Guided by his figures, Rebecca Manley suggested that the total number of evacuated people in the war reached 16.5 million, of which 4.5 million were added in 1942.[65] Her work was criticized by Vadim Dubson, who found these figures highly overstated.[66] Dubson himself, in his survey of refugee statistics, relies on evacuees' cards, drawn up at the discretion of the same CSA. By February 1943 it had issued cards for 6,388,359 evacuees. Based on this and other figures, he believes that the number of refugees during the war amounted to 6.63–7.30 million.[67]

Undoubtedly, during the war the Soviet authorities attached great importance to the registration of refugees. The CSA and evacuation authorities kept trying to lower these statistics, for which lists of refugees were compiled with detailed information about the former place of residence, the gender, age, and nationality. However, the refugees' large numbers and high mobility made this task difficult. As a result, information about the evacuees suffered from inaccuracies and incompleteness. In the comments to the statistical materials, which summarized the information on three million refugees in December 1941, Pamfilov, the head of the Governance of Evacuation, indicated that this figure was incomplete and that in reality more than ten million people had been evacuated.[68] He likely was also relying on the data of the People's Commissariat of Railways.

The report "On the number of evacuated people placed in the rear areas of the USSR," compiled by the CSA on January 20, 1942, helps elucidate the actual situation. According to the document, 6,962,500 evacuees (including, 5,672,900 from the RSFSR, 27,500 from Georgia, 17,800 from Azerbaijan, and 3,500 from Armenia) were placed in the rear.[69] However, these relatively informative statistics were incomplete, since in the republics of Central Asia alone there were only 1,240,800 refugees (i.e., 17.8 percent altogether; see table 8).

From table 8, which presents official Soviet data, we can see that the figure for Kirgizstan is approximate. In fact, according to a study by Kyrgyz demographer Shairgul Batyrbaeva, refugees in Kirgizstan at that time numbered 150,800.[71] The small stated number of refugees in Tajikistan and Turkmenistan is also doubtful.

Table 8. Distribution of registered refugees in the Central Asian republics as of January 20, 1942, according to official data[70]

Area	Number of refugees	Their share in relation to all refugees in Central Asia in %
Uzbekistan	716,500	57.8
Kazakhstan	386,500	31.1
Kirgizstan	100,000	8
Tajikistan	22,800	1.8
Turkmenistan	15,000	1.2
All Central Asia	1,240,800	100

The official statistics that are based on the evacuees' cards suffer from other inaccuracies. I first encountered the incomplete account of the statistics based on these cards while working at the Jerusalem branch of the Commission for Jewish Material Claims against Germany. The requests sent to the Red Cross in Moscow showed that in about a quarter of cases, former refugees were not counted, despite the presence of other evidence of evacuation. The search for several dozen witnesses on the official Soviet cards of Uzbekistan, to which I refer here and who were in the republic during the war, shows that some of them were unregistered.[72] At the same time, it is known that in 1942 alone 340,000 refugees were in Uzbekistan on 250,000 cards (minors were registered on the card of a parent or another caregiver).[73] These refugees constitute 47.5 percent of the 716,500 refugees in Uzbekistan (see table 8) whom the authorities knew about.

Compared to the statistics of "those placed" on the cards, the statistics of the lists that arrived to the same CSA were very far behind. According to the data for February 15, 1942, there were 3,587,766 evacuees according to the CSA lists, including 106,007 in Uzbekistan and only 68 in Armenia.[74] In fact, as of April 1, 1942, there were 4,068 refugees in Armenia.[75] Meanwhile, statistics on "those placed" (6.962 million) are confirmed by Dubson's number of 6.5 million as of July 1942, taken from a memorandum of the USSR's department of labor. Dubson believes these statistics to be reliable.[76]

In reality, these "by the lists" statistics suffer from an undercounting not only in Central Asia but also in Russia. In the Altai territory on October 1, 1941, there were 18,293 evacuees according to the lists, and 32,011 evacuees were listed as "those placed." Discussing this discrepancy, Iulia Mellekhova, who studied the organization of the evacuee population in this region, believes that the unwillingness of some of the refugees to register with the city councils or village councils is the reason for the discrepancies.[77] According to data from the Sterlitamak, there were only 4,500 registered refugees in January 1942, while an inspection carried out by the evacuation department at that time revealed another 3,900; and this was not all, because the authorities had information that there were 12,000 refugees in the town.[78] In Sverdlovsk in February 1942, 42,000 refugees were personally registered on evacuee' cards, while the authorities had information about the presence of 160,000 refugees in the city.[79] The evacuation inspector P. Radionenko in the Mari ASSR complained in October 1942 to Pamfilov that five districts had not submitted lists of refugees.[80] A postwar calculation of the registered cards concluded that 245,013 evacuees were in the Novosibirsk region at the beginning of 1942. This contradicts the operational data from NKVD and the evacuation office of the Novosibirsk region, according to which there were 381,000 evacuees in this region.[81] Undercounting was well known to the evacuation committee.[82]

Among the unregistered refugees there were many Jews, Ukrainians, and Belorussians who until 1939 were Polish citizens. Many Polish Jews were liberated from the camps and exile from August to December 1941 as a result of the amnesty. They fled to the USSR from the western regions of Poland in 1939–1940, and after they refused to accept Soviet citizenship, they were deported to Siberia and to the North.[83] Those Polish Jews who were liberated, as well as those who independently fled to the east after June 22, 1941, tried to avoid registration with the Soviet authorities because of fears of remaining forever in the USSR. According to the same card information on the evacuees, in February 1942 there were only 5,393 Jews in Uzbekistan, who indicated either Poland or, more specifically, the Baranovichi, Białystok, Brest, Warsaw, Vileika, Katowice, Kielce, Kraków, Łódź, Lublin, Pinsk, Poznań, Pomorze, Volyn, Drogobych, L'vov, Rovno, Śląsk, Stanislav, and Tarnopol areas as their places of origins.[84] In fact, the Polish Jews in Uzbekistan, even by 1946 (i.e., after the departure of some of them with the Anders's Polish Army in the USSR to Iran in 1942), in spite of the decline due to the high mortality rate, the call-up to the Soviet-Polish army, and the migration to the west of the USSR and to Poland in 1944–1945, numbered at least 33,692, according to the Union of Polish Patriots (Związek Patriotów Polskich, ZPP).[85] As in other places in the USSR, evacuation departments in Uzbekistan distinguished Polish citizens from general statistics only if there was a need to explain the reduction in the total number of refugees, for example, as a result of being summoned to the Anders's army.[86]

Information on their departure from the USSR helps to estimate the total number of Jews who were Polish citizens. It is known that together with the

Anders's army, 6,000 Polish Jews left the USSR through Iran in 1942.[87] In 1944–1946, 202,000 Polish Jews left for Poland.[88] Another 2,000 left in 1947–1948[89] and 18,743 more in 1955–1959.[90] However, not all Polish Jews left the USSR. Mark Kupovetskii estimates the total number of Polish Jews remaining in the USSR by the 1960s at 15,000. Thus, about 244,000 Polish Jews remained alive in the USSR.[91] Let us now try to reconstruct the number of Polish Jewish refugees at the beginning of 1942. To do this, we subtract 35,000 survivors in the occupied territory according to the 1940 borders,[92] add 25 percent of those who died of hunger and disease in four and a half years (February 1942–June 1946)[93] to the figure that was obtained and then at least 4,000 more who perished in the First and Second Polish armies in 1943–1945.[94] It turns out that in the rear areas of the USSR in early 1942 there were about 282,000 Polish Jews. In a similar status there were about 150,000 Belorussians and Ukrainians,[95] also former Polish citizens who hoped to return to Poland. In contrast to the former Polish citizens, former Romanian citizens before 1940—Jews and non-Jews—did not enjoy protection from the government of Romania and had no hope of returning there. They were registered as Soviet evacuees and therefore appear in general refugee statistics.

Now let's focus on the total number of refugees. Dubson believes that the CSA mistakenly counted refugees in those administrative units that had already been occupied by the Germans. Indeed, the statistics came in late. However, if the refugees fled further, many of them did not have time to register in the intermediate places. Dubson is mistaken when he writes that 183,000 registered evacuees in the Rostov region in October 1941 continued to remain in the reports until the end of that year, despite the occupation of Rostov from November 21 to November 28.[96] In fact, according to the statistics for November 10, 1941, there were only 33,722 evacuees in the region.[97] Dubson also suggests that the authorities included deported Germans in refugee statistics. Indeed, it sometimes happened at the lower level, but it was rare, because, as we have seen above, higher-level administrators corrected these errors. Based on a small number of Germans (32,649) and Finns (4,335) on the general list of evacuees throughout the USSR on December 1, 1941, we can conclude that the deportees were not included.[98]

Given the number of unrecorded refugees, the number of all persons who held the status of "evacuated" as of February 1, 1942, can be estimated at 7.7 million (i.e., after adjusting by almost 10 percent). Note that it is very important to distinguish the statistics of persons who had been in the status of evacuees from the statistics of persons who continued to be in it. The figure includes those who by that time had stopped being a refugee, because they died, perished, or were drafted into the army. The high mortality among refugees from hunger and disease, which even by the most cautious assessments can be estimated at no less than 2.5 percent for the period from July 1, 1941, to February 1, 1942, resulted in the loss of 190,000 people. During the same period, at least 500,000 refugees were drafted into the army.[99] Therefore, on February 1, 1942, about seven million refugees actually remained in the rear. Due to the small number of births and the huge infant mortality rate, the increase because of births among refugees was insignificant.

Now, let's turn to the number of refugees from February through the end of 1942. It would be wrong to add them mechanically to the refugees of the first wave since a large number of them were refugees of the first wave and already entered into the statistics of the evacuees. It is known that many of the 220,000 refugees who arrived in the Krasnodar territory in 1941 with the approach of the front line tried to travel further in 1942.[100] Many refugees from the Ordzhonikidze territory, the North Ossetian and Dagestan ASSRs, and the Voroshilovgrad, Rostov, Kursk, Voronezh, Stalino, and other regions also tried to do this. Having been himself evacuated from Leningrad to the North Caucasus in the spring of 1942, Anatolii Krasnov-Levitin on reports the last days before the occupation of Nal'chik: "I wander among the crowd of those departing—mostly Jews: from Moldavia, from the Baltic states, from Ukraine. All in due time fled from the Germans. Now they are running again." Arriving in Baku, he noted: "A multifaceted, diverse wave of humans, people from Moldavia, Ukraine, Belorussia, Moscow and Leningrad, from Rostov and Odessa, finding themselves evacuated to the North Caucasus, they move through the Caucasus to Baku, and from Baku they are sent to Central Asia."[101]

But not all refugees managed to escape far enough from the Wehrmacht. It is estimated that about 300,000 refugees from the first wave came under occupation. The Jews among them (for full statistics, see below) perished. In addition, not everyone managed to stay alive during the crossing of the Caspian Sea to Central Asia (see the testimony of Boris Shnaider in chapter 1).

The arrival of refugees to the east is confirmed by statistical sources. About half a million passed through the Caspian Sea to Central Asia in that difficult year of 1942.[102] Some of them arrived in Kazakhstan, where the number of refugees in 1942 increased by 141,911 people.[103] In the same year, 421,400 new refugees were deployed in Western Siberia (Altai territory, Omsk, Kemerovo, and Novosibirsk regions).[104] Because of the second wave of evacuation in Chuvashia among all migrants, the proportion of immigrants from Ukraine increased by 32.7 percent. As a result, the proportion of immigrants from Ukraine increased among all refugees from 4.8 percent to 10 percent.[105]

Those Muscovites, Leningraders, and residents of some other cities who left for the east in 1942 should be considered new refugees. According to statistics,

495,000 people left Leningrad in that year; 40,000 left Voronezh region (by July 18, 1942); 23,000 Kalinin region (by July 7, 1942); 20,000 Orël region (by July 7, 1942); 15,000 Rostov region (by July 18, 1942); 15,000 Smolensk region (by June 5, 1942); and 180,000 Stalingrad region (by September 11, 1942). According to the same report, as of October 14, 1942, evacuation from the Kalinin, Leningrad, Voronezh, and Stalingrad regions continued.[106] The reports do not contain statistics on the departure of refugees from the North Caucasus, the Kalmyk ASSR, the Voroshilovgrad and Kharkov regions. Together with immigrants from these areas, the total number of new refugees (i.e., excluding repeat refugees) from February 1 to December 31, 1942, can be estimated at one

German invasion of the Soviet Union, 1941 and 1942

million people. Therefore, the number of all those who held once the status of "evacuated" by January 1, 1942, would be 8.7 million.

In reality, the number of people who kept holding the status of "evacuated" by this time was less. The increase in the number of refugees by one million mainly compensated for the decrease in the number of refugees by 900,000 because of: (a) the conscription in 1942 into the army—estimated at about 200,000 refugees;[107] (b) the 300,000 refugees of the first wave who fell under occupation; (c) the death of about 400,000 refugees from hunger and disease during the difficult period from February 1 to December 31, 1942, estimated at 5 percent. Thus, during these eleven months, the number of refugees in the rear increased from 7 to 7.1 million. From then on, the number of people who kept holding the status of "evacuated" constantly declined due to mortality, mobilization to the front, and re-evacuation.

The Number of Jewish Refugees

According to L. S. Rogachevskaia and V. M. Kabuzan, on the eve of the German attack on the USSR, about 5 million Jews lived there, including new citizens.[108] Mark Kupovetskii gives nearly the same figure, 4.965 million.[109] Mordechai Altshuler's estimate is not much higher—5.082–5.084 million, which includes 3.113 million Jews with "old" Soviet citizenship, 282,000 annexed Romanian Jews, 1,292 million annexed Polish Jews, 150,000 Jewish refugees from Poland, 152,500 Lithuanian Jews, and 95,000 Latvian and Estonian Jews together.[110] Mark Tolts estimates the number of all Jews at that time a little higher—between 5.1 and 5.2 million.[111] Tolts's estimate seems the most accurate, taking into account the average annual growth of the 3,028,538 Soviet Jews (according to the 1939 census).

Having as a basis the census of 1939, none of these authors take into account that some Jews concealed their ethnicity, which we will see further when determining the number of the frontline Jewish soldiers. Besides, children from mixed marriages during this census were often declared non-Jews. Mixed marriages among Jews in the RSFSR were 25 percent for men and 17 percent for women in 1926, and an average of 15 percent in Ukraine and 11–13 percent in Belorussia in 1936.[112] Perhaps a fairer theory, suggested by Arch Getty, Gábor Rittersporn, and Viktor Zemskov, is that some Jews felt assimilated enough to publicly identify with other ethnic groups.[113] In any case, taking these factors into account, it should be recognized that the number of Jews (determined by the mother's ethnicity) by the summer of 1941 was at least several hundred thousand more. In the context under consideration, it is important for us to take into account the fact that, according to the 1939 census, only 355,000

Soviet Jews lived in the territories from which evacuation was not subsequently carried out.[114]

As indicated in the first chapter, according to official statistics of September 15, 1941, the proportion of 486,906 Jews among all registered refugees at the place of arrival was 24.8 percent. However, these statistics covered less than half of the actual number of refugees at that time. At the beginning of October the share of Jews among the highly incomplete statistics increased slightly—to 25.7 percent, and at the beginning of November—to 26.2 percent.[115] According to official statistics, on December 1, 1941, 779,410 Jews were evacuated, making 27.3 percent of all 2,854,419 refugees who have indicated their ethnicity.[116]

By February 1, 1942, there were more than 1,127,200 Leningraders[117] in the evacuation and more than 2,178,500 Muscovites.[118] In total, thus, 3,305,700 people. As we already know, Jews among them amounted to about 12 percent, from which it follows that their total number reached 396,684 (including those of them who were already drafted into the army as evacuees). Because of the stabilization at the front in December 1941 and early January 1942, the remaining population in Moscow, Leningrad, and other places was practically not evacuated, and therefore could not reduce the proportion of Jewish refugees;[119] it is possible to extrapolate the December percentage (27.3 percent) to all 7.7 million people who had held the status of evacuees by February 1, 1942. It turns out that by this time approximately 2.1 million Jews had held the status of evacuees and there were about 1.91 million Jews who had been holding the status of evacuees. In some areas of the USSR, the proportion of Jews among refugees was very high. At the beginning of October 1941, in the Krasnodar territory it was 69.5 percent, Ordzhonikidze territory—67.7 percent, Stalingrad region—55.5 percent, and in the Chkalov region—41.9 percent. The share of Jews in Armenia was much lower—10.5 percent of all refugees for February 1942.[120]

Among the 1 million new refugees who arrived from February to December 1942, the share of Jews hardly exceeded 11–13 percent, since the residents of the Moscow and, mainly, Leningrad regions were predominant there. Among all refugees who arrived in the first half of February 1942 in the Udmurt ASSR, Jews accounted for 12.4 percent. It's not known where they came from, but the general statistics at the exit point show that these were not places with a large percentage of Jews. Among them 57.2 percent were residents of the Leningrad region; 9.8 percent those from the unoccupied part of the Karelo-Finnish SSR; 6.4 percent from the Murmansk region; 5.4 percent from the Moscow region, and so on.[121] Statistics from the Chuvash ASSR confirm the low proportion of Jews among the refugees who arrived there in 1942. On September 15, 1941, Jews made up 15.5 percent of all refugees in this republic,[122] and by December 15, 1942, their number fell to 13.6 percent.[123] The example of Chuvashia is good because in 1942 there were practically no repeat refugees from the south of the RSFSR. Therefore, it can be assumed that from February to December 1942 about 120,000 (i.e., 12 percent of one million) Jewish new refugees arrived as evacuees. However, the number of Jewish refugees did not increase, and even decreased, due to the following: death in the North Caucasus and other places is estimated at about 120,000 Jewish refugees of the first wave;[124] the mobilization to the front of 1942 accounted for about 70,000 already evacuated Jews;[125] the departure in 1942 of 6,000 Polish Jews from the USSR with the Anders's army; a record wartime death rate among refugees in 1942 (estimated at 17,000, i.e., 6 percent for Polish refugees, and 71,500, i.e., 5 percent for the rest). Considering all this, as of January 1, 1943, the total number of Jewish refugees can be estimated at 1.75 million. As for all the Jews who had by that time been evacuated in the USSR, their number would have increased to 2.22 million (see table 9). This is much more than the figure proposed by Raul Hilberg—1.5 million.[126] Although later orphans were found in the liberated areas, the number of Jews among them was hardly significant.

The foregoing and other sources make it possible to distribute these 2,22 million Jewish refugees (including those who in 1942 did not have time to escape further from German occupation) according to the place of exit. A large percentage of them went to Ukraine—42.8 percent (see table 10).

As already mentioned in passing, the Jews in Central Asia turned out to be especially numerous, mainly due to the directions of transport routes from Ukraine, southern Russia, and the Northern Caucasus. In the archives of Solomon Mikhoels, seized after his death in 1948, the authorities found several unsent letters to Stalin. One of them stated: "About one and a half million Jews have been evacuated to Uzbekistan, Kazakhstan, and other Central Asian

Table 9. The total number of all evacuees who had been and were in the status of evacuees, among them Jews and their percentage

Date	All those who had held the status of "evacuee"	Jews among them	Percentage of Jews	All refugees who had been holding the status of "evacuee"	Jews among them	Percentage of Jews
February 1, 1942	7,700,000	2,100,000	27.3	7,000,000	1,910,000	27.3
January 1, 1943	8,700,000	2,220,000	25.5	7,100,000	1,750,000	24.7

Table 10. Distribution of Jews evacuated as of January 1, 1943, according to their place of residence in the summer of 1939 (the number is given in a rounded manner)

Place of origin	Number	Percentage of the total number
RSFSR	580,000[127]	27
Belorussian SSR	200,000	9
Ukrainian SSR	950,000	42.8
Bessarabia and Moldavian SSR	130,000[128]	6.8
Baltic states	40,000[129]	1.8
Poland	280,000	12.6
Total	2,220,000	100

Soviet republics since the beginning of the Patriotic War."[130] Another head of the JAC, Shakhno Epshtein, claimed that more than a million Jewish refugees found refuge in Uzbekistan alone.[131] Redlich cites information from edited by Epshtein *Eynikayt*, according to which in same Uzbekistan there were half a million Jewish refugees.[132] It is clear that in these cases their own estimates are given.

Such information on several million of refugees, based on the data of the CSA of the State Planning Committee of the USSR, is contained in the materials of the evacuation department. According to it, at the beginning of September 1941, Jews made up 44.2 percent of all refugees in Central Asia. By early October, their share increased to 49.8 percent. At the beginning of November of the same year, their share increased even more—to 51.4 percent of all refugees in Central Asia.[133] Calculations of the proportion of Jews according to the existing lists of refugees in two cities of Turkmenistan—Tedzhen (49 percent) and Krasnovodsk (32 percent) partly confirm these overall numbers.[134]

As we can see from table 8, by February 1942, 1,240,800 refugees were registered in Central Asia. Given the underreporting by 25 percent, the total number of them should be about 1,650,000. Then, assuming that in November the proportion of Jews among all refugees was 51.4 percent, we conclude that the total number of Jews in Central Asia by that time was about 845,000. During 1942 some 260,000 Jews arrived there, mainly via the Caspian Sea. They were refugees of both the first and second waves. However, calls to the army (including the departure of 6,000 Polish Jews to Iran with the Anders's army), a small migration from there to other regions (about 14,000),[135] and even greater mortality (15,000 of Polish Jews and 30,000 of the rest) adversely affected the overall population. Considering all this, it is estimated that by the beginning of

Table 11. The number of Jewish refugees in Central Asia and their percentage of all Jewish refugees in the USSR

Date	All Jews who had been holding the status of "evacuee"	Including Jews in Central Asia	Percentage of all Jewish refugees
February 1, 1942	1,910,000	845,000	55.5
January 1, 1943	1,750,000	1,000,000	57.1

1943 there were 1 million Jewish refugees in Central Asia. Just in Tashkent, according to Max Vekselman, during the war 200,000 Jewish refugees were accommodated.[136]

The available statistics for Kazakhstan indicated a large number of Jewish refugees in the republic. According to the NKVD, in the autumn of 1941 there were about 300,000 Jewish refugees there.[137] If by August 30, 1941, Jews in Kazakhstan accounted for 33.9 percent of all refugees, in three months their share grew even larger, to 46.6 percent.[138]

Jewish refugees in the rear, unlike others, were more mobile and willing to move to places where they had relatives who were better off or where the prices were lower and the prospects of finding a job were higher. Postal correspondence played a huge role in reestablishing communication and sharing information. The information service was very helpful in finding relatives who had moved in. However, the movement of refugees from region to region irritated the authorities, as it destabilized work at enterprises and collective farms, as well as congested railway lines. At the war's midpoint, it became increasingly difficult to move because permits for relocation were issued reluctantly. As a result of migration, and often ill-conceived train streams with refugees at the beginning of the war, they were deployed disproportionately across areas, regions, and districts. The proportion of Jews among refugees was also disproportionate. Some administrative units had more than 50 percent of them, while others had barely more than 10 percent. Of the 7.7 million who were in the status of evacuees as of February 1, 1942, some 2.1 million (27.3 percent) were Jews. By January 1, 1943, at the time the evacuation was almost completely stopped, 2.22 of 8.7 million refugees (25.5 percent) were Jews. More than 55 percent of all Jewish refugees found themselves during the war in Central Asia. Statistical analysis also shows that among all Jewish refugees who found themselves in the rear, 42.8 percent came from Ukraine. In the next chapter, we will see what difficulties Jewish refugees faced in the process of re-evacuation.

CHAPTER EIGHT

The Difficult Road Back

Departure

As the western territories of the Soviet Union were liberated, many refugees wanted to return to their homes. The central authorities approached this issue differentially, not based on the economic situation and family circumstances of refugees, but on the state's needs. Higher-level authorities communicated to those below them that "the government can not allow an organized return of all evacuated citizens to their former places of residence all at once."[1]

Factory workers were not universally permitted to return home. People's Commissar for Armaments Ustinov feared the negative impact of re-evacuation on the production of weapons. To prevent this, he ordered "to 'attach' the engineering and technical personnel and workers to the worksite where they are being utilized."[2] Fleishman, the master of a blacksmith shop that had been evacuated with Kirov Plant from Leningrad to Cheliabinsk, said: "In what way are we better than the prisoners? It would have been better if I had deserted from the shop floor, by now I would have been amnestied and gone home."[3] The workers began to both openly protest these policies and escape to their hometowns.[4] When it was necessary to provide the liberated regions with specialists, the central authorities often allowed re-evacuation, despite the shortage of such specialists in the eastern regions of the USSR.

There were instances of local administrations in the rear preventing the specialists from returning home. The director of the Cheboksary plant no. 254, Bunin, did not want to the engineer Arkadii Sul'kin go to Tallinn, as he was the only one with expertise in the plant's equipment. Moreover, the administrator even promised to create for Sulkin conditions to work on a *kandidat nauk* (candidate of sciences).[5] In some cases, due to a shortage of workers, local managers even blocked the departure of janitors and cleaners.[6] In cases of such disputes the central authorities acted as an arbiter.

To some extent, the policy of restrictions on cargo that repatriates were allowed to bring with them prevented their independent return. While organized repatriating refugees had the right to take up to fifteen hundred kilograms per family, those departing alone could carry only 50 kilograms per person.[7] Since the weight verification systems had not had all the kinks ironed out and there were not enough scales, the load was usually checked "by eye."

In general, the return to places of former residence was more organized, as evidenced by materials from the Chuvash ASSR. In April and May 1944 six hundred refugees, mainly the inhabitants of the collective farms rather than workers and employees in the cities, were repatriated to the Smolensk region.[8] In July 1944 an organized re-evacuation to Leningrad was carried out, when 6,357 people were sent by 170 train cars.[9] In the autumn more refugees were sent back to Leningrad and also to the Kalinin region. In June 1945, the last train with those being re-evacuated was sent to Leningrad.[10] In September and October 1945 additional refugees returned by train to the Kalinin region.[11]

The departure of the refugees created a serious problem of labor shortages for the local authorities. The kolkhozes suffered particularly badly since the frontline soldiers who had worked there previously did not want to return to their former serf-like status after demobilization. Military decorations opened up new prospects for employment for them. Because of the labor shortage in 1946, the crops were harvested with great delay, and some remained in the fields.[12]

The reduction of the number of refugees in the rear regions is corroborated by the evidence from the Chuvash ASSR, as well as separately from the Kuvakino and Tsivil'sk districts of this autonomous republic.

With the cancellation of restrictions on the transport of passengers inside the country, starting July 1, 1946, local authorities lost almost all tools to forcibly detain refugees, including the special passes formerly issued by the police.

Table 12. Changes in the number of refugees and Jews among them in the Kuvakino district of the Chuvash ASSR, 1941–1944[13]

Date	All refugees	Jews	Percentage of Jews
October 1, 1941	1,707	114	6.7
February 1, 1942	1,775	127	7.2
June 15, 1942	1,171	68	5.8
December 15, 1942	1,171	68	5.8
August 1, 1943	872	61	7
August 1, 1944	199	11	5.5

Table 13. Changes in the number of refugees and Jews among them in the Tsivil'sk district of the Chuvash ASSR for 1941–1945[14]

Date	All refugees	Jews	Percentage of Jews
October 1, 1941	844	112	13.3
February 1, 1942	2,830	312	11
June 15, 1942	2,502	254	10.2
December 15, 1942	3,390	323	9.5
March 1, 1945	497	47	9.5
June 15, 1945	479	56	11.7
September 17, 1945	303	41	13.5
November 1, 1945	183	7	3.8

Such passes were now required only for return to the border areas. Therefore, the local authorities could only use persuasion to convince the refugees not to leave, promising improvements to their living standards. Knowing about the difficult situation in the western regions of the USSR, they recommended that refugees confirm with the authorities in the places of their former residence that they could in fact reclaim their housing and resume their previous *propiska* (residence permit).[16] Nevertheless, most of the refugees preferred to return. Refugees from the Chkalov region were coming back at a rapid pace, with 27,473 refugees, according to official data, at the beginning of 1946 and 11,393 at the beginning of 1947.[17] According to the information of the RSFSR Resettlement Department, following the July lifting of the restrictions on re-evacuation, 300,744 evacuees returned to the places of their former residence in the second half of 1946, and another 117,260 in 1947. One cannot but agree with Potëmkina, who cites these statistics, that the real number of the re-evacuated was much higher.[18]

The Authorities and Re-evacuation

The easiest way for the authorities to solve the problem was to re-evacuate the population to the northwest regions of the USSR, including the Baltic states. There were no restrictions on leaving for Lithuania.[19] The authorities were preparing to continue the aborted absorption of this republic, which entailed collectivization and internationalization, for which they badly needed non-Lithuanian employees who knew the Lithuanian language well. The authorities were guided by the same motivation when allowing the re-evacuation of refugees to Estonia. In April 1945 a special train returned some evacuees from

Table 14. Changes in the number of refugees and Jews among them in the Chuvash ASSR, 1941–1946[15]

Date	All refugees	Jews	Percentage of Jews
September 1, 1941	41,222	5,722	13.9
October 1, 1941	48,345	7,788	16.1
November 1, 1941	59,154	9,136	15.4
December 15, 1941	62,879	9,636	15.3
February 1, 1942	69,519	11,941	17.2
April 15, 1942	63,785	8,982	14.0
June 15, 1942	64,468	9,043	14.0
December 15, 1942	70,096	9,556	13.6
July 15, 1943	57,352	8,443	14.7
December 1, 1943	54,994	8,029	14.6
January 1, 1946	4,936	unknown	—

Chuvashia to Estonia.[20] In the Chkalov region, too, authorities organized the re-evacuation to Latvia and Estonia.[21]

The decision on the re-evacuation of deported former residents of the Karelo-Finnish SSR was adopted by decree of the Council of People's Commissars of the USSR on March 22, 1945. Even those who worked in the factories and were considered essential specialists were not allowed to stay. In Chuvashia this decision was carried out quickly. Already in April and May, about seven hundred people from the Karelo-Finnish SSR who were not working in factories were sent back, and the rest followed in the summer of the same year.[22] One hundred twenty refugees were also re-evacuated there from the Chkalov region.[23] During the entire period of Stalin's rule, repatriation to the Karelo-Finnish SSR was the only case of the return of deported peoples.

The procedure for returning to Moscow was somewhat different. Almost immediately after the evacuation from that city, many Muscovites began to make attempts to return. However, the majority were not successful, since on September 21, 1941, the executive committee of the Moscow City Council passed a resolution "On the temporary prohibition of entry to Moscow of persons evacuated from the city." In accordance with this resolution, the authorities ordered that tickets to Moscow not be sold without special permits.[24] Anna Bruell writes: "The most difficult thing was to get permission to travel to Moscow. Only two women were able to get out of our city."[25]

Indeed, a small number of refugees managed to return to Moscow without permits. Giving up on getting an official permit, in August 1944 the doctor Khasia Rivlina and her family left Shardrinsk illegally. To do this, she had to give alcohol to the train conductors who accompanied the re-evacuation of the equipment of the ZIS Plant. According to her son's memoirs, several more families traveled to Moscow with them illegally. At the stops, the conductors allowed them out only after checking that nobody was around. After a month of traveling, fearing an inspection in Moscow, they dropped the returning refugees off in a Moscow suburb.[26] Nikolai Zhukov complained about the fact that some refugees from Chuvashia managed to get to Moscow without permits in May 1943.[27]

In June 1944, the executive committee of the Moscow City Council passed a resolution allowing Muscovites to return. However, those wishing to come back had to, by autumn of that year, request permission to return from the local municipal authorities at their former residences and attach payment receipts for a *kvartplata* (housing fee) for the period they were away, as well as notarized documents on servicemen in the family that included where and when they served.[28] The requirement to confirm the *kvartplata* was not a formality: the city council ordered not to even consider requests of Muscovites who had made *kvartplata* payments for three months or longer,[29] and local administrators in the city strictly adhered to this decree. N. Rozman ended up without an apartment, not having managed to pay this fee because of her and her children's illnesses.[30] Because of nonpayment, the authorities also confiscated the apartment of Mordekhai Levin, transferring it to the family of some general.[31]

Even those Muscovites who retained the rights to their homes had to return to Moscow within two months, after which they again lost the rights to their housing. Simultaneously, the city council, using a loophole, deprived of housing those Muscovites and their families who evacuated together with their workplace.[32] Fearing for their housing, many Muscovites hurried back. In the Kemerovo region, out of 6,100 evacuated from Moscow only 1,700 remained by the end of 1945.[33] Perhaps some remained voluntarily, attracted by better housing opportunities and positions in enterprises that were being vacated due to the mass departure.

Re-evacuating with difficulty, many Muscovites and residents of other cities found their apartments occupied. Although housing was guaranteed to all evacuees by the decree of the Council of People's Commissars of the USSR on August 5, 1941, the authorities deceived them. Already on February 16, 1942, the Supreme Soviet of the USSR issued a resolution, mentioned in the beginning of the book. According to it, the evacuees' apartments were to be used temporarily by city authorities to distribute to remaining workers and employees in need of housing. The seizure of housing affected both cities that remained unoccupied by the Wehrmacht and those that were being freed. As a result, many refugees from Odessa to Leningrad were preoccupied with taking back their former housing, if it had not been destroyed.

In 1944–1945, families of Jewish collective farmers who had fled from Crimea could not obtain permissions to return to Snegirëvka and Kalinindorf districts. And those who somehow managed to come back could not get the authorities to help reclaim their homes. Four families returning to Kalinindorf could not get their homes back. The chair of the district executive committee Ivan Kopytko told them, "We did not invite you here, so how you arrange yourselves is not our business." Only the intervention of the writer Ilya Ehrenburg helped to resolve their housing issue.[34] After all, in Jewish kolkhozes housing was exclusively private, unlike in many cities. Only after a bitter struggle, Vera Bakhshi's house in Kerch was returned to her.[35]

The Belorussian leadership pursued a more complex policy on the return of refugees. It began to gather information about the whereabouts of doctors and teachers from Belorussia in the spring of 1942.[36] After liberation from the German occupation, the republic experienced an acute shortage of these and other specialists. For example, in 1945 in Grodno, out of the ninety-one medical doctoral positions, only twenty-one were filled and the rest remained vacant. More than 50 percent of nurses and teachers were missing.[37] Therefore, one should not be surprised by the desire of the republican authorities to have practitioners of these high-demand professions to return. The People's Commissariat of Belorussia, on the eve of the academic year 1944–1945, sent invitations to the eastern regions of the USSR to 6,283 people who hailed from the republic.[38] The former Rechitsa teacher Maria Rubinchik was sent no fewer than three telegrams by the Belorussian Commissariat of Education inviting her to come to Minsk.[39] Klara Fel'dman returned from the evacuation to teach in Ptich', Gomel region, on such invitation. A graduate of the Vitebsk Pedagogical Institute, Aron Roninson, was by that time working as a director of a middle school in the Tambov region. Arriving to Belorussia in October 1944, he was appointed the head of the Pinsk school district.[40] In 1945 the People's Commissariat of Education of the BSSR again sent out summons. Responding to such a call, Liza and Masha Fomins in the summer of that year were re-evacuated to Vitebsk from the Chuvash ASSR. At the same time, a refugee from Vitebsk, the teacher Sara Pomerants, who was now in the Kuibyshev region, in response to her request to return to Minsk received a call-up for herself, her mother, and her younger brother. From there she was assigned to work in Novogrudok.[41]

Even greater efforts were made by the Belorussian leadership to return doctors and nurses. Because of the epidemic of typhus in February 1944, when by no means all of eastern Belorussia had been liberated, at the request of the

Minsk authorities, the USSR's People's Commissariat of Health sent 650 refugee doctors from this republic back. Invitations and summons were also sent to doctors and nurses from the BSSR. These measures were not in vain. In the same Rechitsa, the number of doctors and nurses more than doubled between 1944 and 1948.[42] In passing, we note that after the liberation other western republics of the USSR also encountered a shortage of health care workers. In the Moldavian SSR only 1.7 percent of doctors and 7 percent of nurses, of the state-mandated numbers, remained.[43] Therefore, the People's Commissar for Public Health of the USSR demanded on September 8, 1944, that all medical workers who had worked there before the war return to this republic.[44] Another order from August 24, 1945, put an end to attempts by medical officials of the eastern regions to keep the evacuated doctors in their regions by administration means. According to it, all evacuated doctors were to return within a year's time to the place of their former residence, if they so desired, and the positions that they were vacating should be occupied by demobilized doctors and graduates of medical institutions.[45]

The Belorussian authorities also called upon prominent engineers and directors of enterprises to return. Against the background of the intensifying state antisemitism, the invitations to Jews for high-ranking managerial positions testify to how acute the problem with cadres was. During the war Jews proved to be top-rate factory managers,[46] and after the liberation the Belorussian authorities wished to have them helping with restoration of the economy. The director of the mechanical plant in Alma-Ata, Abram Shteingol'ts, received several urgent summonses to Minsk. The Alma-Ata authorities did not want to let him go, offering him the post of director of the city's bread factory—almost the same position as he occupied in Minsk before the war.[47] Shteingol'ts decided not to return.

The question of the re-evacuation of the rest of the population in Belorussia was settled in a different way. Immediately after liberation, because of the acute shortage of housing, the executive committees of the city councils in Minsk, Mozyr', Mogilëv, and Gomel approached this question very carefully, rigorously examining every request of refugees for return. As a results of this cautious approach, only one train car with twenty re-evacuated refugees—only specialists and their families—was dispatch from Alatyr' to Gomel in August 1944.[48] The lack of statistics on refugee return permits does not allow to conclude whether Jewish refugees received a disproportionately low number of such permits. Nevertheless, the republican authorities' greater efforts to absorb the Belorussians and other Slavs who were being resettled from Poland, as well as the returning *Ostarbeiters* from Germany,[49] among whom there were very few Jews, indirectly indicate such a possibility.

This very selective practice with respect to the repatriation of refugees, which opened up wide opportunities for bribes and extortion, was abolished in September 1944 by the decision of the Council of People's Commissars of the BSSR on the unhindered return of all residents of the republic. The same decree obligated the local authorities to provide them with housing.[50] It is possible that the resolution was issued for purely propagandistic reasons. In June 1945 Rakhil Baranova asked the local authorities in the BSSR for permission to return to Rechitsa, pointing out that her fifteen-year-old son was already there with nobody to take care of him; she was refused because of the absence of a decision on re-evacuation. On the same basis, Rakhil and Polina Kaganovs, who asked to be re-evacuated to Gomel, were refused permission.[51] It is also possible that the leadership of the republic did not inform the authorities of the rear areas about the permission for re-evacuation. In any case, in the early autumn of 1945 the leadership of Belorussia sent letters to the evacuation departments of the eastern regions of the USSR with a request to delay the re-evacuation to this republic because of the severe housing problem.[52] Despite this, the refugees continued to return to Belorussia,[53] sometimes resorting to various tricks.

At the same time, in Belorussia itself Jews gradually withdrew from the highest republican and regional posts and duties. Because of this policy, from 1946 to 1949 the proportion of Jews in these positions decreased from 279 (6.1 percent) to 240 (5.5 percent).[54] However, the situation was even worse with regular jobs. Where no special knowledge was required, preferences were given to non-Jews. In Rechitsa until the mid-1950s, leaders tried not to hire Jews in state institutions and enterprises. After a short difficult organizational period, the Jews responded to this process of economic exclusion with the mass opening of artels. Artels not only saved them from hunger but also helped the entire population cope with the acute shortage of goods.[55]

The surrounding population met the returning Jews, in general, with coldness. Although there were cases of a warm attitude toward returning refugees from neighbors and acquaintances, some residents reacted to the evacuated Jews even with hostility. The negative attitude toward the Jews was due, in part, to the massive antisemitic propaganda that the local population was exposed to during the occupation,[56] but above all it was a reaction to the pressing issue of the return of Jewish dwellings: apartments and houses, both private and municipal. The last one was especially difficult to return. Part of the housing and household property was returned by the new owners voluntarily, some of it was returned only by court order or after appeals to the city administration, and some was never returned.

In the Belorussian town of Rechitsa authorities preferred not to interfere in this process much, so as not to aggravate interethnic relations. It was easier for a demobilized soldier to reclaim a house than for an elderly person or a widow with children. It was especially difficult to recover property seized by the officials. Sheina-Ita Frenkel, who returned to Rechitsa in 1944, discovered that her house was occupied by a policeman. Under the neighbors' pressure, he gave her one room, but later tried to drive the woman out, threatening her with a gun. Frenkel was forced to file a complaint with the court, which ruled in her favor only in 1946. While leaving, the policeman took all of her household possessions.[57] The connivance of the town authorities in relation to the arbitrary seizure of someone else's housing in Rechitsa caused criticism from the executive committee of the Gomel Regional Council of Deputies. Its chair, Koval'chuk, wrote in August 1945 about the arbitrariness in Rechitsa: "Many townspeople do not have apartments, there is no order in the distribution of vacant housing. The decree of the Council of People's Commissars of the USSR on the return of dwellings of those returning home from the evacuation is grossly violated. Many communal houses are not inhabited and are being plundered."[58]

However, in large cities it was precisely the Belorussian authorities' voluntaristic treatment of the houses of evacuated Jews that became a model for the population. In Minsk the city authorities distributed many Jewish apartments in undamaged buildings to party and state officials. Although the complaints of Jews, especially the frontline soldiers among them, prompted the Belorussian Central Committee and the central authorities in Moscow to give orders for the release of housing, the new tenants, the officials, and the city authorities often did not hurry to comply with them. Other new tenants also did not hurry to vacate apartments and houses. As Leonid Smilovitsky shows, this situation was typical for all of postwar Belorussia. Sometimes the struggle to reclaim housing lasted more than five years.[59]

Disappointed by having to return to the former owners the seized housing and property (and even Yiddish music records were taken[60]), some of the local population spread rumors about the cowardice of the Jews at the front and the flight of the total Jewish population to Tashkent.[61] In this way, the non-Jewish population in many places tried to some extent to rehabilitate themselves from the "lived in occupied territory" label that blemished their biographies. The growth of antisemitism was noted in many places in postwar Belorussia. The Galbershtadt family was re-evacuated to Bobruisk in 1946 but were faced there with such strong antisemitism that they returned to the town of their evacuation, Ust'-Kamenogorsk.[62]

The Outbreak of Antisemitism in Ukraine

The authorities' opposition to the return of refugees was stronger in Ukraine than in other Soviet republics. Here, there was no organized return to by special trains at all. To control the repatriation and other migrations, a department for evacuation affairs was established under the Council of People's Commissariat of the Ukrainian SSR. In April 1944, the refugees were informed that they could return to the Kharkov, Sumy, Poltava, Voroshilovgrad, Zaporozh'e, Dnepropetrovsk, and Stalino regions only, for which they needed to obtain special permits from the local police. At the same time, however, it was strictly forbidden to return to the cities of Kharkov, Sumy, Konotop, Shostka, and Romny.[63] It seems that there was a re-evacuation to the Zhitomir region. The Executive Committee of the Zhitomir Regional Council decided to allow the return of refugees starting on July 20, 1944, but the return to the cities of Zhitomir, Berdichev, Korosten', and Novograd-Volynsk was conditional upon the receipt of special permits from the executive committees of these cities.[64] When Bella Margulis from Kanash (Chuvashia) asked permission to return to her native Korosten' for herself, her husband, and her son, a disabled veteran, the authorities allowed only the son to return.[65] Jews almost were not allowed to enter Chernovtsy. Near the entrance to the city a checkpoint was set up and only those Jews who could prove that they lived there before the war were admitted.[66]

The Kiev region was particularly persistently "protected." Even after Aron Sokol, an invalid of the war who two years later was awarded the Order of Glory 3rd Class, came back to Belaia Tserkov' in 1945, the town authorities refused the return of his mother and sister, also local residents, from the evacuation in the Tatar ASSR. The chair of the city executive committee, Malashkevich, told him directly, "I do not need a Jewish kolkhoz here, and there are enough Jews who come here to trade in the bazaars." The permission Sokol received for the arrival of only his mother and sister (but not the latter's children and husband) he considered a mockery.[67]

By means of these restrictions, the Soviet Ukrainian authorities sought to prevent the return of Jewish refugees. Although this was a manifestation of state antisemitism, one should take into account the specifics of this policy in Ukraine. It emerged from the desire to reduce the local population' discontent about the returning Jews, who were demanding their housing and household possessions back. In 1944 M. Mamud complained from Odessa to Ehrenburg: "I was in the evacuation for three years, and have recently returned to my native city. The things and furniture in my apartment have been looted; the apartment is occupied. I have two officer sons protecting the homeland, and I've been lying in the lobby for seven days, which does not bother my neighbor at all. . . . The bureaucrats in the housing office do not want to give me a lease for an apartment."[68] Even when the prosecutor's office ordered the eviction of illegal residents, they did not hurry to leave. The Kiev resident Kiva Vekselman complained to the same Ehrenburg about such an occupant.[69]

Given that Kiev was liberated as early as the beginning of November 1943, one can conclude that the authorities' restrictive measures were successful in maintaining a low proportion of Jews in the city—4.8 percent (15,644) in June 1944.[70] This is despite the fact that in 1939, according to the census, their number in Kiev stood at 224,236, comprising 26.5 percent of the city's residents. In other words, less than 7 percent of all the Jews who had lived there previously returned to Kiev in first half a year after its liberation. Considering, on the one hand, the death of 33,771 Kiev Jews in Babii Yar[71] (which is about 15 percent of the prewar number of Jews) and, on the other hand, the similar death rate between the rest of the Jewish and non-Jewish population during the war, the number of Kiev Jews who were not allowed to return at once is very high.

Jewish refugees complained about the Soviet Ukrainian policies to the JAC and its newspaper *Eynikayt*. In the 1944 letter to Molotov mentioned in chapter 4, along with calls to help the Jews who had survived in occupied Ukraine, the leaders of the JAC asked to facilitate the return of housing to former owners and provide an opportunity for Jewish refugees to return to Ukraine. Molotov shared the letter with the Central Committee, and only Beria suggested taking some measures about the complaints. But his suggested measures concerned only the improvement of the situation of the survivors and the fight against antisemitism, not the return of refugees[72]—and this was not accidental.

Beria was well aware of the views, circulating in different variations in the European part of the USSR, and in Ukraine in particular, that the Jews not only did not fight in the war but also did not not stay to guard their homes and property, thus avoiding the harsh occupation with its hunger and forced labor. Instead, they fled to allegedly bountiful Tashkent, and on their return there they easily got back their housing, which they had not fought or suffered for. In Kiev Dovzhenko retold the rumors brought from Moscow that Jews in Tashkent and Tbilisi had supposedly "bought injured Muscovites" in hospitals to accompany them to Moscow, where they would "purchase residence permits and apartments" for huge amounts of money.[73] The Muscovite Parfënova said during a conversation with a propagandist: "Jews are a cunning people. They can secure good lives for themselves. During the war, more so than others, they took refuge in the rear. Now they are given good jobs and live without need."[74] At the same time, stories circulated in Leningrad that Jews wishing to return to the city used connections to arrange their return wherever they wanted.[75] However, sources show that the Jewish theme was quite marginal in the rumors of these two largest cities of the USSR. Note that even before the war rumors in the USSR were a very important channel for receiving news, given the lack of confidence in the official media. The authorities were unhappy with this alternative channel of information but were powerless to fight it. This channel's role increased even more after the order of the authorities at the beginning of the war for almost all citizens to surrender their radio sets (they were not returned until 1946).

Having survived the German occupation, Ukraine's population was also hostile to the returning Jewish refugees, who, unlike the Ukrainians, were not branded with the "lived in occupied territory" mark. Meanwhile, by 1944 many Ukrainians and Russians began to feel like second-class citizens because of this.[76] According to some information on Vinnitsa region, 81.75 percent of people who were in the occupied territory during the war were ousted from the Communist Party by the beginning of 1947. As for the whole republic, by 1950 about 68,000 persons were expelled from the party, 92.25 percent of all Communists who remained under German occupation.[77]

The rumors circulating in Ukraine and the demands to return housing lead to public insults and beatings of Jews. Former frontline officer Moisei Dargolts, describing to Stalin in November 1945 the indifference of the authorities in the matter of settling the re-evacuated Jews and returning their apartments, stated: "There is terrible, unbridled antisemitism in Kamenets-Podol'sk, which knows no boundaries, which does not meet with resistance from local organizations . . . at every step, the word 'kike' is a common occurrence. And expression like: 'the Jews did not fight,' the medals that Jews wear were bought for money.' A lot of fights, right on the streets, happen for this reason."[78] Upon his return with his family to Zhitomir, Motl Kats saw that their house had been bombed. Then he went to his daughter's apartment. His granddaughter Klara writes that the Ukrainians who had lived there since 1941 chased him away with death threats: "If you do not disappear from here, you will be where your daughter is. We'll kill you! Do you want to go to Bogunia?"[79] This was the name of the forest where the Jews who had remained in the city were shot.

There were several cases of beatings of Jews in Kharkov, one of them, in the farmers market, ending in murder. The peasant-merchants even resisted the arriving police.[80] Semën Abramovich reported in his letters about the rampant antisemitism in the liberated Kharkov region.[81] Doba Belozovskaia describes teenagers (she calls them fascists) beating Jewish girls in the city of Snovsk in the Chernigov region.[82] Throughout the Dnepropetrovsk region, according to the authorities' report, the Jewish children returning from the evacuation were persecuted by their Russian and Ukrainian peers who had remained in the occupied territory.[83] In Dnepropetrovsk itself, according to Genia Kniazeva, one Jew was struck by an ax, and this growth of antisemitism in the city forced Kniazeva's family to move to Chernovtsy.[84] Perhaps historian Victoria Khiterer describes this exact event. According to her data, in Dnepropetrovsk in August 1944, the rioters, indignant at the return of the apartments to the Jews, threw stones at one of them and crushed the apartment of another with an ax. After that, the police broke up the crowd and arrested several assailants.[85] In Krivoi Rog the frontline pilot Fridzon entered his former apartment in June 1944, which was taken over after the execution of his wife and children. The new tenants raised a cry, "The Jews have come and are beating Russians!" causing a crowd to come running from the nearby bazaar. Fridzon was beaten up by the crowd that shouted, "Five mine-shafts for Yids were not enough, all the mines must be filled with them!"[86] When the head of the city's municipal services tried to stop the massacre, a crowd screamed at her: "Bah . . . this Communist came to protect Yids, beat her, beat her!"[87]

It should be noted that the NKGB of the Dnepropetrovsk region did make an effort to fight the growth of antisemitism. With some delay, in the summer of 1945, about a dozen perpetrators of antisemitic rumors were arrested in this region. The most monstrous of these rumors circulated in Krivoi Rog, where a group of three people who told workers about a gang of Jews who allegedly killed Russian children and used them for sausages and hand-pies to sell on the market; they were sentenced to seven years in jail.[88]

In June 1944 in Kiev, a tradeswoman in the bazaar, mistaking Ivan Kartavyi for a Jew, broke his head with a bottle, which required treatment at the clinic. This incident became the starting point for the rapidly spreading rumors in the city that a Jewish woman had killed an officer, who, according to one version of the rumor, was a Hero of the Soviet Union.[89] Due to the inaction of the authorities, one such incident in Kiev morphed into a real pogrom. On September 4, 1945, two demobilized Ukrainian soldiers attached and beat up Lieutenant Iosif Rozenshtein, who was dressed in civilian clothes. When he tried to explain that he was an employee of the People's Commissariat of State Security of Ukraine, he heard in response only, "Bah . . . the Tashkent guerrilla." Running home and putting on his uniform, the lieutenant returned and tried to take the abusers to the police. They resisted, and Rozenshtein shot them. The funeral procession on September 7 passed through the central streets to the Jewish market, along the way growing to a crowd of three hundred people. The mob brutally beat and pelted with stones about a hundred Jews into whom they ran on the street. Among the thirty-six Jews who ended up in the hospital after that, five died on the same day.[90] As a result, all the troops of the Kiev garrison urgently deployed to restore order in the city. According to the testimony of Fridrikh Valler, who was studying at the Kiev Artillery School at the time, the Jews among the cadets were asked to leave the formation and were sent to stand watch at the school, while the rest of the cadets were sent to the city to restore order.[91]

Péter Apor, who studied the pogrom in the village of Kunmadaras (Hungary) in 1946, believed that the main reason behind it was the commercial activity of Jews in the village. This way the pogromists—most of whom were women—tried to protect their families from Jews and achieve social justice.[92] Although in postwar eastern Ukraine the Jews had very few opportunities for independent trading activity, their claim on their homes and property was perceived precisely as an attempt to violate the already accomplished "social justice." Unlike Kunmadaras and the Polish town of Kielce, where an anti-Jewish pogrom also took places in 1946, Soviet authorities in Ukraine did not take pogromists to court. Instead, to appease the local population, Rozenshtein was shot by the decision of the military tribunal of the NKGB. Although in Hungarian and Polish cases the questions of bringing pogromists to justice were also decided on the instructions of Soviet advisers, the Kiev pogromists were not brought to trial because of the very difficult situation in Ukraine. At the time, there was a persistent armed struggle with nationalists, and the Soviet authorities feared that the separatists would take advantage of the pogromists' trial to recruit broad sections of the population into their ranks. Besides, trials in Hungary and Poland were needed by Stalin to demonstrate to the West the democratic character of the governments under the Soviet control and the process of denazification that they were carrying out. There was no such need in Ukraine.

It should be noted that sometimes the use of weapons by Jewish veterans in Ukraine still proved to be an effective method to reclaim housing and did not lead to serious consequences. As Oskar Rokhlin recalls, at the end of 1944 his father, a tank driver, after finding out that the "tenants" in their apartment in Kiev did not want to vacate it, asked for a short leave from the battalion. Arriving,

> he kicked in the door, put the "owner" to the wall, and gave him twenty-four hours to clear the apartment. After four hours, the "owner" left, and we moved into our prewar property. Then my father walked through the apartments of our Ukrainian neighbors and prompted them to return the furniture stolen from us, which was immediately done. At the same time, the neighbors were touchingly saying how glad they were that we had survived and that they managed to hold onto the furniture until our, so joyful for them, return. The sight of an enraged father, with military orders on his chest and a gun on his belt, just turned their worldview upside down, and they immediately loved us like their own. So, we returned to our own apartment.[93]

Antisemitic sentiments in eastern Ukraine were strong even before the war. The diary of a resident of Kiev in the 1930s, Dovzhenko, was full of hatred for the Jews.⁹⁴ However, before the war and even during it, there were no cases of massacres of large groups of Jews by civilians in this part of the republic. It was the struggle for supposed "social justice" that prompted certain groups of local people, after the war, to cross the invisible line separating hatred of Jews from violence against them.

On September 13, 1944, Sergei Savchenko, People's Commissar of the State Security, drew attention of the republic's leadership to the strong wave of antisemitism. His report cited examples of antisemitic utterances and wrongdoings against the Jews, including refusing to hire them, by Ukrainian administrators. Savchenko concluded the report with the recommendation to arrest the instigators of antisemitic rumors. Instead, several apparatchiks from the TsK KP(b) of Ukraine, headed by Viktor Alidin, condemned him. Rejecting almost all the accusations against the administrators, they, in turn, suggested that Savchenko came harder against the increased Zionism in Ukraine.⁹⁵ Semën Ignatiev, known for his role in the Doctors' Plot, noticed Alidin's leadership in this matter, and as soon as the former became Minister of State Security (MGB) of the USSR in August 1951, he appointed Alidin the deputy head of the seventh directorate (field supervision) of the MGB. After Alidin's attack, Nikita Khrushchev, the first secretary of the Ukraine's Central Committee, in a joint meeting of the TsK KP(b) and the Council of People's Commissars of Ukraine, also attacked Savchenko, accusing State Security staff of seizing the best buildings and furniture in Kiev.⁹⁶ This seemed too little to him, however, and, after coming to power ten years later, Khrushchev almost immediately dismissed Savchenko "for professional inadequacy." It did not help Savchenko that in 1946 he "saw the light," and organized repressions against the Zionists, especially in western Ukraine.⁹⁷

Sensing the growth of state Russian chauvinism in Kremlin, the creative intelligentsia of Ukraine tried to expand it to a more general East Slavic chauvinism. It seemed to them that this discourse might allow, if not to eliminate, then at least to neutralize accusations of disloyalty against Ukrainians because of numerous cases of collaboration with the Nazis and separatism. Bringing into focus the particularly large losses borne by Ukrainians on the front line, in comparison with the Jews who allegedly did not fight, was part of the Ukrainian creative intelligentsia's plan. In reading Dovzhenko's diary entries, one can easily guess that he saw the Holocaust victims as an obstacle to this part of the plan.⁹⁸ This position was openly shared by the Ukrainian writer Ostap Vishnia, who in the summer of 1946 published a feuilleton asserting that while the Ukrainians fought, the Jews sat out in Fergana and Tashkent. And now, Vishnia continued, Ukrainians were busy with rebuilding the country, and Jews were engaged in trade.⁹⁹ These attacks did not go unnoticed in Moscow.

Criticizing Vishnia's accusation, among other things, *Pravda* asks on what basis the author chose to target the Soviet people who evacuated because of the German occupation threat.[100]

In March 1943 Khrushchev supported the proposal of the People's Commissar for Internal Affairs of the Ukrainian SSR, Vasilii Sergienko, to remove Natan Rybak from the post of deputy executive secretary of the Union of Soviet Writers of Ukraine (then located in Ufa). Sergienko's proposal cited statements made against Rybak by Ukrainian writers, among whom Dovzhenko, perhaps the instigator of this campaign, distinguished himself by especially antisemitic declarations: "Jews are very harmful to Ukrainian culture. They hated us, hate us, and will hate us. They try to get everywhere and take everything in their hands. The fact that the Union of Soviet Writers of Ukraine is run by the lousy *evreichik* [little Jew] Rybak is outrageous."[101]

It should be noted that the Jew-disliking Khrushchev,[102] sympathized with Ukrainian antisemitism. With special energy he suppressed any attempts to memorialize the Holocaust in Ukraine. The Yiddish poet David Gofshtein was not allowed to organize a memorial rally in Kiev in honor of the dead.[103] When in 1945 the composer Dmitrii Klebanov, a Jew by ethnicity, wrote his Symphony no. 1 (*Babii Yar*), imbued with Jewish mourning melodies, it was banned, and the author was dismissed from the post of chair of the Kharkov branch of the Union of Composers. It is not known whether this message of the Ukrainian creative elite reached the broader strata of the population of Ukraine. In any case, overall, the population did not consider Jewry a victim of genocide and did not feel compassion for it after the war.

Such an attitude in Ukraine is not surprising. It was encoded in all Soviet cinematography and the central press, which often hushed up the massacres of Jews. The Kremlin, on the one hand, feared the emergence of additional rumors about its Judeophilia, and on the other, sought to unify all victims in general: "the perished peace-loving Soviet people." It is possible that in 1944 and the first half of 1945, the authorities believed that broad anti-German propaganda could replace the politically problematic and therefore unnecessary public campaign against antisemitism. Sergei Yekelchyk argued that as the Ukrainian regions were liberated, the authorities intensively cultivated a discourse of hatred toward the Germans among the local population.[104] The postwar public trials of Nazi criminals and collaborators were a part of this policy.

Stalin did not like this nationalist movement of the Ukrainian intelligentsia, as there was a fierce struggle with the nationalist insurgency. Therefore, at the end of 1943 he severely criticized the script of Dovzhenko's film *Ukraine on Fire* for the fact that showed only Ukrainians as leading the fight against the Nazis. In the presence of specially invited Ukrainian writers, Stalin said to him:

"Why didn't you unmask a single Ukrainian bourgeois nationalist? You yourself are infected with nationalism." Because of Stalin's reaction, Khrushchev, who himself sympathized with the Ukrainian case, began to criticize the screenplay, as Dovzhenko recorded in his diary with indignation.[105] At the end of August 1946, a meeting of writers was held in Kiev, at which the third secretary of the TsK KP(b) of Ukraine Konstantin Litvin criticized the recently published textbook *Outline of the History of Ukrainian Literature* by S. Maslov and E. Kiriliuk for nationalism and the *vneklassovyi podkhod* (non-class approach). At the same meeting, the novel *Sofia* of Leonid Smilianskii, several works by other authors, as well as literary magazines *Vitchizna*, *Dnipro*, and *Radian'skii L'viv* were also censured for nationalism. The announcement of the meeting was published in *Pravda*.[106]

Supporting restrictions on entry and residence of Jews in Ukraine, and in view of the continued growth of antisemitism, the Kremlin instructed party organizations to engage quietly in explanatory work, and not only in Ukraine. According to the memoirs of Basia Malinkovich, being the secretary of the party organization of the sewing workshop of Ust'-Kamenogorsk, she was invited to the East Kazakhstan regional party committee, where she and other secretaries were read a secret letter from the Central Committee of the Party about manifestations of antisemitism and the contribution of Jews to the military victory, as well as to science and culture.[107] However, such superficial measures could not be a substitute for the authorities' strong denunciation of antisemitism, which could have come a public address through the mass media.

Having given up on trying to get a permit to return to Ukraine, Jewish refugees made their way there illegally, getting where they wanted to go either by train, with the help of a bribe, or by hitchhiking. In January 1946 Kiev city authorities complained that the restrictions did not prevent the arrival in the Ukrainian capital of tens of thousands of illegal re-evacuees who settled in the city and found jobs.[108] Those of them who went to Kiev, but could not prove their residence there before the war, were evicted.[109] Of the 10,523 written requests from refugees for residence in Kiev, sent to the "provisional commission" specially created to solve the housing problem in the city, the authorities acceded to only 6.[110] However, the commission in the same year permitted the demobilized soldiers and employees arriving independently to work in the republican ministries. This caused indignation from Minister of State Control of Ukraine V. O. Chernovol, who stated that these numbers indicated the absence of a real fight against illegal entry into Kiev. Although Chernovol did not speak openly about the undesirability of Jews settling in the city (even the families of frontline soldiers), the examples cited by him show exactly the anti-Jewish overtones.[111]

Isaak Kotliar, who had been discharged from the army for health reasons and was in the evacuation, faced bureaucratic barriers when he tried to return to his home in Kiev. He was told in court that housing in Kiev was returned only to war veterans or members of their families. But in 1945 the local bureaucratic machine sabotaged all his attempts to request documents confirming that he had served in the army and that one of his sons was killed at the front and the other disappeared without a trace; even appealing to the Prosecutor General of Ukraine, Roman Rudenko, did not help.[112] Khava Ovrutskaia testifies that her husband, a frontline soldier, was only allowed to return to Kiev in 1950, but they were not returned their apartment.[113]

This was very similar to the prerevolutionary situation when Kiev Governor-General Fëdor Trepov opposed the settlement of Jews in Kiev and those who settled there without permission were evicted. The essential difference between the two situations was that the Soviet authorities were harsher toward Jews. Often even those Jewish refugees who had lived there long before the war were not allowed to return. Meanwhile, the measures introduced by Chernovol and other leaders of the republic tightened the passport regime. Persons without a residence permit were sometimes not simply evicted from Kiev but sentenced for up to five years in prison.[114]

As for the complaint of the JAC, on the instructions of Khrushchev, the deputy chair of the Council of People's Commissars of Ukraine, I. S. Senin, prepared a memorandum. Judging by the data given in it and the tone, it was compiled with one goal—to reassure the committee. The refusal of the authorities to receive returning refugees was formally explained by a concern for them: that they would not find themselves in Ukraine in a worse situation with regards to housing and employment than in their places of temporary residence. Besides that, the memorandum glossed over the serious problems Jews faced in recovering their property in the Ukraine.[115]

The administrative restrictions on the re-evacuation introduced on January 1, 1946, delayed the return to Ukraine for about 300,000 evacuees (i.e., 15.4 percent of their total number), according to the Statistical Office of the Ukrainian SSR.[116] The fact that ongoing repressive measures against the "evacuated population" were only directed at the Jews can be seen from a statement made by Khrushchev, as retold by Pavel Sudoplatov:

> I remember how Khrushchev, then the secretary of the Communist Party of Ukraine, called Usman Iusupov, the secretary of the Communist Party of Uzbekistan, and complained to him that Jews who had been evacuated during the war to Tashkent and Samarkand were flocking to Ukraine like crows. In this conversation, which took place in 1947, he also said that he simply did not have enough

places to accept everyone, as the Kiev was destroyed, and that it was necessary to stop this flow, otherwise pogroms would begin in the city. At that moment I was in Iusupov's office, and he related this conversation to me.[117]

One step in reducing the dissatisfaction of the local population of Ukraine with the returning Jews was the resolution adopted on June 28, 1945, at Khrushchev's request by the Council of People's Commissars of the USSR stipulating that those apartments of the refugees that since had been given to the local intelligentsia—academics, professors, writers, distinguished artists, scientists, and actors—were not to be turned over to their previous residents. This decision partially abolished on the territory of Ukraine the countrywide decree of August 5, 1941, on the securing housing. In July 1945 in Belarus, the people's commissar of justice and the prosecutor general requested that the Belorussian republican authorities pass a similar measure, but it is not clear from the available documents how this issue was decided there.[118] Although the decree in the USSR provided for alternative housing for returning owners, it was, if provided at all, much worse than the housing which had been appropriated. Having selected an apartment house for academicians on Morozov Street, the Kiev city authorities did not provide any alternative housing to the family of Vladimir Smoliar. Only after numerous complaints they were housing, but it was in a communal apartment.[119] It should be noted that Khrushchev had been trying to push this decree for a long time. In May 1944 he was indignant that he had no housing in Kiev for academicians and musicians.[120] Thus, discrimination against refugees practiced at the local level was given partial legislative legitimization.

It is fair to say that conflicts over housing in liberated Kiev also occurred among the gentile population, sometimes even with the use of weapons against the police, as happened on September 26, 1944.[121] However, such conflicts did not become an excuse for ethnic clashes. The city and republican bureaucracy (including police, passport offices, courts, and prosecutors) were also interested in exploiting the aggravation of the housing issue in Kiev and in Ukraine in general. The acute shortage of housing in the Ukrainian capital helped them to acquire useful personal connections with the political elite, or became a source of bribes. The bribes ranged from one to ten thousand rubles.[122] Many members of the political elite improved their prewar housing conditions by securing the best apartments in the center of the city, which belonged to refugee families or families that had perished, often moving from one room in a communal apartment to their own three-room apartments.

In Ukraine—as in Belorussia—but much more consistently, another measure that was implemented to appease the local population was the reduction of the number of Jews in high-ranking and managerial positions. When requests were made for elite workers in the liberated areas of Ukraine and the Baltic states in 1945, only representatives of the titular nationalities of these republics hired.[123] In all western republics, Jews were not allowed to serve as secretaries of regional, territorial, and republican committees of the Communist Party. As a result, among the 2,693 chairs of the executive committees, secretaries of city committees, and *raikoms* in Ukraine, only five (0.2 percent) Jews remained in 1946. The process of eliminating Jews in leadership positions in the republic did not end there. By January 1953, their share was reduced to 0.08 percent.[124] It was not much better with regard to middle- and lower-level administrators. In Kamenets-Podol'sk, according to Dargolts's letter to Stalin, Jews who had formerly been party leaders or administrators were not recruited after their return from the front.[125] Mikhail Stakhurskii, the first secretary of the Vinnitsa Regional Committee of the Communist Party, did everything possible to prevent frontline Jews from returning to their prewar positions, claiming that they "fought" in Tashkent. He did not stop there. In just one year of his administration, as Amir Weiner shows, several dozen Jews were "cleansed" from the regional apparatus, so that their share fell from 9.34 percent in 1945 to 7.46 percent in 1946.[126]

The Ukrainian authorities did the same regarding the teaching staff. After the Kiev Commercial Institute's return from the evacuation, Jewish teachers were dismissed.[127] Then the Jews—teachers and deans—were "cleaned" from the Kiev Conservatory.[128] A similar purge was carried out in the Academy of Sciences of Ukraine. According to the complaint from Professor Kalman Bronshtein to the propaganda and agitation department of the TsK KP(b) of Ukraine, in June 1943 it was decided not to repatriate from Ufa eighty teachers of the Kiev Institute of Geological Sciences, the overwhelming majority of whom were Jews.[129] However, as Gennadii Kostyrchenko writes, the elimination of Jewish scholars had begun a year before, but those purges concerned only the social sciences and were carried out in Moscow and Leningrad.[130] Therefore, purges in all the institutes of the Academy of Sciences of Ukraine since 1943 were most likely the result of the personal initiative of the first secretary of the TsK KP(b) of Ukraine, Khrushchev. This is supported by the fact of Stalin's concern with the resentment at the basis of Khrushchev's personnel purges in 1947.[131]

In 1945–1946 quotas were unofficially introduced in the universities of Ukraine that limited not only the enrollment of first-year Jewish students but also transfers from universities outside the republic. With this measure the authorities intended to reassure further the Slavic population of the republic. Bulaevskaia, who wanted to transfer from the university in Alma-Ata to the University of Kiev, received a response that did not beat around the bush: "We accept only 12 percent Jews and the university is overcrowded."[132]

The antisemitic campaign in Ukraine did not skip secondary schools. Vera Belskaia, who returned from Frunze, remembers that she first felt the state antisemitism in postwar Kiev. The pedagogical board of the school, from which she graduated in 1946, decided to present her with a gold medal for excellence in her studies. But the Jewish school principal, who knew the local district's approach to the "Jewish question," warned Belskaia that the board might not approve the decision. This is in fact what happened.[133]

Simultaneously, the Ukrainian authorities took measures to reduce the number of Jews in public institutions. The Kiev prosecutors' office had wanted to hire Bulaevskaia, but after learning of her ethnicity, the personnel department said: "Jews are not respected, people are dissatisfied with you, so you understand it's not possible."[134] In early January 1949 Evgenii Paton, who replaced Aleksandr Palladin as the president of the Academy of Sciences of the Ukrainian SSR, held a hearing on the abolition of the Academy's departments dealing with Jewish culture (departments of literature, folk art, language, and folklore) as failing to inculcate patriotism and, instead, contributing to the disunity of the Soviet peoples. The republican authorities immediately sanctioned the liquidation of these departments.[135]

Perhaps because of Stalin's special plans for the Crimea, which then belonged to the RSFSR, Jewish teachers were also not allowed to be hired there. In June 1946, the head of the Crimean Medical Institute, Iakov Braul, complained in writing to Stalin's secretary Poskrebyshev that the director had forbidden to accept a Jewish pathologist, saying: "What are you doing with me? I am already in hot water with the regional committee for the fact that I have a lot of Jews."[136] Braul cites examples of the dismissal of Jewish directors and refusals of employment in the city council and as directors of the theater; it was openly said that the reason was the Jewish ethnicity of the candidates.[137] However, Jews were not wanted even for lower-level state posts, which, most likely, was part of the unofficial local policy of pushing them out by economic means. In Kerch Vera Bakhshi could not find a job for a long time after the war because of her Jewish patronymic, Abramovna.[138] Just like in Belorussia, many Jews of Ukraine and Crimea found a way out of this situation by opening artels.[139]

This policy, which can be called a "proportionate equalizing," seems so paradoxical for the country whose troops liberated half of Europe, was nevertheless the result of the authorities' realization of their own weakness. "Proportionate equalizing" was one of the measures to counter the agitation of the Organization of Ukrainian Nationalists (OUN) and Ukrainian Insurgent Army (UPA), which attempted to recruit Ukrainians into insurgent groups. Besides, it was a measure to pacify the population of Ukraine, dissatisfied with the ruined economy and the hunger that broke out in 1946–1947. Although the famine in Ukraine was by no means worse than in other places,[140] it contributed to an even greater increase in xenophobia. Some, following the old habit, blamed the Jews. During an election in Kiev, some marked their ballots with demands to remove Jews from state trade and government bodies: "Jews are cheating and swindling the shoppers, they do everything for easy money."[141] This and other manifestations of antisemitism were one of the forms of discontent with the regime. Realizing this, the authorities adopted a compromised version of the "removal of Jews" in order to weaken the discontent, mostly caused not by the return of Jews but by difficulties with grain and bread procurement.[142]

Another method that local authorities used to pacify the Ukrainian population was softer penalties for wartime collaborators. The German researcher Tania Penter noticed that in 1946 only 2.3 percent of the 29,204 collaborators in Ukraine received death sentences, while the rest received relatively light ten-year sentences in labor camps. The leniency toward collaborators was a cause for criticism by the Ministry of Justice toward the Ukrainian prosecutor's office at the end of 1949, after which, in 1950–1951, 94 percent of such defendants began to be sentenced to twenty-five years.[143] It is difficult not to link these changes with the departure of Khrushchev from Ukraine, who was transferred to a new position in Moscow in December 1949. Another attempt to pacify the Ukrainian population was Khrushchev's plan to transfer Crimea to Ukraine. But as he himself said, it was only after Stalin's death that this project could be, and was, realized.[144]

For their part, some Jewish returnees, learning about the annihilation of relatives and destruction or the seizure of dwellings, and also encountering acute hostility in Ukraine, went back to the places of their evacuation or sought alternative places of residence. Klara Kats, already familiar to us, recalls that after they were left without housing in Zhitomir and were living under the stairs, they began asking themselves, "What do we do next? And then our mother made the decision to leave Zhitsomir. For several months she corresponded with the director of shoe factory no. 1 in Tashkent, Prokhorov, where she had worked as a janitor during the war. . . . Prokhorov wrote to mother that he would take her on as an employee. . . . And here there were five of us—grandmother, mother, and us three girls . . . again we went to the east, as in 1941."[145] According to statistics, 12,056 refugees from Ukraine and 5,661 from Belorussia wouldn't or couldn't re-evacuate from Western Siberia.[146]

With regards to this situation, the authorities came up with the idea to revive the stalled Birobidzhan project. On January 26, 1946, the Council of People's Commissars of the RSFSR adopted a resolution "On measures to strengthen and further develop the economy of the JAR (Jewish Autonomous Region)." In March 1946 the first secretary of the regional party committee, Aleksandr

Bakhmutskii, went to Moscow to meet with the members of the JAC, who talked about the great potential of the autonomous region,[147] and in April 1946, an article by writer David Manevich on Birobidzhan's readiness to receive up to 2,500 Jewish families was submitted to the editorial office of *Eynikayt*.[148] After that, five employees of the Odessa garment factory wrote to *Eynikayt* expressing their desire to move to this autonomous region.[149] The campaign was gaining momentum. Kostyrchenko believes that this initiative of resettlement in Birobidzhan belonged to the JAC, which addressed Beria and Kaganovich in June of the same year.[150] However, the release of Jews who were not Soviet citizens prior to 1939 to Romania and Poland[151] testifies that the authorities themselves were looking for ways around the problem of the "extra" Jewish population in the western republics of USSR.

In any case, for about a year Manevich's call did not receive significant support from the authorities; then suddenly, apparently at the direction of Stalin, the resettlement project began to move at a rapid pace. By order of Lazar Kaganovich, to whom the organization of the resettlement was entrusted, the deputy secretary of the Regional Party Committee of the JAR, Ia. S. Sheinin, sent campaigners to the Kherson, Nikolaev, and other regions in Ukraine, and possibly also to Moldavia and Uzbekistan. In a short period of time, they signed up about 5,500 volunteers for resettlement from Ukraine. Then, fearing that the project might be perceived as deportation, the resettlement organizers recommended that those who signed up make formal requests for relocation. As a result, in March 1946 a group from the Vinnitsa region, on behalf of 1,500 people, petitioned the chair of the Presidium of the Supreme Soviet of the USSR, N. M. Shvernik, with a request for their resettlement in the JAR. This request was sent by the central authorities to Khrushchev. He enthusiastically agreed, and in mid-December 1946 a train with 450 settlers went to Birobidzhan.[152] In September 1947 another group of five people on behalf of 2,525 Jews in the Kherson region sent a request for their resettlement directly to the Council of Ministers of the Ukrainian SSR. In the same month, 704 families (644 Jewish, 34 Ukrainian, 25 Russian, 1 Georgian) from Nikolaev and mainly from the Kherson regions sent to the Kherson regional executive committee personal requests to relocate. In May–October 1947 the Ukrainian authorities approved the requests, and in June–November these families were sent to Birobidzhan with food supply for their journey.[153]

In July 1947 activists from Birobidzhan arrived in the Vinnitsa and Kiev regions. At the same time, Crimea was included in the Birobidzhan campaign.[154] Mikhail Shpigel'man recalls that agitators from Birobidzhan came to them in the village of Berëzovka (until 1945, Smidovich village with Sotsdorf collective farm) in the Razdol'noe district (before the war, the Fraidorf Jewish autonomous district). In his estimation, because of strong antisemitism, about 20 percent of all Jews who returned from evacuation to the Crimea were convinced to move. They were sent by train from Dzhankoi in north Crimea.[155] In the JAR, the settlers, the overwhelming majority of whom were urban residents, were mainly assigned to live in kolkhozes. In its Smidovichi district in 1947 and the first half of 1948, 112 families of immigrants from the Vinnitsa, Nikolaev, and Crimea regions were settled.[156]

Because of Khrushchev's request to the Uzbek authorities, in September 1947 a train with two hundred families of Jewish refugees was sent to the JAR from Samarkand. The dispatch was accompanied by great pomp. An orchestra played at the station, city officials gave solemn speeches about the friendship of Soviet peoples and about the glorious work of Jewish refugees in the enterprises and fields of the republic.[157] As part of the same campaign, additional 2,515 Jews left the eastern regions of Ukraine in 1950 (31.2 percent of them from the Kamenets-Podol'sk region).[158] In total, from six to twenty thousand Jews went to the JAR as a result of this campaign.[159] It seems that it was these relocations, within the framework of which lists were drawn up and trains were being prepared, that rumors arose about the preparations for an all-out deportation of Jews.

Although the relocation of Jews to the Far East could not be carried out without Stalin's approval, he was somewhat alarmed by Khrushchev's sympathy for Ukrainian nationalism and antisemitism. He knew about Khrushchev's biases from the numerous complaints of Jewish refugees and also from Savchenko's boss—Beria. To eliminate "errors," Stalin sent Lazar Kaganovich to Ukraine in 1947. As the first secretary of the Central Committee of the Communist Party of Ukraine, he occupied himself with "straightening out" the nationalist line, mainly in historical science, and he returned to Moscow later that year.[160] Khrushchev, who at that time retained the post of chair of the Council of People's Commissars of the republic, once again combined his two posts after the departure of Kaganovich, and two years later he was recalled to Moscow. Knowing Stalin well, he could not perceive Kaganovich's appointment as anything other than the disapproval of his Ukrainian national policy. It is possible that Khrushchev got Stalin to recall Kaganovich, saying that by terrorizing the party leadership, he prevented them from providing a plan for grain procurement, a very important issue in the postwar famine.

～

After liberating and securing the western regions of the USSR from Nazi rule, the Soviet government did not immediately allow refugees to re-evacuate. The Kremlin was afraid that their departure from eastern regions would have a negative impact on the country's economy in general and interrupt the normal provision of the army in particular. Later on, the authorities allowed for the return, first of all, issuing permits to specialists who had an acute need in the liberated or former frontline areas. In many places, the issuance of permits for re-evacuation by local authorities was compelled, as they realized they would have to deal with unpleasant litigation for housing already occupied by other families. It was particularly difficult for Jewish families to obtain permission to return to Ukraine, where antisemitism increased during the occupation years and the first secretary of the Central Committee of the Communist Party of the Republic Khrushchev did not want to irritate the local population. Eyeing economic extrusion, the Ukrainian authorities limited the hiring of Jews and their admission to the institutions of higher education. Stalin was sympathetic to this policy of limiting Jews' return to Ukraine: he, for example, authorized of the resuscitation of the Birobidzhan project. As a consequence, 6,000 to 20,000 Jews, mainly from Ukraine, went to the Jewish autonomous region in the Far East. These figures indicate the failure of the project, given the total number of Jewish refugees from Ukraine of 950,000.

Conclusion

ESPECIALLY AT THE BEGINNING OF THE WAR, the authorities often tried, by various means, to halt the movement of refugees to the east in order to stop the notorious "panic moods." This approach came from Stalin. To some extent, his position was determined by not yet abandoned hopes to implement the prewar precept of "fighting the enemy on their territory." Therefore, the local administrators who did not carry out the evacuation of the population were not afraid of being punished. On the contrary, it was those representatives who evacuated the people too soon who were punished. Therefore, the Jewish refugees mainly had to rely on their own strength to save themselves.

Once permission to evacuate was received, the authorities usually tried to help all those who wished to leave the western regions of the USSR. However, it was difficult to leave because of delayed permits, lack of trains, and destroyed railway tracks, bridges, and cars. Some Jews did not manage to leave the dangerous regions in time and fell under the occupation with all its dramatic consequences or, at best, found themselves under a massive bombing of trains by the aircraft of the advancing German army. As a rule, because of the poor distribution of the swarms of trains with hundreds of thousands of refugees and the congestion of the Soviet railway network, the refugees took a very long time to reach their destinations. Because of the long journey in crowded train cars—hotbeds of epidemics—with a lack of food and hygienic conditions, some of the refugees died or succumbed to infection.

Providing refugees with transportation to the east, the authorities in Moscow and in the regions were guided not by considerations of humanity but by the desire to preserve the human capital for the successful waging of the war. In the memoirs of prominent Soviet workers in the 1970s and 1980s, one can often find the expression "evacuation of the productive forces to the east." Even the very use of the impersonal concept of "productive forces" shows that the authorities saw in refugees not people who were torn from their homes by war but only as one—albeit important—element of the production process. Therefore, the authorities tried to safeguard the refugees in general, not to save each one in particular. Someone may argue that such an attitude was a necessary measure for the sake of a swift victory, but the negligent attitude of administrators to their duties actually delayed the victory rather than sped it up.

Several thousand kilometers from their homes, refugees entered their new world completely without anything—or with minimal means of subsistence. This new world was located on the periphery of a vast country engaged in a fight for its existence. For many refugees, adapting to a new life was a very difficult task. The overwhelming majority of them were forced to change their place of residence two or three times, but doing so four to five times, and even more, was not uncommon. Distances could be short, within a single city or district, or they could be far—in other regions and republics. The frequent change of residence was due to the movement of the front line, relocation or harassment by the authorities, poor relations with homeowners, and the search for better opportunities for survival. Very often the new place turned out to be worse than the old one.

One of the important problems that the Soviet authorities had to face during the years of war was the issue of securing food for the the population. The Soviet population suffered from a lack of food even before the war, and with its beginning the situation deteriorated significantly. There were several reasons for this. In the first years of the war, the Germans seized important areas of the USSR that specialized in grain production: Ukraine, Crimea, Kuban', and part of the Central Black Earth Region, the rest of which was under bombardment. Of the remaining areas, the male population of the most able-bodied age was mobilized. Arriving refugees could not replace them since many of them did not have much experience in agriculture. Although many refugees were involved in grain production, a significant portion of them were burdened by the new work.

Hunger and disease caused a high mortality rate among refugees in their new places of residence, especially in 1942. In total, during the evacuation (including, for many of them, the starving year of 1946), 15–20 percent of all refugees died. Only well-paid work could give refugees the opportunity to survive in new conditions. In addition to their own abilities and luck, the success of the job search was influenced by the attitude of the local party and administrative leaders toward refugees, as well as the general attitude of the local population. It was the first time that the locals were encountering strangers in their midst in such large numbers. They saw them as a threat to the usual order and way of life. Perceiving the refugees as a once prosperous sector of the population, closer to the central power, residents of the eastern regions in some cases even gloated over the refugees' poverty. "They got fat and will be!" they said, justifying their indifference or even hostility to the refugees. The negative attitude toward the refugees on the part of the collective farmers was compounded by the bitterness, accumulated over the course of two decades, caused by the militant measures taken by the Soviet government in the process of collectivization. The obligation imposed on local residents to allow refugees to live with them contributed to their negative views.

The attitude toward Jews, on the whole, was particularly negative because of preexisting prejudices against them, both among the Russian Orthodox population and among Muslims. Besides, the arrival of such a large number of refugees, among whom Jews in a number of places constituted a substantial percentage, caused a rise in the price of food and essential goods on the market, which further increased the negative attitude toward them. In 1941–1943 the local population in Central Asia was particularly irritated by the large proportion of young men among Jewish refugees from former Poland and the Baltic states, whom the authorities at that point did not conscript into the Soviet Army. This contributed to the strengthening of antisemitism. The central authorities, as a rule, fought this antisemitism, as they rightly saw it as a manifestation of hidden discontent with the system. The local authorities took a softer stance on antisemitism, because, on the one hand, they were themselves under the influence of local discontent and, on the other, were often burdened with a new duty to improve the living situation of refugees. This attitude, which contributed to permanent inadequacy and which was influenced by the country's disastrous economic situation, was a cause of suffering for all refugees—and the Jews among them especially.

As was said in the introduction, even before the war Stalin knew about the poor management system in the provinces. To correct the existing party and administrative systems, he expanded the functions of the NKVD at the local level. Despite this measure, the situation in the rear during the war exposed the poor administrative system of the Soviet state. The lower-level administration poorly carried out the duties assigned to it. The repressions of the late 1930s did not teach the lower-level administrators to perform their duties, but rather taught them political maneuvering and the fear of punishment for the manifestation of initiative. Many local administrators waited for instructions on the smallest issues. Penalties for inaction or for the widespread theft of goods and food products during colossal shortages of personnel frightened them less during the war. All of this had a negative impact on the absorption of refugees, as we saw in the examples above.

As we also have seen, the central authorities fought—though not very actively—against manifestations of antisemitism, both among the population and the lower-level administration, mainly because they saw in these manifestations signs of dissatisfaction with the regime. The central authorities did not want a far-reaching and public fight against antisemitism, but not because they, to some extent, disliked Jews (which was the case) but because such a struggle would have increased the rumors about the domination of Jews in the upper echelons of power that were already circulating. Thus, in this Jewish question, the central authority had to pass between Scylla and Charybdis. The success of German antisemitic propaganda in the wartime USSR showed Stalin that it fell on the fertile ground of prerevolutionary antisemitism, which for more than twenty years the Soviets could not overcome. In order to weaken the accusations of sympathy for the Jews, Stalin already in 1942–1943 began to expel them from the arts, film production, literature, and journalism. By the end of the war, Stalin's use of state antisemitism was even more frequent, as the population, who had suffered greatly from the economic crisis and often saw the perpetrators of many troubles in the Jews, liked this policy. While initially only the Jews of Moscow and Leningrad were subjected to state antisemitism, in 1944–1946 it was already extended to the liberated western republics. It was especially widespread in these and subsequent years in Ukraine. There, the return of Jewish refugees caused particular discontent among the population. Obviously, the "de-Judaization" in the eyes of the population culminated in the campaigns of 1948–1953: the case against the JAC, the Night of the Murdered Poets, the fight against "rootless cosmopolitans," and the Doctors' Plot.

The stay of foreign and Soviet Jews in the eastern regions of the USSR, although it saved many from certain death in the territories occupied by the Germans, still led to a significant deterioration in their socioeconomic status. As well as victory at the front, the victory in the rear proved to involve many unjustified losses of life. The refugees who died as a result of resettlement are correctly considered indirect victims of the war.

Notes

Abbreviations of Archives

ACC—Archive of Claims Conference, Tel Aviv
AJC Archives—American Jewish Committee Archives, New York
GAOOGO—Gosudarstvennyi arkhiv obshchestvennykh ob"edinenii Gomel'skoi oblasti (State Archive of Social Associations of Gomel region), Gomel
GARF—Gosudarstvennyi arkhiv Rossiiskoi Federatsii (State Archive of the Russian Federation), Moscow
JDC Archives—Joint Distribution Committee Archives, New York
OHD/ICJ—Department of Oral History, Institute of Contemporary Jewry, Hebrew University, Jerusalem
RGAE—Rossiiskii gosudarstvennyi arkhiv ekonomiki (Russian State Archive of Economics), Moscow
RGASPI—Rossiiskii gosudarstvennyi arkhiv sotsial'no-politicheskoi istorii (Russian State Archive of Social and Political History), Moscow
TsAMO—Tsentral'nyi arkhiv Ministerstva oborony Rossiiskoi Federatsii (Central Archives of the Ministry of Defense of the Russian Federation), Podol'sk
TsDAGOU—Tsentral'nii derzhavnii arkhiv gromads'kikh ob'iednan' Ukraïni (Central State Archives of Public Organizations of Ukraine), Kyiv
TsGAChR—Tsentral'nyi gosudarstvennyi arkhiv Chuvashskoi Respubliki (State Archive of the Chuvash Republic), Cheboksary
TsGARK—Central State Archive of the Republic of Kazakhstan, Almaty
USHMM—United States Holocaust Memorial Museum Archives, Washington, DC
YVA—Yad Vashem Archives, Jerusalem
ZGAR—Zonal'nyi gosudarstvennyi arkhiv v Rechitse (Local State Archive of the Rechitsa, Gomel region)

f.—fond (collection)
op.—opis' (register)
d.—delo (file)

Introduction

1. There is considerable literature on this topic; I, however, refer to only two works here: Shvarts, *Evrei v Sovetskom Soiuze*, 45–47; Pinchuk, *Yehude Berit ha-Mo'atsot*, 86–92.

2. For further information, see Kaganovitch, "Jewish Refugees," 100.

3. For further information, see Kaganovitch, "Stalin's Great Power Politics," 60–68. Iosef Litvak did not distinguish between these two categories of Polish Jews in the USSR. Litvak, *Peliṭim Yehudim*, 362–363. He evidently accepted the Polish government-in-exile's intentional disregarding of distinctions in Soviet legislation relating to all Polish Jews in order to arouse antagonism against the USSR among Jews in the West. Kaganovitch, "Stalin's Great Power Politics," 63–65.

4. Vasilii Agafonov, *Neman! Neman! Ia—Dunai!* (Moscow: Voenizdat, 1967), 34–35 (emphasis added).

5. Nikolai Strokovskii, "Bol'shaia sem'ia," *Izvestiia*, May 26, 1943, 4.

6. Arkadii Perventsev, "My—russkie," *Izvestiia*, May 26, 1943, 3.

7. "V bol'shoi sem'e kuznetsa," *Izvestiia*, August 24, 1955, 1.

8. Stephen Norris considers the story of Abram a revolutionary breakthrough because the myth that all nations suffered equally during the war was widespread in the USSR and information about the Holocaust largely absent. Norris, "Landscapes of Loss," 77–78.

9. Belonosov, "Evakuatsiia naseleniia," 26.

10. *Partiinoe rukovodstvo evakuatsiei*; *Voina i zheleznodorozhnyi transport, 1941–1945*, ed. Georgii Kumanëv (Moscow: Nauka, 1988). Another book that follows the same concept is *Sovetskii tyl v period korennogo pereloma v Velikoi Otechestvennoi voine (noiabr' 1942–1943)*, ed. A. V. Mitrofanova (Moscow: Nauka, 1989), as do a few more contemporary works: Potëmkina, *Evakuatsiia*; Krasnozhënova, "Sotsial'naia pomoshch'," 141–147.

11. See, for example, Chulpan Arslanova, "Evakuirovannoe i deportirovannoe v Bashkirskuiu ASSR naselenie v gody Velikoi Otechestvennoi voiny: 1941–1945" (PhD candidate diss., Ufa State University, 2006); Aleksandr Nikolaenko, "Deiatel'nost' gosudarstvennykh i partiinykh organov po zhizneobespecheniiu evakuirovannogo naseleniia v gody Velikoi Otechestvennoi voiny (na materialakh Arkhangel'skoi i Vologodskoi oblastei)" (PhD candidate diss., Saint Petersburg State University, 2017).

12. Khudalov, *Severnaia Osetiia*; *Bashkiriia v gody Velikoi Otechestvennoi voiny*; Jumadurdy Annaorazov, "Turkmenistan during the Second World War," *Journal of Slavic Military Studies* 25, no. 1 (2012): 53–64. Compared to these works, Zhanguttin's research stands out: Zhanguttin, "Evakuatsiia sovetskogo naseleniia."

13. Ermolov, *Tankovaia promyshlennost' SSSR*; *Oboronnaia promyshlennost'*; *Vo imia pobedy*.

14. Stanisław Ciesielski and Grzegorz Hryciuk, "Warunki egzystencji," in *Życie codzienne polskich zesłańców w ZSRR w latach 1940–1946*, ed. Stanisław Ciesielski, 79–154 (Wrocław, Poland: Uniwersytet Wrocław, 1997).

15. Ibid., 231–261.

16. Srebrakowski, "Stan zdrowia ludnosci polskiej," 209–229.

17. Litvak, *Peliṭim Yehudim*.

18. Levin, "Miklat ara'i," 91–120; Levin, "Yehudey Besarabiyah," 101–118.

19. Shlomo Kless, "Peilut tsiyonit shel' Pelitim Yehudim be-Berit ha-Mo'atsot be-shanim 1941–1945 ve-kesher ha-Yishuv ha-Yehudi ba-Arerets 'imahem (1945–1941)" (PhD diss., Hebrew University of Jerusalem, 1985).

20. Shveibish, "Evakuatsiia i sovetskie evrei," 36–55.

21. Kiril Feferman, "A Soviet Humanitarian Action? Centre, Periphery and the Evacuation of Refugees to the North Caucasus, 1941–1942," *Europe-Asia Studies* 61, no. 5 (2009): 814–815.

22. Ibid., 829.

23. The Southern Front political department reported on August 6, 1941, that the families of the 360th Infantry Regiment's commanding staff had been shot by the Germans in the military town of Balta. The political department ordered the commander of the 9th Army to punish those responsible for abandoning these families. Zhirnov, "Proverka strakhom," 72–73.

24. Redlich, "The Jews under Soviet Rule."

25. Manley, *To the Tashkent Station*.

26. Stronski, *Tashkent*, 124.

27. I will provide a few examples: Hessler, *A Social History*, 281; and Harrison, *Soviet Planning*, 81–85, 118–152. However, since the Second World War, acceptance of Soviet statistics in general has become common among American historians.

28. See, e.g., these statistical studies: Kornilov, *Ural'skoe selo i voina*; Veniamin Alekseev and Vladimir Isupov, *Naselenie Sibiri v gody Velikoi Otechestvennoi voiny* (Novosibirsk, USSR: Nauka, 1986).

29. Vyltsan, "Zhertvy golodnogo vremeni," 166–168; Natalia Aralovets, "Smertnost' gorodskogo naseleniia tylovykh raionov Rossii, 1941–1945," in *Liudskie poteri SSSR v period vtoroi mirovoi voiny*, ed. Rostislav Evdokimov, 154–159 (Saint Petersburg, Russia: Blits, 1995); Veniamin Zima, "O smertnosti sel'skogo naseleniia v sovetskom tylu (po arkhivnym svodkam 1941–1945 gg.)," in ibid., 160–164.

30. Fëdor Sverdlov, *Evrei-generaly Vooruzhënnykh Sil SSSR* (Moscow: n.p., 1993); Fëdor Sverdlov, *Voiny-evrei na frontakh Velikoi Otechestvennoi* (Moscow: Kholokost, 1999); Shneer, *Plen*, vol. 2, 27–87.

31. Dubson, "On the Problem of the Evacuation," 37–56; Levin, "Antisemitism," 191–203.

32. Anna Shternshis, "Between Life and Death: Why Some Soviet Jews Decided to Leave and Others to Stay in 1941," *Kritika: Explorations in Russian and Eurasian History* 15, no. 3 (2014): 477–504; Kirill Feferman, *"If We Had Wings We Would Fly to You": A Soviet Jewish Family Faces Destruction, 1941–42* (Boston: Academic Studies Press, 2020).

33. I have briefly considered some issues related to the stay of Polish Jews in the Soviet rear in Kaganovitch, "Stalin's Great Power Politics," 59–94. For some new aspects of this subject, see Eliyana R. Adler, *Survival on the Margins: Polish Jewish Refugees in the Wartime Soviet Union* (Cambridge, MA: Harvard University Press, 2020).

34. Nikulin, *Vospominaniia o voine*, 210, 226.

35. Gerald Easter, *Reconstructing the State: Personal Networks and Elite Identity in Soviet Russia* (New York: Cambridge University Press, 2007); J. Arch Getty, *Practicing Stalinism: Bolsheviks, Boyars, and the Persistence of Tradition* (New Haven, CT: Yale University Press, 2013).

Chapter 1. Wartime Migration to the Eastern Regions of the USSR

1. *Russkii arkhiv*, vol. 20 (9), 21.
2. Ibid., 52.
3. *Belarus' v pervye mesiatsy*, 157–158.
4. Karel C. Berkhoff, "Total Annihilation of the Jewish Population: The Holocaust in the Soviet Media, 1941–45," *Kritika: Explorations in Russian and Eurasian History* 10, no. 1 (2009): 66.
5. *Sovetskaia Sibir'*, July 13, 1941, 4. Lubaczów was on the border with Poland in 1939, when it was handed over to the Soviet Union by Germany; after the war the USSR returned it to Poland.
6. *Izvestiia*, August 10, 1941, 1; *Krasnaia Zvezda*, August 10, 1941, 4; *Sovetskaia Sibir'*, August 10, 1941, 1.
7. V. Ocharov, "Fashistskie razboiniki," *Pravda*, August 12, 1941, 3.
8. "Ot sovetskogo informbiuro," *Pravda*, August 27, 1941, 3.
9. Vsevolod Ivanov, "Shchit slavy," *Izvestiia*, August 29, 1941, 3.
10. "Ot sovetskogo informbiuro," *Pravda*, August 31, 1941, 3.
11. "Miting predstavitelei evreiskogo naroda," *Vecherniaia Moskva*, August 25, 1941, 3; "Brat'ia evrei vo vsëm mire!," in ibid., August 25, 1941, 3. Similar forms of address began to be widely used in the mass media with respect to other ethnic groups as well. See, for an example, *Krasnaia Zvezda*, January 15, 1943, 4; June 10, 1943, 3; August 8, 1943, 3. As early as 1942 the authorities had detailed information about the mass genocide of the Jewish population not only within the territory of the USSR but in other countries as well. This is attested by extensive coverage in the most important Soviet newspapers: *Krasnaia Zvezda*, May 26, 1942, 3; December 19, 1942, 1; *Izvestiia*, December 19, 1942, 1; December 20, 1942, 4. The fact that the genocide was not completely concealed is evidenced by a book published in Leningrad at the end of 1942, *Zverstva, grabezhi i nasiliia nemetsko-fashistskikh zakhvatchikov*. It includes a protest note from Vyacheslav Molotov dated January 6 of that year, along with other evidence informing the authorities of the killing of Jews in Ukraine: 6,000 in L'vov, 8,000 in Odessa, 8,500 in Kamenets-Podol'sk, 10,500 in Dnepropetrovsk, 3,000 in Mariupol', 7,000 in Kerch (*Zverstva, grabezhi i nasiliia*, 26). This book, like the newspapers, generalized the victims of racism, recounting also the killing of civilians in Belorussian and Smolensk villages, Russian and Ukrainian workers in Kharkov, etc.
12. "Gotovy otrazit' liubye popytki napadeniia fashistov," *Izvestiia*, September 4, 1941, 1.
13. Al'tman, *Zhertvy nenavisti*, 387. I was not able to find any such orders in the previously classified archival materials of the Evacuation Council. Iosif Kazovskii, who held different positions in the Commissariat of Railways during the war, including Deputy Chief of the Military Transportation Directorate, knows nothing about special evacuation of the Jewish population. Interview with Iosif Kazovskii, February 12, 2004, author's personal archive.
14. I discuss this issue in detail in my article "The Propaganda Machine in the USSR about the Holocaust: Based on the Materials of the Soviet Press, 1941–1945," which is being prepared for publication.

Notes to Pages 17–21

15. Makabi-Yoresh, *Kokhav lo ikabeah*, 83.
16. Altshuler, "Ha-Pinui veha-menusah," 129–133.
17. Simonov, *Raznye dni voiny*, vol. 1, 72.
18. Kaganovitch, *The Long Life*, 259–260.
19. Altshuler, "Ha-Pinui veha-menusah," 131–133.
20. Dobrushkin, *Istoriia odnoi sem'i*, 3.
21. USC Shoah Foundation, Visual History Archive, interview with Maria Berlina, Saint Petersburg, Russia, October 8, 1997, segments 1–14, Spielberg Archive.
22. Arkadii Gurevich's memories recorded for the museum of the Daraganovo school, available at http://iremember.ru/memoirs/artilleristi/gurevich-arkadiy-grigorevich/.
23. *Voices of Resilience*, 291.
24. Interview by Grigorii Koifman with Arkadii Viner, available at http://iremember.ru/memoirs/pekhotintsi/viner-arkadiy-vladimirovich/.
25. Roman Karmen, *No pasaran!* (Moscow: Sov. Rossiia, 1972), 31.
26. These memories were woven into Konstantin Simonov's novel *Zhivye i mërtvye* (Moscow: Khudozhestvennaia literatura, 1989), available at http://militera.lib.ru/prose/russian/simonov1/01.html.
27. Leonid Sandalov, *Perezhitoe* (Moscow: Voenizdat, 1961), available at http://militera.lib.ru/memo/russian/sandalov1/05.html.
28. Ehrenburg, *Sobranie sochinenii*, vol. 9, 412.
29. *Belarus' v pervye mesiatsy*, 10–15.
30. Russiianov, *V boiakh rozhdennaia*, 16–17.
31. "Iz istorii Velikoi Otechestvenoi voiny," 211.
32. Kaganovitch, *The Long Life*, 261.
33. Elena Voitenko, "Kholokost na iuge Rossii v period Velikoi Otechestvennoi voiny, 1941–1943 gg." (PhD candidate diss., Stavropol' State University, 2005), 126–127.
34. Mikhail Vodolagin, "Stalingradskii arsenal," in *Kuznitsa Pobedy: Podvig tyla v gody Velikoi Otechestvennoi voiny; Ocherki i vospominaniia*, ed. Ivan Danishevskii (Moscow: Politizdat, 1980), 126.
35. Ehrenburg, *Sobranie sochinenii*, vol. 9, 413–414.
36. Makabi-Yoresh, *Kokhav lo ikabeah*, 83–84.
37. Ivan Konev, "Vospominaniia," in *Na pravom flange Moskovskoi bitvy*, comp. M. Ia. Maistrovskii (Tver', USSR: Moskovskii rabochii, 1991), 62–63.
38. *Organy Gosudarstvennoi bezopasnosti*, vol. 2, part 1, 204.
39. Ibid., 121.
40. Shvarts, *Evrei v Sovetskom Soiuze*, 48–49, and after him Pinchuk, *Yehude Berit ha-Mo'atsot*, 100–101; Altshuler, "Ha-Pinui veha-menusah," 120.
41. Author's personal archive. Because of this, thousands of Pinsk Jews were forced to return home. AJC Archives, interview by Rachel Erlich no. 5 with L. L., Interviews with Polish and Jewish DPs in DP Camps on Their Observations of Jewish Life in Soviet Russia, 4.
42. YVA, O.3/2242, 1.
43. Feigelovich, "Prikliucheniia chetyrëkh," 22–23.
44. AJC Archives, interview by Rachel Erlich no. 6 with J. C., Interviews with Polish and Jewish DPs in DP Camps on Their Observations of Jewish Life in Soviet Russia, 1.

45. Interview by Grigorii Koifman with Meir Toker, available at http://iremember.ru/memoirs/svyazisti/toker-meir-fayvelevich/.
46. Simonov, *Raznye dni voiny*, vol. 1, 28, 195–199.
47. *Organy Gosudarstvennoi bezopasnosti*, vol. 2, part 1, 178. This case, as well as many others, was retold in Simonov's diary. *Raznye dni voiny*, vol. 1, 49, 71.
48. *Organy Gosudarstvennoi bezopasnosti*, vol. 2, part 1, 197.
49. For more details, see the secret order in the papers of the Southwestern Front, TsAMO, f. 229, op. 161, d. 5, 8–9.
50. *Russkii arkhiv*, vol. 16 (5–1), 42–43.
51. Artëm Drabkin, *Ia dralsia v pantservaffe: "Dvoinoi oklad—troinaia smert'"* (Moscow: Iauza, 2007), 156–157.
52. Georgii Beregovoi, *Tri vysoty* (Moscow: Voenizdat, 1986), 13.
53. Asia Adam, "Dalëkoe blizkoe: Tri dnia iiunia 1941," *Novyi mir*, no. 12 (2002): 134–136; I. Voronkova, "Voina obrushilas' na Minsk bombardirovkami," *Vechernii Minsk*, June 20, 1997, 5; Zhirnov, "Proverka strakhom," 72–73; interview by Grigorii Koifman with Arkadii Krasinskii, available at http://iremember.ru/memoirs/partizani/krasinskiy-arkadiy-borisovich/.
54. Altshuler, "Ha-Pinui veha-menusah," 136–137.
55. Russiianov, *V boiakh rozhdennaia*, 17–18.
56. GARF, f. A259, op. 40, d. 3032, 19–20 (copy in YVA, JM/24.678). Without wasting time on evacuation, the republican authorities of Lithuania and Latvia ran to the east as well.
57. Kaganovitch, *The Long Life*, 256.
58. Olekhnovich, "Ot Pripiati—za Volgu," 96–97; *Belarus' v pervye mesiatsy*, 19–28, 36–74.
59. Altshuler, "Ha-Pinui veha-menusah," 142–143.
60. Letter from Fridrikh Valler, June 17, 2001, author's personal archive.
61. Altshuler, "Ha-Pinui veha-menusah," 142–143; *Belarus' v pervye mesiatsy*, 251.
62. Pinchuk, *Yehude Berit ha-Mo'atsot*, 108.
63. L. Skriabina, "K probleme evakuatsii naseleniia Belarusi v tylovye raiony SSSR," in *Belarus' 1941–1945: Podvig, tragediia, pamiat'*, ed. Aleksandr Kovalenia and others (Minsk: Belaruskaia navuka, 2010), vol. 2, 58–59.
64. Kaganovitch, *The Long Life*, 257–258.
65. Amazasp Babadzhanian, *Dorogi pobedy* (Moscow: Molodaia gvardiia, 1975), 216–218.
66. Pëtr Kalinin, *Partizanskaia respublika* (Moscow: Voenizdat, 1964), 41.
67. Ivan Iakubovskii, *Zemlia v ogne* (Moscow: Voenizdat, 1975), 56. The crying of a newborn near its deceased mother during a bombing became the subject of the poem "Birth" by the Yiddish poet Lev (Leiba) Gornshtein. The orphaned child is adopted by a stranger, an old Jewish man who promises to memorialize the tragedy:

I shall adopt this child in his state,
And give him, comrades, such a name,
That shouts his destiny and fate,
That lights our people's hearts aflame.
Let the name fit into his life, like thirst he cannot quench.

What hasn't been before will be at last!
I say we name this child—Revenge!
So people don't forgive the past.

The poem, published in Russian translation from Yiddish in Tashkent (*Tashkentskii Al'manakh*, ed. Khamid Alimdzhan, Vsevolod Ivanov, and Isai Lezhnëv [Tashkent, USSR: Gosizdat UzSSR, 1942], 35), was probably Gornshtein's last publication during his life. All traces of him in Uzbekistan are lost.

68. Ivan Bagramian, *Tak nachinalas' voina* (Moscow: Voenizdat, 1971), 178.

69. Zhirnov, "Nas obmanom vyvezli," 52–53. For information about evacuation of 300,000 from Stalingrad just days before the beginning of the battles in the city, see *Partiinoe rukovodstvo evakuatsiei*, 29. This figure, most certainly, includes wounded soldiers and hospital personnel.

70. Albert Utënkov, "Ia byl mal'chishkoi v ogne Stalingrada," in *Do svidan'ia, mal'chiki: My ne byli svolochami!*, comp. Artëm Drabkin (Moscow: Iauza, Eksmo, 2006), 601, 618. One of those responsible for the evacuation of the population, Major General Pavel Kabanov, was at best insincere when he wrote about the successful evacuation of refugees from Stalingrad in his memoirs. See Pavel Kabanov, *Stal'nye peregony* (Moscow: Voenizdat, 1973), 145–147.

71. "Iz istorii Velikoi Otechestvenoi voiny," 207.

72. Kobylianskii, *Priamoi navodkoi po vragu*, 52.

73. See, e.g., the text of this decree: "On the vacancies of the living space belonging to local councils and enterprises previously occupied by workers and employees evacuated to the east," *Sovetskaia Sibir'*, February 18, 1942, 1.

74. Dokuchaev, *Sibirskii tyl*, 162.

75. *Partiinoe rukovodstvo evakuatsiei*, 13.

76. Altshuler, "Ha-Pinui veha-menusah," 121.

77. Grigorii Gogiberidze, "Eshelony idut na vostok," in *Kuznitsa Pobedy: Podvig tyla v gody Velikoi Otechestvennoi voiny. Ocherki i vospominaniia*, ed. Ivan Danishevskii (Moscow: Politizdat, 1980), 96–97.

78. Fedotov, *Evakuirovannoe naselenie*, 69–70, 74.

79. GARF, f. A259, op. 40, d. 3091, 5–9 (copy in YVA, JM/24.678). The percentage of Jews among all refugees grew slightly over the next month and was 26.8 percent on October 15, 1941. See ibid., 21–22; Dubson, "On the Problem of the Evacuation," 56.

80. *Distribution of the Jewish Population*, 28–30.

81. Koval'chuk, "Evakuatsiia naseleniia Leningrada," 17.

82. Lomagin, *Neizvestnaia blokada*, 586. See also 241, 253, 275.

83. On how antisemitism was the cornerstone of the German propaganda spread in the Leningrad region and its success there, see ibid., 149–150, 159, 163, 197, 199, 237–238, 242, 247, 250, 253, 258, 264, 275–276, 286, 293, 321, 350, 909, 913. The growth of antisemitism became so noticeable that on August 20, 1941, at the meeting of the activists of the Leningrad Communist Party, its head Andrey Zhdanov stated that it was necessary to put an end to pro-fascist agitation against the Jews (ibid., 243). The growth of antisemitism also received special attention at the meeting of the bureau of the Leningrad's Kirovskii District Committee of the Communist Party on August 29, 1941—"On anti-Soviet rumors, antisemitism, and measures to combat them" (ibid.).

On the rise of antisemitism in Moscow, also as a result of German propaganda, see Grigor'ev, *Moskva voennaia*, 117–119; *Organy Gosudarstvennoi bezopasnosti*, vol. 2, part 2, 225.

84. For the breakdown, see TsGAChR, f. P820, op. 8, d. 249, 1–23 (copy in USHMM Archives, RG 22.020). This same list confirms that Jews from eastern Belorussia made up 88.6 percent of all those who arrived in Alatyr'. Ibid.

85. GARF, f. A259, op. 2, d. 164, 151–160 (copy in YVA, JM/23,513).

86. Galina Olekhnovich wrote about a million evacuees from the BSSR in an early article. Olekhnovich, "Ot Pripiati—za Volgu," 88. At the same time, Ivan Belonosov tentatively wrote about more than one million evacuees from Belorussia. Belonosov, "Evakuatsiia naseleniia," 20. The collective work *Ekonomika Sovetskoi Belorussii, 1917–1967*, ed. F. S. Martinkevich, Z. I. Georgidze, M. G. Matusevich, and others (Minsk, USSR: Nauka i tekhnika, 1967), 287–288, mentioned about one million of those evacuated from Belorussia. Although there is an indication that the figure was obtained on the basis of registration lists from November 25, 1942, there is no reference to the source. For the estimation of one and a half million refugees from this republic, see *Sovetskii tyl*, 138; Olekhnovich, *Ekonomika Belorussii*, 6.

87. GARF, f. A259, op. 400, d. 351, 11 (copy in YVA, JM/24.678).

88. Emanuil Iofe, "Evakuatsyia nasel'nitstva BSSR letam 1941 goda: Svedchanni dakumentaŷ, uspaminy vidavochthaŷ, merkavanni dasledchykaŷ," *Belaruski gistarychny chasopis*, no. 6 (2011): 26.

89. Altshuler, "Ha-Pinui veha-menusah," 150–151.

90. Daniil Romanovskii, "Skol'ko evreev pogiblo v promyshlennykh gorodakh Vostochnoi Belorussii v nachale nemetskoi okkupatsii (iiul'–dekabr' 1941 g.)," *Vestnik evreiskogo universiteta v Moskve*, no. 4 (2000): 151–172; Kiril Feferman, "Soviet Investigation of Nazi Crimes in the USSR: Documenting the Holocaust," *Journal of Genocide Research* 5, no. 4 (2003): 593–598; Kaganovitch, *The Long Life*, 269–270.

91. Based on GARF, f. A259, op. 40, d. 3517, 11 (copy in YVA, JM/24.678).

92. RGAE, f. 1562, op. 329, d. 2217, 11.

93. A. V. Skorobogatov, *Kharkiv u chasi nimets'koï okupatsiï, 1941–1943* (Kharkiv, Ukraine: Prapor, 2006), 32.

94. Belonosov, "Evakuatsiia naseleniia," 20.

95. This number is not much larger than Kruglov's estimate, according to which more than 900,000 Jews fled from Ukraine. See Alexander Kruglov, "Jewish Losses in Ukraine, 1941–1944," in *The Shoah in Ukraine: History, Testimony, Memorialization*, ed. Ray Brandon and Wendy Lower (Bloomington: Indiana University Press, 2008), 273.

96. Interview by Grigorii Koifman with Iosif Faigenboim, available at http://iremember.ru/memoirs/svyazisti/faygenboym-iosif-aronovich/.

97. Altshuler, *Soviet Jewry*, 34.

98. Calculated from TsGARK, f. P1137, op. 6, d. 1289, 34 (copy in USHMM Archives, RG 74.002M).

99. Pogrebnoi, "O deiatel'nosti Soveta," 201–206; *Voina i zheleznodorozhnyi transport*, 72–73.

100. GARF, f. A259, op. 40, d. 3028, 79–82 (copy in YVA, JM/24.678). For further information about these evacuation plans, see Manley, *To the Tashkent Station*, 32–40.

Notes to Pages 34–38   247

101. GARF, f. A259, op. 40, d. 3028, 43 (copy in YVA, JM/24.678). In this monograph "Central Asia" denotes the USSR's republics of Turkmenistan, Kirgizstan, Kazakhstan, Uzbekistan, and Tajikistan. This is somewhat broader than the definition used in the USSR, which did not include Kazakhstan.

102. GARF, f. A259, op. 40, d. 3038, 108 (copy in YVA, JM/24.678).

103. *Vo imia pobedy*, vol. 1, 299.

104. Dobrushkin, *Istoriia odnoi sem'i*, 16; TsGARK, f. P1137, op. 6, d. 1283, 41 (copy in USHMM Archives, RG 74.002M).

105. Vaseněva, "Priëm i ustroistvo," 41.

106. "V prokurature Soiuza SSR," *Izvestiia*, January 7, 1942, 4.

107. Manley, *To the Tashkent Station*, 138.

108. *Narody Dagestana v gody Velikoi Otechestvennoi voiny 1941–1945 gg.: Dokumenty i materialy k 60-letiiu pobedy*, ed. A. I. Osmanov and others (Makhachkala, Russia: RAN, 2005), 628–630.

109. For the complete quote and additional details about this "North Caucasian traffic jam," see Kaganovitch, "Estimating the Number," 472–473.

110. TsGARK, f. P1137, op. 6, d. 1279, 48 (copy in USHMM Archives, RG 74.002M).

111. TsGAChR, f. P203, op. 18, d. 220, 53 (copy in USHMM Archives, RG 22.020). Not having withstood the heavy and nerve-fraying work on the organization of the evacuation and accommodation of the population, Pamfilov died in May 1943 from a heart attack.

112. Sergei Luganskii, *Na glubokikh virazhakh* (Alma-Ata, USSR: Kazgoslitizdat, 1963), available at http://militera.lib.ru/memo/russian/lugansky/02.html.

113. *Partiinoe rukovodstvo evakuatsiei*, 24.

114. GARF, f. A259, op. 40, d. 3030, p. 10 (copy in YVA, JM/24.678); *Istoriia Velikoi Otechestvennoi voiny*, vol. 2, 547.

115. TsGAChR, f. P203, op. 18, d. 219, 445 (copy in USHMM Archives, RG 22.020).

116. GARF, f. A259, op. 40, d. 3038, 105–106 (copy in YVA, JM/24.678).

117. *Partiinoe rukovodstvo evakuatsiei*, 30.

118. Koval'chuk, "Evakuatsiia naseleniia Leningrada," 16.

119. TsGARK, f. P1137, op. 6, d. 1278a, 28 (copy in USHMM Archives, RG 74.002M); Belonosov, "Evakuatsiia naseleniia," 22–23.

120. "V prokurature Soiuza SSR," *Izvestiia*, January 7, 1942, 4.

121. Pogrebnoi, "O deiatel'nosti Soveta," 206–207. For the errors with the distribution of the evacuated population, see Belonosov, "Evakuatsiia naseleniia," 26.

122. *Iz istorii poliakov v Kazakhstane*, 130–131.

123. The percent of refugees transported by *teplushka* was calculated on the basis of the information in *Istoriia Velikoi Otechestvennoi voiny*, vol. 2, 548. For the number of passengers in a *teplushka*, see Nikolai Patolichev, *Ispytanie na zrelost'* (Moscow: Politizdat, 1977), 217.

124. *Iz istorii poliakov v Kazakhstane*, 130–131.

125. Aleksandr Gusev, *El'brus v ogne* (Moscow: Voenizdat, 1980), 23.

126. Kobylianskii, *Priamoi navodkoi po vragu*, 58.

127. "V voennoi prokurature Tomskoi zheleznoi dorogi," *Sovetskaia Sibir'*, March 17, 1942, 4.

128. TsGARK, f. P1137, op. 6, d. 1278a, 27 (copy in USHMM Archives, RG 74.002M).
129. "V prokurature Soiuza SSR," *Izvestiia*, January 7, 1942, 4.
130. Efron, *Dnevniki*, vol. 2, 119.
131. Ibid., 121, 124.
132. Vasenëva, "Priëm i ustroistvo," 42.
133. Elena Sologub, "Moia voina," in *Vzrosloe detstvo voiny: Sbornik vospominanii*, ed. Mikhail Kipnis (Ashdod, Israel: Keitar, 2013), vol. 1, 126.
134. Potëmkina, *Evakuatsiia*, 35, 41.
135. *Vo imia pobedy*, vol. 1, 222.
136. Shnaider, "Vniz po reke," vol. 1, 157–158.
137. Belonosov and Makhmut, "Alma-Atinskii elektrotekhnicheskii zavod," 134.
138. Koval'chuk, "Evakuatsiia naseleniia Leningrada," 20.
139. GARF, f. A259, op. 40, d. 3022, 1–6 (copy in YVA, JM/24.678).
140. Stel'man, *Pamiat' i vremia*, 40–41.
141. "V prokurature Soiuza SSR," *Izvestiia*, January 31, 1942, 4.
142. TsGARK, f. P1137, op. 6, d. 1291, 63, 67 (copy in USHMM Archives, RG 74.002M).
143. Ibid., 89.
144. *Evakuatsiia v Kazakhstan*, 51–53.
145. Elza-Bair Guchinova, "Deportation of the Kalmyks (1943–1956): Stigmatized Ethnicity," *Slavic Eurasian Studies*, ed. Uyama Tomohiko (Sapporo, Japan: Slavic Research Center, Hokkaido University, 2007), 190–192.
146. *Organy Gosudarstvennoi bezopasnosti*, vol. 2, part 1, 559–560; ibid., vol. 4, part 2, 251. Stalin's decree on the deportation of Germans from the Moscow region allowed them to take not one ton per family, but two hundred kilograms per family member. Ibid., vol. 2, part 2, 25. Given that four people was the average size of a German family, it still turns out that the refugee family could take three times less.
147. GARF, f. A259, op. 40, d. 3038, 107 (copy in YVA, JM/24.678).
148. Belkovets, *Administrativno-pravovoe polozhenie*, 52; *Organy Gosudarstvennoi bezopasnosti*, vol. 2, part 2, 25, 110.
149. Although at the end of July 1941 the chief of the liaison group with the local organizations of the Evacuation Council, I. Boiukhanov, complained to the deputy chair of this council, A. Kosygin, not only about the lack of doctors on the trains but also about the unsatisfactory medical care at the stations (GARF, f. A259, op. 40, d. 3024, 5–6 [copy in YVA, JM/24.678]), the problem was not resolved.
150. Belkovets, *Administrativno-pravovoe polozhenie*, 69.
151. GARF, f. A259, op. 40, d. 3038, 103 (copy in YVA, JM/24.678). There are also personal testimonies to the fact that the deported Germans were fed along the way: Brul', *Nemtsy v Zapadnoi Sibiri*, vol. 2, 14–16.
152. GARF, f. A259, op. 40, d. 3038, 103 (copy in YVA, JM/24.678). At the same time Babkin did not feel sympathy for the Jews, of whom there were many among the refugees. As part of his duties, he actively fought against Zionist organizations, which resumed work among refugees. See *Iz istorii poliakov v Kazakhstane*, 186.
153. Gribanova, "Evakuatsiia," 233.
154. *Stalinskie deportatsii 1928–1953*, 301–303, 310–311.

155. Brul', *Nemtsy v Zapadnoi Sibiri*, vol. 2, 54, 62.
156. Kaganovitch, "Estimating the Number," 468.
157. *Istoriia stalinskogo Gulaga*, vol. 5, 406. See also Kh.-M. A. Sabanchiev, "Deportatsiia narodov Severnogo Kavkaza v 40-kh gg. XX veka," *Voprosy istorii* 11 (2013): 107–108.
158. *Istoriia stalinskogo Gulaga*, vol. 1, 489.
159. Calculated from ibid., vol. 5, 407.
160. Viktor Zemskov, *Stalin i narod: Pochemu ne bylo vosstaniia* (Moscow: Algoritm, 2014), 92–93.
161. Calculated from *Istoriia stalinskogo Gulaga*, vol. 5, 399.
162. For the details of the order and instructions for the release, see *Stalinskie deportatsii 1928–1953*, 174–176.
163. "Stalin, Beriia i sud'ba," 66.
164. TsGAChR, f. P203, op. 18, d. 218, 161 (copy in USHMM Archives, RG 22.020).
165. For examples in the published sources, see Konstantin, *A Red Boyhood*, 106; Ilana Maschler, *Moskiewski czas* (Warsaw, Poland: Wydawnictwo Krupski I S-ka, 1994), 361; Wat, *My Century*, 311. Some Polish Jews had read the Polish translation of this book, published in 1929, even before the war. See YVA, O.3/10894, 23; Elton, *Destination Buchara*, 185. Translations and publications of this book in Yiddish by Ezra Fininberg (1924) and in Hebrew by Avraham Shlonsky (1932) confirm its great popularity among Jews. The book was also reprinted in Russian in Riga in 1929, and also in translation into German in Germany (1925) and in English in the United States (1927) and England (1930).
166. Parsadanova, "Deportatsiia naseleniia," 43; Mikhail Rogachëv, *Stranitsy pol'skoi istorii: Fakty i dokumenty* (Syktyvkar, Russia: Fond Komi knizhnoe izdatel'stvo, 2002), vol. 5, 364–370.
167. *Documents on Polish-Soviet Relations*, vol. 1, 225; Litvak, *Peliṭim Yehudim*, 185.
168. Parsadanova, "Deportatsiia naseleniia," 43.
169. RGASPI, f. 644, op. 1, d. 15, 6.
170. *Stalinskie deportatsii 1928–1953*, 176–177. Erroneous data apparently showed that 45,000 Polish refugees had been moved there on November 21, 1941. See Litvak, *Peliṭim Yehudim*, 186.
171. Particularly this happened with the family of Bina Boiman; see her *Yalde ha-korpus ha-sheni*, 159–170.
172. *Documents on Polish-Soviet Relations*, vol. 1, 224–225.
173. Parsadanova, "Deportatsiia naseleniia," 43.
174. Moskoff, *The Bread of Affliction*, 37.
175. RGASPI, f. 644, op. 1, d. 16, 69.
176. With reference to RGASPI, f. 644, op. 1, d. 20, 103, see www.soldat.ru/doc/gko/text/1203.html.
177. Stronski, *Tashkent*, 131–132.
178. About this wave, see Litvak, *Peliṭim Yehudim*, 186–187.
179. See, e.g., YVA, O.3/10814, 16–18; Grynberg, *Children of Zion*, 122–123, 132.
180. Manley, *To the Tashkent Station*, 151; Bader-Whiteman, *Escape via Siberia*, 71.
181. On sending representatives there, see Manley, *To the Tashkent Station*, 139.

182. Aleksandr Abramovich, "Epizody evreiskoi evakuatsii 1941–42 gg. v Karagandinskuiu oblast'," in *Evakuatsiia: Voskreshaia proshloe*, ed. Aleksandr Baron and others (Almaty, Kazakhstan: Fortress, 2009), 114–115.

183. Manley, *To the Tashkent Station*, 150–151.

184. *Evakuatsiia v Kazakhstan*, 30–33; YVA, O.3/1568, 8; TsGARK, f. P1137, op. 6, d. 1280, 112, 141, 146–147, 158–159 (copy in USHMM Archives, RG 74.002M); Boiman, *Yalde ha-korpus ha-sheni*, 147; USC Shoah Foundation, Visual History Archive, interview with Aryeh Katsav, Haifa, Israel, April 14, 1997, segment 118, Spielberg Archive; Miller, "Iz perezhitogo."

185. YVA, O.3/2242, 3.

186. GARF, f. A259, op. 40, d. 3028, 107 (copy in YVA, JM/24.678).

187. Anatolii Kotliar, "Stranichka moego detstva," in supplement "Evreiskii kamerton" to *Novosti nedeli*, May 5, 1999, 19.

Chapter 2. The Local Authorities Facing Refugees

1. GARF, f. A259, op. 40, d. 3518, 48a (copy in YVA, JM/24.678).
2. Fedotov, *Evakuirovannoe naselenie*, 75.
3. GARF, f. A259, op. 40, d. 3527, 113 (copy in YVA, JM/24.678).
4. Ibid., d. 3518, 123.
5. TsGARK, f. P1137, op. 6, d. 1278a, 20 (copy in USHMM Archives, RG 74.002M).
6. GARF, f. A259, op. 40, d. 3529, 210 (copy in YVA, JM/24.678).
7. Krasnozhënova, "Sotsial'naia pomoshch'," 142–145.
8. TsGAChR, f. P203, op. 11, d. 66, 88 (copy in USHMM Archives, RG 22.020).
9. Account of the chair of the Executive Committee of the Sundyr' district Ugol'nikov, March 26, 1942, TsGAChR, f. P203, op. 18, d. 218a, 25a (copy in USHMM Archives, RG 22.020).
10. TsGAChR, f. P203, op. 18, d. 118a, 146 (copy in USHMM Archives, RG 22.020).
11. Letter from artel chair A. Ermishev to Vasilii Grigor'ev, Deputy Chair of the Council of People's Commissars of the Chuvash ASSR, TsGAChR, f. P203, op. 18, d. 119, 320 (copy in USHMM Archives, RG 22.020).
12. Classified report by the head of the resettlement department of Chuvashia Nikolai Zhukov to A. M. Matveev of the Council of People's Commissars of this republic, TsGAChR, f. P1263, op. 1, d. 36, 25 (copy in USHMM Archives, RG 22.020).
13. TsGAChR, f. P1263, op. 1, d. 51, 192, 194 (copy in USHMM Archives, RG 22.020).
14. Ibid., d. 46, 67.
15. Ibid., d. 66, 96.
16. Account of the chair of the Executive Committee of the Sundyr' district Ugol'nikov, March 26, 1942, TsGAChR, f. P203, op. 18, d. 218a, 25a (copy in USHMM Archives, RG 22.020).
17. TsGAChR, f. P1263, op. 1, d. 46, 65a (copy in USHMM Archives, RG 22.0200).
18. Ibid., 2.
19. Ibid., f. P827, op. 1, d. 235, 76.
20. Ibid., f. P1263, op. 1, d. 36, 18–18a.

21. TsGAChR, f. P203, op. 18, d. 218a, 125a (copy in USHMM Archives, RG 22.020).
22. Ibid., f. P1263, op. 1, d. 46, 65.
23. Mandel'shtam, *Vtoraia kniga*, 484.
24. See, e.g., TsGAChR, f. P1263, op. 1, d. 66, 80, 94 (copy in USHMM Archives, RG 22.020).
25. Ibid., d. 67, 103.
26. Calculated from ibid., d. 46, 2. On how children didn't attend school for this reason, see also the evacuation inspector A. Nikitina's report on Shumerlia district, ibid., d. 51, 67a.
27. Ibid., f. P835, op. 1, d. 354, 286.
28. GARF, f. A259, op. 40, d. 3529, 212 (copy in YVA, JM/24.678).
29. Ibid., 174–175.
30. Ibid., d. 3518, 48a.
31. TsGAChR, f. P1263, op. 1, d. 36, 18–18a (copy in USHMM Archives, RG 22.020).
32. Ibid., f. P203, op. 18, d. 218a, 145a.
33. TsGAChR, f. P1263, op. 1, d. 51, 67a (copy in USHMM Archives, RG 22.020).
34. Fedotov, *Evakuirovannoe naselenie*, 75.
35. Potëmkina, *Evakuatsiia*, 69–70.
36. "Zabota ob evakuirovannom naselenii," *Sovetskaia Sibir'*, December 19, 1941, 1.
37. TsGAChR, f. P203, op. 26, d. 32, 9–9a (copy in USHMM Archives, RG 22.020); ibid., f. P1263, op. 1, d. 65, 22.
38. Barbara Piotrowska-Dubik, *Kwiaty na stepie: Pamiętnik z zesłania* (Warsaw, Poland: "Soli Deo," 2007), 119.
39. *Izvestiia*, June 6, 1941, 1.
40. TsGAChR, f. P1263, op. 1, d. 51, 132 (copy in USHMM Archives, RG 22.020).
41. Ibid., f. P203, op. 11, d. 66, 40. As a result of this incident, which even came to the attention of the Communist Party Politburo member Mikhail Kalinin, the kolkhoz chair received a ten-year prison sentence. Ibid.
42. Ibid., f. P1263, op. 1, d. 51, 80a.
43. Ibid., d. 46, 206.
44. GARF, f. A259, op. 40, d. 3518, 135, 139 (copy in YVA, JM/24.678).
45. TsGAChR, f. P203, op. 11, d. 15, 190 (copy in USHMM Archives, RG 22.020).
46. Ibid., op. 19, d. 71, 45.
47. http://ru.wikipedia.org/wiki/%D0%A7%D1%83%D0%B2%D0%B0%D1%88%D0%B8%D1%8F#.D0.9A.D0.BB.D0.B8.D0.BC.D0.B0.D1.82.
48. GARF, f. A259, op. 40, d. 3527, 113 (copy in YVA, JM/24.678).
49. TsGAChR, f. P203, op. 19, d. 71, 23 (copy in USHMM Archives, RG 22.020).
50. Ibid., f. P1263, op. 1, d. 46, 194.
51. GARF, f. A259, op. 40, d. 3527, 130 (copy in YVA, JM/24.678).
52. Ibid., d. 3518, 140; TsGAChR, f. P203, op. 11, d. 66, 34, 39, 42 (copy in USHMM Archives, RG 22.020); ibid., f. P1263, op. 1, d. 36, 25a.
53. Ibid., d. 51, 65.
54. Ibid., d. 46, 162–163.
55. Ibid., d. 51, 100.

56. Ibid., 101.
57. Ibid., f. P203, op. 18, d. 219, 305–305a.
58. Ibid., f. P1263, op. 1, d. 51, 62, 67, 80a, 82, 85–86; ibid., d. 66, 95a.
59. Ibid., f. P203, op. 11, d. 66, 31–32.
60. B. Mark, "Ob ustroistve evakuirovannykh," GARF, f. P8114, op. 1, d. 107, 315 (copy in USHMM Archives, RG 220028M).
61. *Chuvashskaia ASSR v period Velikoi Otechestvennoi voiny (1941–1945): Sbornik dokumentov i materialov*, comp. Nikanor Semënov (Cheboksary, USSR: Chuvashskoe knizhnoe izdatel'stvo, 1975), 248.
62. TsGAChR, f. P1263, op. 1, d. 51, 91a (copy in USHMM Archives, RG 22.020).
63. Ibid., f. P1952, op. 1, d. 100, 20.
64. USC Shoah Foundation, Visual History Archive, interview with Roza Bazylianskaia (Amromina), Vitebsk, Belarus, May 2, 1998, segments 65–66, Spielberg Archive.
65. B. Mikhailov, "Zabota ob evakuirovannom naselenii," *Pravda*, February 3, 1942, no. 34, 3.
66. "Evrei na poliakh Kazakhstana," GARF, f. P8114, op. 1, d. 67 (copy in USHMM Archives, RG 220028M).
67. S. Gorodon, "Evreiskie kolkhozniki na poliakh Kuibyshevskoi oblasti," GARF, f. P8114, op. 1, d. 101, 187–187a (copy in USHMM Archives, RG 220028M).
68. Abram Gontar, "Evakuirovannye v kolkhozakh Bashkirii," GARF, f. P8114, op. 1, d. 101, 36 (copy in USHMM Archives, RG 220028M).
69. TsGAChR, f. P835, op. 1, d. 354, 312 (copy in USHMM Archives, RG 22.020).
70. Ibid., f. P1263, op. 1, d. 66, 96.
71. Ibid., d. 65, 21–21a.
72. GARF, f. A259, op. 40, d. 3518, 126 (copy in YVA, JM/24.678); ibid., d. 3527, 127.
73. Ibid., d. 3518, 124, 126.
74. TsGAChR, f. P203, op. 11, d. 66, 39a (copy in USHMM Archives, RG 22.020).
75. Ibid., 21.
76. Ibid., f. P203, op. 19, d. 71, 186.
77. Ibid., f. P1263, op. 1, d. 46, 206.
78. Ibid., d. 51, 180.
79. Kazakhstan: TsGARK, f. P1137, op. 6, d. 1289, 175 (copy in USHMM Archives, RG 74.002M); Ural: GARF, f. A259, op. 40, d. 3529, 209 (copy in YVA, JM/24.678); Potëmkina, *Evakuatsiia*, 106–107; Volga area (Kuibyshev region): GARF, f. A259, op. 40, d. 3527, 31–32 (copy in YVA, JM/24.678).
80. TsGAChR, f. P1263, op. 1, d. 46, 178 (copy in USHMM Archives, RG 22.020).
81. GARF, f. A259, op. 40, d. 3518, 48a (copy in YVA, JM/24.678).
82. Ibid., d. 3527, 115.
83. TsGAChR, f. P203, op. 18, d. 218a, 127 (copy in USHMM Archives, RG 22.020).
84. Ibid., f. P427, op. 9, d. 25, 154. Exactly the same punishment was used in the regional centers of Chuvashia. Ibid., f. P1989, op. 1, d. 96, 9.
85. On such resolutions in the Mordovian ASSR, see *Partiinoe rukovodstvo evakuatsiei*, 34.
86. Kerimbaev, *Sovetskii Kirgizstan*, 62.
87. Miller, "Iz perezhitogo."

88. GARF, f. A259, op. 40, d. 3518, 134–135 (copy in YVA, JM/24.678).
89. Ibid., 122, 124; ibid., d. 3527, 32.
90. TsGAChR, f. P1263, op. 1, d. 36, 23a (copy in USHMM Archives, RG 22.020).
91. Feigelovich, "Prikliucheniia chetyrëkh," 29.
92. GARF, f. A259, op. 40, d. 3518, 126 (copy in YVA, JM/24.678).
93. TsGAChR, f. P203, op. 26, d. 32, 11a (copy in USHMM Archives, RG 22.020).
94. *Evakuatsiia v Kazakhstan*, 34.
95. GARF, f. A259, op. 40, d. 3518, 48 (copy in YVA, JM/24.678).
96. Interview by Lev Aizenshtat with Rachel Rivkina, Saint Petersburg, Russia, December 2004, available at: https://www.centropa.org/biography/rachel-rivkina.
97. GARF, f. A259, op. 40, d. 3518, 48a (copy in YVA, JM/24.678).
98. Ibid., 136.
99. For example, in Kazakhstan, Altai territory, Cheliabinsk region, and Tomsk: *Partiinoe rukovodstvo evakuatsiei*, 35–36, 41–42. In Ul'ianovsk and Penza: Fedotov, *Evakuirovannoe naselenie*, 69. In Western Siberia: *Vo imia pobedy*, vol. 1, 101–102.
100. *Vo imia pobedy*, vol. 1, 158–159, 170.
101. Gusak, *Militsiia Iuzhnogo Urala*, 65.
102. Grantserska-Kadari, *Ha-Meah ha-esrim sheli*, 202–205. The service was better in the city hospital, but even there the patients were starving. Ibid., 207–208.
103. *Krasnoiarskii krai v gody Velikoi Otechestvennoi voiny 1941–1945 gg.: Sbornik dokumentov*, ed. Liudmila Mezit and others (Krasnoiarsk, Russia: Knizhnoe Krasnoiar'e, 2010), 146–147.
104. GARF, f. A259, op. 40, d. 3518, 133 (copy in YVA, JM/24.678).
105. Ibid.
106. Ustinov, *Vo imia Pobedy*, 302–303.
107. GARF, f. A259, op. 40, d. 3518, 135 (copy in YVA, JM/24.678).
108. Ibid., 36.
109. Ibid., d. 3527, 32.
110. Ibid., 33.
111. Ibid., 115.
112. Ibid.
113. Ibid., 130–131.
114. B. Mikhailov, "Zabota ob evakuirovannom naselenii," *Pravda*, February 3, 1942, 3.
115. For examples, see Pulatov, *Andizhanskaia partiinaia organizatsiia*, 16–17.
116. Stronski, *Tashkent*, 137–138.
117. See GARF, f. A259, op. 40, d. 3529, 210 (copy in YVA, JM/24.678). Compare with propagandistic Soviet works describing the additional help to families of front-line soldiers: Salakhutdinov, *Samarkandskaia partiinaia organizatsiia*, 38–44; Pulatov, *Andizhanskaia partiinaia organizatsiia*, 16, 108–109.
118. Krasnozhënova, "Sotsial'naia pomoshch'," 142–145.
119. TsGAChR, f. P1263, op. 1, d. 51, 134, 144 (copy in USHMM Archives, RG 22.020).
120. Ibid., d. 46, 88–90. Brodskaia's statement was confirmed by her landlady's testimony. Ibid.
121. Podlivalov, *Iuzhnoe Zaural'e*, 155–156.

122. GARF, f. A259, op. 40, d. 3518, 141 (copy in YVA, JM/24.678).

123. "V prokurature Soiuza SSR," *Pravda*, January 31, 1942, 4; "V prokurature Soiuza SSR," *Izvestiia*, January 31, 1942, 4.

124. TsGAChR, f. P1263, op. 1, d. 66, 95a (copy in USHMM Archives, RG 22.020).

125. This is verified in a classified report by an inspector of the Council of People's Commissars of the RSFSR from November 1942, who checked on the Kirov region, where 56,600 members of the officers' families were registered. See GARF, A259, f. 40, op. 40, d. 3529, 171–179 (copy in YVA, JM/24678).

126. *Pis'ma Velikoi Otechestvennoi*, 82–83.

127. GARF, f. A259, op. 40, d. 3527, 33 (copy in YVA, JM/24.678).

128. Ibid., d. 3038, 106.

129. TsGAChR, f. P1263, op. 1, d. 51, 174–176, 192 (copy in USHMM Archives, RG 22.020).

130. *Russkii arkhiv*, vol. 17 (6–1), 149–150.

131. Annakurbanov, *Kommunisticheskaia partiia Turkmenistana*, 46.

132. TsGAChR, f. P1263, op. 1, d. 61, 2–2a (copy in USHMM Archives, RG 22.020).

133. *Sovetskaia propaganda*, 622–626.

134. *Organy Gosudarstvennoi bezopasnosti*, vol. 4, part 2, 246.

135. *Russkii arkhiv*, vol. 17 (6–1), 264–265.

136. About this prewar practice, see Christian, *Imperial and Soviet Russia*, 312–315; Fitzpatrick, *Everyday Stalinism*, 104–105.

137. GARF, f. A259, op. 40, d. 3022, 37 (copy in YVA, JM/24.678).

138. A member of the Evacuation Council and Deputy People's Commissar for Communications, Dubrovin complained about train cars with this personal property blocking the railway tracks. See N. F. Dubrovin, "Eshelon za eshelonom," in *Eshelony idut na vostok*, ed. Iurii Poliakov (Moscow: Nauka, 1966), 211.

139. TsGARK, f. P1137, op. 6, d. 143, 43–43a (copy in USHMM Archives, RG 74.002M).

140. GARF, f. A259, op. 40, d. 3022, 37 (copy in YVA, JM/24.678).

141. Hessler, *A Social History*, 301.

142. TsGARK, f. P1137, op. 6, d. 1291, 95–96 (copy in USHMM Archives, RG 74.002M).

143. Potëmkina, *Evakuatsiia*, 78.

144. Fedotov, *Evakuirovannoe naselenie*, 70.

145. TsGAChR, f. P203, op. 18, d. 219, 25–27a, 46–47a (copy in USHMM Archives, RG 22.020). It is curious that this fact was included in the officially published information about the help provided to the evacuated children by the Chuvash authorities, without indicating whose children they were. See *Partiinoe rukovodstvo evakuatsiei*, 47.

146. Viktor Lushnikov, "Normirovannoe raspredelenie produktov v Khakasii i v iuzhnykh raionakh Krasnoiarskogo kraia, 1941–1947 gg.," *Voprosy teorii i praktiki, Seriia: Istoricheskie, filosofskie, politicheskie i iuridicheskie nauki, kul'turologiia i iskusstvovedenie* 7, no. 21 (2012): 120–121.

147. TsGARK, f. P1137, op. 6, d. 1280, 42–43 (copy in USHMM Archives, RG 74.002M).

148. Timofeev, *Dnevnik voennykh let*, part 2, 131.

Notes to Pages 66–70   255

149. Ibid., 152.
150. Ibid., 143–4, 152, 156.
151. In September 1941, Fadeev wrote about their distressed state to the secretary of the Central Committee of the Communist Party Aleksandr Shcherbakov, who oversaw the culture. *Sovetskaia propaganda*, 127.
152. TsGAChR, f. P1263, op. 1, d. 61, 2–2a (copy in USHMM Archives, RG 22.020).
153. Ibid., f. P203, op. 19, d. 71, 14.
154. Ibid., f. P1263, op. 1, d. 46, 175–176a.
155. Novikov, *Vospominaniia diplomata*, 94–95.
156. Willerton, *Patronage and Politics*, 29–33; Fitzpatrick, *Tear Off the Masks!*, 182–202.
157. Oleg Khlevniuk, "Sistema tsentr-regiony v 1930–1950-e gody: Predposylki politizatsii 'Nomenklatury,'" *Cahiers du Monde russe* 44, no. 2/3 (2003): 255–257.
158. Novikov, *Vospominaniia diplomata*, 117–118.
159. Pikhoia, *Moskva. Kreml'. Vlast'*, 24–26.
160. Pëtr Druzhinin, *Ideologiia i filologia: Leningrad, 1940e gody* (Moscow: NLO, 2012), vol. 1, 211–242.
161. Timofeev, *Dnevnik voennykh let*, part 3, 155.
162. TsGAChR, f. P1263, op. 1, d. 51, 57–58a (copy in USHMM Archives, RG 22.020).
163. Ibid., d. 46, 56–56a.
164. GARF, f. A259, op. 40, d. 3529, 207 (copy in YVA, JM/24.678).
165. In Alma-Ata, see ibid., d. 3038, 106–107; in the Chuvash ASSR: TsGAChR, f. P1263, op. 1, d. 46, 206–207 (copy in USHMM Archives, RG 22.020); in the Novosibirsk region, *Vo imia pobedy*, vol. 1, 213. About poor work done at evacuation points, see also Belonosov, "Evakuatsiia naseleniia," 26.
166. TsGAChR, f. P1263, op. 1, d. 46, 163 (copy in USHMM Archives, RG 22.020).
167. GARF, f. A259, op. 40, d. 3518, 36 (copy in YVA, JM/24.678).
168. Calculated based on information in P. Radionenko's report to Konstantin Pamfilov, ibid., 35–36.
169. *Partiinoe rukovodstvo evakuatsiei*, 11.
170. TsGAChR, f. P1263, op. 1, d. 33, 49, 51 (copy in USHMM Archives, RG 22.020). Such a decision was probably the result of a general directive "from above."
171. In the Bashkir ASSR: GARF, f. A259, op. 40, d. 3518, 142a (copy in YVA, JM/24.678); in Kuibyshev region: ibid., d. 3527, 33; Mariinsk district of the Novosibirsk region: ibid., 103; Glazov district of the Udmurt ASSR: ibid., 116.
172. TsGAChR, f. P203, op. 18, d. 219, 314–315 (copy in USHMM Archives, RG 22.020).
173. Ibid., 365–365a, 393.
174. Ibid., f. P835, op. 1, d. 339, 112–119.
175. Ibid., f. P1263, op. 1, d. 46, 128–128a.
176. Ibid., d. 51, 187–187a.
177. Boiman, *Yalde ha-korpus ha-sheni*, 154.
178. TsGAChR, f. P1263, op. 1, d. 51, 132–133 (copy in USHMM Archives, RG 22.020).

179. Ibid., f. P203, op. 11, d. 66, 32.
180. GARF, f. A259, op. 40, d. 3038, 101–103 (copy in YVA, JM/24.678).
181. *Organy Gosudarstvennoi bezopasnosti*, vol. 3, part 1, 108–109.
182. Fitzpatrick, *Everyday Stalinism*, 175–176.
183. TsGAChR, f. P1263, op. 1, d. 46, 128a (copy in USHMM Archives, RG 22.020).
184. Ibid., f. P203, op. 19, d. 71, 94a.
185. Ibid., 211.
186. GARF, f. A259, op. 40, d. 3038, 105 (copy in YVA, JM/24.678).
187. TsGAChR, f. P1263, op. 1, d. 46, 127 (copy in USHMM Archives, RG 22.020).
188. Ibid., f. P203, op. 11, d. 66, 89.
189. GARF, f. A259, op. 40, d. 3529, 207 (copy in YVA, JM/24.678).
190. Ibid., 210.
191. *Vo imia pobedy*, vol. 2, 240.
192. GARF, f. A259, op. 40, d. 3518, 134–135 (copy in YVA, JM/24.678); ibid., d. 3096, 70.
193. *Vo imia pobedy*, vol. 2, 280–281, 293–294.
194. Annakurbanov, *Kommunisticheskaia partiia Turkmenistana*, 45.
195. TsGAChR, f. P203, op. 26, d. 32, 10a (copy in USHMM Archives, RG 22.020).
196. Ibid., op. 18, d. 219, 306–306a.
197. GARF, f. A259, op. 40, d. 3529, 15–17 (copy in YVA, JM/24.678).
198. Ibid., d. 3517, 25.
199. Ibid., d. 3529, 213.
200. Ibid., 208.
201. TsGAChR, f. P203, op. 11, d. 66, 21 (copy in USHMM Archives, RG 22.020). These facts confirmed the report of the head of the territorial group of the Council of People's Commissars of the Chuvash ASSR, S. B. Zubrilin, on the situation in Ichikisy, compiled in February 1942. TsGAChR, f. P1263, op. 1, d. 46, 152–153 (copy in USHMM Archives, RG 22.020).
202. Ibid., 164.
203. GARF, f. A259, op. 40, d. 3028, 107 (copy in YVA, JM/24.678).
204. Ibid., 208.
205. Ibid., d. 3529, 212.
206. Ibid., 209.
207. TsGAChR, f. P2021, op. 3, d. 5, 45–45a (copy in USHMM Archives, RG 22.020).
208. With reference to RGASPI, f. 644, op. 1, d. 40, 85, see http://www.soldat.ru/doc/gko/text/1938.html.
209. Fitzpatrick, *Everyday Stalinism*, 172–174. In the case with Vera Nikitina in Chuvashia described above, an investigation of her economic situation was conducted and assistance was provided.
210. *Sovetskaia propaganda*, 602.
211. TsGAChR, f. P203, op. 18, d. 119, 320 (copy in USHMM Archives, RG 22.020).
212. Ibid., op. 19, d. 71, 58.
213. Podlivalov, *Iuzhnoe Zaural'e*, 122.

214. GARF, f. A259, op. 40, d. 3529, 175 (copy in YVA, JM/24.678).
215. Maria Belkina, *Skreshchenie sudeb* (Moscow: Blagovest—Rudomino, 1992), 310–316.

Chapter 3. "He who does not work, does not eat"

1. Fedotov, *Evakuirovannoe naselenie*, 114.
2. Potëmkina, *Evakonaselenie*, 122. The Urals includes the Sverdlovsk, Cheliabinsk, and Orenburg (Chkalov, in the wartime) regions.
3. *Vo imia pobedy*, vol. 2, 337.
4. Calculated from "The report on the employment of evacuees in the Chuvash ASSR, June 10, 1942," TsGAChR, f. P203, op. 18, d. 218a, 94 (copy in USHMM Archives, RG 22.020).
5. Calculated from "The reference on the employment of evacuees in the Chuvash ASSR, October 1, 1942," TsGAChR, f. P1263, op. 1, d. 39, 55 (copy in USHMM Archives, RG 22.020).
6. Calculated from "The report on the employment of evacuees in the Chuvash ASSR, November 1, 1942," ibid., 58.
7. Calculated from "The report on the employment of evacuees in the Chuvash ASSR, December 15, 1942," ibid., 68.
8. The evacuation inspector Mikhail Kosolapov wrote about such manipulations in the Pervomaiskoe district of the Chuvash ASSR in his report from April 20, 1942. Ibid., d. 46, 168–168a.
9. Ibid., d. 65, 65.
10. *Vo imia pobedy*, vol. 2, 223.
11. Pirimkulov, "Evrei," 132. Pirimkulov, however, having a poor understanding of the situation, presents these archival data as an example of the refugees' reluctance to work.
12. YVA, O.3/11786, 13, 17.
13. Ibid., 12.
14. YVA, O.3/8122, 22; AJC Archives, interview by Rachel Erlich no. 18 with W., Interviews with Polish and Jewish DPs in DP Camps on Their Observations of Jewish Life in Soviet Russia, 3.
15. Aharonson, *Beriḥah le-moledet*, 88.
16. Liuksemburg, *Sozveszdie Mordekhaia*, 123, 135.
17. Keila Pruzanski, *Sunshine and Shadows (Moie Zycie)* (Melbourne, Australia: n.p., 1995), 43–46.
18. Gabel, *Behind the Ice Curtain*, 247–251, 267–268.
19. Moshe Shtrasberg, *Mi-shfelat Polin ve-'ad midbarit 'Uzbekistan* (Ramat-Gan: n.p., 1993), 55–59.
20. USC Shoah Foundation, Visual History Archive, interview with Nathan Brener, New York, March 2, 1995, segments 66–70, Spielberg Archive.
21. Zylbering, "A Survivor Remembers," 44–49.
22. With reference to RGASPI, f. 644, op. 1, d. 58, 11, see http://www.soldat.ru/doc/gko/text/2342.html.
23. TsGAChR, f. P1263, op. 1, d. 51, 231–231a (copy in USHMM Archives, RG 22.020).

24. Riva Draier, "Novyi evreiski tsentr v Alma-Ate," GARF, f. P8114, op. 1, d. 115, 370 (copy in USHMM Archives, RG 220028M).

25. Efim Iankelevich, *Armiia 1943–1945 gg.: Vospominaniia soldata 60 let spustia* (2003), available at http://militera.lib.ru/memo/russian/yankelevich_ea/02.html.

26. Anatolii Tiktiner, *Vospominaniia: Mysli i fakty* (2005), available at http://tiktiner.narod.ru/vosp_tiktiner_titul.html.

27. A. Iuditskii, "Istoriia odnoi arteli," GARF, f. P8114, op. 1, d. 102, 38–38a (copy in USHMM Archives, RG 220028M).

28. USC Shoah Foundation, Visual History Archive, interview with Nathan Brener, New York, March 2, 1995, segments 66–70, Spielberg Archive; Grantserska-Kadari, *Ha-Meah ha-esrim sheli*, 195.

29. "Spekuliantov i vorov pod sud," *Sovetskaia Sibir'*, February 8, 1942, 2.

30. For examples, see YVA, O.3/2242, 3; ibid., O.3/10889, 50–54, 60, 65; Litvak, *Peliṭim Yehudim*, 196–197; Grynberg, *Children of Zion*, 130; Davidson-Rosenblatt, *Keine Zeit für Abschied*, 56–57 (I am grateful to Yael Lantsman for translation of these pages); Wenig, *From Nazi Inferno*, 223, 252–253; Zylbering, "A Survivor Remembers," 44, 46–47; Aharonson, *Beriḥah le-moledet*, 88.

31. USC Shoah Foundation, Visual History Archive, interview with Aryeh Katsav, Haifa, Israel, April 14, 1997, segments 129–130, Spielberg Archive.

32. Isaak Rozenblium, "Bratskoe gostepreimstvo," GARF, f. P8114, op. 1, d. 124, 72–73 (copy in USHMM Archives, RG 220028M).

33. *Dokumenty i materialy po istorii sovetsko-pol'skikh otnoshenii*, ed. Ivan Khrenov (Moscow: Nauka, 1973), vol. 7, 90; *Iz istorii poliakov v Kazakhstane*, 194, 198, 205–207.

34. Gribanova, "Evakuatsiia," 232.

35. TsGAChR, f. P1263, op. 1, d. 36, 18 (copy in USHMM Archives, RG 22.020).

36. Ibid., 25.

37. Ibid., d. 65, 90a–91.

38. Ibid., d. 51, 105.

39. Partially about this, see Gribanova, "Evakuatsiia," 234–235.

40. See copies of both evacuees' cards at: Holocaust Survivors and Victims Database, USHMM, http://www.ushmm.org/online/hsv/person_advance_search.php?Sourceid=20492.

41. Calculated from GARF, f. 7021, op. 85, d. 247–251, 263 (copy in YVA, JM/23.638–23.639). For further information about prewar salaries and other incomes, see Kaganovitch, *Long Life*, 222–224.

42. TsGAChR, f. P203, op. 26, d. 32, 11 (copy in USHMM Archives, RG 22.020); ibid., f. P1263, op. 1, d. 31, 17–18, 35. For comparison, the head and deputy head of the evacuation centers earned, respectively, 900 and 765 rubles. Ibid.

43. Calculated from TsGARK, f. P1137, op. 9, d. 141, 78a–79 (copy in USHMM Archives, RG 74.002M).

44. Calculated from ibid., op. 6, d. 1279, 33–36.

45. *Sovetskaia Sibir'*, February 1, 1942, 4; ibid., March 1, 1942, 4.

46. Grosman, *Ba-arets ha-agadit*, vol. 2, 396–297.

47. USC Shoah Foundation, Visual History Archive, interview with Nathan Brener, New York, March 2, 1995, segments 66–70, Spielberg Archive.

48. Krasnov-Levitin, *Ruk tvoikh zhar*, 133.

49. TsGARK, f. P1952, op. 1, d. 100, 50 (copy in USHMM Archives, RG 74.002M).

50. Luidmila Snegirëva, "Sotsial'no-ekonomicheskie posledstviia reevakuatsii v zapodnosibirskom tylu (1942–1948)," *TSPU Bulletin* 9, no. 162 (2015): 192.

51. *Zdorov'e i zdravookhranenie trudiiashchikhsia SSSR: Statisticheskii sbornik*, ed. Ivan Kraval (Moscow: TsUNKhU Gosplana SSSR and V/O "Soiuzorguchet," 1937), 158.

52. List of doctors who arrived in Alma-Ata as evacuees (January 1943), TsGARK, f. P1137, op. 6, d. 1279, 228–285 (copy in USHMM Archives, RG 74.002M).

53. The table is compiled only based on those lists of doctors in Kazakhstani localities in which the column "nationality" was designated. See ibid., f. P1473, op. 2, d. 21, 1–6.

54. Viacheslav Konstantinov, *Evreiskoe naselenie byvshego SSSR v XX veke* (Jerusalem: Lira, 2007), 219.

55. Calculated from GARF, f. A259, op. 40, d. 3532, 105–106 (copy in YVA, JM/24.678).

56. For the full text of this resolution, see *Vo imia pobedy*, vol. 2, 305.

57. *Oboronnaia promyshlennost'*, 294–295. Publishing archival documents about this, the editor of this collection considered it necessary to omit a few paragraphs that obviously concerned repressive measures connected to the mobilization.

58. Interview by Grigorii Koifman with David Bakas, available at http://iremember.ru/memoirs/svyazisti/bakas-david-moyshevich/. For the same practice of police raids in the wartime Alma-Ata, see Pomerantz and Wallwork-Winik, *Run East*, 64.

59. Grantserska-Kadari, *Ha-Meah ha-esrim sheli*, 194.

60. Iulia Melekhova, "Istoricheskii opyt organizatsii priëma i obustroistva evakuirovannogo naseleniia v gody Velikoi Otechestvennoi voiny (na primere Altaiskogo kraia)" (PhD candidate diss., Altai State Technical University, 2016), 116–117.

61. *Oboronnaia promyshlennost'*, 324, 326.

62. Calculated from ibid., 516–517.

63. For the full text of this resolution, see *Vo imia pobedy*, vol. 2, 304.

64. "V prokurature Soiuza SSR," *Sovetskaia Sibir'*, February 8, 1942, 2.

65. TsGAChR, f. P203, op. 18, d. 218a, 127 (copy in USHMM Archives, RG 22.020).

66. Gusak, *Militsiia Iuzhnogo Urala*, 59, 62–63. According to the author's information, for only one month in March 1943, in order to catch labor "deserters" and other lawbreakers, the police in this area carried out fifty-three roundups. Ibid., 63.

67. "Ob ukreplenii trudovoi distsipliny: Beseda s prokurorom SSSR K. P. Gorsheninym," *Izvestiia*, August 23, 1948, 2; Aleksandr Kodintsev, "Kampaniia po bor'be s dezertirstvom s predpriiatii voennoi promyshlennosti SSSR v 1941–1948 gg.," *Rossiiskaia istoriia* 6 (2008): 103–106.

68. *Oboronnaia promyshlennost'*, 505–509.

69. TsGAChR, f. P835, op. 1, d. 352, 20, 84–87 (copy in USHMM Archives, RG 22.020); ibid., f. P1263, op. 1, d. 50, 80–82; ibid., d. 52, 60–61.

70. For full list of the benefits, see ibid., d. 68, 158.

71. Ibid., d. 61, 26–26a.

72. Calculated from ibid., d. 51, 97a.

73. Calculated from ibid., d. 72, 1, 4a.

74. Ibid., d. 68, 87–90.

75. Belkovets, *Administrativno-pravovoe polozhenie*, 147. In the light of the categories of the population listed in the text who were sent to labor in fisheries, her assertion that the majority of them were German special settlers seems erroneous.

76. Rachel Rachlin and Israel Rachlin, *16 let vozvrashcheniia: Sibirskaia saga* (Moscow: ZubraE, 2005), 84–87; Rachel Rachlin and Israel Rachlin, *Sixteen Years in Siberia* (Tuscaloosa: University of Alabama Press, 1988), 58.

77. TsGAChR, f. P1263, op. 1, d. 81, 66 (copy in USHMM Archives, RG 22.020).

78. Mitsel, "Programmy," 104–105.

79. TsGAChR, f. P1263, op. 1, d. 46, 146–147 (copy in USHMM Archives, RG 22.020).

80. Ibid., f. P 203, op. 11, d. 66, 52.

81. For the full text of this resolution, see *Vo imia pobedy*, vol. 2, 312–313. For the information about its operation in the Chuvash ASSR, see TsGAChR, f. P1263, op. 1, d. 46, 175a (copy in USHMM Archives, RG 22.020).

82. During the above-mentioned forced mobilization to the defense factory Kombinat no. 179, seven people died there in 1943 and six people died in the first five months of 1944 because of industrial accidents. Over the same period, more than a thousand cases of other industrial injuries were registered at this enterprise. *Oboronnaia promyshlennost'*, 653–656.

83. Ibid., 697–699.

84. Arkadii German and Aleksandr Kurochkin, *Nemtsy SSSR v "Trudovoi armii" 1941–1945* (Moscow: Gotika, 1998), 114–115. The authors included a description of the conditions of the Soviet German "labor soldiers" at the same plant no. 65, finding them particularly difficult. Ibid., 116.

85. Liubimov, *Torgovlia i snabzhenie*, 27–28; YVA, O.3/8122, 22; ibid., O.3/10814, 18.

86. YVA, O.3/9722, 8.

87. *Kuibyshevskaia oblast' v gody Velikoi Otechestvennoi voiny (1941–1945 gg.): Dokumenty i materialy*, comp. V. Chistiakov and F. Zakharova (Kuibyshev, USSR: Kuibyshevskoe knizhnoe izdatel'stvo, 1966), 276; Liubimov, *Torgovlia i snabzhenie*, 29–30.

88. *Iz istorii poliakov v Kazakhstane*, 187–189; Pirimkulov, "Evrei," 130–131.

89. *Iz istorii poliakov v Kazakhstane*, 187–189.

90. USC Shoah Foundation, Visual History Archive, interview with Sholom Omri, Holon, Israel, March 1, 1998, segment 120, Spielberg Archive.

91. *Istoriia Velikoi Otechestvennoi voiny*, vol. 2, 554.

92. TsGAChR, f. P203, op. 19, d. 71, 211 (copy in USHMM Archives, RG 22.020).

93. Ibid., TsGARK, f. P1137, op. 6, d. 1289, 175 (copy in RG 74.002M).

94. GARF, f. 9401, op. 2, d. 64, 293–294, cited in *Istoriia v dokumentakh*.

95. Letter from Bella Vladimirskaia, December 19, 1942, Olga Tsarëva's personal archive.

96. Letter dated December 5, 1944, from M. L. Cherniavskii to David Zaslavskii, a journalist at *Eynikayt*, GARF, f. P8114, op. 1, d. 120, 197–197a (copy in USHMM Archives, RG 220028M).

97. For her petition to the authorities, January 18, 1943, see TsGAChR, f. P835, op. 1, d. 354, 225 (copy in USHMM Archives, RG 22.020).

98. Ibid., f. P1263, op. 1, d. 66, 89a.

99. Grosman, *Ba-arets ha-agadit*, vol. 2, 375.
100. TsGAChR, f. P835, op. 1, d. 354, 312 (copy in USHMM Archives, RG 22.020).
101. Hessler, *Social History*, 271–272.
102. *Vo imia pobedy*, vol. 3, 321–322. Consequently, their parents were fined. Ibid.
103. Liberman, *Iz berlinskogo getto*, 175.
104. Podlivalov, *Iuzhnoe Zaural'e*, 132.
105. GARF, f. A259, op. 40, d. 3518, 49 (copy in YVA, JM/24678).
106. Calculated from *Kirgiziia*, 327.
107. *Kirgiziia*, 328–329. Reporting this, the republican authorities asked the central authorities to help with bread for the evacuees.
108. TsGAChR, f. P203, op. 11, d. 66, 136 (copy in USHMM Archives, RG 22.020).
109. Ibid., 46.
110. [Ivan Kharkevich], "Ves' narod sil'no sdal telom: Voina i sovetskii tyl glazami inzhenera I. A. Kharkevicha," *Rossiiskaia istoriia* 6 (2009): 60.
111. TsGAChR, f. P203, op. 11, d. 66, 88 (copy in USHMM Archives, RG 22.020).
112. GARF, f. A259, op. 40, d. 3529, 212 (copy in YVA, JM/24678).
113. TsGAChR, f. P1263, op. 1, d. 36, 17 (copy in USHMM Archives, RG 22.020).
114. Ibid., d. 46, 71a.
115. Heinzen, "A 'Campaign Spasm,'" 125.
116. Ivanova, "Sed'maia tetrad'," 208.
117. *Sovetskaia propaganda*, 653.
118. *Organy Gosudarstvennoi bezopasnosti*, vol. 4, part 1, 218, 235–236.
119. *Sovetskaia propaganda*, 653–654.
120. *Bashkiriia*, 369.
121. *Vo imia pobedy*, vol. 2, 276.
122. *Sovetskie evrei pishut*, 143–144.
123. Wenig, *From Nazi Inferno*, 223–224, 251–253.
124. Ermolinskii, *O vremeni*, 290.
125. Classified report of Head of the Resettlement Department of Chuvashyia Nikolai Zhukov to A. M. Matveev, Council of People's Commissars of the republic, TsGAChR, f. P1263, op. 1, d. 36, 23 (copy in USHMM Archives, RG 22.020).
126. Ibid., d. 51, 133.
127. The evacuation inspector A. Nikitina's report on the Shumerlia district, ibid., 67–67a.
128. Ibid., 192, 194.
129. Ibid., f. P1041, op. 1, d. 512, 23. About this practice in Eastern Siberia, see Shalak, *Usloviia zhizni*, 37.
130. TsGAChR, f. P1263, op. 1, d. 46, 65 (copy in USHMM Archives, RG 22.020).
131. *Vo imia pobedy*, vol. 2, 235.
132. Fedotov, *Evakuirovannoe naselenie*, 76.
133. GARF, f. A259, op. 40, d. 3527, 115 (copy in YVA, JM/24678).
134. Podlivalov, *Iuzhnoe Zaural'e*, 124–125, 157–158.
135. *Bashkiriia*, 369.
136. AJC Archives, interview by Rachel Erlich no. 10 with E. G., Interviews with Polish and Jewish DPs in DP Camps on Their Observations of Jewish Life in Soviet Russia, 8.

137. Viktor Konasov, "Evakuirovannye leningradtsy na Vologodskoi zemle," *Voprosy istorii* 1 (2007): 142.

138. TsGAChR, f. P1263, op. 1, d. 65, 89 (copy in USHMM Archives, RG 22.020).

139. "Khishchenie prodovol'stvennykh kartochek," *Pravda*, January 28, 1942, 4.

140. "V prokurature Soiuza SSR," *Izvestiia*, July 24, 1943, 4.

141. Such warnings were issued because of the widespread theft or forgery of ration cards. However, it did not achieve its goal. In the conditions of famine, these practices continued, as evidenced by the transcript of the secret meeting on combating theft of food in the Novosibirsk Regional Party Committee on July 19, 1943. *Vo imia pobedy*, vol. 2, 208–211.

142. TsGARK, f. P1137, op. 6, d. 1285, 220 (copy in USHMM Archives, RG 74.002M).

143. Ibid., 220–221.

144. Shalak, *Usloviia zhizni*, 36–37.

145. The evacuation inspector A. Nikitina's report on the Shumerlia district, TsGAChR, f. P1263, op. 1, d. 51, 67–67a (copy in USHMM Archives, RG 22.020).

146. GARF, f. A259, op. 40, d. 3518, 36 (copy in YVA, JM/24678).

147. Potëmkina, *Evakuatsiia*, 63.

148. GARF, f. A259, op. 40, d. 3518, 49 (copy in YVA, JM/24678).

149. Ibid., d. 3527, 115.

150. Podlivalov, *Iuzhnoe Zaural'e*, 156.

151. GARF, f. A259, op. 40, d. 3518, 49 (copy in YVA, JM/24678).

152. TsGAChR, f. P1263, op. 1, d. 46, 65 (copy in USHMM Archives, RG 22.020).

153. Shaul' Beilinson, *Moi dolgii put' v Ierusalim* (Jerusalem: n.p., 1995), 59–60, 65–67.

154. Hooper, "A Darker 'Big Deal,'" 158.

155. YVA, O.3/10889, 62.

156. Meletinskii, *Izbrannye stat'i; Vospominaniia*, 507. See about this also USC Shoah Foundation, Visual History Archive, interview with Hildda Busch, London, UK, August 28, 1997, segment 50, Spielberg Archive.

157. *Russkii arkhiv*, vol. 13 (2–2), 265–266.

158. *Organy Gosudarstvennoi bezopasnosti*, vol. 3, part 1, 372–373.

159. V. M. Antropov and E. V. Krotov, "Deiatel'nost' organov BKhSS Altaiskogo kraia v gody Velikoi Otechestvennoi voiny," *Altaiskii iuridicheskii vestnik* 4, no. 12 (2015): 9–10.

160. Archive of the President of the Russian Federation (hereinafter AP RF), f. 3, op. 58, d. 212, 211–212, cited in *Istoriia v dokumentakh*.

161. With reference to RGASPI, f. 17, op. 162, d. 37, 72, see *Istoriia v dokumentakh*; AP RF, f. 3, op. 58, d. 212, 211–212, cited in ibid.; *Organy Gosudarstvennoi bezopasnosti*, vol. 4, part 1, 275.

162. AP RF, f. 3, op. 58, d. 212, 215, cited in *Istoriia v dokumentakh*.

Chapter 4. Famine, Mortality, and Some Help

1. Isupov, *Demograficheskie katastrofy*, 153.
2. GARF, f. A259, op. 40, d. 3529, 212 (copy in YVA, JM/24678).
3. Ivanova, "Sed'maia tetrad'," 210.

4. GARF, f. A259, op. 40, d. 3529, 212 (copy in YVA, JM/24678).
5. TsGAChR, f. P1263, op. 1, d. 51, 180 (copy in USHMM Archives, RG 22.020).
6. Vyltsan, "Zhertvy golodnogo vremeni," 166–167.
7. Interview by Grigorii Koifman with Iosif Faigenboim, available at http://iremember.ru/memoirs/svyazisti/faygenboym-iosif-aronovich/.
8. Osokina, *Our Daily Bread*, 150.
9. YVA, O.3/8122, 24; *Widziałem Anioła Śmierci*, 258; Barkan, "Vospominaniia," 22; Grynberg, *Children of Zion*, 129.
10. Sasonkin, *Zikhronotai*, 239. See also Levin, *Zikhronotai*, 107.
11. *Widziałem Anioła Śmierci*, 219.
12. YVA, O.3/1555, 4; ibid., O.3/5807, 12; ibid., O.3/3656, 6–7; Azrieli, *Na shag vperedi*, 99; *Widziałem Anioła Śmierci*, 60; Elton, *Destination Buchara*, 194.
13. Fabrikant, *Nam dorogi eti*, 151.
14. Mandel'shtam, *Vtoraia kniga*, 363.
15. Zylbering, "A Survivor Remembers," 45.
16. Shikheeva-Gaister, *Deti vragov naroda*, 88.
17. Dunaevskii, *Be-ḥoshekh 'efshar rak laḥlom*, 127.
18. Shikheeva-Gaister, *Deti vragov naroda*, 89.
19. Letter written on October 18, 1942, from the personal archive of Dmitrii Shirochin, whom I thank for giving me the opportunity to consult Tatiana Goikhman's letters.
20. Anatolii Kotliar, "Stranichka moego detstva," in supplement "Evreiskii kamerton" to *Novosti nedeli*, May 19, 1999, 18–19.
21. Bruell, *Autumn in Springtime*, 90–91.
22. Bernard Dov Weinryb, "Polish Jews under Soviet Rule," in *The Jews in the Soviet Satellites*, ed. Peter Meyer (Westport, CT: Greenwood Press, 1971), 356.
23. USC Shoah Foundation, Visual History Archive, interview with Mosheh Atsmon, Kibbutz Nirim, Israel, March 3, 1997, segments 53–56, Spielberg Archive.
24. Jadwiga Ihnatowicz-Suszyńska, *We Will Uproot You* (Lublin, Poland: Arlon, 2005), 273–274.
25. Max Komito, *Between Two Crazy Dictators* (New York: n.p., 1991), 51.
26. Kornilov, "Naselenie Sverdlovska," 105–106.
27. Kornilov, *Ural'skoe selo i voina*, 100.
28. YVA, O.3/8425, 11; Wenig, *From Nazi Inferno*, 245; testimony of Shymon Kupferschmied, March 24, 2003, ACC, F. 90000113.
29. TsGAChR, f. P203, op. 11, d. 66, 87–87a (copy in USHMM Archives, RG 22.020); ibid., f. P1263, op. 1, d. 36, 24.
30. For examples, see: YVA, O.3/12368, 9; Grosman, *Ba-arets ha-agadit*, vol. 2, 332; Grynberg, *Children of Zion*, 116, 125.
31. Grosman, *Ba-arets ha-agadit*, vol. 2, 333, 414; YVA, O.3/10814, 18–21; ibid., O.3/10894, 28.
32. Kornilov, "Naselenie Sverdlovska," 100; Rybakovskii, *Liudskie poteri SSSR*, 92; P. A. Stoliarov-Korol', *Rodina, zanovo obretennaia* (Abakan, Russia: Zhurnalist, 2007), 59.
33. Mataeva (Abramchaeva), *Od tizrah ha-shemesh*, 82–83.
34. Isupov, *Demograficheskie katastrofy*, 124–128.
35. GARF, f. A259, op. 40, d. 3028, 106–107 (copy in YVA, JM/24678).

36. TsGAChR, f. P1263, op. 1, d. 46, 76 (copy in USHMM Archives, RG 22.020).
37. Sinitsyn, *Vsenarodnaia pomoshch' frontu*, 294.
38. YVA, O. 3/9925, 18; TsGAChR, f. P1263, op. 1, d. 46, 76 (copy in USHMM Archives, RG 22.020); USC Shoah Foundation, Visual History Archive, interview with Sabina Austendig, New York, July 6, 1995, segment 39, Spielberg Archive; Grynberg, *Children of Zion*, 142; Rybakovskii, *Liudskie poteri SSSR*, 92. It is significant that even in twenty-six military hospitals located in the Kuibyshev region only 85 percent of the doctors had surgical training. See *Kuibyshevskaia oblast'*, 331.
39. Konstantin, *A Red Boyhood*, 116.
40. Grosman, *Ba-arets ha-agadit*, vol. 2, 280–281; Grynberg, *Children of Zion*, 128–129.
41. GARF, f. A259, op. 40, d. 3028, 107 (copy in YVA, JM/24678).
42. Timofeev, *Dnevnik voennykh let*, part 2, 128.
43. Salakhutdinov, *Samarkandskaia partiinaia organizatsiia*, 44. On the spread of typhus in Samarkand and Central Asia in general at this time, see Levin, "Miklat ara'i," 97, 105, 110; Sasonkin, *Zikhronotai*, 238.
44. "V prokurature Soiuza SSR," *Izvestiia*, March 15, 1942, 4.
45. Konstantin, *A Red Boyhood*, 119.
46. TsGAChR, f. P1263, op. 1, d. 46, 77 (copy in USHMM Archives, RG 22.020).
47. YVA, O.3/12287, 23.
48. Grosman, *Ba-arets ha-agadit*, vol. 2, 328. On large mortality rates among Polish Jewish refugees, also see Grynberg, *Children of Zion*, 143.
49. GARF, f. A259, op. 40, d. 3517, 48 (copy in YVA, JM/24.678).
50. Zylbering, "A Survivor Remembers," 43. USC Shoah Foundation, Visual History Archive, interview with Khava Ovrutskaia, Ashdod, Israel, May 25, 1998, segment 89, Spielberg Archive; interview with Galina Slonim, August 30, 2005, author's personal archive.
51. Sasonkin, *Zikhronotai*, 238–239.
52. Annakurbanov, *Kommunisticheskaia partiia Turkmenistana*, 24–25.
53. USC Shoah Foundation, Visual History Archive, interview with Rita Finver, Tamarac, Fl, January 9, 1996, segment 68, Spielberg Archive.
54. Konstantin, *A Red Boyhood*, 105.
55. Grantserska-Kadari, *Ha-Meah ha-esrim sheli*, 191–193.
56. Letter from Bella Vladimirskaia, December 19, 1942, Olga Tsarëva's personal archive.
57. Boiman, *Yalde ha-korpus ha-sheni*, 222; testimony by Efim Rabinovich on October 13, 2003, ACC, f. 81370306; interview by Nathalia Fomina with Liana Degtiar, Chişinău, Moldova, 2004, available at: https://www.centropa.org/biography/liana-degtiar.
58. Kornilov, *Ural'skoe selo i voina*, 78.
59. RGASPI, f. 644, op.1, d. 20, 195–198.
60. *Iz istorii poliakov v Kazakhstane*, 163–164; Salakhutdinov, *Samarkandskaia partiinaia organizatsiia*, 44; Wenig, *From Nazi Inferno*, 225.
61. *Iz istorii poliakov v Kazakhstane*, 152. In his testimony Dov Auseibel reports on the great value of soap in Central Asia, always prioritizing it when sending packages from Jerusalem. He arrived in Jerusalem from Central Asia via Iranin 1942. See YVA, O.3/8303, 36.

62. Donald Filtzer, *The Hazards of Urban Life in Late Stalinist Russia: Health, Hygiene, and Living Standards, 1943–1953* (New York: Cambridge University Press, 2010), 134–136.
63. TsGARK, f. P1137, op. 6, d. 1281, 97–98 (copy in USHMM Archives, RG 74.002M).
64. YVA, O.3/12287, 9.
65. *Rekviem*, 18.
66. Kornilov, *Ural'skoe selo i voina*, 78.
67. TsGAChR, f. P203, op. 11, d. 66, 39a (copy in USHMM Archives, RG 22.020).
68. Letter from Bella Vladimirskaia, December 19, 1942, Olga Tsarëva's personal archive.
69. Vladimir Isupov, "Naselenie Zapadnoi Sibiri v gody Velikoi Otechestvenoi voiny: Chislennost', sostav, vosproizvodstvo," *Rossiiskaia istoriia* 4, no. 4 (2010): 71.
70. Vladislav Kruglikov, "Gorodskoe naselenie Sverdlovskoi oblasti nakanune i v gody Velikoi Otechestvennoi voiny (1939–1945 gg.)" (PhD candidate diss., Institute of History and Archeology of the Ural Branch of the Russian Academy of Sciences, 2007), 18.
71. Kornilov, *Ural'skoe selo i voina*, 64. However, Kornilov's data on rural areas of the Urals raise doubts when compared with the large increase of mortality in the Sverdlovsk region (part of Ural area), which we saw in Kruglikov's study.
72. Donald Filtzer, "Starvation Mortality in Soviet Home-Front Industrial Regions during World War II," in *Hunger and War Food Provisioning in the Soviet Union during World War II*, ed. Wendy Z. Goldman and Donald Filtzer (Bloomington: Indiana University Press, 2015), 290, 297.
73. *Bashkiriia*, 254–255.
74. Gribanova, "Evakuatsiia," 225.
75. TsGAChR, f. P1263, op. 1, d. 46, 154 (copy in USHMM Archives, RG 22.020).
76. Ibid., f. P203, op. 11, d. 66, 21.
77. Ibid., 46–46a.
78. Azrieli, *Na shag vperedi*, 99.
79. Litvak, *Peliṭim Yehudim*, 188.
80. Interview by Nathalia Fomina with Sarra Shpitalnik, Chişinău, Moldova, 2004, available at: https://www.centropa.org/biography/sarra-shpitalnik.
81. Interview by Aleksei Ivashin with Leonid Shmurak, available at http://iremember.ru/memoirs/pekhotintsi/shmurak-leonid-moiseevich/.
82. *Widziałem Anioła Śmierci*, 382.
83. Interview by Grigorii Koifman with Arkadii Dael', available at http://iremember.ru/memoirs/pulemetchiki/dael-arkadiy-isaakovich/.
84. Interview by Artëm Drabkin with Polina Rivkina, available at http://iremember.ru/memoirs/letno-tekh-sostav/rivkina-polina-filippovna/.
85. YVA, O.3/9722, 7.
86. Grosman, *Ba-arets ha-agadit*, vol. 2, 378.
87. Feigelovich, "Prikliucheniia chetyrëkh," 28–29.
88. AJC Archives, interview by Rachel Erlich no. 1 with R., Interviews with Polish and Jewish DPs in DP Camps on Their Observations of Jewish Life in Soviet Russia, 5; Manley, *To the Tashkent Station*, 193.

89. TsGAChR, f. P1263, op. 1, d. 35, 53–53a (copy in USHMM Archives, RG 22.020); Grynberg, *Children of Zion*, 147. Henryk Grynberg recounts of how the hospital refused to release the body of his younger brother to a Polish Jew, who only managed to obtain and bury it in a Jewish cemetery by means of a bribe. When the mother died three weeks later, he wanted to bury her body in the same place, but he was late—the person in the hospital warden buried her that night in an unmarked place. Ibid., 141.

90. Andrei Suslov, *Spetskontingent v Permskoi oblasti, 1923–1953* (Moscow: Rosspen, 2010), 59–63.

91. Zaron, *Ludnosc polska*, 202.

92. I am grateful to Vadim Geller, psychiatry researcher at Ben-Gurion University of the Negev, for consultation on this issue.

93. Liberman, *Iz berlinskogo getto*, 173.

94. Calculated from GARF, f. A304, op. 1, d. 255, 1–9 (copy in YVA, JM/21915).

95. *Rekviem*, 18.

96. Batyrbaeva, *Tendentsii izmeneniia chislennosti*. Given the very poor record of registration of refugees in the republic, and even more so of the dead among them, as the demographer herself writes, this mortality is hardly traceable in the republic's accounting documents.

97. Calculated from the data in the table "Information about the dead by gender and causes of death" of the Central Statistical Administration of the USSR of February 4, 1949, RGAE, f. 1562, op. 33, d. 2638, 91–94a.

98. Ibid.

99. Isupov, *Demograficheskie katastrofy*, 153.

100. Rybakovskii, *Liudskie poteri SSSR*, 93.

101. Manley, *To the Tashkent Station*, 194.

102. Kornilov, *Ural'skoe selo i voina*, 64–65.

103. Ravilia Khisamutdinova, *Sel'skoe khoziaistvo Urala v gody Velikoi Otechestvennoi voiny* (Orenburg, Russia: Orenburgskii universitet, 2002), 191–196; *Mesto evakuatsii*, 167.

104. Kornilov, *Ural'skoe selo i voina*, 64–65.

105. Ibid., 78.

106. YVA, O.3/8122, 23; ibid., O.3/12287, 9; Levin, "Miklat ara'i," 105; Wat, *My Century*, 357.

107. YVA, O.3/1568, 11.

108. Pirimkulov, "Evrei," 131.

109. Ermolinskii, *O vremeni*, 335–336.

110. Litvak, *Peliṭim Yehudim*, 359.

111. Kostyrchenko, *Tainaia politika Stalina*, 431.

112. Gusak, *Militsiia Iuzhnogo Urala*, 57.

113. YVA, O.3/8122, 21; Elton, *Destination Buchara*, 190; Klevan, *Le-toldot ha-Yehudim*, 118.

114. Aharonson, *Beriḥah le-moledet*, 88; Grantserska-Kadari, *Ha-Meah ha-esrim sheli*, 195. Moshe Grosman writes about the attacks in Samarkand as a common phenomenon in his memoirs: Grosman, *Ba-arets ha-agadit*, vol. 2, 363.

115. YVA, O.3/9521, 25.
116. Interview with Hillel Livshits, March 23, 2006, author's personal archive; Grosman, *Ba-arets ha-agadit*, vol. 2, 327, 373–372; *War through Children's Eyes*, 236.
117. Semën Glikman, "Sladkaia zhizn'," in *Vzrosloe detstvo voiny: Sbornik vospominanii*, ed. Mikhail Kipnis (Ashdod, Israel: Keitar, 2013), vol. 2, 32.
118. YVA, O.3/10496, 17; *"W czterdziestym,"* 221.
119. *War through Children's Eyes*, 63.
120. RGASPI, f. 644, op. 1, d. 69, 15.
121. *Dokumenty po istorii Belarusi v "Osoboi papke" I. V. Stalina*, comp. S. V. Zhumar' (Minsk, Belarus: NARB, 2004), 47, 49. On the elimination of gangs in Kyrgyzstan in 1943, see also *Organy Gosudarstvennoi bezopasnosti*, vol. 4, part 1, 494–495.
122. Statiev, "The Nature, 1942–44," 299.
123. GARF, f. 9401, op. 2, d. 64, 293–294, cited in *Istoriia v dokumentakh*.
124. Podlivalov, *Iuzhnoe Zaural'e*, 125.
125. Postnikov, *V dalekikh garnizonakh*, 23.
126. *Teoriia i praktika*, 410–411. On the deserters' banditry in the Kursk region, see *Organy Gosudarstvennoi bezopasnosti*, vol. 4, part 1, 33–36; in Kalmyk ASSR: ibid., 500–501.
127. See letter from G. Sher to S. Mikhoels and D. Zaslavskii in Redlich, "The Jews under Soviet Rule," 233–234.
128. TsGAChR, f. P203, op. 11, d. 66, 84 (copy in USHMM Archives, RG 22.020).
129. Calculated from "The report on the gardens and seeds provided to evacuated citizens in the Chuvashian Autonomous Republic," TsGAChR, f. P203, op. 18, d. 118a, 137–137a (copy in USHMM Archives, RG 22.020).
130. The campaign in the press for gardening was tracked in Moskoff, *The Bread of Affliction*, 224–226; Berkhoff, *Motherland in Danger*, 98–100.
131. USC Shoah Foundation, Visual History Archive, interview with Jacob Sosniak, Indianapolis, September 21, 1997, segments 102–103, Spielberg Archive.
132. *Evakuatsiia v Kazakhstan*, 73–74, 80.
133. Kaganovitch, *The Long Life*, 217, 222–223.
134. Gabel, *Behind the Ice Curtain*, 266–267.
135. TsGAChR, f. P1263, op. 1, d. 66, 171a (copy in USHMM Archives, RG 22.020).
136. Interview by Nathalia Fomina with Liana Degtiar, Chișinău, Moldova, 2004, available at: https://www.centropa.org/biography/liana-degtiar.
137. *Narodnoe hoziaistvo SSSR v Velikoi Otechestvennoi voine 1941–1945 gg.: Statisticheskii sbornik* (Moscow: Goskomstat, 1990), 109.
138. *Istoriia Velikoi Otechestvennoi voiny*, vol. 2, 555.
139. Joseph Stalin and Vyacheslav Molotov, "O merakh okhrany obshchestennykh zemel' kolkhozov ot razbazarivaniia: Postanovlenie TsK VKP(b) i SNK SSSR," *Pravda*, September 20, 1946, 2.
140. GARF, f. P8114, op. 1, d. 1063, 21–24 (copy in USHMM Archives, RG 22.028M). See also Mikhail Agapov, *Evreisko-palestinskoe soobshchestvo v sovetskoi blizhnevostochnoi politike 1939–1948 gg.* (Tyumen', Russia: Vektor Buk, 2012), 124–126.

141. Nikolai Terenchenko, *My byli suvorovtsami* (Rostov, Russia: Izdatel'stvo ROIU, 1993), 43.

142. About the AJJDC's $1 million donation to the USSR in July 1945 and $1.5 million in 1946, see Mitsel, "Programmy," 115, 118.

143. Yehuda Bauer, *American Jewry and the Holocaust: The American Jewish Joint Distribution Committee, 1939–1945* (Detroit, MI: Wayne State University Press, 1982), 297–298.

144. *Gosudarstvennyi antisemitizm*, 127, 133.

145. *Kommunisticheskaia vlast'*, 181.

146. *Gosudarstvennyi antisemitizm*, 132–133.

147. *Kommunisticheskaia vlast'*, 181.

148. GARF, f. P8114, op. 1, d. 1064, 112 (copy in USHMM Archives, RG 22.028M).

149. *TsK VKP(b) i natsional'nyi vopros*, 822–823.

150. This is indirectly reflected in the memorandum form V. S. Abakumov, December 4, 1948. See *Gosudarstvennyi antisemitizm*, 139–143. On the committee's linking of the "Crimean initiative" with the intensified Jewish question in the USSR, see Redlich, *War, Holocaust and Stalinism*, 48.

151. Dov-Ber Kerler, "The Soviet Yiddish Press: During the War, 1942–1945," in *Why Didn't the Press Shout? American & International Journalism during the Holocaust*, ed. Robert Moses Shapiro (New York: Yeshiva University, 2003), 221–249.

CHAPTER 5. ORPHANAGES, ADOPTION, AND JEWISH CHILDREN

1. From the poem by Gafur Guliam, Khamid Alimdzhan, and Chustii, "Pis'mo uzbekskogo naroda boitsam Velikoi Otechestvennoi voiny" (translation from Uzbek into Russian by L. Pen'kovskii and V. Derzhavin), *Tashkentskii Al'manakh*, ed. Khamid Alimdzhan, Vsevolod Ivanov, and Isaia Lezhnëv (Tashkent, USSR: Gosizdat UzSSR, 1942), 18–22.

2. GARF, f. A304, op. 1, d. 209, 18 (copy in YVA, JM/21916).

3. Aharonson, *Beriḥah le-moledet*, 90–91; YVA, O.3/8303, 31.

4. Bader-Whiteman, *Escape via Siberia*, 78–79.

5. There were twenty-one Latvians and twenty-nine Jews among the fifty children. TsGAChR, f. P1041, op. 1, d. 511, 1 (copy in USHMM Archives, RG 22.020). Iakov Shvarts reports on the placement of children evacuated from Latvia into orphanages in Tatarstan, the Gor'kii, Kirov, and Ivanovo regions, as well as in Tashkent. Shvarts, "Nekotorye voprosy evakuatsii," 204.

6. Pulatov, *Andizhanskaia partiinaia organizatsiia*, 13–14; Dzhuraev, *Kommunisticheskaia partiia Uzbekistana*, 258.

7. *Partiinoe rukovodstvo evakuatsiei*, 48.

8. Annakurbanov, *Kommunisticheskaia partiia Turkmenistana*, 53.

9. Calculated from TsGARK, f. P1137, op. 9, d. 144, 190–194 (copy in USHMM Archives, RG 74.002M); *Kazakhstan v period*, 125.

10. Sinitsyn, *Vsenarodnaia pomoshch' frontu*, 285.

11. TsGARK, f. P1137, op. 6, d. 1289, 176 (copy in USHMM Archives, RG 74.002M).

12. *Kirgiziia*, 321.

13. Fabrikant, *Nam dorogi eti*, 156.

14. Podlivalov, *Iuzhnoe Zaural'e*, 184.
15. Dunaevskii, *Be-ḥoshekh 'efshar rak laḥlom*, 83.
16. Mandel'shtam, *Vtoraia kniga*, 291.
17. Svetlana Somova, "Mne dali imia—Anna": Anna Akhmatova v Tashkente," *Moskva* 3 (1984): 177–193.
18. Shvarts, "Nekotorye voprosy evakuatsii," 205.
19. *Mordoviia*, 244.
20. Sinitsyn, *Vsenarodnaia pomoshch' frontu*, 293.
21. Medvedeva-Natu, "V atmosfere liubvi," 168.
22. *Vo imia pobedy*, vol. 3, 351.
23. *Istoriia Velikoi Otechestvennoi voiny*, vol. 2, 557; Sinitsyn, *Vsenarodnaia pomoshch' frontu*, 304.
24. Dzhuraev, *Kommunisticheskaia partiia Turkmenistana*, 258.
25. Annakurbanov, *Kommunisticheskaia partiia Turkmenistana*, 49.
26. *Kirgiziia*, 336–337.
27. *Zapadnyi Ural—frontu: Trudiashchiesia Permskoi oblasti v bor'be za pobedu v Velikoi Otechestvennoi voine 1941–1945 gg.; Dokumenty i materialy*, comp. Vladimir Lanin (Perm', USSR: Permskoe knizhnoe izdatel'stvo, 1985), 265.
28. TsGAChR, f. P1041, op. 1, d. 512, 23–24 (copy in USHMM Archives, RG 22.020).
29. Ibid., 20.
30. Ibid., 27.
31. The evacuation inspector A. Nikitina's report on the Shumerlia district, ibid., f. P1263, op. 1, d. 51, 67a.
32. Ibid., d. 65, 66.
33. Shalak, *Usloviia zhizni*, 32–33.
34. TsGAChR, f. P1263, op. 1, d. 46, 190–191a (copy in USHMM Archives, RG 22.020).
35. Shalak, *Usloviia zhizni*, 37.
36. *Vo imia pobedy*, vol. 3, 268–269.
37. Viktor Usov, "Oni zhili v sovetskom interdome (tri knigi kitaitsev s vospominaniiami o godakh, provedennykh v SSSR)," *Problemy Dal'nego Vostoka* 3 (2007): 128.
38. Chukovskaia, *Zapiski ob Anne Akhmatovoi*, vol. 2, 29.
39. Medvedeva-Natu, "V atmosfere liubvi," 169.
40. Dunaevskii, *Be-ḥoshekh 'efshar rak laḥlom*, 76, 78, 91.
41. Manley, *To the Tashkent Station*, 190.
42. USC Shoah Foundation, Visual History Archive, interview with Danielle Bell, Montreal, September 17, 1996, segment 98, Spielberg Archive.
43. Boiman, *Yalde ha-korpus ha-sheni*, 202.
44. Medvedeva-Natu, "V atmosfere liubvi," 169.
45. Chukovskaia, *Zapiski ob Anne Akhmatovoi*, vol. 2, 29.
46. TsGAChR, f. P1263, op. 1, d. 46, 185 (copy in USHMM Archives, RG 22.020).
47. Shalak, *Usloviia zhizni*, 61.
48. *Mordoviia*, 232–234.
49. Shalak, *Usloviia zhizni*, 61.
50. Ibid.

51. Kornilov, *Ural'skoe selo i voina*, 74.
52. Ibid., 75.
53. Podlivalov, *Iuzhnoe Zaural'e*, 185–187.
54. TsGAChR, f. P835, op. 1, d. 354, 304 (copy in USHMM Archives, RG 22.020).
55. Ibid., f. P1263, op. 1, d. 46, 12a–15; 197–200.
56. Ibid., d. 51, 117–117a.
57. Igor' Zolotusskii, "Nas bylo troe," *Zvezda* 5 (2010): 43.
58. *Mesto evakuatsii*, 168.
59. Boiman, *Yalde ha-korpus ha-sheni*, 220, 244.
60. *Kazakhstan v period*, 102–103.
61. TsGAChR, f. P1263, op. 1, d. 33, 75 (copy in USHMM Archives, RG 22.020).
62. Manley, *To the Tashkent Station*, 190.
63. Nadezhda Paletskikh, *Sotsial'naia politika na Urale v period Velikoi Otechestvennoi voiny* (Cheliabinsk, Russia: Cheliabinskii agroinzhenernyi universitet, 1995), 11.
64. Dunaevskii, *Be-ḥoshekh 'efshar rak laḥlom*, 76; Iushkovskii, "Dnevnik," 189–190.
65. *Vo imia pobedy*, vol. 3, 211.
66. Boris Khazanov, *Podvig odnogo zavoda* (Moscow: Voenizdat, 1990), 244.
67. *Mordoviia*, 242; Boiman, *Yalde ha-korpus ha-sheni*, 214.
68. Ioanna Ol'chak-Roniker, *V sadu pamiati* (Moscow: NLO, 2006), 255–256.
69. Goldin, "Zakonchilos' detstvo," vol. 2, 40.
70. *Vo imia pobedy*, vol. 3, 177.
71. Ibid., 393.
72. Sinitsyn, *Vsenarodnaia pomoshch' frontu*, 287–288.
73. Postnikov, *V dalekikh garnizonakh*, 19–20.
74. Interview by Grigorii Koifman with Arkadii Dael', available at http://iremember.ru/memoirs/pulemetchiki/dael-arkadiy-isaakovich/.
75. *Kazakhstan v period*, 125; Boiman, *Yalde ha-korpus ha-sheni*, 209.
76. *Kuibyshevskaia oblast'*, 357.
77. TsGARK, f. P1137, op. 6, d. 1285, 38 (copy in USHMM Archives, RG 74.002M).
78. TsGAChR, f. P1263, op. 1, d. 66, 155 (copy in USHMM Archives, RG 22.020).
79. A. V. Plotnikova, "Prebyvanie leningradskogo internata 'Iunye patrioty' v Shadrinske, 1941–1945 gg.," in *Shadrinsk voennoi pory*, ed. Sergei Borisov (Shadrinsk, Russia: Pedinstitut, 1995), vol. 3, 125–140.
80. Iushkovskii, "Dnevnik," 192.
81. Goldin, "Zakonchilos' detstvo," vol. 2, 39.
82. *Istoriia Velikoi Otechestvennoi voiny*, vol. 2, 557.
83. Elena Kononenko, "Ty ne sirota, malysh! (O blagorodnom pochine zhenshchin 'Krasnogo bogatyria')," *Pravda*, January 31, 1942, 3.
84. "My sberezhëm detei: Pochin rabotnits 'Krasnogo bogatyria' podkhvachen sovetskimi materiami (Obzor chitatel'skikh pisem)," *Pravda*, February 23, 1942, 3.
85. "Zabota o detiakh," *Pravda*, February 4, 1942, 1; "Zabota o detiakh, ostavshikhsia bez roditelei," *Izvestiia*, February 19, 1942, 3; "Blagorodnyi pochin sovetskikh patriotov," *Izvestiia*, March 14, 1942, 1; "Moskvichki usynovliaiut sirot," *Izvestiia*, May 29, 1942, 3; "Tatiana TESS, Laska rodiny," *Izvestiia*, October 18, 1942, 2; "Tatiana TESS, Konets odinochestva," *Izvestiia*, December 9, 1944, 3; R. Teplitskii, "Moia mama vernulas'," *Sovetskaia Sibir'*, February 5, 1942, 4.

86. "Kolkhozniki berut na vospitanie evakuirovannykh detei," *Pravda*, February 5, 1942, 2.
87. Dzhuraev, *Kommunisticheskaia partiia Uzbekistana*, 257.
88. For example, in Andizhan; see Pulatov, *Andizhanskaia partiinaia organizatsiia*, 15.
89. Dzhuraev, *Kommunisticheskaia partiia Uzbekistana*, 257.
90. Ivanova, "Zabota ob evakuirovannykh detiakh," 234.
91. Salakhutdinov, *Samarkandskaia partiinaia organizatsiia*, 45; Pulatov, *Iz istorii*, 15–17.
92. Isaak Rozenblium, "Bratskoe gostepreimstvo," GARF, f. P8114, op. 1, d. 124, 72–73 (copy in USHMM Archives, RG 22.028M); Klevan, "'Al Kurot ha-Yahudim," 123; Il'ia Khudaidatov, "Posol bukharskikh evreev v Moskve," *Bukharian Times*, November 3, 2016, 21; Pulatov, *Iz istorii*, 16–18.
93. Levertov, *The Man*, 95–122.
94. Klevan, "'Al Kurot ha-Yahudim," 11.
95. Asia Novitskaia, "Novaia sem'ia," *Vzrosloe detstvo voiny: Sbornik vospominanii*, ed. Mikhail Kipnis (Ashdod, Israel: Keitar, 2013), vol. 1, 112–113.
96. Fabrikant, *Nam dorogi eti*, 152.
97. *Kazakhstan v pervyi god*, 30. Telling this touching story, the editor didn't name Siderman's ethnicity, as they did in other examples of adoption.
98. *Voices of Resilience*, 315–316.
99. TsGAChR, f. P835, op. 1, d. 354, 40, 286, 303 (copy in USHMM Archives, RG 22.020).
100. Klevan, "'Al Kurot ha-Yahudim," 11.
101. *Kuibyshevskaia oblast'*, 358–359.
102. *Kirgiziia*, 313–315.
103. Kerimbaev, *Sovetskii Kirgizstan*, 60.
104. *Kazakhstan v pervyi god*, 30–31.
105. *Kul'turnaia zhizn' v SSSR (Khronika): 1941–1950 gg.*, ed. Maksim Kim and others (Moscow: Nauka, 1977), 41.
106. Roza Bazarova, *Sovetskii Turkmenistan—frontu* (Ashkhabad, USSR: Ilym, 1978), 230; Annakurbanov, *Kommunisticheskaia partiia Turkmenistana*, 51–52.
107. "Tatiana TESS, Laska rodiny," *Izvestiia*, October 18, 1942, 2.
108. *Partiinoe rukovodstvo evakuatsiei*, 46; TsGAChR, f. P221, op. 1, d. 2537, 214 (copy in USHMM Archives, RG 22.020).
109. *Partiinoe rukovodstvo evakuatsiei*, 54.
110. *Vo imia pobedy*, vol. 3, 281, 321–322.
111. Ibid., 288.
112. USC Shoah Foundation, Visual History Archive, interview with Edna Eizenstein, Winnipeg, MB, November 30, 1995, segments 68–71, Spielberg Archive.
113. Kamynska-Myron, "Mi-Pyiṭrkov," 188–193; YVA, O.3/5807, 12; ibid., O.3/12258, 18–25.
114. *Partiinoe rukovodstvo evakuatsiei*, 54.
115. *Vo imia pobedy*, vol. 3, 349–350.
116. *Oboronnaia promyshlennost'*, 546.

117. For example, in the orphanage no. 20, located in Bogdanovka (Kuibyshev region), half of the twenty evacuated children were from Minsk. Of these ten children, seven were Jews. TsGAChR, f. P221, op. 1, d. 2352, 109 (copy in USHMM Archives, RG 22.020).

118. Ibid., d. 2209, 90, 93–99; ibid., d. 2304, 87–100.

119. *Mordoviia*, 210–211. According to official information, a total of 14,000 children from 110 orphanages, 25 kindergartens, 28 pioneer camps, 3 special schools, and 3 children's sanatoriums were sent from Belorussia to the east. *Partiinoe rukovodstvo evakuatsiei*, 15.

120. TsGAChR, f. P221, op. 1, d. 2304, 87–88 (copy in USHMM Archives, RG 22.020).

121. This is evidenced by the treatment of many parents: ibid., 22a, 23a, 26a, 27, 30a, 31a, 32a, 46a, 47–47a, 54a; ibid., d. 2272, 114–115.

122. Ibid., f. P203, op. 19, d. 71, 303; testimony of Ekaterina Rapoport from March 30, 2003, ACC, f. 82447202.

123. TsGAChR, f. P203, op. 18, d. 219, 353 (copy in USHMM Archives, RG 22.020).

124. Ibid., f. P1041, op. 1, d. 511, 1.

125. Calculated from ibid., f. P1263, op. 1, d. 39, 9.

126. Ibid., 72.

127. Ivanova, "Zabota ob evakuirovannykh detiakh," 235–236.

128. Dunaevskii, *Be-ḥoshekh 'efshar rak laḥlom*, 83.

129. Ibid., 86, 98; *Widziałem Anioła Śmierci*, 332.

130. Vaksman and Vaksman, "Vospominaniia brat'ev Vaksman," 127–128.

131. Dunaevskii, *Be-ḥoshekh 'efshar rak laḥlom*, 86.

132. USC Shoah Foundation, Visual History Archive, interview with Lev Levin, Haifa, Israel, May 16, 1996, part 2, segment 33–34, Spielberg Archive.

133. Grynberg, *Children of Zion*, 150.

134. YVA, O.3/9521, 31. *Widziałem Anioła Śmierci*, 66, 71, 216, 222, 233, 283, 286, 376, 440; Grynberg, *Children of Zion*, 152–159; *War through Children's Eyes*, 237.

135. YVA, O.3/1850, 6.

136. *Widziałem Anioła Śmierci*, 66, 175, 213.

137. YVA, O.3/12368, 10; ibid., O.3/8303, 31–33; *War through Children's Eyes*, 237.

138. YVA, O.3/9521, 34.

139. YVA, O.3/12287, 8; Grynberg, *Children of Zion*, 152–159.

140. *Widziałem Anioła Śmierci*, 219, 258, 325.

141. Dunaevskii, *Be-ḥoshekh 'efshar rak laḥlom*, 74–76, 124.

142. Vaksman and Vaksman, "Vospominaniia brat'ev Vaksman," 127–129.

Chapter 6. Culture Clashes

1. USC Shoah Foundation, Visual History Archive, interview with Rachel Glickman, Chicago, June 6, 1997, segment 137, Spielberg Archive.

2. Gabel, *Behind the Ice Curtain*, 244–245.

3. Ermolinskii, *O vremeni*, 289.

4. Ibid., 308–309.

5. See, for example, decree of the State Defense Committee of October 13, 1943, on the postponement of the conscription of men born in 1922–1925, who work in industry and agriculture. With reference to RGASPI, f. 644, op. 1, d. 163, 6, see http://www.soldat.ru.

6. Biriukov, "Dnevnikovye zapisi," 218.

7. Vasenëva, "Priëm i ustroistvo," 47.

8. GARF, f. A259, op. 40, d. 3096, 69 (copy in YVA, JM/24678).

9. Potëmkina, "Evakonaselenie: Opyt vyzhivaniia," 94.

10. Konstantin, *A Red Boyhood*, 121.

11. To avoid punishment for this, David Azrieli had to flee the kolkhoz. Azrieli, *Na shag vperedi*, 96–98.

12. Konstantin, *A Red Boyhood*, 123.

13. Potëmkina, "Evakonaselenie: Opyt vyzhivaniia," 94.

14. TsGAChR, f. P1263, op. 1, d. 46, 146a (copy in USHMM Archives, RG 22.020).

15. Manley, *To the Tashkent Station*, 227–9.

16. Potëmkina, "Evakonaselenie: Opyt vyzhivaniia," 89.

17. GARF, f. A259, op. 40, d. 3529, 212 (copy in YVA, JM/24678).

18. Ibid., d. 3518, 48a.

19. Ibid., d. 3529, 211.

20. Ibid., 208.

21. Interview by Grigorii Koifman with Mikhail Mishnaev, available at http://iremember.ru/memoirs/svyazisti/mishnaev-mikhail-khaimovich/.

22. Potëmkina, *Evakuatsiia*, 150.

23. GARF, f. A259, op. 40, d. 3527, 113–115 (copy in YVA, JM/24678).

24. TsGAChR, f. P1263, op. 1, d. 46, 73a (copy in USHMM Archives, RG 22.020).

25. Ibid., d. 51, 187.

26. Ibid., d. 46, 178a.

27. Ibid., 93.

28. Ibid., 115a., 128a.

29. Ibid., d. 46, 162a.

30. Ibid., d. 51, 80a.

31. Ibid., 213a.

32. USC Shoah Foundation, Visual History Archive, interview with Liudmila Gavrilova, Kiev, Ukraine, February 16, 1998, segment 46, Spielberg Archive.

33. TsGAChR, f. P1263, op. 1, d. 36, 18–18a (copy in USHMM Archives, RG 22.020).

34. Ibid., 80.

35. TsGARK, f. P1137, op. 6, d. 1278a, 20 (copy in USHMM Archives, RG 74.002M).

36. Ibid.

37. Konstantin, *A Red Boyhood*, 117.

38. TsGAChR, f. P203, op. 11, d. 66, 88 (copy in USHMM Archives, RG 22.020); ibid., op. 18, d. 218a, 25a; ibid., f. P1263, op. 1, d. 36, 25a.

39. Ivanova, "Sed'maia tetrad'," 212.

40. Chukovskaia, *Zapiski ob Anne Akhmatovoi*, vol. 1, 256.

41. GARF, f. A259, op. 40, d. 3520, 32 (copy in YVA, JM/24678).

42. Anatolii Tiktiner, *Vospominaniia: Mysli i fakty* (2005), available at http://tiktiner.narod.ru/vosp_tiktiner_titul.html.

43. Dunaevskii, *Be-ḥoshekh 'efshar rak laḥlom*, 91–92.
44. Grosman, *Ba-arets ha-agadit*, vol. 2, 397.
45. Levertov, *The Man Who Mocked the KGB*, 95–122; Dunaevskii, *Be-ḥoshekh 'efshar rak laḥlom*, 119–120; *Widziałem Anioła Śmierci*, 244, 373, 382.
46. Dmitrii Shevelëv, "Pis'ma S. Ia. Borovogo V. I. Pichete v 1939–1946 gg.," *Tsaytshrift* 8 (2013): 206.
47. GARF, f. A259, op. 40, d. 3527, 114 (copy in YVA, JM/24678).
48. Ibid., d. 3518, 48a.
49. Ibid., d. 3527, 114.
50. The evacuation inspector A. Nikitina's report on Shumerlia district, TsGAChR, f. P1263, op. 1, d. 51, 67a (copy in USHMM Archives, RG 22.020).
51. GARF, f. A259, op. 40, d. 3518, 122 (copy in YVA, JM/24678).
52. Zhirnov, "Nas obmanom vyvezli," 54–55.
53. GARF, f. A259, op. 40, d. 3518, 134–135 (copy in YVA, JM/24678).
54. Ibid., d. 3527, 32.
55. Ibid., d. 3096, 69.
56. Fedotov, *Evakuirovannoe naselenie*, 74.
57. GARF, f. A259, op. 40, d. 3518, 35–36 (copy in YVA, JM/24678), 49; ibid., O.3/3096, 57, 59.
58. Krutova, *Evrei na zemle*, 135.
59. GARF, f. A259, op. 40, d. 3518, 126 (copy in YVA, JM/24678).
60. Ibid., d. 3527, 99.
61. Ibid., d. 3096, 68.
62. Fedotov, *Evakuirovannoe naselenie*, 74.
63. TsGAChR, f. P203, op. 18, d. 218a, 31a–37 (copy in USHMM Archives, RG 22.020).
64. Report of evacuation inspector A. Nikitina (no later than May 5, 1942), ibid., f. P1263, op. 1, d. 51, 78–79.
65. Ibid., d. 46, 154.
66. Ibid., d. 36, 14.
67. Ibid., f. P203, op. 19, d. 71, 256–262.
68. Ibid., op. 18, d. 218a, 126.
69. The evacuation inspector A. Nikitina's report on the Shumerlia district, ibid., f. P1263, op. 1, d. 51, 67.
70. Ibid., 225.
71. Ibid., f. P203, op. 11, d. 66, 35.
72. GARF, f. A259, op. 40, d. 3529, 209 (copy in YVA, JM/24678).
73. Ibid.
74. Ibid.
75. *War through Children's Eyes*, 63.
76. "W czterdziestym," 109.
77. Makabi-Yoresh, *Kokhav lo ikabeah*, 110.
78. RGAE, f. 1562, op. 336, d. 257, 16. According to the same census, in Leningrad and in Moscow only 18.5 percent and 20.5 percent Jews, respectively, identified Yiddish as their mother tongue (Altshuler, *Soviet Jewry*, 93). However, it is probable that, because

they were trying to show off during the census how internationalist and enlightened they were, the actual percentage of Jews who used Yiddish to communicate was higher.

79. Aleksandr Shakhmeister, "Sakharok vperedvizhku i vprigliadku," in *Vzrosloe detstvo voiny: Sbornik vospominanii*, ed. Mikhail Kipnis (Ashdod, Israel: Keitar, 2013), vol. 2, 126–127.

80. Hanna Davidson Pankowsky, *East of the Storm: Outrunning the Holocaust in Russia* (Lubbock: Texas Tech University Press, 1999), 63–64.

81. On how this view was widespread in Russian settlements in Turkmenistan, where the population was awaiting the arrival of the German army to liberate them from the Bolsheviks, see YVA, O.3/4197, 26–27.

82. Joon Seo Song, "The Legacy of World War II on the Stalinist Home Front: Magnitogorsk 1941–1953" (PhD diss., Michigan State University, 2007), 10–12.

83. Shkurko, "Demograficheskie," 167–169.

84. TsGAChR, f. P1263, op. 1, d. 51, 128–128a (copy in USHMM Archives, RG 22.020).

85. Ibid., 115a–116.

86. Ibid., 128a.

87. Ibid., f. P203, op. 18, d. 218a, 126a.

88. Interview by Grigorii Koifman with Iakov Karasin, available at http://iremember.ru/memoirs/pekhotintsi/karasin-yakov-tsalelovich/.

89. TsGAChR, f. P1263, op. 1, d. 51, 225a–226 (copy in USHMM Archives, RG 22.020).

90. Ibid., 213a.

91. Potëmkina, *Evakuatsiia*, 149–150.

92. Mikhail Khefets, "Ia togda ne ponimal vsei tiazhesti situatsii," in *Evreiskie bezhentsy i evakuatsiia: Vospominaniia o voennom detstve*, ed. Alla Nikitina, 132–134 (Jerusalem: n.p., 2009).

93. Manley, *To the Tashkent Station*, 233.

94. Letter from Volf Gutman, November 20, 2015, author's personal archive.

95. AJC Archives, interview by Rachel Erlich no. 8 with K. Red, Interviews with Polish and Jewish DPs in DP Camps on Their Observations of Jewish Life in Soviet Russia, 9–10.

96. "W czterdziestym," 210.

97. Fedotov, *Evakuirovannoe naselenie*, 76.

98. Vladimir Barsukov, *Chto ia pomniu* (2005), available at http://www.anr.su/literatura/barsukov/30.html.

99. GARF, f. A259, op. 40, d. 3527, 32 (copy in YVA, JM/24678).

100. Ibid., d. 3518, 37.

101. Vaksman and Vaksman, "Vospominaniia brat'ev Vaksman," 126–129.

102. Goldin, "Zakonchilos' detstvo," vol. 2, 38–39.

103. *Gosudarstvennyi antisemitizm*, 73.

104. Vaksman and Vaksman, "Vospominaniia brat'ev Vaksman," 127–129.

105. Timofeev, *Dnevnik voennykh let*, part 2, 141.

106. Interview by Grigorii Koifman with Elia Gekhtman, available at http://iremember.ru/memoirs/pekhotintsi/gekhtman-elya-gershevich/.

107. Letter from Maria Rubinchik, April 12, 2001, 18, author's personal archive.

108. Miller, "Iz perezhitogo."

109. Rusakova, *Vospominaniia ob ottse*, 205–206.

110. GARF, f. A259, op. 40, d. 3518, 123 (copy in YVA, JM/24678). As seen in the reports, Shklovskii took negative relations with refugees, as well as antisemitism, to heart. He tried to improve the situation as best he could, ignoring possible accusations and preconceptions.

111. Ibid., 123, 129.

112. Odarka Bernadskaia, "Papa vernulsia," in *Vzrosloe detstvo voiny: Sbornik vospominanii*, ed. Mikhail Kipnis (Ashdod, Israel: Keitar, 2013), vol. 2, 28–29.

113. Biriukov, "Dnevnikovye zapisi," 219. The same collection includes a few memoirs of non-Jews, who recount how they picked frozen potatoes during the war from the kolkhoz located in Shadrinsk: *Shadrinsk voennoi pory*, ed. Sergei Borisov (Shadrinsk, Russia: Pedinstitut, 1995), vol. 2, 12–13; vol. 3, 43, 176.

114. Pëtr Poluian, *Moia voina: Vospominanija* (Irkutsk, Russia: Oblastnaia tipografiia no. 1, 1998), available at http://militera.lib.ru/memo/russian/poluyan_pm/03.html.

115. Miller, "Iz perezhitogo."

116. Timofeev, *Dnevnik voennykh let*, part 1, 157.

117. With reference to Central Archive of Federal Security Service of the USSR, see *Istoriia v dokumentakh*.

118. YVA, O.3/10889, 64; Rusakova, *Vospominaniia ob ottse*, 213; Meletinskii, *Izbrannye stat'i*, 501, 510; Grantserska-Kadari, *Ha-Meah ha-esrim sheli*, 279.

119. *Istoriia sotsialisticheskogo Tashkenta: 1941–1965*, ed. Rakhima Aminova (Tashkent, USSR: Fan, 1966), vol. 2, 80; Beniaminov, *Bukharskie evrei* (New York: n.p., 1983), 96.

120. AJC Archives, interview by Rachel Erlich no. 13 with S. Rotshtein, Interviews with Polish and Jewish DPs in DP Camps on Their Observations of Jewish Life in Soviet Russia, 5; Shvarts, *Evrei v Sovetskom Soiuze*, 157–158. For specific examples of this in Kirghizstan, Uzbekistan, and Turkmenistan, see YVA, O.3/11786, 12–13, 15; ibid., d. 10496, 16–17; Bar, *Lelot Ṭashkenṭ*, 143; Begin, *Be-lelot levanim*, 316; Levin, "Antisemitism," 197–201; Gitlin, *Natsional'nye men'shinstva*, 589–590.

121. Kiriak Bendrikov, *Ocherki po istorii narodnogo obrazovaniia v Turkestane (1865–1924)* (Moscow: Akademiia pedagogicheskikh nauk RSFSR, 1960), 442.

122. Grynberg, *Children of Zion*, 129; Efron, *Dnevniki*, vol. 2, 163, 194.

123. Miller, "Iz perezhitogo."

124. Interview by Lev Aizenshtat with Rachel Rivkina, Saint Petersburg, Russia, August 2004, available at: https://www.centropa.org/biography/rachel-rivkina.

125. YVA, M.37/371, 9–11.

126. *Gosudarstvennyi antisemitizm*, 34.

127. Kahan, *Unter di sovietishe himlen*, 441–443.

128. Vladimir Vaisberg, *Strakh* (2002), available at http://rjews.net/berkovich.

129. Petrov, *Escape from the Future*, 303–304.

130. With reference to State Archive of East Kazakhstan region, see Nina Krutova, *Evrei na zemle*, 80.

131. Ibid., 81.

132. Interview by Aleksei Ivashin with Lev Mistetskii, available at http://iremember.ru/memoirs/svyazisti/mistetskiy-lev-fridelevich/.

133. *Gosudarstvennyi antisemitizm*, 32–33. Manley misunderstood this source and inaccurately wrote that the three Jews were killed instead of beaten. Manley, *To the Tashkent Station*, 231.

134. With reference to the Central Archive of Federal Security Service, see *Istoriia v dokumentakh*.

135. Testimony of her daughter Idaliia Sidelnikova, April 28, 1998, author's personal archive.

136. Begin, *Be-lelot levanim*, 316.

137. Grosman, *Ba-arets ha-agadit*, vol. 2, 326.

138. AJC Archives, interview by Rachel Erlich no. 1 with R., Interviews with Polish and Jewish DPs in DP Camps on Their Observations of Jewish Life in Soviet Russia, 6; ibid., interview by Rachel Erlich no. 6 with J. S., 3.

139. Meletinskii, *Izbrannye stat'i*, 512.

140. Levin, "Antisemitism," 197.

141. Ibid., 199.

142. USC Shoah Foundation, Visual History Archive, interview with Alice Vinik, Indianapolis, May 4, 1995, segment 46, Spielberg Archive.

143. USC Shoah Foundation, Visual History Archive, interview with Stefa Bloch, Hallandale Beach, Fl, August 1, 1996, segments 76, 86, 96, 104, Spielberg Archive.

144. Efron, *Dnevniki*, vol. 2, 136.

145. Tatiana Zhdanko and Iurii Rapoport, "Gody voiny v zhizni S. P. Tolstova," *Etnograficheskoe obozrenie* 2 (1995): 72.

146. Chukovskaia, *Zapiski ob Anne Akhmatovoi*, vol. 1, 255.

147. Dovzhenko, *Dnevnikovye zapisi*, 87.

148. Ibid., 63.

149. Shneer, *Plen*, vol. 2, 154–162.

150. Edele, "More Than Just Stalinists," 167.

151. Efron, *Dnevniki*, vol. 2, 140.

152. Anatolii Tiktiner, *Vospominaniia: Mysli i fakty* (2005), available at http://tiktiner.narod.ru/vosp_tiktiner_titul.html.

153. Edele, *Soviet Veterans*, 92–95.

154. AJC Archives, interview by Rachel Erlich no. 5 with L. L., Interviews with Polish and Jewish DPs inDP Camps on Their Observations of Jewish Life in Soviet Russia, 5.

155. YVA, O.3/6085, 3.

156. Robert Frimtzis, *From Tajikistan to the Moon: A Story of Tragedy, Survival and Triumph of the Human Spirit* (Rancho Santa Fe, CA: Ecliptic Publishing, 2008), 56–58, 73.

157. YVA, O.3/6498, 5.

158. AJC Archives, interview by Rachel Erlich no. 6 with J. S., Interviews with Polish and Jewish DPs in *DP* Camps on Their Observations of Jewish Life in Soviet Russia, 3.

159. Testimony of Khaim Kats, January 27, 2009, author's personal archive.

160. YVA, O.3/8425, 11; O.3/9722, 6; Bilich, *What I Will Always Remember*; Boiman, *Yaldeha-korpus ha-sheni*, 152.

161. Bar, *Lelot Ṭashḳenṭ*, 37; Livshits, "Nadezhda umiraet poslednei," 59; Azrieli, *Na shag vperedi*, 96, 98–99; Bilich, *What I Will Always Remember*; Gitlin, *Natsional'nye*

men'shinstva, 561–562; Aharonson, *Beriḥah le-moledet*, 81–82, 86, 98, 104; YVA, O.3/10894, 24; ibid., d. 10864, 21–22; ibid., d. 10843, 22–24.

162. Boiman, *Yalde ha-korpus ha-sheni*, 155–157.

163. USC Shoah Foundation, Visual History Archive, interview with Alexander Masiewicki, Palm Beach, Fl, February 4, 1998, segment 151, Spielberg Archive.

164. Interview by Ella Levitskaya with Sophia Abidor, Uzhgorod, Ukraine, April 2003, available at: https://www.centropa.org/biography/sophia-abidor.

165. USC Shoah Foundation, Visual History Archive, interview with Michael Garber, New York, May 25, 1997, segment 77, Spielberg Archive.

166. Bruell, *Autumn in Springtime*, 88.

167. Borovoi, *Vospominaniia*, 263; Wenig, *From Nazi Inferno*, 198; Aharonson, *Beriḥah le-moledet*, 86–87.

168. YVA, O.3/11786, 13–15; ibid., d. 10814, 18; Grosman, *Ba-arets ha-agadit*, vol. 2, 348–349; Sasonkin, *Zikhronotai*, 238.

169. *Widziałem Anioła Śmierci*, 404.

170. Stronski, *Tashkent*, 122.

171. Wat, *My Century*, 336.

172. Krasnov-Levitin, *Ruk tvoih zhar*, 135.

173. Efron, *Dnevniki*, vol. 2, 137.

174. AJC Archives, interview by Rachel Erlich no. 5 with L. L., Interviews with Polish and Jewish DPs in *DP* Camps on Their Observations of Jewish Life in Soviet Russia, 4.

175. Timofeev, *Dnevnik voennykh let*, part 2, 128.

176. *Teoriia i praktika*, 435–441.

177. About this desertion, see *Organy Gosudarstvennoi bezopasnosti*, vol. 3, part 2, 395, 400–402.

178. *Teoriia i praktika*, 464–468; *Organy Gosudarstvennoi bezopasnosti*, vol. 3, part 2, 393, 395, 400–402; interview by Grigorii Koifman with Samuil Rozenberg, available at http://iremember.ru/memoirs/pekhotintsi/rozenberg-samuil-iosifovich/.

179. YVA, O.3/10894, 25; Gurkov, *Sefer ha-zikhronot*, 121; Sasonkin, *Zikhronotai*, 238; Zamir, *Sheliḥut ḥayai*, 77.

180. Grynberg, *Children of Zion*, 131.

181. Sasonkin, *Zikhronotai*, 238.

182. Gurkov, *Sefer ha-zikhronot*, 121.

183. Borovoi, *Vospominaniia*, 263–264.

184. Kostyrchenko, *Tainaia politika Stalina*, 431.

185. USC Shoah Foundation, Visual History Archive, interview with Mania Beizer, Caulfield South, Australia, October 28, 1996, segment 48–59, Spielberg Archive.

186. *Widziałem Anioła Śmierci*, 244.

187. Ibid., 318.

188. Kostyrchenko, *Tainaia politika Stalina*, 243.

189. Calculated from *Gosudarstvennyi antisemitizm*, 34.

190. YVA, O.3/6498, 5.

191. Zhanguttin, "Evakuatsiia sovetskogo naseleniia."

192. Interview with Sara Garber (Kiselëva), March 5, 2006, author's personal archive.

193. Stronski, *Tashkent*, 123.
194. Ivanov, *Dnevnik*, 104.
195. Zylbering, "A Survivor Remembers," 45.
196. AJC Archives, interview by Rachel Erlich no. 10 with E. G., Interviews with Polish and Jewish DPs in DP Camps on Their Observations of Jewish Life in Soviet Russia, 6–7.
197. AJC Archives, interview by Rachel Erlich no. 15 with Ent., Interviews with Polish and Jewish DPs in DP Camps on Their Observations of Jewish Life in Soviet Russia, 3.
198. Letter from Shlomo Leizer, May 27, 2007, author's personal archive.
199. Petrov, *Escape from the Future*, 303.
200. Grosman, *Ba-arets ha-agadit*, vol. 2, 371–372; Bar, *Lelot Ṭashḳenṭ*, 143–144; YVA, O.3/10814, 18; ibid., d. 10894, 24; ibid., d. 11786, 12.
201. Ivanov, *Dnevnik*, 117. Mikhail Golodny (whose real name was Epshtein) was a Soviet poet.
202. Kostyrchenko, *Tainaia politika Stalina*, 251.
203. Petrov, *Escape from the Future*, 303–304.
204. Ehrenburg, *Sobranie sochinenii*, vol. 9, 377.
205. *Gosudarstvennyi antisemitizm*, 34. However, Ortenberg's cautiousness did not prevent him falling into disfavor several months later, when he was dismissed as part of the campaign that was unfolding in the USSR to "cleanse" administrative and cultural-educational structures from Jews. Kostyrchenko, *Tainaia politika Stalina*, 244. See also Kena Vidre, "Kakaia ona byla Frida Vigdorova," *Zvezda* 5 (2000): 112–113.
206. Klevan, "'Al Kurot ha-Yahudim," 124; *Organy Gosudarstvennoi bezopasnosti*, vol. 4, part 1, 196–197, 247.
207. With reference to GARF, f. 9401, op. 2, d. 65, 168–169, see *Istoriia v dokumentakh*.
208. Grosman, *Ba-arets ha-agadit*, vol. 2, 327.
209. Kaganovich, "Ha-rekʻa ha-midini veha-sotsio-'ekonomi," 40–42.
210. Levin, "Antisemitism," 195.
211. Levin, "Miklat ara'i," 111.
212. Kamynska-Myron, "Mi-Pyiṭrkov," 191.
213. Honig, *From Poland to Russia*, 130–131.
214. *Sovetskaia povsednevnost' i massovoe soznanie, 1939–1945 gg.*, comp. A. Livshin and I. Orlov (Moscow: Rosspen, 2003), 435.
215. Pirimkulov, "Evrei," 131; *Iz istorii poliakov v Kazakhstane*, 180–181; M'eyr Kozhin, "Be'ayot be-heker ḳorotehem shel Pelitim Yehudim be-Berit ha-Mo'atsot be-yeme Milḥemet ha-'olam ha-sheniyah," *Yad Vashem* 3 (1959): 118; Litvak, *Peliṭim Yehudim*, 148; Gutman, "Yehudim be-tsava Anders," 176–212.
216. Klevan, *Le-toldot ha-Yehudim*, 118.
217. Letter from Shlomo Leizer, May 27, 2007, author's personal archive.
218. Pirimkulov, "Evrei," 131.
219. Livshits, "Nadezhda umiraet poslednei," 59.
220. Toby Klodawski Flam, *Toby: Her Journey from Lodz to Samarkand* (Toronto: Childe Thursday, 1989), 56.
221. Kamynska-Myron, "Mi-Pyiṭrkov," 187–193.
222. Gabel, *Behind the Ice Curtain*, 438.

223. USC Shoah Foundation, Visual History Archive, interview with Doba Belozovskaia, Kiev, December 12, 1996, segment 178, Spielberg Archive.

224. Interview by Nathalia Fomina with Liana Degtiar, Chişinău, Moldova, 2004, available at: https://www.centropa.org/biography/liana-degtiar.

225. Iushkovskii, "Dnevnik," 182–183.

226. Testimony of Khaim Kats, January 27, 2009, author's personal archive.

227. USC Shoah Foundation, Visual History Archive, interview with Roza Bazylianskaia (Amromina), Vitebsk, Belarus, May 2, 1998, segment 67, Spielberg Archive.

228. YVA, O.3/10864, 19, 21.

229. Interview by Artëm Drabkin with Polina Rivkina, available at http://iremember.ru/memoirs/letno-tekh-sostav/rivkina-polina-filippovna/.

230. Interview by Grigorii Koifman with Grigorii Refas, available at http://iremember.ru/memoirs/pekhotintsi/refas-grigoriy-irmovich/.

231. USC Shoah Foundation, Visual History Archive, interview with Anna Solov'eva, Moscow, November 1, 1996, segment 55, Spielberg Archive; ibid., interview with Anna Tolochinskaia, Saint Petersburg, Russia, January 30, 1997, segment 72; interview with Gutia Turk, Smolensk, Russia, November 23, 1996, segment 46; interview with Nina Notkina, Moscow, October 13, 1996, segments 66–70.

232. Ibid., interview with Anna Tolochinskaia, Saint Petersburg, Russia, January 30, 1997, segments 74–77.

233. Ibid., interview with Nina Notkina, Moscow, October 13, 1996, segments 66–70.

234. TsGAChR, f. P1263, op. 1, d. 51, 53 (copy in USHMM Archives, RG 22.020).

235. Maurice Halbwachs, *On Collective Memory* (Chicago: University of Chicago Press, 1992).

236. In addition to the above-mentioned sources about the spread of antisemitism in Leningrad and Moscow, see also Grosman, *Ba-arets ha-agadit*, vol. 2, 372; M. V. Andrienko and S. I. Linets, *Naselenie Stavropol'skogo kraia v gody Velikoi Otechestvennoi voiny: Otsenka povedencheskikh motivov* (Piatigorsk, Russia: Izdatel'stvo PGTU, 2006), 52–53.

237. Shkurko, "Demograficheskie," 169–170.

238. GARF, f. A259, op. 40, d. 3518, 36 (copy in YVA, JM/24678).

239. Stronski, *Tashkent*, 123.

240. Kaganovitch, *The Long Life*, 217, 221.

241. See, for example, reports on Moscow and on the Anders's Polish army in the USSR: Grigor'ev, "Moskva voennaia," 117–119; *Russkii arkhiv*, vol. 14 (3–1), 90–91, 102–103.

242. *TsK VKP(b) i natsional'nyi vopros*, 657.

243. GARF, f. A259, op. 40, d. 3527, 113 (copy YVA, JM/24678).

244. Krutova, *Evrei na zemle*, 142.

245. Kostyrchenko, *Tainaia politika Stalina*, 243; Isak Grinberg, *Evrei v Alma-Ate* (Almaty, Kazakhstan: Mitsva, 2005), 109.

246. Levin, "Antisemitism," 199–202.

247. AJC Archives, interview by Rachel Erlich no. 10 with E. G., Interviews with Polish and Jewish DPs in DP Camps on Their Observations of Jewish Life in Soviet Russia, 6–7.

248. Potëmkina, *Evakuatsiia*, 150.
249. TsDAGOU, f. 1, op. 23, d. 4138, 1–7 (copy in YVA, M. 37/210).
250. TsGAChR, f. P821, op. 4, d. 97, 133 (copy in USHMM Archives, RG 22.020).
251. With reference to the Archive of the Council of Ministers of the Union of Belorussian SSR, see Olekhnovich, "Ot Pripiati—za Volgu," 90.
252. TsGAChR, f. P835, op. 1, d. 352, 13 (copy in USHMM Archives, RG 22.020).
253. Ibid.
254. Ibid., f. P203, op. 18, d. 218a, 125–127.
255. Ibid., op. 11, d. 16, 190.
256. Barkan, "Vospominaniia," 24.
257. Liuksemburg, *Sozveszdie Mordekhaia*, 139–142.
258. Aizik Sheinman, "Evreiskaia religioznaia obshchina v gorode Frunze," GARF, f. P8114, op. 1, d. 82, 530–531 (copy in USHMM Archives, RG 220028M).
259. Aharon Elyahu Gershuny, *Ḳidush ha-Shem: Parashiyot mesirut nefesh etsel Yehudim be-Berit ha-Mo'atsot* (Jerusalem: Moshabim, 1995), 14.
260. Sasonkin, *Zikhronotai*, 246, 220; *Toldot Chabad*, 336; Gurkov, *Sefer ha-zikhronot*, 122–123; Levin, *Zikhronotai*, 106–107.
261. Sasonkin, *Zikhronotai*, 251; *Toldot Chabad*, 337; Gurkov, *Sefer ha-zikhronot*, 124.
262. Shakhno Epshtein, "Evrei v Uzbekistane," GARF, f. P8114, op. 1, d. 88, 435 (copy in USHMM Archives, RG 22.028M); Gurkov, *Sefer ha-zkhronot*, 124.
263. AJC Archives, interview by Rachel Erlich no. 4 with Traitman, Interviews with Polish and Jewish DPs in DP Camps on Their Observations of Jewish Life in Soviet Russia, 3; Kahan, *Unter di sovietishe himlen*, 326–328.
264. Levin, *Zikhronotai*, 111–113.
265. Osipova, *Khasidy*, 126–131.
266. Sasonkin, *Zikhronotai*, 251; Gershuny, *Yehudim ve-Yahadut*, 178.
267. Kaganovitch, "Stalin's Great Power Politics," 79.
268. "Thousands of Jews Celebrate Passover in the Uzbekistan for First Time," *Chicago Sentinel*, April 16, 1942, 24.
269. Shakhno Epshtein, "Sovetskii patriotizm bukharskikh evreev," GARF, f. P8114, op. 1, d. 87, 308 (copy in USHMM Archives, RG 220028M).
270. I. Okrutnyi, "Balutskie tkachi v Samarkande," GARF, f. P8114, op. 1, d. 134, 85 (copy in USHMM Archives, RG 22.028M); YVA, O.3/8122, 25; ibid., O.3/10889, 65; Levin, *Zikhronotai*, 107.
271. Pirimkulov, "Evrei," 133.
272. YVA, O.3/6498, 5.
273. See specific examples of this in Matayeva (Abramchaeva), *Od tizrah ha-shemesh*, 8; Aharonson, *Beriḥah le-moledet*, 85–86.
274. AJC Archives, interview by Rachel Erlich no. 10 with E. G., Interviews Polish and Jewish DPs in DP Camps on Their Observations of Jewish Life in Soviet Russia, 8.
275. Feygenblum, "Be-mokorot volfram be-'Uzbekistan," 119–120.
276. Klevan, *Le-toldot ha-Yehudim*, 103; Davison-Rosenblatt, *Keine Zeit für Abschied*, 50–51. These same practices seeped into liberated territories of Ukraine and Belorussia. Even the intelligentsia was involved in this process. See documents in *Kommunisticheskaia vlast'*, 165.
277. Litvak, *Peliṭim Yehudim*, 199.

278. Ro'i, "The Reconstruction," 187.
279. Yehezk'el Keitelman, "Pedyon ha-met," *Amot* 4 (1963): 106–109.
280. Calculated from Altshuler, *Yahadut ba-makhbesh ha-sovyeti*, 399–487. On the growth of national self-awareness in these years, see Ro'i, "The Reconstruction," 187.
281. AJC Archives, interview by Rachel Erlich no. 15 with Ent., Interviews with Polish and Jewish DPs in DP Camps on Their Observations of Jewish Life in Soviet Russia, 3.
282. Altshuler, *Yahadut ba-makhbesh ha-sovyeti*, 477. It appears that the opening of this synagogue was mentioned in a report from that same year by Ibadov, Commissioner of the Council for the Affairs of Religious Cults. YVA, JM/11268, 29.
283. Ibid., 83.
284. Ibid., 122, 128, 130.
285. Vekselman, "The Struggle," 346–360.
286. Grosman, *Baarets ha-agadit*, vol. 2, 412.
287. Ibid., 387–388.
288. USC Shoah Foundation, Visual History Archive, interview with Zofia Sznicer, Sidney, October 26, 1995, segment 55, Spielberg Archive; YVA, O.3/3656, 6–7; ibid., O.3/7866, 23–24; ibid., O.3/11688, 27–28; Levin, "Miklat ara'i," 110; Litvak, *Peliṭim Yehudim*, 201–202, 242–243; Barkan, "Vospominaniia," 21–22; Natalie Belsky, "Fraught Friendships: Polish and Soviet Jews on the Soviet Home Front during the Second World War," in *Shelter from the Holocaust: Rethinking Jewish Survival in the Soviet Union*, ed. Mark Edele, Sheila Fitzpatrick, and Atina Grossmann (Detroit: Wayne State University Press, 2017), 161–184; Betsalel Shif, "Vospominaniia," in *Vosemnadtsat'* (Jerusalem: Shamir, 1989), 262–263; *Halutsim nodedym be-drakhim*, ed. Tsvyka Dror (Lohame hagyt'oot, Israel: Beyt lohamey hagyt'oot, 1989), 158; Gabel, *Behind the Ice Curtain*, 420–427, 438; Max Vekselman, "The Lubavich Hasidim in Uzbekistan 1918–1995," *Shvut* 8, no. 24 (1999): 136; Davidson-Rosenblatt, *Keine Zeit fur Abschied*, 48, 57; Pomerantz and Winik, *Run East*, 79–81; Honig, *From Poland to Russia*, 140–143, 197.
289. Grosman, *Ba-arets ha-agadit*, vol. 2, 397.
290. AJC Archives, interview by Rachel Erlich no. 14 with H., Interviews with Polish and Jewish DPs in DP Camps on Their Observations of Jewish Life in Soviet Russia, 13.
291. For example, see AJC Archives, interview by Rachel Erlich no. 10 with E. G., Interviews with Polish and Jewish DPs in DP Camps on Their Observations of Jewish Life in Soviet Russia, 4; Gabel, *Behind the Ice Curtain*, 420–424; USC Shoah Foundation, Visual History Archive, interview with Zofia Sznicer, Sidney, October 26, 1995, segment 56, Spielberg Archive; ibid., interview with Isaac Geiman, New York, January 5, 1998, segments 80–81, 86; USC Shoah Foundation, Visual History Archive, interview with Sabina Austendig, New York, July 6, 1995, segment 31.
292. Vladimir Vaisberg, *Strakh* (2002), available at http://rjews.net/berkovich.
293. Gershuny, *Yehudim ve-Yahadut*, 266.
294. Sasonkin, *Zikhronotai*, 242–243; David Abraham Mendelboim, *Teḥela Le-David* (Jerusalem: Makhon 'Emry David, 1992), 238–239.
295. Gurkov, *Sefer ha-zkihronot*, 123.
296. Sasonkin, *Zikhronotai*, 245–246; Osipova, *Khasidy*, 129. Relatives of Rabbi Sasonkin lived in the house of Bukharan Jews in Samarkand. See Zamir, *Sheliḥut ḥayai*, 76–77.

297. Grosman, *Ba-arets ha-agadit*, vol. 2, 311; Klevan, *Le-toldot ha-Yehudim*, 103–104; Levin, "Miklat ara'i," 110; Sasonkin, *Zikhronotai*, 242–243; Mataeva (Abramchaeva), *Od tizrah ha-shemesh be-haloni*, 7–8.

298. YVA, O.3/11516, 18–22.

299. Barkan, "Vospominaniia," 23.

300. Levin, *Zikhronotai*, 112.

301. YVA, O.3/8425, 11–12.

302. Begin, *Be-lelot levanim*, 315–316.

303. Feygenblum, "Be-mokorot volfram be-'Uzbekistan," 124.

304. Dunaevskii, *Be-ḥoshekh 'efshar rak laḥlom*, 84.

305. USC Shoah Foundation, Visual History Archive, interview with Dorothy Abend, Tucson, AZ, November 4, 1995, segments 124–125, Spielberg Archive.

306. Il'ia Khudaidatov, "Posol bukharskikh evreev v Moskve," *Bukharian Times*, November 3, 2016, 21.

307. For some examples of assistance from Bukharan Jews, see: YVA, O.3/3104, 22; Feygenblum, "Be-mokorot volfram be-'Uzbekistan," 125–126; Davison-Rosenblatt, *Keine Zeit für Abschied*, 48, 57; Gitlin, *Natsional'nye men'shinstva*, 618–619.

308. Interview with David Lipkind, September 20, 1966, OHD/ICJ, collection 169, file 12.

309. Shakhno Epshtein, "Sovetskii patriotizm bukharskikh evreev," GARF, f. P8114, op. 1, d. 83, 308, 311–312, 320–322 (copy in USHMM Archives, RG 220028M).

310. See examples: Beniaminov, *Bukharskie evrei*, 97; Bekhor Barukh (Malaev), *Byt' chelovekom: Rav Eliahu ben Efraim (Abdurakhmanov)* (Jerusalem: n.p., 2001), 22–24; Iakhiia Ashurov and Khanan Shimonov, *Bukharsko-russko-evreiskii slovar': Lugati-Bukhori-Rusi-Ivrit* (Jerusalem: n.p., 1990), 6; Mataeva (Abramchaeva), *Od tizrah ha-shemesh be-haloni*, 7; interview with Ekiiahu Akbashev, July 21, 2005, author's personal archive.

311. YVA, O.3/10846, 8.

312. Ibid., d. 7285, 10; ibid., d. 8122, 24; ibid., d. 11786, 12; ibid., d. 10889, 63–65, 67; Cherpichnik, "Ba-aretz ha-zahav ha-lavan," 256; Mikhail Margolin, *Pamiat' serdtsa* (2003), available at http://www.sem40.ru/ourpeople/destiny/4392/.

313. Levertov, *The Man Who Mocked the KGB*, 95–122.

314. AJC Archives, interview by Rachel Erlich no. 10 with E. G., Interviews with Polish and Jewish DPs in DP Camps on Their Observations of Jewish Life in Soviet Russia, 6.

315. Grynberg, *Children of Zion*, 129.

316. About this crisis, see Kaganovich, "Ha-rek'a ha-midini veha-sotsio-'ekonomi," 35–38.

317. *Widziałem Anioła Śmierci*, 83.

318. Ibid., 174.

319. Interview with Berta Guliamov, March 20, 1986, OHD/ICJ, collection 199, file 46, film 4874.

320. Levin, "Miklat ara'i," 110.

321. Iu. Gert, "A ty poplach', poplach' . . .," *Vestnik*, July 23, 2003, no. 15 (326), available at http://www.vestnik.com/issues/2003/0723/koi/gert.htm.

322. Grosman, *Ba-arets ha-agadit*, vol. 2, 332, 378; Sasonkin, *Zikhronotai*, 243–244; *Toldot Chabad*, 223.

323. On how Polish documents became subjects of sale and purchase by the summer of 1942, reported by Barnaul committee of the Union of Polish Patriots, see *Sud'by: Vospominaniia, dnevniki, pis'ma, stikhi, materialy ekspeditsii, doklady, protokoly doprosov*, comp. N. I. Razgon and others, ed. V. A. Skubnevskii (Barnaul, Russia: Piket, 2001), 316.

324. *Widziałem Anioła Śmierci*, 174.

325. JDC Archives 1933–1944, folder 1056.

326. AJC Archives, interview by Rachel Erlich no. 10 with E. G., Interviews with Polish and Jewish DPs in DP Camps on Their Observations of Jewish Life in Soviet Russia, 7.

327. Grosman, *Ba-arets ha-agadit*, vol. 2, 326.

328. YVA, O.3/10889, 63–65, 67. In that interview, he also testified that the Bukharan Jews didn't help them.

329. YVA, O.3/6498, 5. It's possible, however, that the disallowance for Jewish refugees to visit this synagogue was the fulfillment of the authorities' conditions, which allowed Bukharan Jews to open it in 1943.

330. Cherpichnik, "Ba-aretz ha-zahav ha-lavan," 256.

331. Feygenblum, "Be-mokorot volfram be-'Uzbekistan," 119–120. Barukh Cherpichnik also writes that Bukharan Jews treated them with suspicion. Cherpichnik, "Baretz ha-zahav ha-lavan," 256.

332. Bar, *Lelot Ṭashkent*, 146. The wide range of terror among Bukharan Jews, caused by the repression, is evidenced by the fact that in Samarkand the majority of Jewish religious literature was either buried in the graveyard or even used to wrap products sold in the city market. Grosman, *Ba-arets ha-agadit*, vol. 2, 381.

333. AJC Archives, interview by Rachel Erlich no. 14 with H., Interviews with Polish and Jewish DPs in DP Camps on Their Observations of Jewish Life in Soviet Russia, 10.

Chapter 7. Statistics on Refugees and Their Migration

1. Interview by Nathalia Fomina with Esfir Dener, Chișinău, Moldova, 2004, available at: https://www.centropa.org/biography/esfir-dener.

2. Manley, *To the Tashkent Station*, 42–43.

3. Ibid., 155.

4. Kornilov, *Ural'skoe selo i voina*, 95.

5. See, for example, the data on the placement of evacuees in Surkhan-Dar'ia region (Uzbekistan), of February 23, 1942, GARF, f. A259, op. 40, d. 3532, 49 (copy in YVA, JM/24678). Another example, for the Altai territory, see Brul', *Nemtsy v Zapadnoi Sibiri*, vol. 2, 21, 27.

6. TsGARK, f. P1137, op. 6, d. 1279, 168 (copy in USHMM Archives, RG 74.002M).

7. For example, they were divided this way in the memorandum by the deputy head of the evacuation department at the Council of People's Commissars of Kazakhstan, M. Iakovlev, in January 1942. TsGARK, f. P1137, op. 6, d. 1289, 173 (copy in USHMM Archives, RG 74.002M).

8. GARF, f. A259, op. 40, d. 3092, 105 (copy in YVA, JM/24.678).

9. *Partiinoe rukovodstvo evakuatsiei*, 17.
10. Dubson, "Toward a Central Database," 104.
11. TsGAChR, f. P835, op. 1, d. 339, 41 (copy in USHMM Archives, RG 22.020).
12. *Organy Gosudarstvennoi bezopasnosti*, vol. 2, part 1, 559–560.
13. Fedotov, *Evakuirovannoe naselenie*, 70.
14. Kornilov, *Ural'skoe selo i voina*, 100; Potëmkina, *Evakuatsiia*, 128.
15. Potëmkina, *Evakuatsiia*, 128.
16. Calculated from TsGAChR, f. P820, op. 8, d. 247, 48–135 (copy in USHMM Archives, RG 22.020).
17. Ibid., 115–116.
18. Refusal for permission to travel there came to the most reasonable requests, such, for example, as enrollment in nursing courses arranged by the Latvian military division. See responses to the requests of Riva Vainer, Berta Grober, Eiga Cherniak, and others: ibid., f. P827, op. 1, d. 234, 194.
19. Ibid., f. P1263, op. 1, d. 61, 41–41a.
20. Ibid., 49.
21. Ibid., f. P835, op. 1, d. 352, 65.
22. YVA, M. 37/726, 2. On the spread of malaria in Central Asia during the war years, see Aharonson, *Beriḥah le-moledet*, 92.
23. Kaganovitch, *The Long Life*, 120.
24. Arkadii Perventsev, *Dnevniki 1941–1945* (Moscow: Veche, 2011), 160–161.
25. TsGAChR, f. P827, op. 1, d. 234, 109 (copy in USHMM Archives, RG 22.020).
26. USC Shoah Foundation, Visual History Archive, interview with Galina Stevenzat, Smolensk, Russia, November 13, 1997, segment 46, Spielberg Archive.
27. USC Shoah Foundation, Visual History Archive, interview with Anna Tolochinskaia, Saint Petersburg, Russia, January 30, 1997, segment 72, Spielberg Archive.
28. TsGAChR, f. P827, op. 1, d. 234, 11–12 (copy in USHMM Archives, RG 22.020).
29. Interview with Evgeniia Ioffe, May 1, 1994, OHD/ICJ, collection 126, file 217, film 4012a.
30. Semën Gol'dberg, *Semeinye istorii* (2012), available at http://berkovich-zametki.com/2012/Starina/Nomer4/SGoldberg1.php.
31. Ibid.
32. Liuksemburg, *Sozveszdie Mordekhaia*, 82–88.
33. GARF, f. A259, op. 40, d. 3014, 19, 23 (copy in YVA, JM/24678).
34. Ibid., d. 3030, 43.
35. Calculated from ibid., d. 3518, 131.
36. Ivanova, "Zabota ob evakuirovannykh detiakh," 233.
37. Interview by Grigorii Koifman with Emmanuil Karp, available at http://iremember.ru/memoirs/pekhotintsi/karp-emmanuil-lvovich/.
38. Stel'man, *Pamiat' i vremia*, 45.
39. Calculated from TsGAChR, f. P827, op. 1, d. 234, 1–197 (copy in USHMM Archives, RG 22.020).
40. Calculated from ibid., f. P1263, op. 1, d. 39, 37–37a.
41. Calculated from TsGAChR, f. P1243, op. 11, d. 23, 1–5 (copy in USHMM Archives, RG 22.020); ibid., d. 57, 1–39a; ibid., f. P1263, op. 1, d. 83, 90–91a.

42. Calculated from ibid., 86.
43. Calculated from ibid., 192.
44. Calculated from ibid., f. P821, op. 4, d. 103, 66; ibid., f. P835, op. 1, d. 352, 60a; ibid., f. P1263, op. 1, d. 39, 11, 37–37a, 42–42a, 69–69a.
45. Ibid.
46. Calculated from ibid., d. 83, 87a.
47. Calculated from ibid., 96–97; ibid., f. P820, op. 8, d. 249, 1–23.
48. Ibid., f. P821, op. 4, d. 103, 20.
49. Calculated from ibid., f. P1263, op. 1, d. 39, 12, 32–32a; 38–38a, 43–43a, 52–52a, 70–70a.
50. Calculated from GARF, f. A259, op. 40, d. 3517, 4–6 (copy in YVA, JM/24678).
51. Ibid., d. 3520, 66.
52. Calculated from Khudalov, *Severnaia Osetiia*, 56.
53. Calculated from Kerimbaev, *Sovetskii Kirgizstan*, 60.
54. For example, among the 850 families who found themselves in the Alatyr' districts of the Chuvash ASSR, 75.7 percent were evacuees from the Moscow region, 7.9 percent from east Belorussia, 3.7 percent from the Smolensk region, 3.3 percent from the Białystok region, 3 percent from Lithuanian SSR, 2.8 percent from Karelo-Finnish SSR, only 2.3 percent from Ukrainian SSR, and no one from Moldavian SSR. TsGAChR, f. P820, op. 8, d. 247, 148 (copy in USHMM Archives, RG 22.020).
55. Calculated from TsGARK, f. P1137, op. 6, d. 1289, 34 (copy in USHMM Archives, RG 74.002M).
56. Interview by Artëm Drabkin with Valentin Smolentsev, available at http://iremember.ru/memoirs/artilleristi/smolentsev-valentin-nikolaevich/.
57. GARF, f. A259, op. 40, d. 3091, 84–110 (copy in YVA, JM/24709).
58. Among them, refugees from the Odessa region accounted from 15 to 35.5 percent.
59. Lithuania and Latvia, as well as Arkhangelsk, Sverdlovsk, Smolensk, and Orël regions.
60. GARF, f. A259, op. 40, d. 3517, 11–17 (copy in YVA, JM/24678).
61. Ibid., d. 3032, 45. See this document also translated into English: Dubson, "On the Problem of the Evacuation," 49. Of these, 4.3 million were removed by August 20, 1941. See GARF, f. A259, op. 40, d. 3032, 28 (copy in YVA, JM/24678).
62. Belkovets, *Administrativno-pravovoe polozhenie*, 58.
63. *Partiinoe rukovodstvo evakuatsiei*, 27; Kumanëv, "Evakuatsiia naseleniia SSSR," 145.
64. Harrison, *Soviet Planning*, 72.
65. Manley, *To the Tashkent Station*, 50.
66. Dubson, "Toward a Central Database," 96, 106.
67. Ibid., 103.
68. GARF, f. A259, op. 40, d. 3014, 24 (copy in YVA, JM/24678).
69. Ibid., d. 3517, 14.
70. The table is based on ibid., d. 3517, 14; Pulatov, *Iz istorii*, 15. Same number of evacuees across Kazakhstan appears in the report of evacuation department of Kazakhstan SSR, which contains data on persons who arrived into this republic from August 1941 to January 1942. *Kazakhstan v period*, 433.
71. Batyrbaeva, *Tendentsii izmeneniia chislennosti*.

72. For this research, I used cards on registered Jewish refugees in Uzbekistan, copied and scanned by the United States Holocaust Memorial Museum Archives in Washington, DC: Holocaust Survivors and Victims Database, USHMM, http://www.ushmm.org/online/hsv/person_advance_search.php?Sourceid=20492.
73. Ibid.
74. GARF, f. A259, op. 40, d. 3517, 24 (copy in YVA, JM/24678).
75. Ibid., d. 3533, 149.
76. Dubson, "Toward a Central Database," 103, 115.
77. Iulia Melekhova, "Organizatsiia uchëta evakuirovannogo naseleniia v 1941–1943 gg. (po materialam Altaiskogo kraia)," *Izvestiia Altaiskogo gosudarstvennogo universiteta* 2, no. 84 (2014): 173.
78. GARF, f. A259, op. 40, d. 3518, 140 (copy in YVA, JM/24678).
79. Kornilov, *Ural'skoe selo i voina*, 96.
80. GARF, f. A259, op. 40, d. 3518, 35 (copy in YVA, JM/24678).
81. Mikhail Belenko, "Chislennost' evakuirovannogo grazhdanskogo naseleniia v Novosibirskuiu oblast' v 1941–1942," in *Zapadnaia Sibir' v Velikoi Otechestvennoi voine, 1941–1945 gg.*, ed. Vladimir Isupov and others (Novosibirsk, Russia: Nauka-Tsentr, 2004), 66–68.
82. GARF, f. A259, op. 40, d. 3030, 43–45 (copy in YVA, JM/24678).
83. *Katyn'*, 412–414. On the categories of Polish Jews who were incarcerated in camps for various reasons, see Litvak, *Peliṭim Yehudim*, 175–182.
84. Holocaust Survivors and Victims Database, USHMM, http://www.ushmm.org/online/hsv/person_advance_search.php?Sourceid=20492.
85. Zaron, *Ludnosc polska*, 280.
86. GARF, f. A259, op. 40, d. 3532, 49 (copy in YVA, JM/24678).
87. Gutman, "Yehudim be-tsava Anders," 206–212.
88. Kaganovitch, "Stalin's Great Power Politics," 75.
89. *Najnowsze dzieje zydow w Polsce: W zarysie; Do 1950 roku*, ed. Jerzy Tomaszewski (Warsaw, Poland: Wydawnictwo Naukowe PWN, 1993), 419.
90. Jan Czerniakiewicz, *Przemieszenia ludnosci polskiej z ZSRR 1944–1959* (Warsaw, Poland: Wydawn. Wyższej Szkoły Pedagogicznej TWP, 2004), 68. A similar number is given by the calculation from Anatol' Vialiki, *Belarus'—Pol'shcha y XX stagoddzi: Neviadomaia repatryiatsyia, 1955–1959 gg.* (Minsk, Belarus: NARB, 2007), 239, 297–309.
91. Kupovetskii, "Liudskie poteri," 143.
92. This estimation draws upon documents in Kaganovitch, "Stalin's Great Power Politics," 66–67; Yitzhak Arad, *The Holocaust in the Soviet Union* (Lincoln and Jerusalem: University of Nebraska Press and Yad Vashem, 2009), 524.
93. Litvak estimates a 35–40 percent mortality rate among Jewish refugees from Poland, including those who died in the Red Army, in Anders's army, and in the camps. Litvak, *Peliṭim Yehudim*, 359. Cholawsky gives more moderate estimate of their mortality, 30 percent. Shalom Cholawsky, *The Jews of Bielorussia during World War II* (Amsterdam: Harwood Academic Publishers, 1998), 32n20.
94. Of the 20,000 Polish Jews in these armies, 16,000 survived. Litvak, *Peliṭim Yehudim*, 315, 358. As early as mid-July 1943, 1,924 Polish Jews were sent from Kazakhstan to the First Polish Army, while there weren't many more Poles sent—2,106. *Iz istorii poliakov v Kazakhstane*, 275–277. According to the memoirs of Barukh Cherpichnik,

five hundred Jews fought in his division, of which twenty-five survived after the first battles. Cherpichnik, "Ba-aretz ha-zahav ha-lavan," 257.

95. According to Beria's note to Stalin on January 15, 1943, there were 64,883 Polish Belorussians and Polish Ukrainians in the rear areas of the USSR. *Katyn'*, 412–414. Most likely, this figure reflects only the registered persons. It is known that in 1940, 132,463 Belorussians and Ukrainians were deported, the so-called *osadniki* (Polish colonists-settlers). GARF, f. P9479, op. 1c, d. 61, 121 (copy in YVA, JM/24681). Even considering that 17,000 of them could have died in two and a half years, the Beria's data seem to be seriously miscalculated. In addition to those deported, former Polish Belorussians and Polish Ukrainians who were involved in the Soviet power structures could come to the eastern regions.

96. Dubson, "Toward a Central Database," 100.

97. GARF, f. A259, op. 40, d. 3092, 3 (copy in YVA, JM/24678).

98. Calculated from ibid., d. 3517, 11.

99. Based on the fact that, in the first eight months of the war, eleven million people were drafted into the Red Army. *Rossiia i SSSR*, 212.

100. *Partiinoe rukovodstvo evakuatsiei*, 33.

101. Krasnov-Levitin, *Ruk tvoikh zhar*, 52, 56.

102. Annakurbanov, *Kommunisticheskaia partiia Turkmenistana*, 29. Not all of them were placed in Central Asia. See testimony of Liudmila Dvorson in Potëmkina, *Evakuatsiia*, 48, 207.

103. *Kazakhstan v period*, 433.

104. *Vo imia pobedy*, vol. 1, 35.

105. Calculated from TsGAChR, f. P1263, op. 1, d. 39, 10, 70, 70a (copy in USHMM Archives, RG 22.020).

106. *Vo imia pobedy*, vol. 1, 308–309.

107. Proceeding from the fact that from May to December 1942, 5,328,392 were drafted into the army. *Rossiia i SSSR*, 212.

108. *Naselenie Rossii v XX veke: Istoricheskie ocherki*, ed. Iurii Poliakov (Moscow: ROSSPEN, 2001), vol. 2, 10.

109. Kupovetskii, "Liudskie poteri," 145.

110. Altshuler, *Soviet Jewry*, 8–9.

111. Mark Tolts, "Migration since World War I," in *The YIVO Encyclopedia of Jews in Eastern Europe*, ed. G. D. Hundert (New Haven, CT: Yale University Press, 2008), 1429.

112. Ibid., 1433.

113. Getty, Rittersporn, and Zemskov, "Victims," 1029.

114. Calculated from *Distribution of the Jewish Population*, 9–12.

115. Calculated from GARF, f. A259, op. 40, d. 3091, 1–33 (copy in YVA, JM/24678).

116. Calculated from ibid., d. 3517, 11. Based on this document, Dubson also tried to calculate the percentage of Jews from the total number of evacuees, but he did not previously subtract a category "undistributed by nationality" from the total number. As a result, he received an incorrect figure, 26.94 percent. Dubson, "Toward a Central Database," 102.

117. Calculated for December 1941 from Danilov, "Evakuatsiia naseleniia," 56–59.

118. This is the data for September 9, 1941. See M. M. Gorinov, "Budni osazhdënnoi stolitsy: Zhizn' i nastroeniia moskvichei (1941–1942 gg.)," *Otechestvennaia istoriia* 3

(1996): 3. According to other sources, two million Muscovites were evacuated by mid-November 1941. *Partiinoe rukovodstvo evakuatsiei*, 24.

119. Danilov, "Evakuatsiia naseleniia," 58; *Sovetskii tyl*, 139; Gavrilova, "Demograficheskii portret Moskvy," 119–120.

120. Calculated from TsGAChR, f. P1263, op. 1, d. 3533, 144–149 (copy in USHMM Archives, RG 22.020).

121. Calculated from ibid., 214–218.

122. Ibid., d. 39, 8.

123. Ibid., 70–70a. During the same fifteen months the number of Jews in Chuvashia grew from 7,906 to 9,556, an increase of 121 percent.

124. This number is based on records in Yad Vashem's Central Database of Names of Shoah Victims Recording. According to them, 939 Jewish refugees from Ukraine perished in the Krasnodar territory, 946 in the Ordzhonikidze territory, over 1,000 in the Rostov region (the database does not show the number of killed refugees over 1,000), 507 in the Caucasus, 72 in the Kabardino-Balkar ASSR, 24 in the Chechen-Ingush ASSR, and 46 in the Dagestan ASSR. According to these records, refugees were also killed during the occupation of the Voroshilovgrad, Kursk, Voronezh, Stalino, and some other regions. In addition to Jewish refugees from Ukraine, Jewish refugees from Belorussia, Russia, Moldavia, Romania, and Poland also died in these places. It is unlikely that the records reflect more than 10 percent of all deaths.

125. Based on the generally accepted number of 500,000 Jews at the front line, it can be assumed that during the entire war 200,000 (40 percent) of them were called up for service from the places of their evacuation. This mass mobilization to the front is indirectly evidenced by the fact that all ten Jewish Heroes of the Soviet Union, who were called up from Uzbekistan, were refugees. It is not known exactly who was the first to make the estimate of 500,000 Jews at the front. Mordechai Altshuler, considering that it was introduced by Yakov Kantor in 1963, notes that this figure was not proved by anyone. Altshuler, "Antisemitism," 49. See also Redlich, "The Jews under Soviet Rule," 129. Nevertheless, it is trustworthy, which can be justified as follows. According to relatively recent studies, the losses in the army have taken 8,668,400 from all 29,574,900 frontline soldiers. See *Rossiia i SSSR*, 217–218. Thus, losses accounted for 29.3 percent. It is known that among the perished frontline soldiers, 142,500 were Jews. Ibid., 228. The 500,000 frontline Jews made up 28.5 percent, which isn't much less than the calculated percent of losses among all frontliners. On the other hand, considering that one fifth of Jews were hiding their Jewish identity (for example, their Jewish nationality hid 22 percent of war medal recipients, who were born in Rechitsa [Kaganovitch, *The Long Life*, 277], and according to some overestimated Ion Degen's guess of one-third, available at http://iremember.ru/memoirs/tankisti/degen-ion-lazarevich/), the real number of Jews killed at the front should be 171,000. Accepting this as 29.3 percent, it turns out the total number of Jews serving the front line could have been 584,000.

126. Hilberg, *The Destruction*, 190.

127. 440,000 from the Moscow and Leningrad regions, and 140,000 from other regions.

128. Kaganovitch, "Estimating the Number," 470. By the summer of 1939, the majority of Bessarabia belonged to Romania. As a result of changing borders, all of Bessarabia was included into Moldavian ASSR in August 1940.

129. Dov Levin judged the number of Jewish refugees from the Baltic states in the Soviet rear as follows: 3,000 from Estonia, 15,000 from Latvia, and 22,000 from Lithuania. See *Pinkas ha-kehilot Latvia ve-Estonia*, ed. Dov Levin (Jerusalem: Yad Vashem, 1988), 32, 311; *Pinkas ha-kehilot Liṭa*, ed. Dov Levin (Jerusalem: Yad Vashem, 1996), 82.
130. *Gosudarstvennyi antisemitizm*, 142.
131. Shakhno Epshtein, "Evrei v Uzbekistane," GARF, f. P8114, op. 1, d. 88, 433 (copy in USHMM Archives, RG 220028M).
132. Redlich, "The Jews under Soviet Rule," 119.
133. Calculated from GARF, f. A259, op. 40, d. 3091, 1–33 (copy in YVA, JM/24678).
134. GARF, f. A259, op. 40, d. 3091, 84–110 (copy in YVA, JM/24709).
135. As we already saw, part of the refugees left after being disappointed with the conditions in Central Asia. A part of the refugees already returned to Moscow in 1942. Gavrilova, "Demograficheskii portret Moskvy," 119–120.
136. Vekselman, "The Struggle," 344.
137. *Iz istorii poliakov v Kazakhstane*, 186.
138. Calculated from TsGARK, f. P1137, op. 9, d. 141, 79, 89 (copy in USHMM Archives, RG 74.002M).

Chapter 8. The Difficult Road Back

1. TsGAChR, f. P203, op. 24, d. 2, 27 (copy in USHMM Archives, RG 22.020).
2. Ustinov, *Vo imia Pobedy*, 301.
3. Potëmkina, *Evakuatsiia*, 204.
4. Aleksandr Vakser, *Leningrad poslevoennyi, 1945–1982 gg.* (Saint Petersburg, Russia: Ostrov, 2005), 8–9.
5. TsGAChR, f. P203, op. 24, d. 2, 184 (copy in USHMM Archives, RG 22.020).
6. Ibid., 243.
7. Potëmkina, *Evakonaselenie*, 185.
8. TsGAChR, f. P821, op. 4, d. 103, 50, 57 (copy in USHMM Archives, RG 22.020).
9. Ibid., f. P807, op. 3, d. 76, 18, 25.
10. Ibid., f. P203, op. 24, d. 3, 404–404a; ibid., f. P1263, op. 1, d. 81, 73.
11. Ibid., f. P807, op. 3, d. 76, 54.
12. Pikhoia, *Moskva. Kreml'. Vlast'*, 60.
13. Calculated from TsGAChR, f. P821, op. 4, d. 103, 66 (copy in USHMM Archives, RG 22.020); ibid., f. P1263, op. 1, d. 39, 11, 37–37a, 42–42a, 69–69a.
14. Calculated from ibid., 10, 37–37a, 42–42a, 69–69a; ibid., P807, op. 3, d. 76, 13, 48, 51–52, 63.
15. Calculated from TsGAChR, f. P1263, op. 1, d. 39, 6, 12, 20, 30, 38–38a, 41–41a, 43–43a, 47–47a, 57–57a, 70–70a (copy in USHMM Archives, RG 22.020); ibid., d. 65, 22–25; ibid., op. 4, d. 9, 82.
16. Ibid., 128.
17. *Mesto evakuatsii*, 71.
18. Potëmkina, *Evakuatsiia*, 183.
19. TsGAChR, f. P807, op. 3, d. 76, 108 (copy in USHMM Archives, RG 22.020).
20. Ibid., f. P820, op. 8, d. 250, 154.
21. *Mesto evakuatsii*, 70.

22. TsGAChR, f. P1263, op. 1, d. 33, 50a (copy in USHMM Archives, RG 22.020); ibid., f. P203, op. 24, d. 2, 243, 392.
23. *Mesto evakuatsii*, 70.
24. TsGAChR, f. P1263, op. 1, d. 46, 152–153 (copy in USHMM Archives, RG 22.020); N. I. Komarov and G. A. Kumanev, *Velikaia bitva pod Moskvoi: Letopis' vazhneishikh sobytii; Kommentarii* (Moscow: Institut rossiiskoi istorii RAN, 2002), 89.
25. Bruell, *Autumn in Springtime*, 117.
26. Lazar' Fredgeim, "Stranitsy shadrinskoi zhizni voennykh let," in *Shadrinsk voennoi pory*, ed. Sergei Borisov (Shadrinsk, Russia: Pedinstitut, 1995), vol. 3, 237.
27. TsGAChR, f. P1263, op. 1, d. 65, 26–26a (copy in USHMM Archives, RG 22.020).
28. Ibid., f. P821, op. 4, d. 103, 64.
29. Ibid.
30. Ibid., f. P1041, op. 1, d. 599, 184.
31. Iosif Roitman and Garri Fel'dman, *Povedai o tom detiam i vnukam svoim* (Netania, Israel: Elbron, 2007), 252.
32. TsGAChR, f. P821, op. 4, d. 103, 64 (copy in USHMM Archives, RG 22.020).
33. Dokuchaev, *Sibirskii tyl*, 163.
34. *Sovetskie evrei pishut*, 151–156, 176.
35. USC Shoah Foundation, Visual History Archive, interview with Vera Bakshi, Simferopol', March 16, 1997, segment 103, Spielberg Archive.
36. Olekhnovich, *Ekonomika Belorussii*, 9.
37. *Osvobozhdënnaia Belarus'*, vol. 2, 240, 342.
38. Ibid., vol. 1, 45, 213.
39. Upon arrival in Minsk, Rubinchik received several offers for positions of a high school principal in west Belorussia, but she preferred to return to Rechitsa, where she was happily accepted by the local education department. Kaganovitch, *The Long life*, 362n15.
40. Iosif Liberman, "Evakuatsiia evreev—put' k spaseniiu," in *Istoriia, Pamiat', Liudi*, ed. Aleksandr Baron (Almaty, Kazakhstan: Mitsva, 2011), 98–99.
41. Kim Pomerants, "Kak sovpalo: Voina, beda, mechta i . . . detstvo," *Neva* 5 (2015): 64–66; TsGAChR, f. P1263, op. 1, d. 118, 212 (copy in USHMM Archives, RG 22.020).
42. GAOOGO, f. 342, op. 1, d. 11, 105.
43. Pëtr Shornikov, *Tsena voiny: Krizis sistemy zdravookhraneniia i demograficheskie poteri Moldavii v period Velikoi Otechestvennoi voiny* (Chişinău, Moldova: n.p., 1994), 70.
44. *Zdravookhranenie v gody Velikoi Otechestvennoi voiny 1941–1945: Sbornik dokumentov i materialov*, comp. L. I. Zavalishchenko and others (Moscow: Meditsina, 1977), 449.
45. Snegirëva, Sotsial'no-ekonomicheskie posledstviia, 192.
46. The growing numbers of Jewish managers and high-ranking engineers in the USSR defense industry points to it clearest of all. Despite the rise of government antisemitism in the middle of the war, the number of Jews in these positions increased from 14 (19.2 percent) to 26 (22.2 percent) between June 1941 and January 1946. Calculated from Kostyrchenko, *Tainaia politika Stalina*, 610. Among them were Isaak Sal'tsman,

the director of the Kirov tank plant (Tankograd) in Cheliabinsk, and Semën Belen'kii, the director of the ammunition plant no. 254.

47. *Evakuatsiia v Kazakhstan*, 47.

48. TsGAChR, f. P820, op. 8, d. 250, 125 (copy in USHMM Archives, RG 22.020).

49. *Osvobozhdënnaia Belarus'*, vol. 2, 111–118, 276–280.

50. Ibid., vol. 1, 189–190. The editorial team's selective choice of documents for this collection that aimed to demonstrate the "affirmative action" of the part of the republic's authorities led to accusations of manipulation.

51. TsGAChR, f. P1263, op. 1, d. 118, 152, 156 (copy in USHMM Archives, RG 22.020).

52. Ibid., d. 125, 1.

53. Ibid., f. P807, op. 3, d. 76, 108.

54. Leonid Smilovitskii, "Evrei Belorussii v pervoe poslevoennoe desiatiletie," *Vestnik Evreiskogo Universiteta v Moskve* 8, no. 26 (2003): 216.

55. Kaganovitch, *The Long Life*, 290–293. The artels' economic role in postwar western Soviet republics is still awaiting research.

56. The success of Nazi propaganda on occupied territory of eastern Belorussia is evidenced by the wishes of many peasants not to restore the kolkhozes. See *Osvobozhdënnaia Belarus'*, vol. 1, 64–65. The self-identification of the inhabitants of Belorussia also changed. This is evident from the letter of the head of the Political Directorate of the First Belorussian Front, S. F. Galadzhaev to P. K. Ponomarenko in June 1944. Here Galadzhaev states that the majority of the inhabitants of the liberated areas did not call the Red Army troops "ours" but referred to them as "Russians" or "Reds." Ibid., 82.

57. Kaganovitch, *The Long Life*, 287.

58. ZGAR, f. 342, op. 1, d. 3, 151.

59. Leonid Smilovitsky, "Struggle of Belorussian Jews for the Restitution of Possessions and Housing in the First Postwar Decade," *East European Jewish Affairs* 30, no. 2 (2000): 59–67.

60. This is evidenced by the order no. 65 of Rechitsa's mayor Karl Gerhard, given in May 1942, on the returning of taken Yiddish records. YVA, JM/11218, 14, 1.

61. On the spread of these rumors in Rechitsa, see letter from Zlata Chechik, March 3, 1998; letter from Faina Vinnik, April 4, 1998; letter from Sofia Zherebovich, June 20, 1999; letter from Liubov' Tsirkina, September 11, 1999, author's personal archive.

62. Krutova, *Evrei na zemle*, 151.

63. TsGAChR, f. P821, op. 4, d. 103, 59 (copy in USHMM Archives, RG 22.020).

64. Ibid., f. P1263, op. 1, d. 81, 55.

65. Ibid., d. 118, 191–191a.

66. GARF, f. P8114, op. 1, d. 1173, 46 (copy in USHMM Archives, RG 220028M).

67. Ibid., d. 1055, 37–38.

68. *Sovetskie evrei pishut*, 148.

69. Ibid., 149–150.

70. Calculated from *Gosudarstvennyi antisemitizm*, 57.

71. Karel C. Berkhoff, "Dina Pronicheva's Story of Surviving the Babi Yar Massacre: German, Jewish, Soviet, Russian, and Ukrainian Records," in *The USC Shoah in Ukraine: History, Testimony, and Memorialization*, ed. Ray Brandon and Wendy Lower (Bloomington: Indiana University Press, 2008), 292.

72. *TsK VKP(b) i natsional'nyi vopros*, 822–824.
73. Dovzhenko, *Dnevnikovye zapisi*, 278.
74. *Moskva poslevoennaia, 1945/47: Arkhivnye dokumenty i materialy*, ed. Mikhail Gorinov and others (Moscow: Mosgorarkhiv, 2000), 129.
75. Lomagin, *Neizvestnaia blokada*, 335.
76. These moods were reflected in the diary entries by Dovzhenko, *Dnevnikovye zapisi*, 87, 152, 207.
77. Weiner, *Making Sense of War*, 122.
78. YVA, M.37/1319, 3. Even though, according to 1945 reports by local authorities, the claims of Jews for apartments were answered favorably 94 percent of the time, and claims for returned belongings were 64 percent, it's evident these statistics were hastily generated in response to receiving a copy of Dargolts's letter. Ibid., 6–7.
79. Kats-Fridman, "Dve evakuatsii odnoi sem'i."
80. Shvarts, *Evrei v Sovetskom Soiuze*, 160.
81. Feygenblum, "Be-mokorot volfram be-'Uzbekistan," 127.
82. USC Shoah Foundation, Visual History Archive, interview with Doba Belozovskaia, Kyiv, Ukraine, December 12, 1996, segment 34, Spielberg Archive.
83. YVA, M.37/1332, 4.
84. *Voices of Resilience*, 317.
85. Victoria Khiterer, "We Did Not Recognize Our Country: The Rise of Antisemitism in Ukraine before and after World War II (1937–1947)," *Polin: Studies in Polish Jewry* 26 (2014): 371.
86. YVA, M. 37/1332, 3.
87. Ibid., 4.
88. Mitsel, *Evrei Ukrainy*, 126–129.
89. Blackwell, "Regime City," 361.
90. YVA, M.37/196, 6–8. See also Weiner, *Making Sense of War*, 192; Mitsel, *Evrei Ukrainy*, 34, 38–41, 54–55, 63–66.
91. Letter from Fridrikh Valler, June 17, 2001, author's personal archive.
92. Péter Apor, "The Lost Deportations and the Lost People of Kunmadaras: A Pogrom in Hungary, 1946," *Hungarian Historical Review* 2, no. 3 (2013): 575–578.
93. Oskar Rokhlin, "Kiev: 1945–1955," *Zametki po evreiskoi istorii*, no. 2–3 (2015): 4.
94. Dovzhenko, *Dnevnikovye zapisi*, 92, 96, 193, 214, 226, 231, 325, 346, 745. However, his diaries are full of scornful views about many eastern ethnic groups. Ibid., 131, 278–279. In one instance he confesses himself: "I never liked eastern people." Ibid., 709.
95. *Gosudarstvennyi antisemitizm*, 40–44; Altshuler, "Antisemitism," 49–70.
96. Dovzhenko, *Dnevnikovye zapisi*, 266.
97. Kostyrchenko, *Tainaia politika Stalina*, 359.
98. Dovzhenko, *Dnevnikovye zapisi*, 109, 207, and especially 231.
99. Blackwell, "Regime City," 370.
100. "Nepravil'noe vystuplenie gazety Radians'ka Ukraïna," *Pravda*, August 29, 1946, 3.
101. TsDAGOU, f. 1, op. 23, d. 685, 82–87 (copy in YVA, M. 37/161). See the translation of this document into English: Mordechai Altshuler, "Were a Majority of the Ukrainian Creative Intelligentsia Antisemitic?," *Jews in Eastern Europe* 2, no. 42 (2000):

76–85. The fact that Khrushchev agreed to remove Rybak from his position is indirectly indicated by the award list on him, according to which he had been working in the frontline newspaper *Stalinskii Sokol* since June 1943. See http://www.podvign aroda.ru/?#id=27867308&tab=navDetailDocument.

102. On Khrushchev's antisemitic statements, see Weiner, *Making Sense of War*, 200–201, 233–234. In this regard, Nikita Khrushchev's assertion that he had never been an antisemite is not credible. See Khrushchev's memoirs, heavily edited by his son Sergei: Nikita Khrushchev, *Vospominaniia: Izbrannye fragmenty* (Moscow: Vagrius, 1997), 309.

103. Altshuler, "Antisemitism," 44.

104. Yekelchyk, *Stalin's Citizens*, 9–24.

105. Dovzhenko, *Dnevnikovye zapisi*, 272–273, 346. Pid sofitami sekretnikh sluzhb (dokumenti z papki-formuliaru na O. P. Dovzhenka), *Z arkhiviv VUChK-GPU-NKVD-KGB*, no. 1/2 (1995): 235–280.

106. *Pravda*, September 2, 1946, 2.

107. Letter from Fridrih Valler, June 17, 2001, author's personal archive.

108. Blackwell, "Regime City," 136.

109. Yisrael Gutin, *Kur'oni: Reshimot, demuyot, zikhronot* (Tel Aviv: ʿEḳed, 1979), 247–250.

110. Blackwell, "Regime City," 138.

111. Ibid., 139–140.

112. Leonid Kotliar, *Vospominaniia evreia-krasnoarmeitsa* (Moscow: Veche, 2011), 130–133.

113. USC Shoah Foundation, Visual History Archive, interview with Khava Ovrutskaia, Ashdod, Israel, May 25, 1998, segment 96, Spielberg Archive.

114. T. V. Pastushenko, "Spadok viini: Politiko-pravove stanovishche repatriantiv u povoennomu radians'komu suspil'stvi," *Ukraïns'kii istorichnii zhurnal* 3 (2010): 118–119.

115. *TsK VKP(b) i natsional'nyi vopros*, 835–836.

116. RGAE, f. 1562, op. 329, d. 2217, 11.

117. Pavel Sudoplatov, *Razvedka i Kreml': Zapiski nezhelatel'nogo svidetelia* (Moscow: Geia, 1996), 347.

118. *Osvobozhdënnaia Belarus'*, vol. 2, 294.

119. Fabrikant, *Nam dorogi eti*, 195–196.

120. Blackwell, "Regime City," 60–61.

121. Ibid., 238–239.

122. Ibid., 63; Viktor Krupina, "Partiino-derzhavna nomenklatura povoennoï Ukraïni," in *Povoenna Ukraïna: Narisi sotsial'noï istoriï (druga polovina 1940-kh—seredina 1950-kh rr.)*, ed. V. M. Danilenko (Kyiv, Ukraine: Institut istoriï NAN Ukraïni, 2010), vol. 1, 170.

123. Potëmkina, *Evakuatsiia*, 192–193.

124. Viktor Krupyna, "Kadrovaia politika v sovetskoi Ukraine v period pozdnego stalinizma: Natsional'nyi aspekt," in *Sovetskie natsii i natsional'naia politika v 1920–1950-e gody*, ed. M. A. Ailamazian (Moscow: Politicheskaia entsiklopediia, 2014), 660–661.

125. YVA, M.37/1319, 2.

126. Weiner, *Making Sense of War*, 115–117.

127. Shvarts, *Evrei v Sovetskom Soiuze*, 160.

128. Altshuler, "Antisemitism," 45.
129. Blackwell, "Regime City," 354–355.
130. Kostyrchenko, *Tainaia politika Stalina*, 251–275.
131. Ibid., 356–357. After assuming the position of secretary general in 1953, Khrushchev made sure to destroy documents implicating him in purges in Ukraine. Feliks Chuev, *Molotov: Poluderzhavnyi vlastelin* (Moscow: OLMA-Press, 1999), 430.
132. *Sovetskie evrei pishut*, 276.
133. *Voices of Resilience*, 294–295.
134. *Sovetskie evrei pishut*, 276.
135. YVA, M.37/5, 213.
136. *Gosudarstvennyi antisemitizm*, 74–75.
137. Ibid.
138. USC Shoah Foundation, Visual History Archive, interview with Vera Bakshi, Simferopol', March 16, 1997, segment 103, Spielberg Archive.
139. USC Shoah Foundation, Visual History Archive, interview with Doba Belozovskaia, Kyiv, Ukraine, December 12, 1996, segment 182, Spielberg Archive.
140. Veniamin Zima, *Golod v SSSR 1946–1947 godov: Proiskhozhdenie i posledstviia* (Moscow: Institut Rossiiskoi istorii RAN, 1996), 67–95, 160–171; Nicholas Ganson, *The Soviet Famine of 1946–47 in Global and Historical Perspective* (New York: Palgrave Macmillan, 2009), 48–67.
141. Vasil' Shvidkii, "Golod 1946–1947 rr. iak chinnik splesku deviantni iavishch v Ukraïni," *Ukraïns'kii istorichnii zhurnal* 1 (2010): 151.
142. On grain procurement, see Oleksandra Veselova, "Pisliavoienna tragediia: Golod 1946–1947 rr. v Ukraïni," *Ukraïns'kii istorichnii zhurnal* 6 (2000): 105–109. As a side note, Veselova didn't approach Nikita Khrushchev's memoirs, where he tried to justify himself, with the necessary criticism.
143. Tanja Penter, "Soviet War Crimes Trials under Stalin (1943–1953)," *Cahiers du Monde russe* 49, no. 2/3 (2008): 356.
144. Dovzhenko, *Dnevnikovye zapisi*, 484.
145. Kats-Fridman, "Dve evakuatsii odnoi sem'i."
146. L. I. Snegirëva and T. A. Safonova, "Evakuatsiia grazhdanskogo naseleniia iz Zapadnoi Sibiri v gody Velikoi Otechestvennoi voiny (1942–1945 gody)," *Vestnik TGPU, Seriia: Gumanitarnye nauki* 4, no. 41 (2004): 29.
147. GARF, f. P8114, op. 1, d. 1064, 129–139 (copy in USHMM Archives, RG 220028M).
148. David Manevich, "Birobidzhan gotov priniat' novykh pereselentsev," GARF, f. P8114, op. 1, d. 47, 19–20 (copy in USHMM Archives, RG 220028M).
149. David Manevich, "Rastët tiaga v Evreiskuiu avtonomnuiu oblast'," ibid., 114–115.
150. Kostyrchenko, *Tainaia politika Stalina*, 489.
151. About release to Poland, see Kaganovitch, "Stalin's Great Power Politics," 59–94. About release to Romania, see ibid., 78.
152. Mitsel, *Evrei Ukrainy*, 104, 109–110.
153. TsDAGOU, f. 1, op. 23, d. 4350, 1–56, (copy in YVA, M.37/213).
154. GARF, f. P8114, op. 1, d. 1056, 99–100 (copy in USHMM Archives, RG 220028M).

155. *Vospominaniia zhitelei evreiskikh poselenii v Krymu*, ed. E. Rivkina and M. Tiaglyi (Simferopol': Khesed Shimon, 2004), 15–16. About this resettlement see also, ibid., 23.

156. A. Lerman, "Obustroim i zakrepim pribyvshikh pereselentsev," GARF, f. P8114, op. 1, d. 108, 227–229 (copy in USHMM Archives, RG 220028M).

157. I. Liumkis, "Iz Samarkanda v Birobidzhan," GARF, f. P8114, op. 1, d. 118, 426–428 (copy in USHMM Archives, RG 220028M).

158. TsDAGOU, f. 1, op. 24, d. 94, 39, 91 (copy in YVA, M.37/235).

159. For this estimation, see Nora Levin, *The Jews in the Soviet Union since 1917: Paradox of Survival* (New York: New York University Press, 1988), vol. 1, 492.

160. For further information, see Yekelchyk, *Stalin's Empire*, 72–87.

Selected Bibliography

Aharonson (Kyesh), Mirym. *Beriḥah le-moledet.* Yavne, Israel: Shiluvym, 2005.
Al'tman, Il'ia. *Zhertvy nenavisti: Kholokost v SSSR 1941–1945.* Moscow: Kovcheg, 2002.
Altshuler, Mordechai. "Antisemitism in Ukraine toward the End of the Second World War." *Jews in Eastern Europe* 22, no. 3 (1993): 40–81.

———. "Ha-Pinui veha-menusaḥ shel Yehudim mi-Byelorusyah ha-Mizraḥit be-tkufat ha-sho'ah, yuniy—'ogusṭ 1941." *Yahadut zmaneynu* no. 3 (1986): 119–158.

———. *Soviet Jewry on the Eve of the Holocaust.* Jerusalem: Hebrew University of Jerusalem and Yad Vashem, 1998.

———. *Yahadut ba-makhbesh ha-sovyeṭi—beyn dat le-zehut yahudit be-Berit ha-Mo'atsot 1941–1964.* Jerusalem: Merkaz Zalman Shazar, 2007.

Annakurbanov, Aganiiaz. *Kommunisticheskaia partiia Turkmenistana—organizator pomoshchi evakuirovannomu naseleniiu i invalidam v gody Velikoi Otechestvennoi voiny.* Ashkhabad, USSR: Ylym, 1984.
Azrieli, David. *Na shag vperedi.* Jerusalem: Yad Vashem, 2002.
Bader-Whiteman, Dorit. *Escape via Siberia: A Jewish Child's Odyssey of Survival.* New York: Holmes & Meier, 1999.
Bar, Miryam. *Lelot Tashkent.* Tel Aviv: A. Levin-Epshtyin, 1970.
Barkan, Nota. "Vospominaniia." In *Vosemnadtsat',* edited by Zeev Vagner, 15–30. Jerusalem: Shamir, 1989.
Bashkiriia v gody Velikoi Otechestvennoi voiny: Sbornik dokumentov i materialov. Edited by T. Kh. Akhmadiev, G. D. Irgalin, and others. Ufa, Russia: Kitam, 1995.
Batyrbaeva, Shaiyrkul. *Tendentsii izmeneniia chislennosti naseleniia Kazakhstana v 1939–1959 gg.* Available at http://www.history.krsu.edu.kg/index.php?option=com_content&task=view&id=453&Itemid=72.
Begin, Menahem. *Be-lelot levanim: Sipur ma'asaro va-hakirato shel Menahem Begin.* Tel Aviv: Devir, 1995.
Belarus' v pervye mesiatsy Velikoi Otechestvennoi voiny, 22 iiunia–avgust 1941 gg.: Dokumenty i materialy. Edited by Vladimir Adomushko and others. Minsk, Belarus: NARB, 2006.
Belkovets, Larisa. *Administrativno-pravovoe polozhenie rossiiskikh nemtsev na spetsposelenii 1941–1955 gody.* Moscow: Rosspan, 2006.

Belonosov, Ivan. "Evakuatsiia naseleniia iz prifrontovoi polosy v 1941–1942 gg." In *Eshelony idut na vostok*, edited by Iurii Poliakov, 15–30. Moscow: Nauka, 1966.

Belonosov, Oleg, and Kamal' Makhmut. "Alma-Atinskii elektrotekhnicheskii zavod— detishche evakuatsii." In *Evakuatsiia: Voskreshaia proshloe*, edited by Aleksandr Baron and others, 132–141. Almaty, Kazakhstan: Fortress, 2009.

Berkhoff, Karel C. *Motherland in Danger: Soviet Propaganda during World War II.* Cambridge, MA: Harvard University Press, 2012.

Bilich, Lev. "What I Will Always Remember." *Memoirs of Holocaust Survivors in Canada* 31 (2004). Available at http://migs.concordia.ca/memoirs/bilich_lev/lev_bilich_01.htm.

Biriukov, Vladimir. "Dnevnikovye zapisi 1941–1945 gg." In *Shadrinsk voennoi pory*, edited by Sergei Borisov, vol. 2, 209–232. Shadrinsk, Russia: Pedinstitut, 1995.

Blackwell, Martin J. "Regime City of the First Category: The Experience of the Return of Soviet Power to Kyiv, Ukraine, 1943–1948." PhD diss., Indiana University, 2005.

Boiman, Bina. *Yalde ha-korpus ha-sheni: Yetomot be-Sibir uve-'Arvot Kirgizyah.* Jerusalem: Yad Vashem, 2007.

Borovoi, Saul. *Vospominaniia.* Moscow: Evreiskii universitet v Moskve, 1993.

Bruell, Anna. *Autumn in Springtime: Memories of World War II.* Melbourne: [A. Bruell], 1995.

Brul', Viktor. *Nemtsy v Zapadnoi Sibiri.* Topchikha, Russia: n.p., 1995.

Cherpichnik, Baruch. "Ba-Aretz ha-zahav ha-lavan." In *Sefer Kostopol: Khaeya ve-muta shel kehila*, edited by Ar'e Lerner, 255–259. Tel Aviv: Irgun Yots'e Kostopol', 1967.

Christian, David. *Imperial and Soviet Russia: Power, Privilege, and the Challenge of Modernity.* New York: Palgrave Macmillan, 1997.

Chukovskaia, Lidia. *Zapiski ob Anne Akhmatovoi.* Moscow: Vremia, 2007.

Danilov, Pavel. "Evakuatsiia naseleniia i oborudovaniia iz Leningrada v 1941–1943 gg." *Otechestvennaia istoriia*, no. 3 (2006): 55–64.

Davidson-Rosenblatt, Bronia. *Keine Zeit für Abschied: Von Polen durch den Ural nach Samarkand und zuruck bis Amsterdam.* Konstanz, Germany: Hartung-Gorre Verlag, 2000.

Distribution of the Jewish Population of the USSR 1939. Edited by Mordechai Altshuler. Jerusalem: Hebrew University of Jerusalem, 1993.

Dobrushkin, Lev. *Istoriia odnoi sem'i.* New York: n.p., 1998.

Documents on Polish-Soviet Relation, 1939–1945. Vols. 1–2. Edited by Edward Raczynski and others. London: Heinemann, 1961–1967.

Dokuchaev, Georgii. *Sibirskii tyl v Velikoi Otechestvennoi voine.* Novosibirsk, Russia: Nauka, 2013.

Dovzhenko, Aleksandr. *Dnevnikovye zapisi, 1939–1956.* Kharkiv, Ukraine: Folio, 2013.

DP Camps on Their Observations of Jewish Life in Soviet Russia. New York: American Jewish Committee, 1948.

Dubson, Vadim. "On the Problem of the Evacuation of Soviet Jews in 1941 (New Archival Sources)." *Jews in Eastern Europe* 40, no. 3 (1999): 37–56.

———. "Toward a Central Database of Evacuated Soviet Jews' Names, for the Study of the Holocaust in the Occupied Soviet Territories." *Holocaust and Genocide Studies* 26, no. 1 (2012): 95–119.

Dunaevskii, Dov. *Be-ḥoshekh 'efshar rak laḥlom.* Pardes Hanah, Israel: Muzah, 2008.

Dzhuraev, Turab. *Kommunisticheskaia partiia Uzbekistana v gody Velikoi Otechestvennoi voiny*. Tashkent, USSR: Uzbekistan, 1964.
Edele, Mark. "More Than Just Stalinists: The Political Sentiments of Victors 1945–1953." In *Late Stalinist Russia: Society between Reconstruction and Reinvention*, edited by Juliane Fürst, 167–191. New York: Routledge, 2006.
———. *Soviet Veterans of the Second World War: A Popular Movement in an Authoritarian Society, 1941–1991*. New York: Oxford University Press, 2008.
Efron, Georgii. *Dnevniki*. Moscow: Vagrius, 2004.
Ehrenburg, Ilya. *Sobranie sochinenii v deviati tomakh*. Moscow: Khudozhestvennaia literatura, 1967.
Elton (Elbaum), Zyga. *Destination Buchara*. Ripponlea, Australia: Dizal Nominees, 1996.
Ermolinskii, Sergei. *O vremeni, o Bulgakove i o sebe*. Moscow: Agraf, 2002.
Ermolov, Arsenii. *Tankovaia promyshlennost' SSSR v gody Velikoi Otechestvennoi voiny*. Moscow: n.p., 2009.
Evakuatsiia v Kazakhstan. Edited by Isaak Grinberg, Gul'nar Karataeva, and Nikolai Krapivnitskii. Almaty, Kazakhstan: Fortress, 2008.
Fabrikant, David. *Nam dorogi eti pozabyt' nel'zia*. Available at http://www.netzulim.org/R/OrgR/Library/Fabrikant/Kniga2.pdf.
Fedotov, Viktor. *Evakuirovannoe naselenie v Srednem Povolzh'e v gody Velikoi Otechestvennoi voiny (1941–1945 gg.): Problemy razmeshcheniia, sotsial'noi adaptatsii i trudovoi deiatel'nosti*. Samara, Russia: Samarskii gosudarstvennyi tekhnicheskii universitet, 2005.
Feigelovich, Aron. "Prikliucheniia chetyrëkh." In Shaul Beilinson, *Moi dolgii put' v Ierusalim*. Jerusalem: n.p., 1995.
Feygenblum, Aharon. "Be-mokorot volfram be-'Uzbekystan." *Yalkut mureshet* 63 (1997): 119–127.
Fitzpatrick, Sheila. *Everyday Stalinism: Ordinary Life in Extraordinary Times: Soviet Russia in the 1930s*. New York: Oxford University Press, 1999.
———. *Tear Off the Masks! Identity and Imposture in Twentieth Century Russia*. Princeton, NJ: Princeton University Press, 2005.
Gabel, Dina. *Behind the Ice Curtain*. New York: CIS Publishers, 1992.
Gavrilova, Irina. "Demograficheskii portret Moskvy v gody Velikoi Otechestvennoi voiny." *Voprosy istorii*, no. 1 (2000): 118–126.
Gershuny, Aharon Eliahu. *Yehudim ve-Yahadut be-Berit ha-Mo'atsot: Yahadut Rusyah mi-tekufat Stalin ve-'ad ha-zeman ha-aharon*. Jerusalem: Feldhaym, 1970.
Getty, Arch, Gábor T. Rittersporn, and Viktor Zemskov. "Victims of the Soviet Penal System in the Pre-War Years: A First Approach on the Basis of Archival Evidence." *American Historical Review* 98, no. 4 (1993): 1017–1049.
Gitlin, Semën. *Natsional'nye men'shinstva v Uzbekistane: Evrei v Uzbekistane*. Vol. 2. Tel Aviv: Gibor, 2004.
Goldin, Sergei. "Zakonchilos' detstvo." In *Vzrosloe detstvo voiny: Sbornik vospominanii*, edited by Mikhail Kipnis, vol. 2, 34–42. Ashdod, Israel: Keitar, 2013.
Gosudarstvennyi antisemitizm v SSSR ot nachala do kul'minatsii 1938–1953: Dokumenty. Compiled by Gennadii Kostyrchenko. Edited by Aleksandr Iakovlev. Moscow: MFD Materik, 2005.

Grantserska-Kadari, Bina. *Ha-Me'ah ha-'esrim sheli: Resise zikhronot*. Tel Aviv: Moreshet, 2008.

Gribanova, Elena. "Evakuatsiia glazami partiinogo kontrolia." In *Evakuatsiia: Voskreshaia proshloe*, edited by Aleksandr Baron and others, 221–242. Almaty, Kazakhstan: Fortress, 2009.

Grigor'ev, R. "Moskva voennaia, 1941 god . . .: Novye istochniki iz sekretnykh arkhivnykh fondov." *Istoriia SSSR*, no. 6 (1991): 101–122.

Grosman, Moshe. *Ba-Arets ha-agadit ha-keshufa: Sheva shenot ḥayim be-Berit ha-Mo'atsot*. Tel Aviv: N. Twersky, 1951.

Grynberg, Henryk. *Children of Zion*. Evanston, IL: Northwestern University Press, 1997.

Gurkov, Meir. *Sefer ha-zikhronot: Divrey ha-yamim 1917–1947 be-Russia ha-sovyeṭit*. Kfar Hab'ad, Israel: 'Ayid'elm'an, 1977.

Gusak, Vladimir. *Militsiia Iuzhnogo Urala v gody Velikoi Otechestvennoi voiny 1941–1945 gg*. Cheliabinsk, Russia: Cheliabinskii iuridicheskii institut, 2007.

Gutman, Israel. "Yehudim be-tsava Anders be-Berit ha-Mo'atsot." *Yad Vashem Studies* 12 (1977): 171–213.

Harrison, Mark. *Soviet Planning in Peace and War, 1938–1945*. Cambridge: Cambridge University Press, 2002.

Heinzen, James. "A 'Campaign Spasm': Graft and the Limits of the 'Campaign' against Bribery after the Great Patriotic War." In *Late Stalinist Russia: Society between Reconstruction and Reinvention*, edited by Juliane Fürst, 123–141. New York: Routledge, 2006.

Hessler, Julie. *A Social History of Soviet Trade: Trade Policy, Retail Practice, and Consumption, 1917–1953*. Princeton, NJ: Princeton University Press, 2004.

Hilberg, Raul. *The Destruction of the European Jews*. New York: Holmes & Meier, 1985.

Honig, Samuel. *From Poland to Russia and Back, 1939–1946*. Windsor, ON: Black Moss Press, 1996.

Hooper, Cynthia. "A Darker 'Big Deal': Concealing Party Crimes in the Post–Second World War Era." In *Late Stalinist Russia: Society between Reconstruction and Reinvention*, edited by Juliane Fürst, 142–163. New York: Routledge, 2006.

Istoriia stalinskogo Gulaga: Konets 1920-kh—pervaia polovina 1950-kh godov. Vols. 1–7. Edited by N. Vert and S. Mironenko. Moscow: ROSSPEN, 2004.

Istoriia v dokumentakh. Arkhiv Aleksandra Iakovleva. Available at http://www.alexanderyakovlev.org/.

Istoriia Velikoi Otechestvennoi voiny Sovetskogo Soiuza. Vol. 2. Edited by Pëtr Pospelov. Moscow: Voenizdat, 1961.

Isupov, Vladimir. *Demograficheskie katastrofy i krizisy v Rossii v pervoi polovine XX veka: Istoriko-demograficheskie ocherki*. Novosibirsk, Russia: Sibirskii khronograf, 2000.

Iushkovskii, Daniil. "Dnevnik, kotorogo ne bylo." In *Evreiskie obshchiny Sibiri i Dal'nego Vostoka*, edited by Viktor Iushkovskii, issue 5, 174–195. Tomsk, Russia: Tomskii universitet, 2001.

Ivanov, Vsevolod. *Dnevnik*. Moscow: IMLI RAN; Nasledie, 2001.

Ivanova, Izolda. "Sed'maia tetrad': Poimi voinu! V evakuatsii." *Neva*, no. 1 (2006): 207–215.

Ivanova, T. "Zabota ob evakuirovannykh detiakh." In *Tashkentskii Al'manakh*, edited by Kh. Alimdzhan, V. Ivanov, and I. Lezhnëv, 233–236. Tashkent, USSR: Gosizdat UzSSR, 1942.
Iz istorii poliakov v Kazakhstane. Edited by Liudmila Degitaeva. Almaty, Kazakhstan: Izdatel'skii dom Kazakhstan, 2000.
"Iz istorii Velikoi Otechestvennoi voiny." *Izvestiia TsK KPSS*, no. 7 (1990): 193–219.
Kaganovitch, Albert. "Estimating the Number of Jewish Refugees, Deportees, and Draftees from Bessarabia and Northern Bukovina in the Non-Occupied Soviet Territories." *Holocaust and Genocide Studies* 27, no. 3 (2013): 464–482.
———. "Ha-rekʻa ha-midini veha-sotsio-'ekonomi shel Berit ha-Moʻatsot le-bryḥat yahude Bukharah mi-'syah ha-Tykhonah (1920–1930)." *AB"A* 2 (2008): 33–45.
———. "Jewish Refugees and Soviet Authorities during World War II." *Yad Vashem Studies* 38, no. 2 (2010): 85–121.
———. *The Long Life and Swift Death of Jewish Rechitsa*. Madison: University of Wisconsin Press, 2013.
———. "Stalin's Great Power Politics, the Return of Jewish Refugees to Poland, and Continued Migration to Palestine, 1944–1946." *Holocaust and Genocide Studies* 26, no. 1 (2012): 59–94.
Kahan, Yaakov. *Unter di sovietishe himlen: Iberlebungen fun tefise lager un fun der Sovietisher frey*. Tel Aviv: Y. L. Perets, 1961.
Kamynska-Myron, Ida. "Mi-Pyiṭrkov ve-ʻad kolḥoz ha-ṭurkmeni be-Bukharah." *Yalkut mureshet* 24 (1977): 179–196.
Kats-Fridman, Klara. "Dve evakuatsii odnoi sem'i." *Evreiskaia starina*, 2012, no. 74. Available at http://berkovich-zametki.com/2012/Starina/Nomer3/Sokolov1.php.
Katyn', mart 1940 g.—sentiabr' 2000 g.: Rasstrel. Sud'by zhivykh. Ekho Katyni; Dokumenty. Edited by Natal'ia Lebedeva. Moscow: Ves' mir, 2001.
Kazakhstan v period Velikoi Otechestvennoi voiny Sovetskogo Soiuza 1941–1945: Sbornik dokumentov i materialov. Vol. 1. Edited by Sergei Pokrovskii. Alma-Ata, USSR: Nauka, 1964.
Kazakhstan v pervyi god Otechestvennoi voiny protiv nemetsko-fashistskikh zakhvatchikov. Edited by M. Abdykalykov. Alma-Ata, USSR: KazOGIZ, 1943.
Kerimbaev, Suiun. *Sovetskii Kirgizstan v Velikoi Otechestvennoi voine 1941–1945 gg*. Frunze, USSR: Ilim, 1985.
Khudalov, Temirsoltan. *Severnaia Osetiia v Velikoi Otechestvennoi voine 1941–1945*. Vladikavkaz, Russia: Sev.-Osetinskii institut gumanitarnykh issledovanii, 1992.
Kirgiziia v gody Velikoi Otechestvennoi voiny 1941–1945 gg.: Sbornik dokumentov i materialov. Edited A. K. Kazakbaev and I. E. Semënov. Frunze, USSR: Kyrgyzstan, 1965.
Klevan, Avraham. "'Al Kurot ha-Yahudim be-Asyah ha-sovyeṭit be-shnot milḥemet-ha-ʻolam ha-shniah." *Yalkut mureshet* 29 (1980): 121–125.
———. *Le-toldot ha-Yehudim be-Asyah ha-Tikhonah ba-meʼot ha-tesha-ʻesreh veha-ʻesrim*. Jerusalem: Makhon Ben Tsevy, 1989.
Kobylianskii, Isaak. *Priamoi navodkoi po vragu*. Moscow: Iauza, Eksmo, 2005.
Kommunisticheskaia vlast' protiv religii Moiseia: Dokumenty 1920–1937 i 1945–1953 gg. Edited by L. I. Kilimnik. Vinnitsa, Ukraine: Globus-Press, 2005.
Konstantin, Anatole. *A Red Boyhood: Growing Up under Stalin*. Columbia: University of Missouri Press, 2008.

Kornilov, Gennadii. "Naselenie Sverdlovska v voennye gody." *Rossiiskaia istoriia*, no. 4 (2010): 94–106.

———. *Ural'skoe selo i voina: Problemy demograficheskogo razvitiia*. Ekaterinburg, Russia: Uralagropres, 1993.

Kostyrchenko, Gennadii. *Tainaia politika Stalina*. Moscow: Mezhdunarodnye otnosheniia, 2001.

Koval'chuk, V. M. "Evakuatsiia naseleniia Leningrada letom 1941 goda." *Otechestvennaia istoriia*, no. 3 (2000): 15–24.

Krasnov-Levitin, Anatolii. *Ruk tvoikh zhar (1941–1956)*. Tel Aviv: Krug, 1979.

Krasnozhënova, Elena. "Sotsial'naia pomoshch' sem'iam voennosluzhashchikh v Nizhnem Povolzh'e. 1941–1945 gg." *Voprosy istorii*, no. 3 (2012): 141–147.

Krutova, Nina. *Evrei na zemle Vostochnogo Kazakhstana, nachalo XVIII—XXI*. Ust'-Kamenogorsk, Kazakhstan: Shygys-Poligraf, 2012.

Kuibyshevskaia oblast' v gody Velikoi Otechestvennoi voiny: Dokumenty i materialy. Edited by Lenar Khramkov. Samara, Russia: Samarskii Dom pechati, 1995.

Kumanëv, Georgii. "Evakuatsiia naseleniia SSSR: Dostignutye rezul'taty i poteri." In *Liudskie poteri SSSR v period Vtoroi mirovoi voiny*, edited by Rostislav Evdokimov, 137–146. Saint Petersburg, Russia: Blits, 1995.

Kupovetskii, Mark. "Liudskie poteri evreiskogo naseleniia v poslevoennykh granitsakh SSSR v gody Velikoi Otechestvennoi voiny." *Vestnik Evreiskogo universiteta v Moskve* 9, no. 2 (1995): 134–155.

Levertov, Moshe. *The Man Who Mocked the KGB*. Brooklyn, NY: M. Levertov, 2002. Available at http://www.chabad.org/library/article_cdo/aid/312437/jewish/Central-Asia.htm.

Levin, Dov. "Miklat ara'i im bitakḫon mugbal: Pelitim yehudim mi-Liṭa be-tokhekhei Berit ha-Mo'atsot." *Dapim le-kheker tkufat ha-Sho'ah* 5 (1987): 91–120.

———. "Yehudey Besarabiyah be-shilton ha-sovyeṭi be-yamey milḥemet-ha-'olam ha-shniah, 1940–1945." *Shvut*, no. 4 (1976): 101–118.

Levin, Yisrael-Yehuda. *Zikhronotai mi-yamey yalduti be-Rusia ha-sovyeṭit 'ad yetsiyati misham ve-hegiyani benisim unifla'ot 'ad halom*. Kfar Hab'ad, Israel: n.p., 1995.

Levin, Zeev. "Antisemitism and the Jewish Refugees in Soviet Kirgizia, 1942." *Jews in Russia and Eastern Europe* 50, no. 1 (2003): 191–203.

Liberman, Mishket. *Iz berlinskogo getto v novyi mir*. Moscow: Progress, 1979.

Litvak, Yosef. *Peliṭim Yehudim mi-Polin be-Berit ha-Mo'atsot, 1939–1946*. Tel Aviv: Kibbutz Meuhad, 1988.

Liubimov, Aleksandr. *Torgovlia i snabzhenie v gody Velikoi Otechestvennoi voiny*. Moscow: Ekonomika, 1968.

Liuksemburg, Mordehai. *Sozvezdie Mordekhaia*. Jerusalem: Shamir, 1990.

Livshits, Inessa. "Nadezhda umiraet poslednei." *Mishpokha*, no. 9 (2001): 58–59.

Lomagin, Nikita. *Neizvestnaia blokada*. Moscow: Olma-Press, 2002.

Makabi-Yoresh, Ania. *Kokhav lo yikabeah*. Tel Aviv: Kibbutz Meuhad, 1991.

Mandel'shtam, Nadezhda. *Vtoraia kniga*. Moscow: Moskovskii rabochii, 1990.

Manley, Rebecca. *To the Tashkent Station: Evacuation and Survival in the Soviet Union at War*. Ithaca, NY: Cornell University Press, 2009.

Matayev (Abramchaev), Berta. *Od tizraḥ ha-shemesh be-ḥaloni: Perkey ḥayim*. Tel Aviv: I. Golan, 2003.

Medvedeva-Natu, Olga. "V atmosfere liubvi k strane Sovetov." In *Istoriia, Pamiat', Liudi: Materialy VI mezhdunarodnoi nauchno-prakticheskoi konferentsii*, edited by Aleksandr Baron, 162–191. Almaty, Kazakhstan: Mitsva, 2013.
Meletinskii, Eliazar. *Izbrannye stat'i. Vospominaniia.* Moscow: RGGU, 1998.
Mesto evakuatsii: Chkalovskaia oblast'. Edited by S. M. Muromtseva. Orenburg, Russia: Dimur, 2010.
Miller, Zinovii. "Iz perezhitogo." In *Evreiskaia starina* 80, no. 1 (2014). Available at http://berkovich-zametki.com/2014/Starina/Nomer1/Manin1.php.
Mitsel, Mikhail. *Evrei Ukrainy v 1943–1953: Ocherki dokumental'noi istorii.* Kyiv, Ukraine: Dukh i litera, 2004.
———. "Programmy Amerikanskogo evreiskogo ob"edinënnogo raspredelitel'nogo komiteta v SSSR 1943–1947." *Vestnik Evreiskogo universiteta v Moskve* 26, no. 8 (2003): 95–122.
Mordoviia v gody Velikoi Otechestvennoi voiny 1941–1945 gg.: Dokumenty i materialy. Edited by Aleksandra Zakharkina and others. Saransk, USSR: Mordovskoe knizhnoe izdatel'stvo, 1962.
Moskoff, William. *The Bread of Affliction: The Food Supply in the USSR during World War II.* New York: Cambridge University Press, 1990.
Nikulin, Nikolai. *Vospominaniia o voine.* Saint Petersburg, Russia: Ermitazh, 2008.
Norris, Stephen. "Landscapes of Loss: The Great Patriotic War in Central Asian Cinema." In *Central Asian Cinema: Rewriting Cultural Histories*, edited by Michael Rouland and Gulnara Abikeyeva, 73–87. London: I. B. Tauris, 2013.
Novikov, Nikolai. *Vospominaniia diplomata: Zapiski o 1938–1947 godakh.* Moscow: Politizdat, 1989.
Oboronnaia promyshlennost' Novosibirskoi oblasti v gody Velikoi Otechestvennoi voiny: Sbornik dokumentov. Edited by I. M. Savitskii. Novosibirsk, Russia: Oblastnoi gosudarstvennyi arkhiv, 2005.
Olekhnovich, Galina. *Ekonomika Belorussii v usloviiakh Velikoi Otechestvennoi voiny, 1941–1945.* Minsk, USSR: BGU, 1982.
———. "Ot Pripiati—za Volgu." In *Eshelony idut na vostok*, edited by Iurii Poliakov, 87–104. Moscow: Nauka, 1966.
Organy Gosudarstvennoi bezopasnosti SSSR v Velikoi Otechestvennoi voine: Sbornik dokumentov. Edited by N. P. Patrushev, V. P. Iampol'skii, and others. Moscow: Rus', 2000.
Osipova, Irina. *Khasidy: "Spasaia narod svoi . . ."; Istoriia khasidskogo podpol'ia v gody bol'shevistskogo terrora (po materialam otchëtov OGPU-NKVD-MGB i sledstvennykh del zakliuchennykh).* Moscow: Formika-C, 2002.
Osokina, Elena. *Our Daily Bread: Socialist Distribution and the Art of Survival in Stalin's Russia, 1927–1941.* Armonk, NY: M. E. Sharpe, 2001.
Osvobozhdënnaia Belarus': Dokumenty i materialy. Edited by Vladimir Adamushko and others. Minsk, Belarus: NARB, 2004.
Parsadanova, Valentina. "Deportatsiia naseleniia iz Zapadnoi Ukrainy i Zapadnoi Belorussii v 1939–1941 gg." *Novaia i noveishaia istoriia*, no. 2 (1989): 26–44.
Partiinoe rukovodstvo evakuatsiei v pervyi period Velikoi Otechestvennoi voiny 1941–1942 gg. Edited by Mikhail Likhomanov, Larisa Pozina, and Evgenii Finogenov. Leningrad: Izdatel'stvo Leningradskogo universiteta, 1985.

Petrov, Vladimir. *Escape from the Future*. Bloomington: Indiana University Press, 1973.
Pikhoia, Rudol'f. *Moskva. Kreml. Vlast'*. Vol. 1. Moscow: Novyi Khronograf, 2009.
Pinchuk, Ben-Cion. *Yehude Berit ha-Mo'atsot mul pene ha-Sho'ah*. Tel Aviv: Makhon le-heker ha-tfutsot, 1979.
Pirimkulov, Shodmonkul. "Evrei v sostave pol'skikh grazhdan, deportirovannykh v Kazakhstan." In *Evrei v Kazakhstane: Istoriia, religiia, kul'tura (Materialy 1 Mezhdunarodnoi nauchno-istoricheskoi konferentsii)*, edited by Isaak Grinberg, 123–138. Almaty, Kazakhstan: Mitsva, 2003.
Pis'ma Velikoi Otechestvennoi: Sbornik dokumentov. Edited by V. L. D'iachkov and M. M. Doroshina. Tambov, Russia: TOGUP, 2005.
Podlivalov, Valerii. *Iuzhnoe Zaural'e v gody Velikoi Otechestvennoi voiny*. Kurgan, Russia: Kurganskii gosudarstvennyi universitet, 2009.
Pogrebnoi, Lavrentii. "O deiatel'nosti Soveta po evakuatsii." In *Eshelony idut na vostok*, edited by Iurii Poliakov, 201–207. Moscow: Nauka, 1966.
Pomerantz, Jack, and Lyric Wallwork Winik. *Run East: Flight from the Holocaust*. Urbana: University of Illinois Press, 1997.
Postnikov, Stanislav. *V dalekikh garnizonakh*. Moscow: Rolygon-press, 2004.
Potëmkina, Marina. *Evakuatsiia v gody Velikoi Otechestvennoi voiny na Urale: Liudi i sud'by*. Magnitogorsk, Russia: MaGU, 2002.
———. "Evakonaselenie v Ural'skom tylu: Opyt vyzhivaniia." *Otechestvennaia istoriia*, no. 2 (2005): 86–98.
———. *Evakonaselenie v Ural'skom tylu (1941–1948 gg.)*. Magnitogorsk, Russia: MaGU, 2006.
Pulatov, Isak. *Andizhanskaia partiinaia organizatsiia v gody Otechestvennoi voiny*. Tashkent, USSR: Gosizdat UzSSR, 1960.
———. *Iz istorii uchastiia narodov Srednei Azii v Velikoi Otechestvennoi voine*. Tashkent, USSR: FAN, 1966.
"Razvitie partizanskogo dvizheniia." *Izvestiia TsK KPSS*, no. 7 (1990): 210–211.
Redlich, Shimon. "The Jews under Soviet Rule during World War II." PhD diss., New York University, 1968.
———. *War, Holocaust and Stalinism: A Documented Study of the Jewish Anti-Fascist Committee in the USSR*. Luxembourg: Harwood Academic Publishers, 1995.
Rekviem pamiati evakuirovannykh leningradtsev, zakhoronennykh v Vologodskoi oblasti v gody Velikoi Otechestvennoi voiny. Vol. 1. Vologda, USSR: Vologodskii gosudarstvennyi pedagogicheskii institut, 1990.
Ro'i, Yaacov. "The Reconstruction of Jewish Communities in the USSR, 1944–1947." In *The Jews Are Coming Back: The Return of the Jews to Their Countries of Origin after WW II*, edited by David Bankier, 186–205. Jerusalem and New York: Yad Vashem and Berghahn Books, 2005.
Rusakova, Alla. "Vospominaniia ob ottse." *Zvezda*, no. 6 (2015): 193–226.
Russiianov, Ivan. *V boiakh rozhdennaia . . .* Moscow: Voenizdat, 1982.
Russkii arkhiv: Velikaia Otechestvennaia. Vols. 13 (2–2), 14 (3–1), 16 (5–1), 17 (6), 20 (9). Moscow: Terra, 1994–1997.
Rybakovskii, Leonid. *Liudskie poteri SSSR i Rossii v Velikoi Otechestvennoi voine*. Moscow: Institut sotsial'no-politicheskikh issledovanii RAN, 2001.

Salakhutdinov, Farid. *Samarkandskaia partiinaia organizatsiia v gody Velikoi Otechestvennoi voiny*. Samarkand, USSR: Samarkandskii universitet, 1961.
Sasonkin, Naḥum Shemaryah. *Zikhronotai: Pirḳe zikhronot mas'irim u-meratḳim*. Jerusalem: Maḥshevet, 1988.
Shalak, Aleksandr. *Usloviia zhizni i byt naseleniia Vostochnoi Sibiri v gody Velikoi Otechestvennoi voiny, 1941–1945*. Irkutsk, Russia: IGEA, 1998.
Shikheeva-Gaister, Inna. *Deti vragov naroda: Semeinaia khronika vremën kul'ta lichnosti 1925–1953*. Moscow: Vozvrashchenie, 2012.
Shkurko, Emma. "Demograficheskie, kul'turnye, psikhologicheskie posledstviia evakuatsii evreev v Bashkirskuiu ASSR." In *Evakuatsiia: Voskreshaia proshloe*, edited by Aleksandr Baron and others, 158–174. Almaty, Kazakhstan: Fortress, 2009.
Shnaider, Boris. "Vniz po reke." In *Vzrosloe detstvo voiny: Sbornik vospominanii*, edited by Mikhail Kipnis, vol. 1, 157–158. Ashdod, Israel: Keitar, 2013.
Shneer, Aron. *Plen*. Jerusalem: Noi, 2003.
Shvarts, Iakov. "Nekotorye voprosy evakuatsii naseleniia." In *Gor'kovskaia oblast' v Velikoi Otechestvennoi voine: Vzgliad cherez 50 let*, edited by Arkadii Kulakov and others, 204–206. Nizhnii Novgorod, Russia: Izdatel'stvo Nizhnii Novgorod, 1995.
Shvarts, Solomon. *Evrei v Sovetskom Soiuze s nachala vtoroi mirovoi voiny (1939–1945)*. New York: Amerikanskii evreiskii rabochii komitet, 1966.
Shveibish, Semën. "Evakuatsiia i sovetskie evrei vo vremia Kholokosta." *Vestnik evreiskogo universiteta v Moskve* 9, no. 2 (1995): 36–55.
Simonov, Konstantin. *Raznye dni voiny: Dnevnik pisatelia*. Moscow: Grifon M, 2005.
Sinitsyn, Andrei. *Vsenarodnaia pomoshch' frontu*. Moscow: Voenizdat, 1985.
Smilovitsky, Leonid. "Struggle of Belorussian Jews for the Restitution of Possessions and Housing in the First Post War Decade." *East European Jewish Affairs* 30, no. 2 (2000): 53–70.
Sovetskaia propaganda v gody Velikoi Otechestvennoi voiny. Edited by A. Ia. Livshin and I. B. Orlov. Moscow: Rosspen, 2007.
Sovetskie evrei pishut Il'e Erenburgu, 1943–1966. Edited by M. Altshuler, I. Arad, and Sh. Krakovskii. Jerusalem: Tsentr po issledovaniiu dokumentatsii vostochnoevropeiskogo evreistva, 1993.
Sovetskii tyl v period Velikoi Otechestvennoi voiny. Edited by Georgii Kumanëv. Moscow: Nauka, 1988.
Srebrakowski, Alexander. "Stan zdrowia ludnosci polskiej." In *Życie codzienne polskich zesłańców w ZSRR w latach 1940–1946*, edited by Stanisław Ciesielski, 209–229. Wrocław, Poland: Uniwersytet Wrocław, 1997.
"Stalin, Beriia i sud'ba armii Andersa v 1941–1942 gg. (Iz rassekrechennykh arkhivov)." *Novaia i noveishaia istoriia*, no. 2 (1993): 59–90.
Stalinskie deportatsii 1928–1953. Edited by Nikolai Pobol' and Pavel Polian. Moscow: Materik, 2005.
Statiev, Alexander. "The Nature of Anti-Soviet Armed Resistance, 1942–44: The North Caucasus, the Kalmyk Autonomous Republic, and Crimea." *Kritika: Explorations in Russian and Eurasian History* 6, no. 2 (2005): 285–318.
Stel'man, Lev. "Pervye dni Velikoi voiny." In *Pamiat' i vremia*, edited by V. N. Akopian and others, 13–47. Minsk, Belarus: Medisont 2014.

Stronski, Paul. *Tashkent: Forging a Soviet City, 1930–1966.* Pittsburgh, PA: University of Pittsburgh Press, 2010.
Teoriia i praktika zapadnoukrainskogo natsionalizma v dokumentah NKVD, MVD i MGB SSSR (1939–1956): Sbornik dokumentov. Edited by Nikolai Samokhvalov and others. Moscow: Ob"edinënnaia redaktsiia MVD Rossii, 2010.
Timofeev, Leonid. "Dnevnik voennykh let." *Znamia*, 1, no. 6 (2002): 139–185; 2, no. 12 (2003): 127–159; 3, no. 7 (2004): 152–161.
Toldot Chabad be-Erets ha-Kodesh: Ba-shanim 1777–1949. Edited by Shalom Duber Levin. New York: Kraney hod ha-Torah, 1989.
TsK VKP(b) i natsional'nyi vopros. Vol. 2, *1933–1945.* Edited by L. S. Gatogova and others. Moscow: ROSSPEN, 2009.
Ustinov, Dmitrii. *Vo imia Pobedy.* Moscow: Voenizdat, 1988.
Vaksman, Viktor, and Leonid Vaksman. "Vospominaniia brat'ev Vaksman." In *Evreiskie bezhentsy i evakuatsiia: Vospominaniia o voennom detstve*, edited by Alla Nikitina, 125–129. Jerusalem: n.p., 2009.
Vasenëva, T. V. "Priëm i ustroistvo evakuirovannogo naseleniia v Kurgane v 1941 g." *Arkhivy Urala*, no. 9–10 (2006): 36–48.
Vekselman, Max. "The Struggle of the Tashkent Ashkenazi Community for the Return of Its Synagogue Building." *Shvut* 17–18, no. 1–2 (1995): 342–360.
Voices of Resilience. Edited by Svetlana Shklarova. Calgary, AB: Jewish Family Service Calgary, 2010.
Vo imia pobedy: Evakuatsiia grazhdanskogo naseleniia v Zapadnuiu Sibir' v gody Velikoi Otechestvennoi voiny v dokumentakh i materialakh. Edited by Liudmila Snegirëva and Tatiana Safonova. Tomsk, Russia: Tomskii universitet, 2005.
Vyltsan, M. A. "Zhertvy golodnogo vremeni (po arkhivnym materialam NKVD-MVD)." In *Liudskie poteri SSSR v period vtoroi mirovoi voiny*, edited by Rostislav Evdokimov, 165–173. Saint Petersburg, Russia: Blits, 1995.
"W czterdziestym nas matko na Sibir zesłali . . .": Polska a Rosja 1939–42. Edited and compiled by Irena Grudzińska-Gross and Jan TomaszGross. London: Aneks, 1983.
War through Children's Eyes: The Soviet Occupation of Poland and the Deportations, 1939–1941. Edited and compiled by Irena Grudzińska-Gross and Jan Tomasz Gross. Stanford, CA: Stanford University Press, 1981.
Wat, Aleksander. *My Century: The Odyssey of a Polish Intellectual.* Berkeley: University of California Press, 1988.
Weiner, Amir. *Making Sense of War: The Second World War and the Fate of the Bolshevik Revolution.* Princeton, NJ: Princeton University Press, 2001.
Wenig, Larry. *From Nazi Inferno to Soviet Hell.* Hoboken, NJ: Ktav Pub. House, 2000.
Widziałem Anioła Śmierci: Losy deportowanych Żydów polskich w ZSRR w latach II wojny światowej. Composed by Maciej Siekierski and Feliks Tych. Warsaw, Poland: Rosner & Wspólnicy, 2006.
Willerton, John. *Patronage and Politics in the USSR.* Cambridge: Cambridge University Press, 1992.
Yekelchyk, Serhy. *Stalin's Citizens: Everyday Politics in the Wake of Total War.* Oxford: Oxford University Press, 2014.
———. *Stalin's Empire of Memory: Russian-Ukrainian Relations in the Soviet Historical Imagination.* Toronto: University of Toronto Press, 2004.

Zamir, Rahel. *Shelihut hayai: Korot hyaim.* Tel Aviv: n.p., 2000.
Zaron, Piotr. *Ludnosc polska w Zwiazku Radzieckim w czasie II wojny swiatowej.* Warsaw, Poland: PWN, 1990.
Zhanguttin, Baurzhan. "Evakuatsiia sovetskogo naseleniia v Kazakhstan, 1941–1942 gg." *Novyi istoricheskii vestnik* 14 (2006), no. 1. Available at http://www.nivestnik.ru/2006_1/6.shtml.
Zhirnov, Evgenii. "Nas obmanom vyvezli iz Moskvy." *Kommersant-Vlast'*, no. 17 (May 5, 2005): 52–58.
———. "Proverka strakhom." *Kommersant-Vlast'*, no. 24 (June 20, 2005): 72–73.
Zylbering, Abraham. "A Survivor Remembers: The Gulag and Central Asia." *Memoirs of Holocaust Survivors in Canada* 26. Montreal: Concordia University, 2002.

Index

Abbasov, Shukhrat, 6
Agitprop (Department of Agitation and Propaganda), 5, 169
AJJDC (American Jewish Joint Distribution Committee), 120–121
Akhmatova, Anna, 57, 105, 125, 138, 149, 164
Alatyr', 31, 90, 140, 191, 194, 196, 216
Alma-Ata, 35–36, 39, 41, 45–46, 57, 62, 64–65, 71, 74, 80, 84–85, 107, 116, 118, 136–137, 162–163, 169, 171, 174, 178, 180, 194, 216, 229
Altai territory, 63, 72, 78, 84, 86, 90, 110, 124, 200
Altshuler, Mordechai, 25, 32, 289n125
Aminov, Avraam, 181
Anders army, 43, 45, 141, 185, 201–202, 207–208, 287n93
Andizhan, 82, 112, 135, 165–166, 178
artels, 79–80, 81, 83–84, 93, 120, 179, 217, 230
Ashkhabad, 45, 109, 164

Babadzhanian, Amazasp, 26
Babkin, Aleksei, 36, 41–42, 70, 248n152
Bagramian, Ivan, 27
Baku, 35, 74, 203
Bashkiria, Bashkir ASSR, 56, 63, 68–69, 111, 116
Belorussia, Belorussian SSR (BSSR), 8, 14–15, 17–20, 23–27, 32–34, 120, 126, 135, 154, 175, 197–198, 205, 208, 215–218, 228, 231
Belorussians, 3, 15, 201–202
Beria, Lavrenty, 43, 70, 101–102, 113, 118, 167, 220, 232–233, 288n95
Białystok, 15, 32, 79, 139, 201
blood libel, 155, 170
bombardment and victims of, 17–20, 22, 26–28, 33–34, 37, 43, 46, 71, 138–139, 235–236, 244n67
Brest, 15, 19, 139, 201
Brezhnev, Leonid, 64
Buinsk (village in Chuvash ASSR), 48, 95, 149
Bukharan Jews, 170, 178, 180–186, 284n332
Buriat-Mongolian ASSR, 88

Caucasus (and North Caucasus), 33, 35, 41, 105, 109, 117, 159, 196–198, 203–204, 207
Central Asia, 34–37, 43–45, 78–79, 85–86, 101, 105–109, 111, 113–114, 116–117, 124, 136, 145, 148–150, 153–154, 160–161, 164–167, 170, 176–181, 185, 187, 191–192, 196–197, 199–200, 203, 207–209, 237, 247n101, 264n61
Chardzhou, 39, 72, 109, 127, 161
Cheboksary, 36, 56–57, 130, 148, 152, 156, 196, 210

Cheliabinsk, 39, 87, 110–111, 151, 190, 192, 210
ChGK (Soviet Extraordinary State Commission), 32
Chimkent, 40, 81, 134, 136
Chkalov and region, 56–57, 62–63, 66, 94, 106, 108, 111, 116, 132, 146, 150–151, 206, 212–213
Chukovskaia, Lidia, 128–129, 164
Chuvashia, Chuvash ASSR, 13, 48–55, 65, 71, 73, 75, 77–78, 80–81, 88, 90, 92, 97, 108, 111, 127–128, 131, 137, 139–140, 147, 152, 156, 172, 175, 191–192, 194–196, 203, 206–207, 211–215
"close cities of the first category," 35, 191
complaints, 48, 55, 60, 62–63, 68–76, 82–83, 121, 128, 148, 156–159, 168–170, 172–173, 218–220, 228, 233
conscription, draft, 4, 8, 17, 34, 42, 105, 114, 117, 144, 160, 167, 188, 202, 205–206, 273n5, 288n99
Crimea, 116, 121, 197–198, 215, 230–233, 236
Crimean Tatars, 43
CSA (Central Statistical Administration), 189, 198–200, 202, 208

Der Nister (Pinkhas Kaganovich), 180
deserters of army, 117–118, 167
deserters of labor, 45, 87, 259n66
Dnepropetrovsk and region, 64, 124, 219, 221–222
Dubson, Vadim, 9, 189, 199–200, 202, 288n116
Dunaevskii, Dov, 106, 129, 140–141, 182
Dzhambul, 37, 81, 116, 162, 177, 179, 181

Efron, Georgii, 38, 165–166
Ehrenburg, Ilya, 15, 19, 97, 169, 215, 219
Eliezerov (Kazarnovskii), Shlomo, 181
employment, 44, 53, 61–62, 68–69, 77–86, 190–191, 211, 227, 230
Epshtein, Shakhno, 15, 121–122, 178, 183, 208
Ermolinskii, Sergei, 97, 143

Estonia, Estonian SSR, 3, 11, 32, 176, 197, 212–213; Jews of, 205, 290n129
Eynikayt, 121, 176, 178, 183, 208, 220, 232

Fadeev, Aleksandr, 65, 255n151
Faigenboim, Iosif, 33, 105
Faizi, Rakhmat, 6
family communication, 192–195, 209
Fedin, Konstantin, 65
Finns, 41, 190, 202
Fitzpatrick, Sheila, 67, 75
flight to the east, 4, 8, 14–34, 197, 203, 207, 218
Frunze and region, 62, 94, 125, 136, 169, 176, 180

Galadzhaev, Sergei, 292n56
German anti-Jewish propaganda, 16–17, 163–164, 169–170, 173, 217, 238, 245n83
Germans, Soviet citizens or Soviet Germans, 29, 41–42, 90, 189–190, 199, 202
GKO (State Defense Committee), 16, 20, 44, 96
GlavPur (Main Political Management of the Red Army), 63
Gogiberidze, Grigorii, 30
Gorodetskii, Simkha, 181
Gomel and region, 18, 25, 196, 216–218
Gor'kii and region, 36, 63, 94, 98, 174, 192
Grosman, Moshe, 117, 181, 185, 267n114
Grushevoi, Konstantin, 64
Gulag, 42, 86, 91

harassment, 82
Hasidism, 177, 181, 183–184; Braslav Hasidim, 177, 182; Chabad, 177, 179, 181–182, 184
ḥeder, 162, 177, 182
Holocaust, 10, 14–17, 138, 176, 179, 207, 220, 225, 242n11
housing problem, 23, 56–62, 68–69, 108, 111, 151, 163, 173, 181–182, 186, 190, 212, 214–223, 226–228, 234

Iakovlev, M., 36, 40, 64
Iakubovskii, Ivan, 27
invalids, disabled people, 121, 162–165, 168–169, 219
Irkutsk and region, 88–89, 198
Iuditskii, Avraham, 179–180
Iusupov, Usman, 102, 136, 227–228
Ivanov, Vsevolod, 15, 168–169
Ivanova, Izolda, 96, 104, 149

JAC (Jewish Anti-Fascist Committee), 116, 120–122, 167, 220, 227, 232, 238
JAR (Jewish Autonomous Region), 231–233

Kabardino-Balkar ASSR, 47, 55–57, 59, 151
Kaganovich, Lazar, 38, 65, 72, 232–233
Kalinin, Mikhail, 71–72, 251n41
Kalinin, Pëtr, 27
Kalinin (city) and region, 21, 31, 39, 204, 211
Kamenets-Podol'sk, 15, 33, 221, 229, 233, 242n11
Kanibadam, 106, 168, 179
Karelo-Finnish SSR, 31, 189, 206, 213
Karmen, Roman, 218
kashrut, 106
Kazakhstan, Kazakh SSR, 13, 34, 37, 44–45, 63, 70, 79, 84–85, 90, 92, 106, 109, 111, 116, 119, 124, 126, 137, 143, 148, 161–162, 167, 170–171, 174, 197–198, 200, 203, 207, 209, 226
Keitelman, Ehezkiel, 179–180
Kermine, 182
Kharkov, 33, 39, 80, 219, 221
Khatyrchi, 179, 182
Khrushchev, Nikita, 28, 224–229, 231–234, 294n101, 294n102
Khudaidatov, Ilia, 182
Khudaidatov, Rafael, 182
Kiev, 18, 82, 124, 155, 219–220, 222–231
Kirgizstan, 44–45, 56, 59, 84, 102, 114, 163–164, 166, 170–171, 174, 176, 196, 198–200

Kirov and region, 49–50, 62–63, 73–74, 95–96, 104, 149, 157, 192, 254n125
Konev, Ivan, 21
Kostyrchenko, Gennadii, 229, 232
Krasnodar territory, 20, 31, 147, 158, 203, 206, 289n124
Krasnoiarsk and territory, 58, 129
Krasnovodsk, 45, 56, 109, 181, 197–198
Krasnozhënova, Elena, 6, 48, 60
Kuibyshev and region, 35, 38, 40, 45, 56, 59, 62, 63, 67, 69, 77, 98–99, 118, 136–137, 139, 190
Kumanev, Georgii, 6, 190, 199
Kurgan and region, 35, 38, 63, 75, 94, 98, 116, 118, 145
Kzyl-Orda, 34, 165, 167, 186, 197

Latvia, 3, 11, 18, 21, 32, 53, 57, 175, 197, 213, 244n56, 268n5; Jews of, 152, 156, 175, 196, 205, 290n129
League V, 16, 120
Leninabad, 98, 168, 174, 179, 184
Leningrad and region, 29, 31, 37, 39–41, 47–48, 51, 58, 63, 71, 90, 104, 120, 123, 125, 134, 174, 181, 190, 192, 196, 198, 204, 206, 211, 215, 220, 229, 238
Levertov, Moshe, 136, 150, 184
Levin, Dov, 7, 184, 290n129
Lithuania, 3–4, 11, 21, 66, 197, 212; Jews of, 90, 100, 181–182, 205, 290n129
Litvak, Yosef, 7, 116, 179, 240n3, 287n93
L'vov, 33, 121, 201

Makabi-Yoresh, Ania, 20, 153
Makhachkala, 35, 112, 159–160
Mandel'shtam, Nadezhda, 49, 105, 125
Manley, Rebecca, 8–9, 45, 115, 131, 146, 156, 189, 199, 277n133
Mari ASSR, 59, 69, 157, 170, 201
Mekhlis, Lev, 96
Merkulov, Vsevolod, 190
Mikhalkov, Sergei, 5, 65
Mikhoels, Solomon, 15, 120–122, 164, 207
Minsk and region, 14–15, 19, 23–24, 121, 126, 132, 139, 197, 215–216, 218

minyan, 176–177, 179, 181
Moldavia, Moldavian SSR, 34–35, 197, 203, 208, 216; Jews of, 15, 181, 232
Molotov, Viacheslav, 72, 102, 121, 220, 242n11
Molotov (city), 36, 63, 153
Mordovia, Mordovian ASSR, 22, 129, 139
mortality in the rear, 9, 32, 42, 74, 91, 94, 107–118, 122, 124, 126, 131, 133, 136, 159, 176–177, 179, 201–203, 205, 207–208, 236
mortality in transit, 27, 39, 42–43
Moscow and region, 15, 22, 24, 31, 63, 65, 71, 99, 106, 123, 131, 135, 137, 160, 174, 177, 196, 198, 206, 213–214, 220, 229, 238

newspapers, 5, 15–17, 51, 61–62, 71–72, 83, 119, 121, 127, 135, 169, 179, 183, 242n11
Niiazov, Iurii, 184
NKVD, NKGB, MGB, OGPU, 13, 21–22, 35, 41–42, 60, 63–64, 70, 73, 86, 91, 101–102, 113, 134, 150, 153, 155, 169–170, 174–175, 177–179, 190, 222, 224, 237
nomenklatura, 63–65
North Ossetia, North Ossetian ASSR, 59, 98, 150, 196, 203
Novosibirsk and region, 35, 56, 63, 81–82, 86, 91, 97–98, 128, 132, 138, 150, 152, 188, 201, 203

Odessa, 37, 125, 138, 159, 215, 232, 242n11
Omsk and region, 35, 84, 137, 196
Ordzhonikidze territory, 52, 150, 203, 206
Orël and region, 31, 204
orphanage, 20, 41, 49, 53, 107, 114, 120, 122–142, 149–150, 182, 268n5, 272n117
Osh and region, 62, 112, 136, 165, 169

Pale of Settlement, 30–32, 173–174
Palestinian Socialist League. *See* League V

Pamfilov, Konstantin, 36, 149, 201, 247n111
Passover, 170, 178
Penza and region, 34–35, 38, 45, 66, 70, 77, 88, 151, 174, 190
Perventsev, Arkadii, 5
pogrom, 155–156, 160, 162–163, 166, 168–169, 222–223, 228
Poland, 3–4, 78, 137, 168, 189, 201–202, 216, 223
Poles, 3–4, 44, 153, 157, 170–171, 189, 287n94
Polish Jews, 3–4, 6, 8, 11–12, 33, 43, 45, 79, 81, 106, 111, 164–166, 168, 170–171, 178, 181–182, 184–186, 198, 201–202, 205, 207–208, 232, 237, 240n3, 287n94
Ponomarenko, Panteleimon, 14, 19, 25, 32, 174–175
Potëmkina, Marina, 6, 77, 145–146, 156, 212

Rechitsa, 17–18, 24, 26, 82, 118, 173, 216–218, 289n125
Red (also Soviet) Army, 4, 8, 16–17, 19, 33, 63, 67, 159; Jews in, 16, 160, 179, 203, 205, 207, 287n93
re-evacuation, 114, 119, 176, 195, 205, 209–219, 227
Romanian Jews, 3, 78, 122, 176, 181, 199, 202, 205, 232
Rostov-on-Don (also Rostov) and region, 36, 171, 202
rumors, 17, 21, 109, 144, 154–155, 158, 162, 166, 168, 170, 218, 220–222, 224–225, 233, 238
Russian chauvinism, 5, 169, 224
Russiianov, Ivan, 19

Samarkand, 45, 62, 79, 83, 92, 101, 105–106, 108–110, 112, 117, 135–136, 150, 160, 163, 167, 177–182, 184, 186, 227, 233
Saratov, 34, 37, 48, 60, 63, 66, 90, 132, 192
Sasonkin, Nakhum-Shmeriiagu, 105, 109, 167, 177, 182, 184

Index

Semipalatinsk and region, 40, 64, 85, 174
Shamakhmudovs, Sha'khmed and Bakhri, 5–6, 135–136
Shcherbakov, Aleksandr, 15–16, 62–63, 96, 169
Shklov, 17
Shklovskii, 55, 59, 158
Shvernik, Nikolai, 52, 157, 176, 232
Siberia, 30, 34, 37, 45–46, 51, 78, 85–86, 105–107, 110, 129–130, 143, 145, 155, 161, 165, 196–197, 201, 203, 231
Simonov, Konstantin, 17–18, 22
Smolensk and region, 27, 32, 204, 211, 286n54
Sovinformburo (Soviet Information Bureau), 15
Stalin, Joseph, 12, 15–16, 19–20, 22, 25, 28, 32, 44, 65, 72, 96, 102, 116, 121–122, 169, 174, 178, 223, 225–226, 229–235, 237–238
Stalinabad, 80, 100, 149, 165, 169, 180,
Stalingrad and region, 20, 28, 34, 120, 133, 166, 204, 206, 245n69, 245n70
Sterlitamak, 57, 72, 94, 151, 201
Stronski, Paul, 9, 44, 166, 173
suicides, 52, 60, 74–76
Sverdlovsk and region, 35, 62, 92, 106, 110–111, 116, 118–119, 132, 156, 190, 196, 201
synagogue, 15, 121, 163, 177, 179–180, 182, 186

Tajikistan, 109, 137, 199–200
Tajiks, 136, 149, 168, 175, 185
Tambov and region, 34, 62, 66, 101, 215
Tashkent, 9–10, 40, 43, 45–46, 57, 60, 81, 84, 86, 93, 101, 105–108, 112, 115, 117, 124–126, 128–129, 131, 135–136, 140–141, 146, 149–150, 154–155, 160, 163–166, 168, 170, 177–180, 182–184, 186, 209, 218, 220, 222, 224, 227, 229, 231
Tatars, 81, 161

Tsvetaeva, Marina, 38, 57, 75
Turkmenistan, 35, 45, 117, 124, 137, 198–200

Udmurt ASSR, 73, 111, 116, 129, 206
Ufa, 35, 58–59, 61, 155, 173, 225, 229
Ukraine, 8, 15, 20, 27, 29, 32–36, 64, 99, 120, 124, 132, 135, 155, 197–198, 203, 205, 207, 209, 218–234, 236, 238, 242n11
Ukrainians, 3, 81, 164, 201–202, 221, 224–225, 230, 288n95
UNRRA (United Nations Relief and Rehabilitation Administration), 97
Urals, 30, 34–35, 37, 39, 43, 45, 77–78, 85, 105–107, 109–111, 116, 131, 143, 145, 154, 156, 161, 165, 196–197, 265n71
Ustinov, Dmitrii, 58, 210
Uzbekistan, Uzbek SSR, 5–6, 43–45, 62, 78–79, 83, 90, 101–102, 105–106, 109, 113, 117, 124, 128, 131, 133, 135–136, 138, 140–141, 149–150, 163, 166, 170, 175, 178, 184–185, 190, 192, 194, 198, 200–201, 207–208, 232, 289n125
Uzbeks, 9, 44, 81, 117, 136–137, 145, 149–150, 153–154, 160–161, 166–171, 179

Vladimirovskaia, Bella, 92, 109–110
Volga area, 28–30, 36, 41, 43, 75, 105–106, 113, 147, 150, 154, 157, 161, 196–197
Voronezh and region, 63, 194, 203–204,

Yakutia, Yakut ASSR, 88, 90
Yeshiva, 83, 167, 177, 181, 184
Yiddish, 43, 122, 141, 154, 181, 183, 274n78

Zadionchenko, Semën, 64
Zhukov, Georgii, 22–23, 34
Zhukov, Nikolai, 43, 78, 128, 148, 191, 214
Zionism, 186, 188, 224

www.ingramcontent.com/pod-product-compliance
Lightning Source LLC
Chambersburg PA
CBHW070818250426
43672CB00031B/2786